CONCEALED AND REVEALED
A YEAR IN THE OLD AND NEW TESTAMENTS

by
John A. Carroll

Author of
Cover to Cover: Through the Bible in 365 Days

Concealed and Revealed
A Year in the Old and New Testaments
by John A. Carroll

Unless otherwise noted, all Scripture quotations are from The Holy Bible, English Standard Version®, copyright © 2001 by Crossway Bibles, a publishing ministry of Good News Publishers. Used by permission. All rights reserved.

Scripture quotations marked KJV are from the *King James Version* of the Bible

Paperback Version: ISBN-13: 978-1-7321724-2-5

Cover Design — Robert Baddorf

Published by John A. Carroll
jacarroll71@gmail.com

To my grandchildren

Grandchildren are the crown of the aged,
And the glory of children is their fathers. Proverbs 17:6

Table of Contents

Preface

The words "consider," "reflect" and "think" inform the framework of a robust devotional life. "I meditate on your precepts and consider your ways" (Ps. 119:15 NIV). "Consider what I say, for the Lord will give you understanding in everything" (2 Tim. 2:7 NASB). "I will reflect at night on who you are, O LORD; therefore I obey your instructions" (Ps. 119:55 NLT). "Or what do you think the Scripture means when it says that the Holy Spirit, whom God has placed within us, watches over us with tender jealousy?" (James 4:5 TLB).

Each of these verses speaks of a meditation on the Scripture. The beauty of John Carroll's *Concealed and Revealed* is that he challenges us to read, consider, and apply what we have read. He gives guidance on how to do this. In each daily reading he has "Reflections" and "Think about It" sections. John wants us to not just know the facts, but to apply the facts of Scripture to our lives. In each reading there is a topic which comes from a passage in the Old and New Testaments. They are practical as well as theological. For example:

"When Theory Becomes Reality" (July 29)

"Authenticity in Worship and Work" (October 4)

"Our Role in Culture: Finding the Balance" (October 31)

This places the Scriptures right in the middle of our daily lives. John's summary comments are both instructive and challenging. His two decades as Navigator Staff, theological education and service as a pastor in a local church ground what he writes in the messiness and reality of life. It reflects the great truths of Scripture in ways that challenge as well as teach. He shows how the Old and New Testaments complement and connect. They are, as the title states, *Concealed and Revealed*. You can read these devotional thoughts daily or spread them out over a year or two, reading and re-reading them. But, most importantly, they draw you to the daily readings which are arranged to bring you through the entire Bible.

People have asked me what the primary discipline I would put above all others. There are many spiritual disciplines that I practice and which I recommend to others. After reflection, I concluded that the one spiritual discipline I would fight to keep is a daily time with God in the Word and prayer. I have practiced this discipline for many decades. Certainly, I have missed days. It is not just a legalistic, check-off-the-box habit. But it is like brushing my teeth —a habit that I know I need for my health.

I also keep a simple journal to remind me of what I have read. Admittedly, I did not always understand what I was reading. In my younger years (and even today) I would whisk through the Old Testament, longing for the Psalms and the New Testament. Yet I dutifully sludged through it. Occasionally, I would turn to a devotional guide that would give me some insight. I knew I needed help in grasping both concepts and historical understanding. *Concealed and Revealed* is the kind of book that would have helped me grasp so much more of what I was reading.

I developed the habit of daily reading in both the Old and New Testaments to balance the full impact of the Bible. Reading God's Word is like eating a gourmet meal. It is to be tasted and savored, not gulped down and rushed. Thus, our prayer is:

"I delight in your decrees; I will not neglect your word. . . . Open my eyes that I may see wonderful things in your law. . . . Your word is a lamp to my feet and a light on my path" (Ps. 119:16, 18, 105 NIV).

Jerry E. White, PhD
International President Emeritus, The Navigators
Major General, USAF, Retired

Introduction

Welcome to a year in the Bible. I hope you will benefit greatly as we read and think together about the most important book ever written.

The title of this book comes from the idea that the New Testament is concealed in the Old and that the Old Testament is revealed in the New. As I wrote these chapters I was continually amazed at the connections between the two Testaments and how they shed light on each other. Truly the Bible is one book with one Author, the triune God who made heaven and earth.

Although we will be reading the Old Testament and New Testament simultaneously, these Testaments do not describe simultaneous events. The plan I am proposing here begins in Genesis in the Old Testament and Matthew in the New Testament. About 2000 years of history elapsed between the writing of the early Old Testament books and the birth of Jesus Christ, which opens the New.

One of the advantages of this reading plan is that we immediately get into the New Testament without neglecting a careful reading of the Old. We get an appreciation for the great cosmic events which set the backdrop for all the rest of the Bible and for human history.

We who are serious Christians or who are considering the Christian faith should make Bible reading a regular part of our lives. But if you have never read through the Bible, you will see that it is a massive undertaking. It can be done and I have done it annually for many years. I do not recommend attempting a faster reading. I find it preferable to read daily at a steady pace, taking some time to reflect on some of the verses.

If you prefer to read at a slower pace, you could opt to read only one of the assignments each day and complete the entire Bible in two years instead of one.[1] Either way, the important thing is to get started and keep going. I will be sharing my gleanings from each day's readings and pray they will be an encouragement to you.

John A. Carroll

---

[1] As a third alternative, you may want to consider reading straight through the Bible using my book *Cover to Cover: Through the Bible in 365 Days*, available at Amazon.com in Kindle or print format.

In the Beginning

Today's Reading: Genesis 1-2; Matthew 1

Selected Verses

> *And God saw everything that he had made, and behold, it was very good. And there was evening and there was morning, the sixth day.*
>
> Gen. 1:31

> *She will bear a son, and you shall call his name Jesus, for he will save his people from their sins.*
>
> Matt. 1:21

Reflections

As you read today, consider the God of creation presented in Genesis 1-2. He shows His care for the universe and for man. The Creator makes the first human couple in His image with an implied purpose to reflect His glory. He gives them a very good world with meaningful work.

When we turn to Matthew, it's obvious that something has gone wrong with the world. Sin has intruded into the life of the first humans. The birth of Jesus is surrounded with scandal as his mother, Mary, turns up pregnant. Her husband-to-be, Joseph, knows he could not be the father. He would not shame her publicly, but he was about to divorce her when an angel appeared to him. The angel tells him that Mary's baby, a son, was conceived not by any immorality of Mary, but by the power of the Holy Spirit. The pregnancy is miraculous. Moreover, Mary's son will save His people from their sins.

Tomorrow we will learn in Genesis how sin entered into human history making necessary a Savior. For now, please note that in Matthew 1 there are four mothers mentioned in the genealogy besides Mary. We will meet them all later in our Old Testament readings and learn details of their lives that show the grace of God to each of them. Even in the lineage of Jesus there was a need for deliverance from the ravages of sin.

Think about It

The God of the Bible is one of power, love, and justice. His Word shows the urgency of understanding how He has acted to create us and to save all those who trust in Him from the devastation of sin. Before we finish, we will see that He will restore all things and establish new heavens and a new earth in which righteousness dwells forever (2 Peter 3:13).

How would greater trust in God change your outlook right now?

January 2 / Day 2
Battle Lines Drawn

Today's Reading: Genesis 3-5; Matthew 2

Selected Verses

I will put enmity between you and the woman, and between your offspring and her offspring; he shall bruise your head, and you shall bruise his heel.

Gen. 3:15

Then Herod, when he saw that he had been tricked by the wise men, became furious, and he sent and killed all the male children in Bethlehem and in all that region who were two years old or under, according to the time that he had ascertained from the wise men.

Matt. 2:16

Reflections

In Genesis 3, temptation and sin enter the human experience. By listening to the serpent and eating the forbidden fruit of the tree of the knowledge of good and evil, Adam and Eve fail the test of trust in and obedience to God. They are confronted, exposed, convicted, and sentenced, but even here there is hope of ultimate salvation (Gen. 3:15) while the conflict with the serpent continues down through the ages.

Indeed, that conflict plays out in the lives of the first siblings, Cain and Abel, culminating in murder. It continues through subsequent generations leading up to a judgment on all mankind which we will read about tomorrow.

God would have been just to execute the sinning first couple immediately, but instead He promises an ongoing conflict in which the serpent's head will be crushed by the offspring of the woman, whom we will later learn is none other than Jesus Christ (Heb. 2:14, 15). More about that later.

In Matthew 2, the birth of Jesus is met with both international recognition and royal rejection. King Herod's scheme to kill the infant is thwarted and prophecies are fulfilled through that heinous action. Here the serpent, through the king, strikes at the heel of the woman's offspring (figuratively speaking).

In these readings, God's holiness, sovereignty, and mercy are clearly seen as He rules over the earth, blessing those who believe in Him, and using evil to work out His plans and purposes for good (Rom. 8:28).

Think about It

The battle lines are drawn in Genesis 3. That battle continues in our time but the victory has been secured through Jesus Christ. Do you trust in Him, the woman's offspring who crushed the serpent's head by His death and resurrection? Are you relying upon Him as your Savior?

Water: Judgment or Deliverance?

Today's Reading: Genesis 6-8; Matthew 3

Selected Verses

*Then Noah built an altar to the Lord and took some of every clean animal and
some of every clean bird and offered burnt offerings on the altar. And when the
Lord smelled the pleasing aroma, the Lord said in his heart, "I will never again curse
the ground because of man, for the intention of man's heart is evil from his youth."*

Gen. 8:20-21a

*Then Jesus came from Galilee to the Jordan to John, to be baptized by him.
John would have prevented him, saying, "I need to be baptized by you,
and do you come to me?" But Jesus answered him, "Let it be so now, for
thus it is fitting for us to fulfill all righteousness." Then he consented.*

Matt. 3:13-15

Reflections

God exercises His power in judgment on sinful mankind with a universal
flood. Even in the flood, He shows His grace and mercy by sparing Noah and his
family along with a male and a female of each animal. Sadly, only this small
group of eight people believes and finds salvation from the waters. The rest are
lost. So it will be in the final judgment. All will not be saved, but only those who
by grace through faith believe in Christ (Eph. 2:8-9).

Notice Noah's immediate response to this deliverance. He builds an altar to
the Lord and offers sacrifices in gratitude to Him.

Matthew tells us of the events surrounding the beginning of Jesus' public
ministry. John the Baptist, son of the high priest Zechariah and Elizabeth,
impacts the nation through his preaching and baptizing. Jesus comes to John for
baptism, showing His submission to fulfill all righteousness. Jesus will perfectly
fulfill the law of God.

The Apostle Peter (1 Pet. 3:18-22) ties both of these passages together,
showing that God's mercy to Noah in the flood is a foreshadowing of Jesus
Christ's deliverance of His people from the judgment for sin. The water of the
flood brought God's just judgment on mankind, but the water of baptism in
Christ Jesus symbolizes cleansing from sin, deliverance from judgment and
assurance of salvation to all who believe in Him.

Think about It

Do you have assurance that you are delivered from the judgment to come?
Give thanks to the Lord Jesus Christ that He submitted perfectly to God's law in
His life and death. Through faith in Him, we are made righteous (1 Cor. 1:30).
Like Noah we who trust in Christ are safe from the flood of judgment to come.

A Call to Repent

Today's Reading: Genesis 9-11; Matthew 4

Selected Verses

*So the Lord dispersed them from there over the face
of all the earth, and they left off building the city.*

Gen. 11:8

From that time Jesus began to preach, saying, "Repent, for the kingdom of heaven is at hand."

Matt. 4:17

Reflections

Following the flood, God commands Noah and his sons to be fruitful and multiply. And multiply they do! You might get dizzy reading all the names of their descendants.

But some things never change. In the midst of these generations of human beings who are listed for us, the cosmic battle between sin and righteousness continues. It divides the sons of Noah with a blessing on Shem and a curse on Canaan. Mankind, united by one language and forgetting the lessons learned from God's judgment through the flood, seeks to unite and build a tower of rebellion against God and for self-glorification. Again God acts in judgment, creating division through language differences. The spiritual hostility is not eliminated but is hampered as God creates the boundaries of culture to point man to Himself (Acts 17:26-27).

We should not conclude that God's plan has failed. Rather, that plan has not completely unfolded. In Genesis 11, we meet Abram. Soon we will see what a pivotal role he plays in God's plan of redemption. Abram is going to be a blessing to the whole earth.

In Matthew, we follow the inauguration of Jesus' ministry. He proclaims the arrival of the Kingdom of God. "Repent," He commands, "for the Kingdom of heaven is at hand" (Matt. 4:17). The same God who acted in judgment is calling all to come to Him in faith and repentance beginning with the Jews, but (as we shall see) extending to all nations, tribes, and languages.

Think about It

God deserves praise. Praise Him for His wisdom in planning the redemption of His people. Praise Him for His sovereignty in carrying out this plan over the millennia of history. He will surely bring it to completion at the end of time. Praise Him that we can know of our adoption as His children and of the assurance that He will take us all the way home. His eternal purposes will be fulfilled though we pass through dark and difficult times on our journey through life. Meanwhile, let us repent of our sins and believe in His salvation.

Holiness: The Struggle

Today's Reading: Genesis 12-14; Matthew 5:1-26

Selected Verses

*So Pharaoh called Abram and said, "What is this you have done
to me? Why did you not tell me that she was your wife?"*

Gen. 12:18

*For I tell you, unless your righteousness exceeds that of the scribes
and Pharisees, you will never enter the kingdom of heaven.*

Matt. 5:20

Reflections

A reality for every believer is the awareness that our actions are often inconsistent with our profession of faith. We veer between the heights of faithfulness and the pits of sin.

Abram shows exemplary faith in his response to God's call (Gen. 12:4). He shows generosity and love toward his nephew Lot. He shows a profound understanding that his integrity was not for sale in his interactions with the pagan kings. However, his deceptive dealing with Pharaoh reveals another side of the patriarch. Gripped by fear, he reverts to deception that even the Egyptian ruler found appalling, passing off his wife as his sister.

In Jesus' Sermon on the Mount, we learn that God looks on the heart of His people. Mere outward conformity to the law is unacceptable. This got the Pharisees in trouble. Their sins would not have been as observable as Abram's famous lie, yet their righteousness was insufficient to gain entrance into the kingdom of heaven. They were insensitive to their failure to truly obey God. If they would find eternal life they would have to recognize their utter inability to be perfect. They would need to learn that only faith in a perfect priest and a perfect sacrifice would open the kingdom of God to them.

Think about It

How do you view your spiritual ups and downs? Do you trust in your own goodness when you seem to be walking in obedience? Do you doubt your acceptance before God when you sin? Our acceptance before God is based on His grace through faith in Christ the perfect priest who gave Himself, the perfect offering, for our sins. It cannot be based on our performance. Our faith will bear increasing fruit of obedience but that will not be perfect until we see the Lord (1 John 3:2). Meanwhile, seek to keep believing God's promises to save us by grace through faith and never quit the struggle to grow in God-glorifying holiness.

God Counts Faith as Righteousness

Today's Reading: Genesis 15-17; Matthew 5:27-48

Selected Verses

And he believed the Lord, and he counted it to him as righteousness.

Gen. 15:6

You therefore must be perfect, as your heavenly Father is perfect.

Matt. 5:48

Reflections

God made Man to live in a perfect world without strife and hostility. After the fall, God begins to reveal His plan to crush the serpent and bless through His chosen servant, Abram, all the families of the earth.

Abram has begun to grow anxious about God's timing in fulfilling His promises. Sarai remains childless. In today's reading, God, in a vision, reassures Abram of His covenant and seals it with a solemn act involving the sacrifice of five animals. In spite of this dramatic event, Abram's faith falters. Sarai suggests he take a surrogate wife, her servant Hagar. Although Hagar conceives Ishmael by Abram, the plan backfires and serious conflict arises between Sarai and Hagar, resulting in a temporary departure of Hagar, still pregnant with Ishmael.

After thirteen years, God again appears to Abram. This time the Lord changes Abram's name to Abraham and gives him a sign, circumcision. God is serious about fulfilling His covenant promises, but He will do it in His way and in His time. Clearly, Abraham needs reassurance continually in order to believe God. Yet, God counts his faith as righteousness.

The blessing promised to all families of the earth will come through Abraham's descendant, not Ishmael, but Jesus the Christ, born of a virgin, born to be a king of a spiritual, heavenly kingdom composed of people from every tribe and tongue.

That descendant whose life we follow in Matthew's Gospel today declared that in His kingdom the righteousness that would be practiced would not be merely outward but would be deeply inward: unfeigned love toward others, even enemies; purity of thought toward the opposite sex; utter fidelity in marriage; faithful keeping of commitments; ready forgiveness and service toward those in need. Jesus said, "You must be perfect, as your heavenly Father is."

Think about It

How are we to be perfect as God is?

We will only be perfect in the same way Abraham was. By faith. He believed and was counted righteous by his faith (Rom. 4:22-25). God counts us righteous by our faith in the Lord Jesus Christ who gives to us His righteousness earned by His perfect life and His death and resurrection. Believe in Him. In Him we are clothed with righteousness and He will work in us growth in holiness, culminating in our being conformed to His image in glory (Rom. 8:26-30). Think about that.

What's Important? I Forget

Today's Reading: Genesis 18-19; Matthew 6

Selected Verses

The sun had risen on the earth when Lot came to Zoar. Then the Lord rained on Sodom and Gomorrah sulfur and fire from the Lord out of heaven. And he overthrew those cities, and all the valley, and all the inhabitants of the cities, and what grew on the ground.

Gen. 19:23-25

But seek first the kingdom of God and his righteousness, and all these things will be added to you.

Matt. 6:33

Reflections

What should we be worried about? To put it another way, what's really important?

We would be clueless, if God had not revealed His holiness and His will to us through special revelation (the Bible). A secular, materialistic mindset tells us to live for ourselves (like the people of Sodom and Gomorrah). "Give no thought to God but only to indulging your own desires. What judgment?" they say.

Lot learned the hard way that God can reduce you to nothing in an instant. What should we be worried about? Not trying to hang on to this world, our position, our stuff.

Jesus told His disciples not to worry about their lives but to focus on the kingdom of God and His righteousness.

Think about It

It's time for a reality check. What's important? It's supremely important to seek His kingdom and His righteousness. Food and drink and clothing are necessary. God knows that, but seeking His kingdom is the priority. He will see that we do not lack what we need.

And we do not get what we need by phony, prayer chants. God is not moved by many words and empty phrases. The prayer Jesus taught was simple, brief, and thoughtful. Prayer should honor God by following those guidelines.

What is important?

- A single-minded focus on the eternal, glorious, righteous kingdom of God.

- Simple prayer.

Ask God to help you keep this straight today.

Faith that Works

Today's Reading: Genesis 20-22; Matthew 7

Selected Verses

After these things God tested Abraham and said to him, "Abraham!" And he said,
"Here I am." He said, "Take your son, your only son Isaac, whom you love, and
go to the land of Moriah, and offer him there as a burnt offering on one of the
mountains of which I shall tell you." So Abraham rose early in the morning.

Gen. 22:1-3a

Everyone then who hears these words of mine and does them
will be like a wise man who built his house on the rock.

Matt. 7:24

Reflections

As unsteady as it was, Abraham's faith translated into action. Abraham did not withhold his own son, Isaac, but took steps to offer him as a sacrifice to God. Later in our reading, we will see that Abraham did not expect the outcome that came. The writer of Hebrews tells us that Abraham assumed God would let him follow through with the sacrifice and, afterwards, raise Isaac from the dead (Heb. 11:17-19).

It is curious, in light of the comment in Hebrews, that Abraham told an anxious Isaac, "God will provide for himself the lamb for a burnt offering, my son" (Gen. 22:8). That statement is loaded with meaning. God has provided for himself a lamb for a burnt offering, His own Son, Jesus Christ. In that case, the offering was not interrupted but completed. The resurrection that Abraham anticipated for Isaac occurred for Jesus, who not only was raised from the dead but ascended to the right hand of God, where He sits in glory and power (Phil. 2:1ff).

Abraham's actions demonstrate that faith works. In Matthew, we find Jesus telling His disciples to demonstrate faith in both actions and attitudes. Faith is not merely holding a correct theological view but of living in the light of that theological view. This action results in knowing God and being known by Him, so that in the judgment it will be that relationship that carries us into His welcoming presence, not the works that we did.

Think about It

Works demonstrate faith but it is not works but faith that saves us. Show your faith through works, but trust Him, not those works, for salvation. Remember, Abraham was saved by his faith, demonstrated in his works, and not lost by his failures and inconsistencies (Rom. 4). The grace of God in Christ made the difference. Isn't that true for you as well? Think about that.

The Dramatic and the Mundane

Today's Reading: Genesis 23-24; Matthew 8

Selected Verses

After this, Abraham buried Sarah his wife in the cave of the field of Machpelah east of Mamre (that is, Hebron) in the land of Canaan. The field and the cave that is in it were made over to Abraham as property for a burying place by the Hittites.

Gen. 23:19-20

And the men marveled, saying, "What sort of man is this, that even winds and sea obey him?"

Matt. 8:27

Reflections

Life unfolds mostly in ordinary, everyday ways. Mostly. But then there are days that one senses a turning point has been reached.

In today's reading in Genesis, Abraham takes care of business. Not unimportant business, but business just the same. He arranges for Sarah's burial and Isaac's marriage. God has promised him the whole land, but he pays the exorbitant asking price for a cemetery. He is generous, because his God is generous. God guides Abraham's servant to a wife for Isaac, making the choice obvious. Blessed is the man who is given a wife by the Lord. Isaac was blessed, but none of these events is totally unexpected. This is normal life, sort of.

In Matthew, however, Jesus' ministry schedule is filled with the dramatic: healing, teaching, and calming a storm to the amazement of the disciples. The One who rocked crowds with His authoritative teaching (Matt. 7:28-29) now shakes the kingdom of darkness by casting out demons and demonstrating His authority over the weather. This is not everyday life in the first century, or any century. History is being made here and the world is being challenged to trust Jesus Christ.

Think about It

God works in both the mundane and the dramatic; don't be complacent in the former or fearful in the latter. Today your life may seem normal, even a little humdrum, but God is not slumbering. On the other hand, this could be a day when all hell breaks loose, but God is not distracted during your trials.

Either way, trust Him and be faithful.

Crisis and Failure Is Not Hopeless

Today's Reading: Genesis 25-26; Matthew 9:1-17

Selected Verses

Jacob said, "Sell me your birthright now." Esau said, "I am about to die; of what use is a birthright to me?" Jacob said, "Swear to me now." So he swore to him and sold his birthright to Jacob. Then Jacob gave Esau bread and lentil stew, and he ate and drank and rose and went his way. Thus Esau despised his birthright.

Gen. 25:31-34

But when he heard it, he said, "Those who are well have no need of a physician, but those who are sick. Go and learn what this means: 'I desire mercy, and not sacrifice.' For I came not to call the righteous, but sinners."

Matt. 9:12, 13

Reflections

How do you face a crisis? How do you handle failure, sin, and guilt?

Isaac faced a crisis—a famine, to be precise. He considered immigrating to Egypt, but God appeared to him and reassured him of His presence and provision. Isaac rested upon God's promises and stayed in the land. Isaac's faith honored God and kept him from a bad decision.

Esau faced a crisis or two. He came home starved from his hunting trip. He gave in to his hunger and sold his birthright for Jacob's delicious stew. Later, Esau wanted a wife. He married a local pagan woman rather than follow the family tradition of marrying within their clan. Esau could not tolerate any delay in the gratification of his physical needs in order to make wise and godly decisions. In both of these cases, his choices had devastating consequences for him and his family.

I admire Isaac's faith and I am repulsed by Esau's undisciplined appetites, but it is easier for me to be like Esau than like Isaac. Do I consistently resist temptation and sin? No. I do not always choose to trust God and to endure whatever difficulty may come without complaining or choosing the path of least resistance.

Yet Jesus gives me hope. He was observed eating with tax collectors and sinners, the low-lifes of society. When questioned about this, He replied: "Those who are well have no need of a physician, but those who are sick. . . . For I came not to call the righteous, but sinners."

Think about It

We fail. We sin. But Jesus Christ came for sinners like us. He came to call us to repentance. He came to heal us. How do you deal with a crisis or the failure to deal with it well? Don't be like Esau, who failed to obtain the grace of God (Heb. 12:14-17). Seek to face a crisis with faith. When you fail, and you sometimes will, repent, confess sin, and find forgiveness from Christ. Get up, press on.

21

Solving the Labor Shortage

Today's Reading: Genesis 27-28; Matthew 9:18-38

Selected Verses

. . . and in you and your offspring shall all the families of the earth be blessed.

Gen. 28:14b

The harvest is plentiful, but the laborers are few; therefore pray earnestly to the Lord of the harvest to send out laborers into his harvest.

Matt. 9:37-38

Reflections

God's revealed will for Abraham, Isaac, and Jacob and their descendants was to bless all the families of the earth. That blessing was far greater than even those patriarchs could have imagined. They would probably envision personal prosperity, security, and long life, the kind of material things most of us long for today.

The blessing God planned for all the families of the earth would involve God Himself becoming flesh and living among us. Jacob's dream of a ladder from heaven pictured a direct connection between the eternal God and mankind. This dream was fulfilled when Jesus came (John 1:51).

Matthew shows how Jesus blessed people through meeting their physical needs, even raising the dead. As we saw yesterday, Jesus wasn't about merely meeting physical needs but about calling sinners to repentance. The promised blessing for all the families of the earth was redemption from sin and reconciliation with God through the atonement of the Messiah, Jesus Christ. This will become clearer as we go forward in our reading.

But Jesus told His disciples there was a problem. The harvest was plentiful, but the laborers were few.

God ordained that the blessing He planned to pour out on the world would be made known through messengers He would send. Jesus said there was a labor shortage. He told His disciples to pray for laborers to go out into the harvest.

Think about It

How do we get laborers to bring in the harvest of souls? God sends them. What can we do about the need for laborers? Ask God to send them. Simple. You can participate right now wherever you are. But beware! He may send *you* as a laborer—across the street or around the world. Tomorrow we will see that Jesus sent the same ones to labor whom He told to pray for laborers. You may become the answer to your own prayer.

Understanding Family Hostility

Today's Reading: Genesis 29-30; Matthew 10:1-23

Selected Verses

When Rachel saw that she bore Jacob no children, she envied her sister. She said to Jacob, "Give me children, or I shall die!"

Gen. 30:1

Brother will deliver brother over to death, and the father his child, and children will rise against parents and have them put to death, and you will be hated by all for my name's sake. But the one who endures to the end will be saved

Matt. 10:21-22

Reflections

Does family hostility always prove God's displeasure? From today's readings, we learn that wonderful harmony at home may elude even those who faithfully follow Christ. We should not pursue unity among relatives at all costs.

Jacob got where he got by several deceptive moves (taking advantage of his brother and father). He met his match with Laban who married off his homely daughter to him and tricked him out of 14 years of labor for the wife he really wanted. This led to conflict between the competing wives. The family would experience lifelong misery. Still, Jacob generally did what God called him to do.

Jesus warned the disciples that those who followed him would be hated by all for His name's sake and even experience conflict with their closest family members. The faithful disciple would not be able to count on support where he might expect it.

Think about It

What goes through your mind when you face rejection or conflict with those you love as a result of your faith in the Lord? Do you wonder if you are truly being a faithful disciple of Christ? Do you doubt your faith? Dr. Steven Lawson wrote about the life of Job: "When all hell breaks loose, you might be doing something right."

As the twelve disciples took on an increasingly public role in proclaiming the gospel of their master, they could expect increasing hostility. So can you and I, but remember, we have a promise: "the one who endures to the end will be saved."

January 13 / Day 13
Fearful Followers Reassured

Today's Reading: Genesis 31-32; Matthew 10:24-42

Selected Verses

Then Jacob was greatly afraid and distressed. He divided the people who were with him, and the flocks and herds and camels, into two camps, thinking, "If Esau comes to the one camp and attacks it, then the camp that is left will escape."

Gen. 32:7-8

And do not fear those who kill the body but cannot kill the soul. Rather fear him who can destroy both soul and body in hell.

Matt. 10:28

Reflections

In both readings today, we meet people who are called by God to enter uncharted territory and are understandably fearful of what looms ahead.

Although Jacob has seen God grant him material success and a peaceful parting with Laban, he is more than a little anxious about meeting Esau after so many years. A man appears to Jacob at night and wrestles with him. We understand the mysterious, unnamed man to be the Angel of the Lord as clarified in Hosea 12:2-6.

God is gracious to Jacob to send His angel to bless him when he most needed reassurance.

Jesus also talks to His disciples about fear. He is sending them out as His messengers, into a hostile world. They will naturally tend to be fearful, but whom should they fear? Not someone who can only kill their bodies and then have no further power. Not an Esau, who might be holding a grudge after twenty years. Jesus tells the Twelve to fear God, the One who has power over our eternal destiny.

Jacob learns that God is with him as he goes back to his homeland and his brother. The disciples learn that God will be with them and keep their souls even if their ministry arouses rejection and death.

Think about It

In a sense, every new day presents uncharted territory for us even when life seems predictable and routine. How confident are you of God's power to keep you wherever He sends you and in whatever He calls you to do? Do not fear Man, not if by faith in Christ you have eternal life and you are ready to die. Don't deny real danger but replace the fear of Man with the fear of God. He will be with His own to the end.

God's Election and the Free Offer of Salvation

Today's Reading: Genesis 33-35; Matthew 11

Selected Verses

So Jacob said to his household and to all who were with him, "Put away the foreign gods that are among you and purify yourselves and change your garments. Then let us arise and go up to Bethel, so that I may make there an altar to the God who answers me in the day of my distress and has been with me wherever I have gone."

Gen. 35:2, 3

At that time Jesus declared, "I thank you, Father, Lord of heaven and earth, that you have hidden these things from the wise and understanding and revealed them to little children; yes, Father, for such was your gracious will. All things have been handed over to me by my Father, and no one knows the Son except the Father, and no one knows the Father except the Son and anyone to whom the Son chooses to reveal him."

Matt. 11:25-27

Reflections

God is sovereign over all things, including His call and election of people to Himself by grace through faith for salvation. He hides truth from those who are wise and understanding in this world but reveals it to little children. The Son has authority to reveal the Father to whom He chooses.

But this does *not* mean that there are some who desperately want to be saved but cannot be, because God turns them away. On the contrary, Jesus makes this offer: "Come to me, all who labor and are heavy laden, and I will give you rest. Take my yoke upon you, and learn from me, for I am gentle and lowly in heart, and you will find rest for your souls. For my yoke is easy, and my burden is light" (Matt. 11:28-30).

God's sovereignty in calling people to Himself is seen in the life of Abraham, Isaac, and Jacob. The lives of all three show serious flaws. Jacob, for example, tolerated his family members serving idols. None deserved God's grace. God chose them freely, not based on their merits. Likewise, God did not choose people from cities like Chorazin, Bethsaida, and Capernaum, even though Jesus had performed "most of his mighty works" there. They refused to repent, in spite of the compelling evidence that Jesus was the Christ. So they bore their own responsibility for their condition.

Think about It

Pride in one's own wisdom is an insurmountable obstacle to faith—and thus, to salvation. Pray for a childlike spirit, for grace to believe and repent. Come to the One who will give your soul rest and your life a purpose, yoked with Him in His redemptive work. You will discover His election of you to salvation.

Sons Who Suffer for Others

Today's Reading: Genesis 36-37; Matthew 12:1-21

Selected Verses

Now Israel loved Joseph more than any other of his sons, because he was the son of his old age. And he made him a robe of many colors. But when his brothers saw that their father loved him more than all his brothers, they hated him and could not speak peacefully to him.

Gen. 37:3, 4

I tell you, something greater than the temple is here. And if you had known what this means, "I desire mercy, and not sacrifice," you would not have condemned the guiltless. For the Son of Man is lord of the Sabbath.

Matt. 12:6-8

Reflections

Jesus Christ, God's Son, came to earth through the sinfully flawed lineage of Abraham, Isaac, and Jacob, into a society steeped in legalistic fear. He came not to merely make things better, but to begin to bring the nations to His kingdom and under His lordship. Not surprisingly, our Lord collided with "the powers that be," including the Pharisees and their over-scrupulous preoccupation with law-keeping—or at least, as *they* interpreted the law. Matthew records two of these collisions here in which Jesus' practice upset the status quo.

In the context of these incidents, Jesus teaches that He is Lord of the Sabbath. He alone is qualified to interpret the true meaning of the Sabbath. His teaching and practice shows that faithfulness to God's law means giving priority to mercy over sacrifice, to the well-being of man, and *not* to the satisfaction of the arbitrary rules the Pharisees had appended to that law.

The story of Joseph's early life in today's reading further demonstrates the depravity of man. Jacob's sons are from four different mothers, which by itself lays the groundwork for discord. Jacob's favoritism toward Joseph exacerbates the tension and competition. Joseph is the favored son, but he will suffer much for that status.

It is not hard to draw parallels between Joseph and Jesus. Both are favored sons of their fathers. They suffer at the hands of their brothers. Both remain faithful, even in the face of undeserved mistreatment. Their suffering ultimately results in the saving of those who caused their anguish.

Think about It

Jesus is Lord of the Sabbath, but not just the Sabbath. He is Lord of *all*: all things, *all* people, *all* of the universe. Today we can see how this is demonstrated in Scripture and in human history. Let us follow our Lord, through suffering if necessary, to the end when His kingdom will fully triumph.

Jesus: Judge or Savior?

Today's Reading: Genesis 38-40; Matthew 12:22-50

Selected Verses

And Judah took a wife for Er his firstborn, and her name was Tamar. But Er, Judah's firstborn, was wicked in the sight of the Lord, and the Lord put him to death.

Gen. 38:6, 7

Whoever is not with me is against me, and whoever does not gather with me scatters. Therefore I tell you, every sin and blasphemy will be forgiven people, but the blasphemy against the Spirit will not be forgiven. And whoever speaks a word against the Son of Man will be forgiven, but whoever speaks against the Holy Spirit will not be forgiven, either in this age or in the age to come.

Matt. 12:30-32

Reflections

God reveals Himself in His Word as a holy Judge. As Creator, He has every right over us and we have every obligation to serve and obey Him. Does He not have the right to execute sinful and rebellious creatures? Didn't Jesus preach about judgment?

God brought the judgment of death on the sons of Judah, Er and Onan. Jesus warned of judgment on those who blaspheme against the Holy Spirit. He spoke of the day of judgment on which the people of Nineveh would rise up and condemn the evil, adulterous, sign-seeking generation of His day that refused a greater prophet than Jonah and a greater king than Solomon.

A common misconception is that Jesus never suggested that there would be judgment, that He only spoke of love and peace. Not so. Rather, Jesus called His hearers to repent and believe the gospel. He warned of a sin that would never be forgiven. He taught that there would be condemnation for careless words and that contemporary society of that day was worse than wicked Nineveh.

But Jesus also gave hope to repentant sinners who recognize their lost, hopeless condition, who receive the revelation of God in Christ, who don't demand other signs, and who flee from the wrath to come.

Think about It

Jesus Christ is Judge of those who reject Him, but the Savior of those who believe in Him. He came to save His people from their sin, but not all are His people. In eternity, will you know Him as Savior or as Judge? Make sure you know you are His.

Providence and Human History

Today's Reading: Genesis 41; Matthew 13:1-32

Selected Verses

And Pharaoh said to his servants, "Can we find a man like this, in whom is the Spirit of God?" Then Pharaoh said to Joseph, "Since God has shown you all this, there is none so discerning and wise as you are. You shall be over my house, and all my people shall order themselves as you command. Only as regards the throne will I be greater than you."

Gen. 41:38-40

He put another parable before them, saying, "The kingdom of heaven is like a grain of mustard seed that a man took and sowed in his field. It is the smallest of all seeds, but when it has grown it is larger than all the garden plants and becomes a tree, so that the birds of the air come and make nests in its branches."

Matt. 13:31, 32

Reflections

God's providence controls all the events of history to bring about His eternal purposes, and because of this, He causes seemingly insignificant things to have a completely unforeseeable impact.

For example, God used a chain of sad and painful events in Joseph's life to bring an amazing outcome. His kidnapping led to his being sold as a slave. As a slave, he was imprisoned on false charges. But in prison he interpreted the dreams of Pharaoh's baker and butler. That resulted in his recognition by Pharaoh for his ability to interpret dreams and give wise advice. Joseph ended up the second-in-command to Pharaoh. From that position, Joseph was able to save Egypt and his own long-lost family from starvation. Jacob and all his family relocated to Egypt where, over a four-century period, they would grow into a mighty nation. Their descendants would be prepared to return to the Promised Land and conquer it for their homeland.

Jesus likened the kingdom of heaven to a man planting a tiny mustard seed in the ground. The seed was hardly visible before it was planted, and, after it was planted, it could not be seen at all. Yet that seed grew into a huge plant, the largest in the garden and able to provide a nesting place for the birds.

Think about It

How have you seen God bring about mighty outcomes from practically unknown people or unfortunate events? How have you seen the kingdom of heaven manifest its greatness where it was previously tiny or even non-existent?

Praise God for His providence! He does wondrous things as He grows His kingdom!

Why Is God So Good?

Today's Reading: Genesis 42-43; Matthew 13:33-58

Selected Verses

> *He said to his brothers, "My money has been put back; here it is in the*
> *mouth of my sack!" At this their hearts failed them, and they turned*
> *trembling to one another, saying, "What is this that God has done to us?"*
>
> Gen. 42:28

> *And they took offense at him. But Jesus said to them, "A prophet is not*
> *without honor except in his hometown and in his own household."*
> *And he did not do many mighty works there, because of their unbelief.*
>
> Matt. 13:57-58

Reflections

"Why does God allow so much suffering and pain in our lives?" It's a question I often hear. And we might more wisely ask, "Why does God allow so much goodness and pleasure?" Before there can be salvation from our sin, we must recognize that we are guilty and deserve punishment. Joseph pushed his guilty brothers to show repentance for their sin toward him. When they did, he showed them mercy by providing the food they needed and returning their money to them. Joseph literally saved his evil brothers from death at no cost to them.

Jesus graciously came into the world to save sinners. He warned of coming judgment. Yet it was in His hometown where He had the most resistance. Those who had seen Him grow up there were perplexed by the authority and wisdom of His teaching, but, instead of submitting to Him, they took Him to be some kind of upstart. They took offense at Him. The consequence of this was He did not do many mighty works there.

Paul wrote to the Romans "...do you presume on the riches of his kindness and forbearance and patience, not knowing that God's kindness is meant to lead you to repentance?" (Rom. 2: 4). In God's plan, before there can be forgiveness, salvation, and reconciliation, there must be recognition of personal responsibility for sin leading to repentance.

Think about It

Have you seen the goodness of God toward you, or do you get stuck on all the suffering you have experienced? Joseph's brothers got it and received salvation. The people of Nazareth didn't.

Are you more like those repentant brothers or like the resistant Nazarenes? Ask God for a heart changed by Jesus Christ, so that you do not take offense at Him but rather bow before Him in contrite faith.

Big Boys Do Cry

Today's Reading: Genesis 44-45; Matthew 14:1-21

Selected Verses

Then Joseph could not control himself before all those who stood by him. He cried, "Make everyone go out from me." So no one stayed with him when Joseph made himself known to his brothers. And he wept aloud, so that the Egyptians heard it, and the household of Pharaoh heard it. And Joseph said to his brothers, "I am Joseph! Is my father still alive?" But his brothers could not answer him, for they were dismayed at his presence.

Gen. 45:1-3

He sent and had John beheaded in the prison, and his head was brought on a platter and given to the girl, and she brought it to her mother. And his disciples came and took the body and buried it, and they went and told Jesus. Now when Jesus heard this, he withdrew from there in a boat to a desolate place by himself.

Matt. 14:10-13a

Reflections

In western society, we swing back and forth to extremes. Decades ago, in my youth, we said glibly, "Big boys don't cry." More recently, the "feeling male" has become the hero, or at least less of a villain than "Rambo," the earlier granite superhero stereotype of cool hardness.

Once again, the Bible shows a different perspective than we generally see in our culture.

John the Baptist preached against sin at the highest levels of society. He paid for that boldness with his head. When Jesus heard the news, He sought solitude and a private place to grieve. That time was interrupted by crowds who came seeking Him. The Lord responded to them without delay, but notice that Jesus felt fully the pain of others, in this case, John the Baptist.

Joseph, too, was moved by the pain of his brothers, deserved though it was. They had suffered long the guilt of their actions toward him, but when he saw their grief he wept and immediately assured them of forgiveness. He even explained how they ought to look at what they had done as a series of events used by God to bring blessing to them all.

Think about It

Both Jesus and Joseph wept for the pain of others. Big boys do cry, but they aren't crybabies nor whiners. The Bible never portrays a godly man as cold and heartless. But neither is he an emotional basket case, unable to take necessary action in a timely way. In today's reading, both Jesus and Joseph showed deep feelings, but both were able to function even with their emotions raw. Let these examples instruct you in Christlike living.

Lessons about Time

Today's Reading: Genesis 46-48; Matthew 14:22-36

Selected Verses

Then Israel said to Joseph, "Behold, I am about to die, but God will be with you and will bring you again to the land of your fathers. Moreover, I have given to you rather than to your brothers one mountain slope that I took from the hand of the Amorites with my sword and with my bow."

Gen. 48:21-22

And after he had dismissed the crowds, he went up on the mountain by himself to pray. When evening came, he was there alone.

Matt. 14:23

Reflections

Jesus, after hearing about the death of John the Baptist, sought to be alone, but crowds came seeking Him (Matt. 14:13). He patiently and lovingly ministered to them, including feeding five thousand with a couple of fish and some bread. That work completed, He dismissed the people and sent the disciples off in a boat while He went alone to a desolate place. Here are a few observations about these incidents:

- Jesus took time to be alone. Too often, people in Christian ministry become exhausted because they see their work as too important to take time for rest and prayer. Jesus recognized His need for time alone.

- Jesus accepted interruptions to His personal life. When the crowds came, He served them, postponing His time alone. Too often, people in Christian ministry put their own needs above those of others and show no flexibility or sensitivity to others. Jesus delayed His time alone.

- Jesus returned to His disciples at their time of need. Once His time alone was concluded, Jesus went right back to the Twelve who were in the midst of a severe storm on the sea. Too often, people in Christian ministry who take time to rest begin to enjoy it so much they never return to the work. Jesus did not shirk His responsibilities by overextending His time alone.

- Jesus had a sense of timing in His life and ministry. He balanced private prayer and public ministry perfectly. He did His Father's will peacefully and confidently.

In our Genesis reading today, Jacob (Israel) also shows sensitivity to God's timing in his life. He anticipates his coming death and takes care of final matters. Too many people act like they will live forever and do not take care of matters that will make it easier on their surviving family and friends when they pass away.

31

Think about It

Time is a gift from God. The length of our life is determined by Him. Besides that, the happenings of each of our days are also providentially directed by God Eternal. We are stewards of our time who must manage it for His glory. Are you developing a sense of God's timing in your life? Do you balance personal prayer and service to others so that both get needed attention? Are you taking care of matters that need to be done by you before God calls you home? Live wisely, knowing that your days are numbered and you are a steward of them.

Looking for Loopholes in God's Law

Today's Reading: Genesis 49-50; Matthew 15:1-20

Selected Verses

My father made me swear, saying, "I am about to die: in my tomb that I hewed out for myself in the land of Canaan, there shall you bury me." Now therefore, let me please go up and bury my father. Then I will return.

Gen. 50:5

For God commanded, "Honor your father and your mother," and, "Whoever reviles father or mother must surely die." But you say, "If anyone tells his father or his mother, 'What you would have gained from me is given to God,' he need not honor his father." So for the sake of your tradition you have made void the word of God.

Matt. 15:4-6

Reflections

Joseph had promised to bury his father, Jacob, in the land of Canaan. Upon his father's death, Joseph asked Pharaoh for permission to return to Canaan and fulfill his commitment to Jacob. Permission was granted and Joseph fulfilled his promise.

Honoring one's parents is the right thing to do both in life and at death. God's law given later through Moses specified that all were to "Honor your father and your mother, that your days may be long in the land that the Lord your God is giving you" (Exod. 20:12). There was a reward of long life held out to those who kept this commandment. Conversely, there is an implied threat of early death for not keeping it.

Yet in Jesus' day, certain religious leaders gutted the original intent of that commandment. They advocated the practice of withholding support to needy parents by designating resources as "given to God." Jesus told His contemporaries that they were using their tradition to make God's word void. They had added tradition on top of the law giving them a seeming loophole to disobey clear commandments.

In a different context but in a similar spirit, the writers of the Westminster Confession of Faith warned those who, because of the corruption of man, are "apt to study arguments, unduly to put asunder" their marriage vows for unlawful reasons (*Westminster Confession of Faith*, ch. 24, par. 6).

Think about It

Beware of seeking ways to skirt the clear teaching of God's Word. Avoid the ungodly practice of those who "study arguments to unduly" break God's law. Yet the good news remains that Christ died for the disobedient loophole-seeker who repents. Trust Him for forgiveness and trust Him for strength and wisdom to walk in obedience to His Word.

We Groan, But Does God Know?

Today's Reading: Exodus 1-3; Matthew 15:21-39

Selected Verses

And God heard their groaning, and God remembered his covenant with Abraham, with Isaac, and with Jacob. God saw the people of Israel—and God knew

Exod. 3:24-25

He healed them, so that the crowd wondered, when they saw the mute speaking, the crippled healthy, the lame walking, and the blind seeing. And they glorified the God of Israel.

Matt. 15:30b-31

Reflections

Exodus opens with an update on the descendants of Jacob (Israel) who by this time had remained in Egypt for 400 years. They no longer enjoyed favored status as they had in the days of Joseph. Their presence threatened the Egyptians who subjected them to slavery. The authorities insisted that the midwives execute all male babies. Things got worse and worse, and the Israelites groaned. Did God know?

Indeed, He did. God heard, remembered, saw, and knew as the passage above points out. He had chosen Moses to deliver them. But first Moses needed to go through a strange training program. He was raised as a son of Pharaoh's daughter. Then, he spiraled down. His first attempts at leadership ended in his committing murder. He fled to the wilderness with this question ringing in his ears, "Who made you a prince and judge over us?" Forty years passed. Finally, God appeared to a now-insecure eighty-year-old Moses. The Lord assured him that he would lead the Israelites out of slavery to the land of the Canaanites, a land that God had promised to Abraham. Israel would be free (Acts 7:30).

But that earthly kingdom of Israel would only be a shadow of the ultimate kingdom. Jesus came announcing the arrival of the kingdom of God. He set people free from the ravages, not of an earthly tyrant, but of the spiritual tyrant, Satan, through whom the world lived and lives in bondage to sin, sickness, and death. Jesus demonstrated His power as the king to liberate those who were bound. The eternal kingdom has already come in part, and we are promised that Jesus will come again to finalize its establishment. Meanwhile we pray, trust God, and wait in the confidence that He knows our groaning, remembers His covenant, and will fulfill all His promises.

Think about It

Do you know that God knows your groaning today? He does. Trust Him. Deliverance is coming.

How Long, O Lord?

Today's Reading: Exodus 4-6; Matthew 16

Selected Verses

*Say therefore to the people of Israel, "I am the Lord, and I will bring you out
from under the burdens of the Egyptians, and I will deliver you from slavery to
them, and I will redeem you with an outstretched arm and with great acts of
judgment. I will take you to be my people, and I will be your God, and you shall
know that I am the Lord your God, who has brought you out from under the burdens
of the Egyptians. I will bring you into the land that I swore to give to Abraham,
to Isaac, and to Jacob. I will give it to you for a possession. I am the Lord."*

Exod. 6:6-8

*For the Son of Man is going to come with his angels in the glory of his Father,
and then he will repay each person according to what he has done.*

Matt. 16:27

Reflections

God's promises are clear, but from our human viewpoint the fulfillment of
those promises is slow in coming. It was true for Israel in Egypt. It was good
news that God sent Moses to them with assurances that the Lord was going to
deliver them from slavery and take them to the land He had promised Abraham,
but in the short run all they got was more oppression. Pharaoh made them find
their own straw and required the same daily production of bricks.

Jesus promised that a day would come in which He, the Son of Man, would
come with His angels in the glory of His Father, and repay each person according to
what he has done. That day has still not come. Meanwhile, those who follow Him
are called to carry a cross. We, no less than the Israelites, must wait in faith that the
Lord Jesus Christ will come on His schedule and bring just and final judgment.

For now we cry with the psalmist:

How long, O Lord? Will you forget me forever?
How long will you hide your face from me?
How long must I take counsel in my soul
and have sorrow in my heart all the day?
How long shall my enemy be exalted over me?

Ps. 13:1-2

Think about It

How long? The answer is "as long as God wills." Even though we cry for His
kingdom to come, we have His promises and His loving presence to sustain us
till then. Are you carrying a cross? You aren't the first. So did Jesus. And His
disciples. You are in good company. Press on.

Heart Responses to God

Today's Reading: Exodus 7-8; Matthew 17

Selected Verses

But Pharaoh hardened his heart this time also, and did not let the people go.

Exod. 8:32

He was still speaking when, behold, a bright cloud overshadowed them, and a voice from the cloud said, "This is my beloved Son, with whom I am well pleased; listen to him." When the disciples heard this, they fell on their faces and were terrified.

Matt. 17:5-6

Reflections

The God of the Bible has revealed Himself in human history, but the responses are mixed. Some, like Pharaoh, harden their hearts. Others, like Peter, James, and John, fall on their faces, terrified.

Pharaoh saw God's power bringing plagues upon him and the nation. In the first two instances, his magicians were successful in reproducing the same results. With the third plague, the magicians failed to produce gnats and concluded that it is "the finger of God." In the fourth case, there is no mention of the magicians even attempting to compete with God's power. Despite the increasing intensity of the plagues, Pharaoh kept hardening his heart.

The disciples on the mountain with Jesus also saw wondrous things. Jesus was transfigured. His face and garments shone with intense light. Moses and Elijah appeared. Staring at this sight, Peter started babbling about making tents for each of them. Then he and the other disciples heard the voice of God. The staring and babbling ended and they fall in terror before God.

How do you account for these contrasting responses to displays of God's power and presence? God hardens Pharaoh's heart, but does a gracious work in the hearts of the disciples. Believers in biblical history always fall before God's revelation of Himself. Unbelievers, like Pharaoh, merely shrug off the evidence of God's presence and power as if it were a mere coincidence. To Pharaoh, the plagues were an inconvenience, not a sign indicating that the eternal, omnipotent God was near.

Think about It

How do you respond to God's revelation of Himself? If you believe, you will have a proper fear of Him—not horror that makes you run from Him, but awe that causes you to fall before Him in worship and reverence.

Fear God for His majesty and power in creation and providence. Fear God for, as the *Westminster Shorter Catechism* (question 4) says, He is "a spirit, infinite, eternal, and unchangeable, in his being, wisdom, power, holiness, justice, goodness and truth." Praise God if He has given you, not a hardened heart, but a tender, believing heart that fears Him.

Who's the Greatest?

Today's Reading: Exodus 9-10; Matthew 18:1-20

Selected Verses

But when Pharaoh saw that the rain and the hail and the thunder had ceased, he sinned yet again and hardened his heart, he and his servants. So the heart of Pharaoh was hardened, and he did not let the people of Israel go, just as the Lord had spoken through Moses.

Exod. 9:34-35

At that time the disciples came to Jesus, saying, "Who is the greatest in the kingdom of heaven?" And calling to him a child, he put him in the midst of them and said, "Truly, I say to you, unless you turn and become like children, you will never enter the kingdom of heaven."

Matt. 18:1-3

Reflections

A daily question in our society is, "Who's the greatest of them all?" The same question has these variations: "Who's the greatest athlete? the greatest celebrity? the most powerful leader? the richest person?" We may even ask, "Who is the worst of all?" Maybe a notorious gangster or traitor comes to mind.

The assumption is that superiority in certain categories like money, beauty, intelligence, physical strength, political power and influence make a person worthy of fame and adulation. We honor those who excel in the areas we consider important.

On a number of occasions, Jesus' disciples showed a competitiveness among themselves for superior positions. Maybe that was in the back of their minds when they asked Him the question in today's reading.

Jesus showed them that the categories generally considered important by society are of no value in the kingdom of heaven. Superiority in those categories is therefore meaningless. A little child showing characteristic humility is held above the proud and haughty.

What a contrast—a little child and the great Pharaoh! The Egyptian ruler's experience certainly demonstrates the destruction that comes to the proud, the hard-hearted, and the spiritually blind. A Pharaoh may impress the masses with his power and prestige, but without a change of heart, he will not even enter the kingdom of heaven, much less be given a place of honor there.

Think about It

What categories of superiority do you value most? Beware of idolizing that which has no importance in the kingdom of heaven. Pray that God may grant you the humility of a child and deliver you from the foolish, temporal values of this world.

Forgiveness: Pay It Forward

Today's Reading: Exodus 11-12; Matthew 18:21-35

Selected Verses

The Lord said to Moses and Aaron in the land of Egypt, "This month shall be for you the beginning of months. It shall be the first month of the year for you."

Exod. 12:1-2

"And should not you have had mercy on your fellow servant, as I had mercy on you?" And in anger his master delivered him to the jailers, until he should pay all his debt. So also my heavenly Father will do to every one of you, if you do not forgive your brother from your heart.

Matt. 18:33-35

Reflections

God created time. He also instructed His people to observe certain periodic days to remember important events and the theological truths connected with those events. The Passover was one of those events. God commanded that it be observed annually and that it coincide with the New Year.

The Passover definitively set apart the Israelites from the Egyptians. The blood of unblemished lambs marked the homes of those who believed and distinguished them from those who did not. The blood protected the inhabitants of those homes from death. The lamb paid the price and the people were saved.

Christ, too, paid the price as the Lamb of God who takes away the sin of the world, our Passover lamb (John 1:29; 1 Cor. 5:7). Just as the ancient Israelites celebrated their deliverance from slavery by an annual Passover celebration, we as God's people today celebrate corporately, by the sacrament of the Lord's Supper or Communion. We are remembering the fulfillment of a greater Lamb whose offering made a once-for-all atonement for sin.

Think about It

Imagine being in an Israelite home in Egypt on the night of the Passover. You have placed the blood of a lamb on the doorposts. You wait inside, trusting that the blood will protect your firstborn son from the angel of death. What relief when the angel passes over your house and you are safe! That is a graphic picture of what God has done for us who trust in the Lamb of God to take away our sins and deliver us from deserved death. Will we not forgive as we have been forgiven? Paul admonished the Christians in Ephesus: "Be kind to one another, tenderhearted, forgiving one another, as God in Christ forgave you" (Eph. 4:32).

The deliverance and forgiveness which Jesus Christ obtained for us ought to be manifested in lives of forgiveness towards others. Be vigilant to show grace and mercy toward those who owe you, not as the unforgiving servant in Jesus' parable.

How to Know You've Learned

Today's Reading: Exodus 13-15; Matthew 19:1-15

Selected Verses

*When they came to Marah, they could not drink the water of Marah
because it was bitter; therefore it was named Marah. And the
people grumbled against Moses, saying, "What shall we drink?"*

Exod. 15:23-24

*Then children were brought to him that he might lay his hands on them and pray.
The disciples rebuked the people, but Jesus said, "Let the little children come
to me and do not hinder them, for to such belongs the kingdom of heaven."*

Matt. 19:13-14

Reflections

Not much changed in people, even God's people, from the time of Moses to the time of Jesus Christ. Not much has changed from those times until today. Don't we struggle to apply what we think we have learned in the past to current problems and challenges?

The Israelites saw God deliver them from Egypt by a series of plagues. Then Pharaoh's army jeopardized their exodus and pursued them. They cried to God in desperation, and God delivered them again. They rejoiced as the cadavers of their enemies washed up on the shores of the Red Sea while they watched safely. Could God deliver them from anything—repeat, *anything*? Yes, yes, a thousand times, YES!

But within hours they were complaining about the lack of water, and when they found water, they complained that it was bitter. Sure enough, they had forgotten the lesson of the Red Sea.

Jesus taught the disciples that the greatest in the kingdom of heaven is a child (Matt. 18:1-3), but when little children were brought to Jesus those same disciples rebuked the parents who brought them. They forgot the lesson of the little child quickly.

Think about It

God is patient with His slow-learning, thick-headed disciples. We really don't get it, do we? Let's face it; we are often repeating the same foolish mistakes of the Israelites and the disciples. How many times do we need to be re-taught the same lessons of faith, patience, and prayer? How quickly we forget what He has done in the past and cave in to doubt, complaining, whining, and panic.

Trust Him to act. Call upon Him with confidence to do more than you can ask or think (Eph. 3:20-21). Transfer what you learned before to the trials and uncertainties of today. Then you will know that you have really learned. Oh, and praise God for His patience. He has a bigger plan than we know.

Leave All; Plod On

Today's Reading: Exodus 16-18; Matthew 19:16-30

Selected Verses

And the people of Israel said to them, "Would that we had died by the hand of the Lord in the land of Egypt, when we sat by the meat pots and ate bread to the full, for you have brought us out into this wilderness to kill this whole assembly with hunger."

Exod. 16:3

Then Peter said in reply, "See, we have left everything and followed you. What then will we have?"

Matt. 19:27

Reflections

God calls His people to leave all and follow Him. The Israelites experienced hunger, thirst, and war after their exodus from Egyptian slavery. Their faith faltered. They thought about the comforts and delicacies of Egypt. Selectively, they remembered the good times and tasty foods in Egypt and forgot the daily quotas of brick production, the scrounging for straw, and the beatings by the taskmasters. They filtered out the bad memories and complained about present conditions. That was their default position.

Jesus, too, called His disciples to leave all behind and follow Him. Peter waxed nostalgic, it seems, as he pondered the cost of following the Lord. "What then will we have?" he asks.

Jesus is quick to reassure him. What will they have?

- A new world where Jesus Christ will sit on His glorious throne.
- Thrones where the apostles would have power and authority to judge the twelve tribes of Israel.
- All that they had given up 100 times over.
- Eternal life.

Think about It

How do Jesus' promises sound to you? They sound sublime to me. Can we plod on another day, maybe many more days? I think so. Whatever it takes.

Nah, I don't miss Egypt.

Do you?

Who Would Begrudge Grace?

Today's Reading: Exodus 19-21; Matthew 20:1-16

Selected Verses

Now these are the rules that you shall set before them.

Exod. 21:1

*Am I not allowed to do what I choose with what
belongs to me? Or do you begrudge my generosity?*

Matt. 20:15

Reflections

In today's reading in Exodus, God gives His law to Moses for Israel. This law includes moral, political, and ceremonial aspects. Can you find any indication of grace in this law system? Yes, but it can be easily overlooked. The ceremonial law established a priesthood and offerings for sin, to atone for the breaking of the law. It points to a need for a permanent offering for sin. It anticipates the grace of God that would be revealed in Jesus Christ.

Nevertheless, the tone of the law sounds like justice, equity, and being responsible to do what is right. The political or civil law designated proper responsibilities for restitution to injured parties, ethical treatment of slaves, and so forth. It is easy for those under law to get a mentality of doing what is specified and no more. The minimum required tends to become the maximum rendered.

As John 1:17 tells us, "…the law was given through Moses; grace and truth came through Jesus Christ."

Accordingly, Jesus' parable of the laborers in the vineyard show how God pours His grace out on some. The master of the house paid the early workers their due but the later arriving workers got the same amount. The former complained about the disparity. They show they do not understand nor accept the graciousness of the master.

The law was given to show us our sin (Rom. 3:19-20), but, having seen it, we are called to seek God who deals with His children with grace, giving what we have not earned nor deserved.

Think about It

Who would begrudge grace? Those who see themselves as righteous, not needing grace. Resentment toward God for His grace toward others indicates never having received His grace. Be warned. Seek the God of grace who in Jesus Christ, His Son, kept the law perfectly and made an offering for sin that covers all who turn to Him in faith and repentance.

Good Intentions Gone Bad

Today's Reading: Exodus 22-24; Matthew 20:17-34

Selected Verses

Then he took the Book of the Covenant and read it in the hearing of the people. And they said, "All that the Lord has spoken we will do, and we will be obedient." And Moses took the blood and threw it on the people and said, "Behold the blood of the covenant that the Lord has made with you in accordance with all these words."

Exod. 24:7-8

Jesus answered, "You do not know what you are asking. Are you able to drink the cup that I am to drink?" They said to him, "We are able."

Matt. 20:22

Reflections

Here we see a clear parallel between human nature under the old covenant and the new covenant. In both cases, people swore to do certain things: to be obedient, to drink the cup of suffering with Jesus Christ. In both cases, as we will see, they failed to live up to their promises and good intentions. They fully intended to carry through. There was not a trace of doubt in their minds or voices. "We will be obedient, we will do *all* the Lord has spoken," they said (emphasis mine).

The Israelites were moved by the thunder and lightning and smoke and trumpet sounds on Mt. Sinai as the Law was given. They trembled. Motivated by fear, they were willing to promise anything, but their good intentions proved insufficient.

The sons of Zebedee, James and John, had aspirations to a place of honor in the coming Kingdom. Their mother supported or, perhaps, instigated this appeal. She asked for this honor to be assured by the Lord. Motivated by pride and ambition, they were certain they could handle the cost of drinking the cup, but when it came time to sip, they fled with the rest and left Jesus alone.

Think about It

I am not very different from the Israelites or the Zebedee family. I, too, have had great intentions of serving God, of obeying Him, of doing all that He has commanded, of drinking the cup of suffering with Him, but my follow-through has fallen far short. How about you?

What does this tell me? It tells me I need forgiveness. I am guilty as charged. I need someone to bail me out, but I do not deserve it and I cannot earn it. It is by grace alone that God Himself would make atonement for my sins.

The Apostle Paul wrote that in His Son we have "...redemption through his blood, the forgiveness of our trespasses, according to the riches of his grace" (Eph. 1:7). This forgiveness covers our empty promises and every other failure to do and be what we should do and be. Think about that. If you know this applies to you, praise God for His forgiveness of your good intentions gone bad.

God Always Initiates

Today's Reading: Exodus 25-26; Matthew 21:1-22

Selected Verses

There I will meet with you, and from above the mercy seat, from between the two cherubim that are on the ark of the testimony, I will speak with you about all that I will give you in commandment for the people of Israel.

Exod. 25:22

"Say to the daughter of Zion,
'Behold, your king is coming to you,
humble, and mounted on a donkey,
on a colt, the foal of a beast of burden.'"

Matt. 21:5

Reflections

Although it is humanity that has rebelled and offended God, it is God who initiates reconciliations and makes the way for people to find Him. It is God who gives Moses a plan for a tabernacle and an ark upon which the Lord promises to meet with him and speak with him. All of the rituals of the tabernacle would point to Jesus Christ, God's Anointed One, who came to Zion in humility, riding a donkey.

In Jerusalem, crowds gathered to see the prophet Jesus from Nazareth of Galilee as He rode into the city. They spread their cloaks and tree branches in His path and proclaimed, "Hosanna to the Son of David!" They recognized Him as the heir to the throne of David, the kingdom that would last forever.

The Triune God always initiates. He always made the first move and He continues to make the first move. Adam hid from God. God sought him anyway. He came to Moses and met him above the mercy seat of the ark in the tabernacle. He came to Jerusalem, cleansed the temple, and healed the sick.

Think about It

He comes to us. He graciously makes the move to restore us to Himself, though we deserve nothing but judgment, punishment, and eternal death. We have tried to hide from Him. We naturally flee His holy presence, not willing to admit that we are dead in sin without Him. We cannot respond until He breathes into us and gives us new life that inevitably results in faith and repentance.

Praise God for reaching out to His own people, for grasping hell-bent sinners and rescuing them from His just wrath. Will we to whom He has come imitate His grace and reach out to those who need forgiveness and good news of salvation through Jesus Christ?

Authority Abused

Today's Reading: Exodus 27-28; Matthew 21:23-46

Selected Verse

For Aaron's sons you shall make coats and sashes and caps. You shall make them for glory and beauty. And you shall put them on Aaron your brother, and on his sons with him, and shall anoint them and ordain them and consecrate them, that they may serve me as priests.

Exod. 28:40-41

And when he entered the temple, the chief priests and the elders of the people came up to him as he was teaching, and said, "By what authority are you doing these things, and who gave you this authority?"

Matt. 21:23

Reflections

God instructed Moses to establish the priesthood of Aaron for His people Israel. They were duly installed within the law governing the priesthood. At the time of Jesus the priests had exercised this authority for centuries.

It seems appropriate that the chief priests and the elders should be concerned about anyone teaching among the people. Was this teacher from God or merely speaking on his own? Their concern was appropriate but their attitude was not. They jealously guarded that authority given to them in the Law of Moses. They were ready to silence anyone whose teaching was not from God.

Jesus' popularity was a threat to the priests control, just as John the Baptist's had been. Jesus wisely uncovered their hypocrisy showing that they were more fearful of getting into trouble with the crowds than in protecting the people from false teachers. They pretended to be concerned about Jesus' source of authority, but their true motivation was to maintain their own authority and power at all costs.

What began "for glory and beauty" had become ugly and corrupted. A showdown was imminent in which the Jewish and Roman leaders of that first century society would join forces to stop Jesus.

Think about It

We should be warned here to hold any proper authority we have (in the church, in the home, in the marketplace, in government) as a stewardship from God. It is to be used for His purposes "for glory and beauty" but not to be held at all costs. Do you use your authority for God's glory, and not your own? Think about it.

How to Be Properly Dressed for Heaven

Today's Reading: Exodus 29-30; Matthew 22:1-22

Selected Verses

> *I will dwell among the people of Israel and will be their God. And they*
> *shall know that I am the Lord their God, who brought them out of the*
> *land of Egypt that I might dwell among them. I am the Lord their God.*
>
> Exod. 29:45-46

> *But when the king came in to look at the guests, he saw there a man*
> *who had no wedding garment. And he said to him, "Friend, how did*
> *you get in here without a wedding garment?" And he was speechless.*
>
> Matt. 22:11-12

Reflections

God seeks true worshipers to enjoy His fellowship (John 4:23). The problem is humankind is sinful and cannot come to God in that natural, fallen state. This is clear in both of today's readings.

God gave Israel the priesthood as an essential means for them to recognize their ongoing need for forgiveness of sin in order to be acceptable before Him. He wanted them to be acceptable because He purposed to live among them and to be their God. The ordination of priests in Israel was foundational to the orderly administration of the sacrificial system.

In Jesus' parable, a king invites people to the marriage of his son. Many completely ignore his gracious invitation, so the king invites any who will come. Yet one who comes doesn't dress properly for this occasion. The king finds and expels him for being so haughty as to show up without a wedding garment. Jesus wants all to grasp the inadequacy of approaching God in our own natural state, without the proper clothing of His righteousness.

In the gospel, we learn that Jesus Christ is our great High Priest. He has fulfilled all righteousness (Matt. 3:15) and He commands us to seek God's righteousness (Matt. 6:33). He credits His righteousness to the account of those who come to Him in faith (1 Cor. 1:30). As the old hymn, "The Solid Rock" by Edward Mote says so poignantly,

> *When He shall come with trumpet sound,*
> *Oh, may I then in Him be found;*
> *Dressed in His righteousness alone,*
> *Faultless to stand before the throne.*

Think about It

God calls us to His fellowship, but we may not come in our natural state. We must be clothed properly; then we may enjoy Him forever. Will you be there dressed in Christ's righteousness?

True Worship of the True God

Today's Reading: Exodus 31-33; Matthew 22:23-46

Selected Verses

And he received the gold from their hand and fashioned it with a graving tool and made a golden calf. And they said, "These are your gods, O Israel, who brought you up out of the land of Egypt!" When Aaron saw this, he built an altar before it. And Aaron made a proclamation and said, "Tomorrow shall be a feast to the Lord."

Exod. 32:4-5

And he said to him, "You shall love the Lord your God with all your heart and with all your soul and with all your mind. This is the great and first commandment."

Matt. 22:37-38

Reflections

When Jesus was asked, "Which is the great commandment in the law?" He immediately identified it as wholehearted love for the Lord your God. That devotion toward God includes our hearts, minds, and souls, that is, our entire being. It is both outward and inward. It involves our thoughts, our emotions, and our wills. Nothing that is us is left out. We may not reserve a corner of our hearts for another god, an idol of our own making.

The Israelites at Mt. Sinai showed the folly of attempting to create their own god. Aaron caved in to the fears and demands of the people to have some physical object to look at and worship. He seems to have been unwilling to fully renounce the God who had brought them out of Egypt, but he was willing to introduce a golden calf as a means to worship the Lord.

Think about It

We live in a pragmatic society whose methods and values too often seep into the church. Many worship practices are justified because "they work." But in what sense do they work? They may work to induce the "me generation" to attend and give, but do they truly honor God? Do they conform to what God says in His Word?

The reformers identified the marks of a true church as the accurate preaching of the Bible, the observance of the sacraments (baptism and the Lord's Supper), and the right administration of discipline. Let us be sure our worship, whether corporately or privately, is of the one true and living God and according to His commands, with no eclectic golden calves permitted. In other words, let ours be true worship of the true God.

Two Keys to Blessing Too Often Missing

Today's Reading: Exodus 34-36; Matthew 23:1-22

Selected Verses

*So the people were restrained from bringing, for the material
they had was sufficient to do all the work, and more.*

Exod. 36:6b-7

*The greatest among you shall be your servant. Whoever exalts himself
will be humbled, and whoever humbles himself will be exalted.*

Matt. 23:11-12

Reflections

Humility and obedience are two qualities which bring blessing but are
usually in short supply. In Jesus' day, the Pharisees turned religion into a means
to prestige and honor in their society. They taught truth but made a great show
of their piety and exempted themselves from doing what they taught. They were
neither humble nor obedient. Jesus pointed them out as negative examples.

By contrast, there was a time following the Exodus during which the
Israelites showed a notable degree of humility and obedience. When called upon
to offer materials for the construction of the tabernacle and its furnishings, the
people went all out; so much so that Moses turned away would-be donors. Their
obedience and humility was demonstrated in generosity.

A few years ago I participated in a capital funds drive in my church. It had
some of the same characteristics of the collection for the tabernacle in Exodus 36.
We set a challenging goal for our small congregation but soon we began to hear
stories of how empty nest moms were taking jobs in order to give more.
Someone paid off a mortgage early, freeing up money for the campaign. Families
delayed replacing their old cars in order to contribute. The proceeds from the
campaign stunned the fundraising consultant as the congregation far surpassed
his expectations. The people rejoiced as they saw the new building take shape
and fill up for the dedication of the beautiful facility.

Think about It

What if humility and obedience flourished in our personal lives and in our
congregations? Would God not be greatly glorified, and the people enriched with
blessing? Pray that becomes reality and that you will do your part to make it so.

Don't Miss the Point

Today's Reading: Exodus 37-38; Matthew 23:23-39

Selected Verses

Bezalel made the ark of acacia wood.

Exod. 37:1a

*O Jerusalem, Jerusalem, the city that kills the prophets and stones those who
are sent to it! How often would I have gathered your children together
as a hen gathers her brood under her wings, and you were not willing!*

Matt. 23:37

Reflections

What great irony between the events of these two passages separated as they
are by many centuries!

In Exodus, we find Bezalel skillfully making the tabernacle and the
furnishings which go in it. It will be the center of Israelite worship from the time
of Moses until King Solomon builds a real temple in Jerusalem. The tabernacle
was a temporary replica of Solomon's temple which would be a temporary replica
of the true temple in heaven.

Despite the terms "temporary" and "replica" there is a sense of excitement
about the building of the tabernacle and, later, the temple. There is a hopefulness
that these earthly constructions would point them to eternal truth and the one,
true God. The people anticipate God-honoring worship to be offered here.

But what happened to all this expectancy and hopefulness?

When Jesus Christ, the promised Messiah, came to Jerusalem and to the
temple, He found not God-honoring worship nor spiritually hungry people, but
hypocritical Pharisees, descendants of their prophet-murdering forefathers. They
strained to appear righteous but failed to see that their hearts were no different
than those who had gone before them. They missed three truths that the
tabernacle and the temple should teach them. God is holy and unapproachable
by humans in their fallen condition. A sacrifice is necessary to reconcile us to
God. And God in His mercy will offer His own Son as the only final, acceptable
offering for the sin of the world. Ironically, these same Pharisees along with the
High Priest, the Sanhedrin, and Pontius Pilate were about to collude to crucify
the Son of God. Their actions would prove the truth of Jesus' cry, "O Jerusalem,
Jerusalem."

Think about It

The Pharisees missed the point. Let us beware that we do not miss it, too.
Have you been willing to come to Jesus and be gathered to Him? If not, may
God make you willing.

The Temple Destroyed

Today's Reading: Exodus 39-40; Matthew 24:1-22

Selected Verses

*And Moses saw all the work, and behold, they had done it; as the Lord
had commanded, so had they done it. Then Moses blessed them.*

Exod. 39:43

*But he answered them, "You see all these, do you not? Truly, I say to you, there
will not be left here one stone upon another that will not be thrown down."*

Matt. 24:2

Reflections

The workers under Moses' leadership followed the God-given instructions
for the details of the tabernacle and the furnishings. Moses reviewed their work
and saw that it was done correctly.

Many paragraphs in this part of Exodus explain the exact design of the
tabernacle and its furnishings. Then we get a description of what was actually
done to show that those in charge of the work did everything according to
specification. They carried it out and God's presence filled the tabernacle as a
great cloud. God was pleased. He accepted the work they had done.

But then we fast-forward to the time of Jesus and the second temple. It is
well to note that the first temple was built by Solomon to replace the tabernacle.
That temple was destroyed in the Babylonian conquest. Jesus predicted the
destruction of the second temple. Roman armies under Titus carried this out in
70 AD. The construction of the tabernacle and the temples had been done
according to God's plan but they were never intended to be permanent.

Jesus, as we will see in John's Gospel, referred to Himself as the temple, a
temple that would be torn down at His crucifixion, but raised again on the third
day, never to be destroyed again (John 2:13-22).

Think about It

Praise God for giving us His Son, in Whom we have a permanent place of
spiritual safety and wholeness. By His mercy and mediation, we come not to an
earthly temple that can be invaded and destroyed, but a heavenly one which will
never end (Heb. 9:24-28).

Can We Please God?

Today's Reading: Leviticus 1-3; Matthew 24:23-51

Selected Verses

> *And the priest shall burn all of it on the altar, as a burnt offering, a food offering with a pleasing aroma to the Lord.*

Lev. 1:8a

> *Blessed is that servant whom his master will find so doing when he comes. Truly, I say to you, he will set him over all his possessions.*

Matt. 24:46-47

Reflections

What God commands pleases Him, but it is also beneficial to those who obey Him. God does not ask His people to do things which are detrimental to themselves. Obeying God is a "win-win" proposition.

Furthermore, it is not hard to know what pleases God. His Word reveals what He wants us to do. We need not attempt to guess what pleases Him. It is clear. Read the Bible.

First, to please Him, we need an offering for our sin. In Leviticus the Israelites were told what their priests needed to do to present a pleasing aroma to God. There were various kinds of offerings: guilt, grain, peace, etc. There is a phrase which is repeated here: "a pleasing aroma to the Lord." Leviticus can come alive to us if we realize that our sin deeply offends the holy God who made us. Our sin is complex in that it permeates our best actions and our whole beings. Our actions are sinful. Our minds are sinful. Our motives are sinful. We commit both sins of omission and commission, that is, we do not do what we ought and we do what we ought not to do. We desperately need an offering for all this sin.

Leviticus shows us that we need an offering and sets the stage for the coming of our Lord Jesus Christ, the only sufficient offering for sin.

Secondly, Leviticus tells us that a proper offering for sin averts the just wrath of God. Furthermore, that proper offering pleases God. In our Matthew reading Jesus teaches that, just as the master was pleased with his servant, we too can please our Master by doing what He commands. Obedience begins with faith in the One who offered Himself for the sin of His people (Matt. 1:21).

Think about It

As you read Leviticus, don't miss the point that Christ is the One who fulfills all these necessary offerings. Seek to do what He commands, for He promised to return for us. May He find us doing what He has commanded! May we be blessed on that day because we believed Him and sought to obey Him! There will be rewards for this. Can we please God? Yes, by grace through faith in Jesus Christ, we please Him.

Do Jesus' Parables Teach Salvation by Works?

Today's Reading: Leviticus 4-6; Matthew 25:1-30

Selected Verses

And the priest shall make atonement for them, and they shall be forgiven.

Lev. 4:20b

And cast the worthless servant into the outer darkness.
In that place there will be weeping and gnashing of teeth.

Matt. 25:30

Reflections

In today's reading in Leviticus is the oft-repeated phrase, "he (or they) shall be forgiven." In yesterday's reading the emphasis was on "a pleasing aroma to the LORD." The sacrifices described in Leviticus resulted in God being pleased and the worshipers being forgiven. God does not merely show restraint in not punishing the sin of true believers, He forgives them and He is pleased with the offering they make.

Of course, we know from the New Testament that these offerings all pointed toward Jesus Christ, the final and complete offering for the sins of His people. In Him, God is pleased and we who believe in Him are forgiven.

So, what does the parable of the talents in Matthew have to do with this? Here we see God's judgment portrayed on one who failed to invest his talent for the master's benefit. He is not forgiven. In fact, he loses the one talent he had and is cast out of his master's presence. A similar judgment falls upon the unprepared virgins.

In light of these parables, we might wonder if Jesus is teaching that we are acceptable before God based on our works or personal preparedness. In fact acceptance before God depends on faith in the offering for sin made by Christ. On the other hand, the reality of our faith is demonstrated in fully employing the talent or gift God has given us and in having an expectant attitude about the Lord's coming in power and judgment.

Think about It

Many trust in their own good works for salvation, only to be lost in the end. Others believe that their trust in Christ only needs to be demonstrated once through repeating a prayer, being baptized, or some other outward profession. These self-deceived people fail to show the fruits of faith in their lives. According to the Bible they will also be lost in the end. Jesus never taught salvation by works. Rather He taught that faith bears observable fruit (Matt. 7:15-20). Ground your faith in Jesus Christ's offering for sin. But be sure your faith shows itself in your life by diligent use of the means of grace (God's word and prayer and the sacraments) both personally in your home and corporately in your local church.

The Gift Acceptable to God

Today's Reading: Leviticus 7-9; Matthew 25:31-46

Selected Verses

And Moses and Aaron went into the tent of meeting, and when they came out they blessed the people, and the glory of the Lord appeared to all the people. And fire came out from before the Lord and consumed the burnt offering and the pieces of fat on the altar, and when all the people saw it, they shouted and fell on their faces.

Lev. 9:23-24

And these will go away into eternal punishment, but the righteous into eternal life.

Matt. 25:46

Reflections

In offering sacrifices to the Lord, Aaron was careful to do exactly as God through Moses instructed him. It must have been a relief and thrill when God showed His acceptance by sending fire to consume the sacrifice.

Jesus taught that in the final judgment there would be sheep and goats, separated as acceptable and not acceptable to God. The righteous are acceptable and enter into eternal life but the unrighteous are unacceptable and go to eternal punishment.

Think about It

Will you be found with the righteous, the sheep, on that day? Is your sacrifice to God acceptable? It can be acceptable, and you can know that it is.

In Romans 12:1-2 we read, "I appeal to you therefore, brothers, by the mercies of God, to present your bodies as a living sacrifice, holy and acceptable to God, which is your spiritual worship. Do not be conformed to this world, but be transformed by the renewal of your mind, that by testing you may discern what is the will of God, what is good and acceptable and perfect."

We are called to present our bodies to God to serve Him. But take note, verse 1 says "therefore" which means this call is written in light of what Paul said earlier. Paul explained the fallen condition of every human. He emphasized the need to be justified by faith in Jesus Christ. So God calls us to present our bodies as a living sacrifice as the result of our having been justified by faith. Christ redeems us by His offering of Himself to God. We offer ourselves to the Lord not in order to earn acceptability before Him. That is already ours. If you are Christ's, you will offer yourself to God and He will find your offering acceptable, yes, even holy. Think about it.

Death at Church

Selected Verses

*Now Nadab and Abihu, the sons of Aaron, each took
his censer and put fire in it and laid incense on it and
offered unauthorized fire before the Lord, which he had
not commanded them. And fire came out from before
the Lord and consumed them, and they died before
the Lord. Then Moses said to Aaron, "This is what
the Lord has said: 'Among those who are near
me I will be sanctified, and before all the people
I will be glorified.'" And Aaron held his peace.*

Lev. 10:1-3

*In pouring this ointment on my body, she has done it to
prepare me for burial. Truly, I say to you, wherever
this gospel is proclaimed in the whole world, what
she has done will also be told in memory of her.*

Matt. 26:12-13

Reflections

Here we have a dramatic contrast between people who sought to make offerings to God. In the Leviticus reading, the two sons of Aaron offer unauthorized fire before the Lord. In Matthew a woman pours expensive ointment on Jesus. God punished the former with death; but Jesus honored the latter and made her an icon of faithfulness.

What made the difference here? Why did God accept the actions of one and not the actions of the others? God is not capricious. He has made His will clear in His word. The sons of Aaron were careless and, maybe, arrogant in their presumption. They exceeded their authority as priests before God, doing what was not commanded in God's law. God showed that worship and the offerings to Him were serious business. Above all, God was to be sanctified, set apart from the common and ordinary. No one may worship Him casually or according to their personal preferences and whims.

Jesus was the Messiah whom God promised to Israel. One's response to Him, whether in disbelief or in faith, was and is crucial. In anointing Jesus with ointment, the woman showed faith which emanated from her love for Him. As a result the Lord lavishly commended her action toward Him.

Think about It

What makes the difference between an acceptable and unacceptable offering to God? The unnamed woman glorified Christ. Aaron's sons exalted themselves. If you hold a position of authority in the church, such as a preacher or teacher, remember the warning of the Apostle James: "Not many of you should become teachers, my brothers, for you know that we who teach will be judged with greater strictness" (James 3:1). Will you glorify God today? Seek to lift Him up before the watching world.

Spiritual Oblivion

Today's Reading: Leviticus 13; Matthew 26:20-54

Selected Verses

And the priest shall examine him again on the seventh day, and if the diseased area has faded and the disease has not spread in the skin, then the priest shall pronounce him clean. . . . And the priest shall look, and if the eruption has spread in the skin, then the priest shall pronounce him unclean; it is a leprous disease.

Lev. 13:6a, 8

Peter answered him, "Though they all fall away because of you, I will never fall away." Jesus said to him, "Truly, I tell you, this very night, before the rooster crows, you will deny me three times." Peter said to him, "Even if I must die with you, I will not deny you!" And all the disciples said the same.

Matt. 26:33-35

Reflections

In our reading from Matthew Jesus institutes what we now call "the sacrament of the Lord's Supper" or "Communion" or the "Eucharist." In doing so He reveals the depth of His love for His own. He is about to give His body and shed His blood for them. Do they understand this?

No, because they are in oblivion. Their immediate and unanimous response is that they will stand by Him and die. He assures them that they will not stand by Him, rather they will all abandon Him. They repeat their assertions. Do they make good on their enthusiastic promises? No, not at all.

The disciples were like lepers who tell themselves they are clean when they are actually very sick with no possibility of healing. In ancient Israel lepers and all who had skin eruptions had to consult with the priest or one of his sons. Sick people ran the risk of spreading disease among the members of the community. They were not to be trusted to diagnose themselves. That was the responsibility of the priest.

So, too, Jesus diagnosed His disciples. Their own diagnosis was completely wrong, but Jesus told them the truth. They were cowards. They were liars. They could talk the talk, but not walk the walk. But they could not even recognize the depth of their sin and need.

That is precisely why He died. He died to save His people from their sin, which should have been as obvious as incurable leprosy, erupting on every inch of their bodies. But before they could be saved, they would need to see how utterly unworthy they were. They had horrific, spiritual leprosy coupled with serious spiritual oblivion. Is it bad? It is fatal. Eternally fatal.

Think about It

Unlike the priests in the old covenant days, Jesus could not only diagnose the illness. He could and did cure it at the cost of His own body and blood. Are you speechless? I am.

Depth of Sin; Pervasiveness of Corruption

Today's Reading: Leviticus 14; Matthew 26:55-75

Selected Verses

This is the law for any case of leprous disease: for an itch, for leprous disease in a garment or in a house, and for a swelling or an eruption or a spot, to show when it is unclean and when it is clean. This is the law for leprous disease.

Lev. 14:54-57

Then he began to invoke a curse on himself and to swear, "I do not know the man." And immediately the rooster crowed. And Peter remembered the saying of Jesus, "Before the rooster crows, you will deny me three times." And he went out and wept bitterly.

Matt. 26:74-75

Reflections

Sin, disease, and death permeate everything in the world from human beings to houses and clothing.

One of the saddest stories in the entire Bible is the story of Peter's denial. Over-confident Peter had declared his allegiance to Jesus Christ only a few hours earlier. Now in the courtyard of the high priest we find him calling down curses on himself, swearing to his own destruction that he does not even know Him. What corruption lies in the human heart! This is a deplorable action but one of which I could also be guilty.

In the reading in Leviticus we learn that disease can infest a home endangering the inhabitants. The priest had detailed instructions about how to diagnose the severity of the problem. In some happy cases cleansing was successful, an offering was made, and the property could be re-inhabited. This was not always the case; sometimes nothing short of demolition of the dwelling would suffice. Again, we see the pervasive effects of the fall which brought disease and death.

Think about It

No self-help book can fix the human condition. Ten easy steps will not lead to the perfection of character. Only at the cross of Christ can we find deliverance, forgiveness, and cleansing. That is where our sins were paid for at the cost of the only sinless man's life. Peter needed that cross. So do we.

Jesus proclaimed the arrival of the kingdom of heaven where sin is eradicated and all suffering and disease is banished forever. Lord, may your kingdom come soon in all its fullness.

I am ready for it. Are you?

The Anguish of Guilt

Today's Reading: Leviticus 15-17; Matthew 27:1-31

Selected Verses

*Aaron shall offer the bull as a sin offering for himself
and shall make atonement for himself and for his house.*

Lev. 16:6

*And throwing down the pieces of silver into the temple,
he departed, and he went and hanged himself.*

Matt. 27:5

Reflections

If any single theme runs through these two readings today it is guilt, human guilt for sin. That theme runs through history since the first sin committed by the first created couple in the garden (Gen. 3).

In Leviticus the high priest must offer a sacrifice for his own sin before he can offer a sacrifice for the sin of the people. He is high priest, but he is as sinful and guilty as the rest of the rank and file. As we have been seeing, the Aaronic priesthood was imperfect and temporary. It pointed to a need for a better priesthood, one that would later be established by the Lord Jesus Christ. All of this will be even clearer when we get to the Epistle to the Hebrews.

The circumstances surrounding Judas' betrayal and Jesus' arrest and trial also reveal how the various parties showed the ravages of their guilt. Judas was tormented by the realization that he had betrayed an innocent man. He sought to rid himself of this guilt by returning the money he received. The chief priests and elders rejected his effort. He then hanged himself.

Pilate and his wife agonized over the case before him and the phony accusations against Jesus. Pilate looked in vain for a way out. He seemed to finally be moved by the eager willingness of the crowd to accept any blame for this execution.

Think about It

Guilt tears apart the human soul, but if God is gracious to us His Spirit moves us beyond guilt to repentance and faith in the true High Priest who offered Himself for the sin of His people. In Him we find forgiveness (not through a diluting of our guilt but) through an offering that is so infinitely worthy it purchased redemption for every single one of God's elect people (Eph. 1:7-10).

Praise Him, my believing friend, for deliverance through Christ from not only the anguish of our guilt but the due consequences of all our sin.

Jesus' Claims: True or False?

Today's Reading: Leviticus 18-19; Matthew 27:32-66

Selected Verses

You shall not steal; you shall not deal falsely; you shall not lie to one another.

Lev. 19:11

"Sir, we remember how that impostor said, while he was still alive,
'After three days I will rise.' Therefore order the tomb to be made secure
until the third day, lest his disciples go and steal him away and tell the people,
'He has risen from the dead,' and the last fraud will be worse than the first."

Matt. 27:63b-64

Reflections

The law of Moses commanded truthfulness. It needed to be commanded because honesty died early in human history when the serpent lied and deceived the woman in the garden. Jesus referred to the devil as the father of lies (John 8:44). All enter into his realm by natural birth. Only by a new birth are we set free from this kingdom of lies and deceit.

The scribes and Pharisees knew the claim Jesus made that He would rise from the dead on the third day. The disciples hid, fearing that Jesus might be gone forever. Meanwhile, the religious leaders worried that people might actually believe Jesus' prediction about rising from the dead. Was there really a danger of the disciples stealing the body and starting a rumor that the Lord had risen? I doubt it. After all, they had shown no courage when Jesus was arrested (Matt. 26:56b). Nevertheless, the stated position of Jesus' enemies was that He had made a false claim and that the disciples would lie to cover for it creating a hoax of monumental magnitude.

It was their stated position. But, I suspect, some of those opponents wondered if Jesus would make good on the claim. Tomorrow we will see how this all worked out and, in the end, the unbelievers inadvertently enhanced the claim that Jesus had risen from the dead.

Think about It

Truth is essential. The claims of Jesus Christ rest on actual historical events, not merely philosophical theory. Consider the historical evidence for the death, burial, and resurrection of the Lord. It is either true or false. Everyone must face the truth. Jesus was no imposter. His claims were proven true and we must all take them seriously.

Missions: Going in Christ's Name

Today's Reading: Leviticus 20-21; Matthew 28

Selected Verses

They shall be holy to their God and not profane the name of their God. For they offer the Lord's food offerings, the bread of their God; therefore they shall be holy.

Lev. 21:6

And Jesus came and said to them, "All authority in heaven and on earth has been given to me. Go therefore and make disciples of all nations, baptizing them in the name of the Father and of the Son and of the Holy Spirit, teaching them to observe all that I have commanded you. And behold, I am with you always, to the end of the age."

Matt. 28:18-20

Reflections

God revealed His name to mankind. He directed the Israelites to worship Him and warned the priests not to profane His name. Jesus revealed the Father and sent His disciples to go and make more disciples of all nations, baptizing them in the name of the Father, the Son, and the Holy Spirit.

Obviously, the name of God is to be hallowed and reverenced. People must not take the name of God lightly or in vain. Jesus' disciples function on His authority, not their own. They go with a purpose which includes making disciples and baptizing them in the name of the Triune God.

This Great Commission is serious business. Missionaries go. Churches send them and support them with money and prayer. Christians in every nation reach out with the gospel and seek to make disciples. All of this is because of the name of God who has revealed Himself beginning with the first man and woman to whom He promised a seed that would crush the head of the deceiving Serpent (Gen. 3:15).

Think about It

The priests of ancient Israel took great care not to profane the sacred name of God. We, as disciples of Jesus Christ, go commissioned in His name to all the world, making disciples and calling them to be baptized in the holy name of God who is Father, Son, and Holy Spirit. In the words of the great hymn by Edith G. Cherry (1895):

> *We rest on Thee, our Shield and our Defender!*
> *We go not forth alone against the foe;*
> *Strong in Thy strength, safe in Thy keeping tender,*
> *We rest on Thee, and in Thy Name we go.*

Let us hallow God's name, take this commission seriously, and go in His name.

Time and Timing

Today's Reading: Leviticus 22-23; Mark 1:1-22

Selected Verses

The Lord spoke to Moses, saying, "Speak to the people of Israel and
say to them, 'These are the appointed feasts of the Lord that you
shall proclaim as holy convocations; they are my appointed feasts.'"

Lev. 23:1-2

Now after John was arrested, Jesus came into Galilee, proclaiming
the gospel of God, and saying, "The time is fulfilled, and the
kingdom of God is at hand; repent and believe in the gospel."

Mark 1:14-15

Reflections

At Creation God gave time to humanity. He divided it into segments: evening and morning, days, seasons, and years (Gen. 1:5,14-19). In Leviticus the Lord gave the Israelites feasts which marked the transitions in the agricultural calendar and celebrated God's gracious acts in their history.

Jesus appeared on schedule when the time was fulfilled (Gal. 4:4, 5). The kingdom of God was at hand. There was to be a new chapter in God's unfolding redemptive story. The Lord proclaimed that the moment had come to repent and believe the gospel.

What would life be without time, without seasons and cycles, without beginnings and endings? Surely, we cannot imagine it. Time is a good gift of God to us. His providence refers to His active working in our time and space as He fulfills His plans and purposes down through human history.

Think about It

We live in a day unlike any other. Our access to global communication, transportation, and technology is unparalleled. The rapid changes which are occurring leave us somewhere on a scale between awestruck and disoriented. Yet the gospel is still true. God is still God. Man is still sinful, needing redemption. Christ's work still stands as the only means for reconciliation with the Creator, the Holy Eternal God.

God works in all things for His glory and all the advances which we make only serve to make His majesty more amazing. The final culmination of this world, the end of history, is still ahead. It may be near or distant to our day, but the message is still true: repent and believe the gospel. Carpe diem: seize the day. Time's a-wasting.

Redeemed to Be His Friends

Today's Reading: Leviticus 24-25; Mark 1:23-45

Selected Verses

> *For it is to me that the people of Israel are servants. They are my servants whom I brought out of the land of Egypt: I am the Lord your God.*

Lev. 25:55

> *And he said to them, "Let us go on to the next towns, that I may preach there also, for that is why I came out." And he went throughout all Galilee, preaching in their synagogues and casting out demons.*

Mark 1:38, 39

Reflections

Provision was made in the law for those who had fallen on hard times and had to sell themselves as servants. The Israelites were God's people. They belonged to Him and could not belong to anyone else, at least not permanently. The law encouraged people to pay a ransom for their enslaved relatives. If there was no one to do this, servants were to be freed automatically at the Year of Jubilee.

So too, Jesus went throughout Galilee preaching and casting out demons, redeeming people not from physical slavery but from spiritual bondage to Satan and sin. The people heard of Jesus' power. Crowds sought Him. The demands on His time increased. What did He do? He went out before daybreak to pray. His disciples found Him and told Him how the crowds were looking for Him. But Jesus had other plans. He and the disciples moved on to the other towns in Galilee.

In reading this passage in Mark's Gospel, it seems clear that Jesus lived purposefully each day without anxiety or confusion. He was not controlled by the many needs around Him. Instead, through prayer He sought the Father's guidance for His day.

Jesus Christ's redemption of lost souls was pictured in the redemption of Old Testament slaves. Just as slaves needed someone to free them from physical slavery, so lost souls need Someone to free them from spiritual bondage.

Think about It

Jesus said, "No longer do I call you servants, for the servant does not know what his master is doing; but I have called you friends, for all that I have heard from my Father I have made known to you" (John 15:15). Our Savior proclaims freedom from sin to all who repent and believe. Trust in Him and be free. In Him there is true freedom to be His servant, but not only His servant but His friend. He redeems us to be His friends.

Does Sin Make Us Sick?

Today's Reading: Leviticus 26-27; Mark 2

Selected Verses

But if you will not listen to me and will not do all these commandments, if you spurn my statutes, and if your soul abhors my rules, so that you will not do all my commandments, but break my covenant, then I will do this to you: I will visit you with panic, with wasting disease and fever that consume the eyes and make the heart ache.

Lev. 26:14-16

And when Jesus saw their faith, he said to the paralytic, "Son, your sins are forgiven."

Mark 2:5

Reflections

The picture God painted for the Israelites of life in the Promised Land, pending full obedience on their part, is nothing short of glorious. Everything the heart could legitimately long for was included as long as the people were careful to obey God's law. The contrasting consequences, should they not be faithful, is a nightmare. They would experience disease, famine, insecurity, families torn apart, and, ultimately, ejection from the land.

As we will see in the ensuing centuries, despite the warning, Israel did disobey and they experienced all of God's foretold consequences. Even so, the Messiah came to them. Jesus Christ came and healed the sick, cast out demons, preached the good news of the kingdom of God, and forgave the sins of a paralyzed man.

Jesus never taught that there was always a direct correspondence between a person's sins and his diseases (John 9:1-3). But He did show that He had power to forgive sin and to eradicate its impact on our bodies.

Think about It

Have you wondered if the sickness you or others suffer is some kind of divine punishment for sin? In a general sense, all the disease and suffering in this world is a result of our rebellion against God. But in a sense, it is seldom possible to connect our sin to our sicknesses in a direct cause-and-effect relationship.

Not all sickness is caused by our personal sin. But sickness may bring us to Christ, who defeated both sin and sickness. When we come to Him seeking a solution to our felt needs (sickness, relational problems, depression, etc.), we find that He will address our real needs (forgiveness and eternal life). Trust Him completely for what He knows you need today and forever.

Is There a Secret to the Number Twelve?

Today's Reading: Numbers 1-2; Mark 3:1-21

Selected Verses

These are those who were listed, whom Moses and Aaron listed with the help of the chiefs of Israel, twelve men, each representing his fathers' house.

Num. 1:44

And he went up on the mountain and called to him those whom he desired, and they came to him. And he appointed twelve (whom he also named apostles) so that they might be with him and he might send them out to preach and have authority to cast out demons.

Mark 3:13-15

Reflections

Twelve tribes, twelve representatives, twelve apostles. It is hard to miss the repetition of the number twelve in the Bible, even when you are not reading simultaneously in the Old and New Testaments, as we are. There seems to be a certain kind of completeness in that number.

In our reading of Matthew, we saw this statement: "Jesus said to them, 'Truly, I say to you, in the new world, when the Son of Man will sit on his glorious throne, you who have followed me will also sit on twelve thrones, judging the twelve tribes of Israel.'" (Matt. 19:28).

So there is a connection between the twelve tribes and the twelve disciples (later called apostles). Is this fully explained? I haven't found it yet. I am okay with not knowing all of God's reasons and purposes now or ever. We should not attempt to go beyond what God has made clear in His Word. He certainly lets us know all that we need to know for life and godliness. As the Apostle Peter wrote: "His divine power has granted to us all things that pertain to life and godliness, through the knowledge of him who called us to his own glory and excellence" (2 Peter 1:3).

Peter went on to point out that the apostles did not follow cleverly devised myths when they preached the good news of Jesus Christ (2 Peter 1:16). Some have tried to make too much out of the secret meaning of numbers in the Bible. It sounds a lot like cleverly devised myths.

Think about It

Even though God does not always reveal to us His reasons for the things He decrees, we can understand all we need to know to come to life in Him. Perhaps when His kingdom comes fully, we will know the reasons we do not yet understand. On that day, we will have even more reasons to praise Him for His infinite wisdom. Meanwhile, start now by faith praising Him for that wisdom.

Eternal Family Ties

Today's Reading: Numbers 3-4; Mark 3:22-35

Selected Verses

*These are the names of the sons of Aaron, the anointed priests, whom he ordained to
serve as priests. But Nadab and Abihu died before the Lord when they offered unauthorized fire before the Lord in the wilderness of Sinai, and they had no children.
So Eleazar and Ithamar served as priests in the lifetime of Aaron their father.*

Num. 3:3-4

*And he answered them, "Who are my mother and my brothers?" And looking
about at those who sat around him, he said, "Here are my mother and my brothers!
For whoever does the will of God, he is my brother and sister and mother."*

Mark 3:33-35

Reflections

Jesus' human family members took Him to be insane. "And when his family
heard it, they went out to seize him, for they were saying, 'He is out of his
mind,'" Mark 3:21. They tried to intervene and stop His teaching and ministry.
Perhaps they were afraid of embarrassment. Maybe they meant well. But they did
not believe in Him (John 7:5).

In the case of Aaron's sons, Nadab and Abihu, their status as sons of the high
priest did not exempt them from obedience to the law. They seem to have
presumed that they could veer from the commands of the law concerning
offerings to God. It cost them their lives.

Jesus said, "Whoever does the will of God, he is my brother and sister and
mother." This is good news for us. It means that although we never physically
saw Jesus nor are we related to Him through natural descent, we are related to
Him based on a common relationship to God, the Father. He is the first born of
many brothers (Rom. 8:29).

Think about It

Spiritual bonds supersede natural, family relationships. Therefore, obedience
to God is more important than blood ties.

Perhaps your human family has problems, conflicts, grudges, and even
bitterness. But if you have been adopted into the Father's family by the new
birth, you are tied eternally to Jesus Christ and to all who are His. Rejoice! And
seek to bear the family resemblance today.

Bear Fruit and Be Blessed

Today's Reading: Numbers 5-6; Mark 4:1-20

Selected Verses

The Lord spoke to Moses, saying, "Speak to Aaron and his sons, saying,
Thus you shall bless the people of Israel: you shall say to them,
> *The Lord bless you and keep you;*
> *the Lord make his face to shine upon you and be gracious to you;*
> *the Lord lift up his countenance upon you and give you peace.*
"So shall they put my name upon the people of Israel, and I will bless them."

Num. 6:22-27

But those that were sown on the good soil are the ones who hear the word
and accept it and bear fruit, thirtyfold and sixtyfold and a hundredfold.

Mark 4:20

Reflections

God wills that His people be blessed and flourishing. He gave a stirring benediction for Aaron to pass on to Israel. But God's blessings depend on the obedience of His people. Sin and disobedience thwart God's best gifts. As Jesus taught in the parable of the soils, people must hear His word, hold it fast, and be careful to let it bear fruit in their lives.

This does not always occur. We could even say it frequently does not occur. If we are honest, there are too many lapses in our hearing, holding fast, and bearing fruit. The word gets snatched away because it never even penetrates our minds. We have an immediate enthusiastic, but superficial, response which results in short term impact but long-term death. This is the result of shallow penetration of the truth into our hearts and minds. Then come the cares of the world, the deceitfulness of riches, and the desires for other things that kill the potential fruit when the seed does take root and grow. When we overcome these obstacles, the seed will bear fruit and the blessing will be poured out.

Think about It

True blessing comes from God and it comes to those who hear the Word, hold it fast, and remain vigilant to let it bear fruit. Beware of the obstacles to fruitfulness. As Jesus told His disciples, "By this is my Father glorified, that you bear much fruit and so prove to be my disciples," John 15:8. Real disciples bear fruit. They are blessed. And that glorifies God as we were meant to do.

The God who Quiets Terrified Sinners

Today's Reading: Numbers 7; Mark 4:21-41

Selected Verses

And when Moses went into the tent of meeting to speak with the Lord, he heard the voice speaking to him from above the mercy seat that was on the ark of the testimony, from between the two cherubim; and it spoke to him.

Num. 7:89

He said to them, "Why are you so afraid? Have you still no faith?"
And they were filled with great fear and said to one another,
"Who then is this, that even the wind and the sea obey him?"

Mark 4:40-41

Reflections

From start to finish the Bible reveals a God who is in constant contact with His creation and in communication with humanity in particular.

In the tabernacle God gave a concrete picture of His love by giving Moses a plan for the Ark of the Covenant which included a gold lid upon which stood two cherubim of gold. Between these cherubim was a space called "the mercy seat." At this place God spoke to Moses, and in future generations He would meet with the high priest on the Day of Atonement. My study Bible notes say that the Greek term for the mercy seat (hilasterion) may be translated the "seat of propitiation." Propitiation refers to the process of satisfying just anger through a sacrificial gift or offering. That is what God did when He offered His Son on the cross for sin (1 John 2:1-2).

Jesus Christ, the Son of God, took on human flesh and revealed the Father to us. The disciples struggled at times to grasp who He was (and is). On the sea they were terrified as He slept peacefully through a terrific storm. They woke Him. He calmly quieted the storm but also rebuked them for their lack of faith.

Think about It

God makes Himself known for His mercy and His power. He makes a sacrifice for the sins of all who believe in His Son and quiets His own just wrath. He stilled the storm for the panicked disciples. Do you know His quieting actions of mercy and power in your life?

Whatever terrifies you today, whether the mounting debt of failures you are amassing through everyday sin or the stress of life's storms bearing down on you, trust Him to see you through to the peace and joy He promises to His own.

God's Glory in Christ's Power

Today's Reading: Numbers 8-10; Mark 5:1-20

Selected Verses

*And whenever the ark set out, Moses said, "Arise, O Lord, and let your
enemies be scattered, and let those who hate you flee before you." And when
it rested, he said, "Return, O Lord, to the ten thousand thousands of Israel."*

Num. 10:35-36

*As he was getting into the boat, the man who had been
possessed with demons begged him that he might be with him.*

Mark 5:18

Reflections

It was a creepy scene. Jesus, unfazed, met a demonic man in a cemetery.
Three times the man begged the Lord for something. First, he plead with Jesus
not to torment him. Second, the demons through the man begged not to be sent
out of the country. Third, after being delivered from the demonic possession, he
begged Jesus to allow him to be with Him.

What attitudes drove the man who begged these things from Jesus?

First, fear of torment. Despite being possessed by an unclean spirit, the
demonic understood his guilt before the "Son of the Most High God." He could
only beg for mercy because torment was what he deserved. Jesus had the power
to torment him but He showed him mercy.

Second, dread of destruction. Jesus had power to send the demons to hell.
Instead, He sent them into the pigs. The herd stampeded and drowned. Legion
was delivered.

Third, desire to be with Jesus. After deliverance, the now-healed man wanted
to continue with the Lord. He sent the saved man back to his Gentile family and
neighbors to tell them what God had done. So the man obeyed and returned to
his people proclaiming to God's glory what Jesus had done for him. The
response? The people were afraid of Jesus but they marveled at the testimony of
the formerly demon possessed man.

In our Numbers reading, God's glory shone through the Israelites as He
guided them on their journey to the Promised Land. Like Legion, Israel saw
God's power to save His people from slavery in Egypt and then to lead them to
their own land with freedom to serve Him.

Think about It

From Bible times right down till today, Christ's power delivers, heals, and
sends His people as His witnesses for His glory in every nation. Has this been
your story, too?

Belief or Unbelief: That Is the Question

Today's Reading: Numbers 11-13; Mark 5:21-43

Selected Verses

So they brought to the people of Israel a bad report of the land that they had spied out, saying, "The land, through which we have gone to spy it out, is a land that devours its inhabitants, and all the people that we saw in it are of great height. And there we saw the Nephilim (the sons of Anak, who come from the Nephilim), and we seemed to ourselves like grasshoppers, and so we seemed to them."

Num. 13:32, 33

And they laughed at him. But he put them all outside and took the child's father and mother and those who were with him and went in where the child was. Taking her by the hand he said to her, "Talitha cumi," which means, "Little girl, I say to you, arise." And immediately the girl got up and began walking(for she was twelve years of age), and they were immediately overcome with amazement.

Mark 5:40-42

Reflections

Here we have two cases of overwhelming odds. Both cases involved life or death. The twelve spies entered into the land of Canaan, the Promised Land. But ten of them only saw terrifying giants, walled cities, and invincible armies. "We cannot take this land," they concluded. In the other case there was a twelve-year-old girl who had died. The friends and neighbors laughed when Jesus said she was only sleeping.

Unbelief is powerful. Unbelief looks only at what humans can or cannot do. Unbelief does not count on God's power, loving kindness, or providence. Unbelief laughs, scorns, ridicules, and trembles.

But unbelief can be overcome by a clear-eyed look at God, His power, and His promises.

It appears that Jairus and his wife believed Jesus. They entered with Him into their daughter's room and within moments received her back from death. The Israelites persisted in their unbelief. Later, we shall see that they earned a sentence of death in the wilderness rather than enter the land they had been promised. It was a costly lesson.

Think about It

God doesn't always raise the dead when we pray, but neither does He always "repay us according to our iniquities" (Ps. 103:10). In God's goodness, we often get far more than we deserve. Nevertheless, trust in Him will never be disappointed because He will make all things result in our good and His glory (Rom. 8:28).

What dead daughters and hostile armies do you face today? If God has promised to work, trust Him to do the impossible according to His wise will.

God's Providence: It's a Mystery

Today's Reading: Numbers 14-15; Mark 6:1-32

Selected Verses

Now if you kill this people as one man, then the nations who have heard your fame will say, 'It is because the Lord was not able to bring this people into the land that he swore to give to them that he has killed them in the wilderness.

Num. 14:15-16

And the king was exceedingly sorry, but because of his oaths and his guests he did not want to break his word to her. And immediately the king sent an executioner with orders to bring John's head. He went and beheaded him in the prison.

Mark 6:26-27

Reflections

God threatened to destroy the entire nation of Israel for their rebellion and unbelief and to start over again forming a new nation with Moses. In a rather unique and wise prayer, Moses appealed to God to spare them on the basis of what would result in greater glory for the Lord. Certainly this was one of Moses' best moments in which he showed more concern for God's glory than for his own. So God spared the guilty Israelites once again.

In our reading in Mark we come to the sad account of the hideous beheading of John the Baptist. John died because he dared to stand up to corruption in high places. It is not hard to surmise that Herod carried the guilty weight of this execution to his dying day.

In both of our readings the providence of God is evident but is not predictable nor understandable, not fully. It is mysterious and complex. Although they suffered discipline and forty years of wandering in the wilderness, the Lord spared the guilty. On the other hand, the bold and faithful John died a horrible death.

Think about It

God does not reveal all of His reasons for the providential circumstances He decrees for His children, but we see enough examples to know that it's not about karma where every good deed gets rewarded and every bad deed gets punished.

Are you perplexed about some inexplicable event? Do not despair even if you never understand it before you reach glory. Trust God that He has a wise plan and ultimately will resolve all things for our good and His glory in the age to come.

The Fearsome Presence of God

Today's Reading: Numbers 16-17; Mark 6:33-56

Selected Verses

And the people of Israel said to Moses, "Behold, we perish, we are undone, we are all undone. Everyone who comes near, who comes near to the tabernacle of the Lord, shall die. Are we all to perish?"

Num. 17:12-13

For they all saw him and were terrified. But immediately he spoke to them and said, "Take heart; it is I. Do not be afraid."

Mark 6:50

Reflections

As we have seen, God who created all things also maintains constant contact with His creation and with His creatures whether they are conscious of Him or not. In both biblical history as well as my personal experience, it is evident that we easily forget that God is there all the time every day. We grow comfortable with attitudes of pride and acts of presumption as if there were no God to whom we must answer. We turn to our own resources to solve our problems rather than seeking His guidance and power.

Korah and his party in the wilderness rebelled against God's appointed leader Moses. They had time to repent but no inclination to do so. They died an horrific death. Then God gave them another sign of His choice of Aaron to head the priesthood by making Aaron's staff to bud as the staffs of the other tribes remained dry sticks.

The people of Israel recognized that they were "undone" and that they were all in danger of perishing for their persistent rebellion. God revealed His presence and taught them to fear Him.

When the disciples saw Jesus walking on the water, they were terrified. The Lord immediately reassured them that it was Him. God again revealed His presence and taught the disciples to fear Him but also to trust Him.

Think about It

The lesson of God's fearsome presence is one that the Israelites and the disciples would have to re-learn. I suspect that you and I will have to re-learn it too. Yet we who know Christ have assurance and comfort that we are God's own adopted children and that He is merciful and gracious to us.

Be aware of God's presence in your life today. He is fearsome, but He is on our side (Rom. 8:31). Thank Him for His patience with us who must re-learn these lessons.

When Leaders Fail

Today's Reading: Numbers 18-20; Mark 7:1-13

Selected Verses

And the Lord said to Moses and Aaron, "Because you did not believe in me, to uphold me as holy in the eyes of the people of Israel, therefore you shall not bring this assembly into the land that I have given them."

Num. 20:12

"You leave the commandment of God and hold to the tradition of men." And he said to them, "You have a fine way of rejecting the commandment of God in order to establish your tradition!"

Mark 7:8-9

Reflections

In both readings today, we find grievous examples of leaders abusing or misusing their authority for personal advantage. Some who criticize biblical faith will point this out as evidence that our faith is erroneous because some characters in Scripture were inconsistent and hypocritical.

Moses failed as a leader by using God's power to gain glory for himself. In striking the rock to bring water for the people, he failed to show that it was God's work and he took the credit due to God. He paid the price of dying before the nation was able to go into the Promised Land.

Jesus condemned the Pharisees who, though they were highly esteemed for strict adherence to the law, created a legal loophole in order to avoid fulfilling their financial responsibilities to their parents. He told them they put their traditions above God's law.

Think about It

All leaders are sinners, including Christian leaders. This does not mean they should not be respected and followed when they lead us in God's ways. It does mean they need God's grace and mercy just as much as other believers who have less visibility and prominence. James warned would-be teachers that they will be subject to stricter judgment (James 3:1-2). The fact that all Christian leaders sometimes fail to measure up to God's standards and a few leaders fail grievously does not negate the truth of the gospel which announces that we are only saved by the grace of our Lord Jesus Christ.

Support godly leaders through prayer, proper respect, and encouragement, but do not follow them blindly. They are able to err, and they may at times need to receive correction from those who follow them. Never assume any mantle of leadership lightly. If you are a leader, be mindful of your responsibility before God.

Was God Unfair to Balaam?

Today's Reading: Numbers 21-23; Mark 7:14-8:10

Selected Verses

And God came to Balaam at night and said to him, "If the men have come to call you, rise, go with them; but only do what I tell you." So Balaam rose in the morning and saddled his donkey and went with the princes of Moab. But God's anger was kindled because he went, and the angel of the Lord took his stand in the way as his adversary.

Num. 22:20-22

There is nothing outside a person that by going into him can defile him, but the things that come out of a person are what defile him.

Mark 7:15

Reflections

The Lord told Balaam to go with the princes of Moab. When he went, God's anger was kindled against him. Was God unfair? On the surface it seems like Balaam got punished for obeying.

If this were true, it would make God's direction contradictory and duplicitous. We who believe in a holy, just, and all-wise God can never admit to such a possibility. What is no doubt the explanation is that God was disciplining Balaam for an attitude of his heart to which we are not privy. As we shall see later in our reading, Balaam wanted to curse Israel and would have done so had the Lord not restrained him. Balaam was eager for the reward and the prestige of assisting the Moabites.

Think about It

Outward behavior can look quite upright and proper, but God looks at our hearts. The Pharisees in Jesus' day were focused on outward appearances of righteousness. Jesus told them that it was not what was outside that defiles them but what comes out of their hearts. He went on to elaborate, in verses 21-23, "For from within, out of the heart of man, come evil thoughts, sexual immorality, theft, murder, adultery, coveting, wickedness, deceit, sensuality, envy, slander, pride, foolishness. All these evil things come from within, and they defile a person."

Balaam had several of these attitudes in his heart that day when the Lord opened his donkey's mouth to speak to him. How do I know? Keep reading to learn how he would later find a devious way to trap and hurt the Israelites.

Beware of the sin lurking in your heart. Confess and repent. God could send you a talking donkey to get your attention.

A Man in Love with the World

Today's Reading: Numbers 24-27; Mark 8:11-38

Selected Verses

So Israel yoked himself to Baal of Peor. And the anger of the Lord was kindled against Israel.

Num. 25:3

For what does it profit a man to gain the whole world and forfeit his soul? For what can a man give in return for his soul?

Mark 8:36-37

Reflections

God warns us to beware of loving the world (1 John 2:15-17). In today's reading, Jesus asked "what does it profit a man to gain the whole world and forfeit his soul?" Famous conquerors like Alexander the Great, Napoleon, and Hitler gained large portions of the earth. In science fiction, evil schemers like Darth Vader or Lex Luther attempt to take over the world or the cosmos. They are Satanic figures who repel us.

Even if a real, historic figure could find a way to take control of the world, he would do so at the cost of his soul. Balaam loved the world and he paid the price.

Balaam failed to curse Israel because God restrained him, but he thought of another way to bring God's curses on Israel. He advised the Moabites to invite the Israelites to the sacrifices of their gods (Num. 31:16). He knew that if the Israelites participated in what would end up being a wild orgy, God would unleash His wrath upon them. The scheme worked for a while, but the guilty, including Balaam, were executed and God's wrath was satisfied.

Think about It

Let this be a lesson to us. Beware of what you love. Beware of loving the wealth, pleasures, power, and prestige which this life affords. People in ancient Israel died because they failed to be vigilant against these temptations. In the gospel of Jesus Christ, we learn that no one is innocent of sin. Only by repenting of our spiritual adultery and trusting in the One who died for His elect people can the sentence of death be stopped.

Love not the world. Love the Creator of the world, of all things, and of us.

Can We Trust the Bible?

Today's Reading: Numbers 28-29; Mark 9:1-29

Selected Verses

So Moses told the people of Israel everything just as the Lord had commanded Moses.

Num. 29:40

And there appeared to them Elijah with Moses, and they were talking with Jesus.

Mark 9:4

Reflections

In the era of fake news and alternative facts it is not surprising that many wonder where you can find truth that conforms to reality. For millennia, Christians have claimed to believe in the Bible as the inerrant Word of God. Today's readings provide an important reason for this confidence.

The Bible contains sixty-six books. It claims to be the revelation of the Eternal God to humankind. As such, it is a revelation which was given in stages over thousands of years. Scholars attribute Numbers to Moses who led the Israelites out of Egypt toward the Promised Land. As God's prophet to them he gave them precise truth which he received from God. As the selected verse above indicates, Moses told them all that God commanded him.

It is reasonable to ask what evidence of unity there is in this book that was received in separate stages over so many years. Notice this. When we jump ahead two thousand years to the Gospel of Mark, what do we find? Jesus meets with this same Moses and another prophet, Elijah.

The incident on the Mount of Transfiguration demonstrates the powerful connection between the Book of Numbers and the Gospel of Mark. Furthermore, we find verification of Jesus' authenticity as the Son of God. Moses and Elijah, God's servants who represent the Law and the Prophets, appeared with Jesus and talked with Him. Israel had utterly failed to keep the law God through Moses had given them. But Jesus would fulfill that law perfectly. He would bring justification to all His chosen people from every tribe and tongue. There never would have been perfect law keepers. Only Jesus Christ could fulfill the just demands of the law that God gave to Moses and Moses gave to Israel.

Think about It

The Transfiguration should reinforce our confidence in the trustworthiness of the Bible and its claims about Jesus Christ. He is our eternal prophet, priest, and king. May His kingdom come soon! Meanwhile, trust the Bible not alternate facts and fake news.

A Warning about Causing People to Sin

Today's Reading: Numbers 30-31; Mark 9:30-50

Selected Verses

> The Lord spoke to Moses, saying, "Avenge the people of Israel on the Midianites. Afterward you shall be gathered to your people." So Moses spoke to the people, saying, "Arm men from among you for the war, that they may go against Midian to execute the Lord's vengeance on Midian.
>
> Num. 31:1-3

> Whoever causes one of these little ones who believe in me to sin, it would be better for him if a great millstone were hung around his neck and he were thrown into the sea.
>
> Mark 9:42

Reflections

God's final assignment to Moses was to bring judgment on the Midianites for the way they had seduced the Israelites into sin. Indeed, as we saw in our March 1 reading, the Israelites paid a severe price for their foolish sin, but now God sends Moses to repay their tempters for causing His people to sin.

The disciples were beginning to show their true colors as the thought of Jesus' death dawned on them. They began to jockey for positions of leadership and wanted to curtail any would-be competitors that they had not authorized. In a forceful statement, Jesus warned them of the danger of defiling little ones who believe in Him. The Reformation Study Bible note explains that the phrase "little ones" may refer either to children or to those who are "insignificant believers." So the warning has broad application. The disciples saw those who were not following them as insignificant and worthy of rebuke (Mark 9:38).

Think about It

Who are the little ones in your life? Are they children? Are they just the so-called insignificant believers? Remember that God holds them in high esteem. He gave His Son for their salvation. Beware of causing others to sin who look up to you either because of your age or status. Treat them all as children of the King for, as believers, that is what they are. If you have failed in this regard, repent of all known sin, confess to God and those offended. Seek the Lord's grace and forgiveness through Christ. God has promised: "If we confess our sins, he is faithful and just to forgive us our sins and to cleanse us from all unrighteousness" (1 John 1:9).

The Obedient Life: Cost and Rewards

Today's Reading: Numbers 32-33; Mark 10:1-31

Selected Verses

Then they came near to him and said, "We will build sheepfolds here for our livestock, and cities for our little ones, but we will take up arms, ready to go before the people of Israel, until we have brought them to their place. And our little ones shall live in the fortified cities because of the inhabitants of the land. We will not return to our homes until each of the people of Israel has gained his inheritance.

Num. 32:16-18

Peter began to say to him, "See, we have left everything and followed you." Jesus said, "Truly, I say to you, there is no one who has left house or brothers or sisters or mother or father or children or lands, for my sake and for the gospel, who will not receive a hundredfold now in this time, houses and brothers and sisters and mothers and children and lands, with persecutions, and in the age to come eternal life.

Mark 10: 28-30

Reflections

In two incidents separated by centuries, God's people were called to leave their homes behind in order to obey Him. In the first case, the tribes of Reuben and Gad and the half-tribe of Manasseh requested permission to take possession of the eastern lands that were conquered before the nation crossed the Jordan. Moses warned them that they would discourage the other tribes and possibly bring judgment on themselves similar to what the nation experienced when the spies had discouraged everyone from entering the Promised Land forty years earlier. The response of the tribes was excellent. They committed to fight till all the other tribes got their territories also. Moses found their commitment satisfactory. Stay tuned to find out how this turned out.

In the second case, the disciples of Jesus left their homes to follow Him. Peter sounds wistful, but Jesus reassures him that they will receive much more than they gave up.

Think about It

What about you? How has being obedient to God been costly to you? Have you given up home, relationships, or career possibilities? Trust Him that His rewards to His faithful followers are blessings out of this world.

Law and Grace: A Contrast

Today's Reading: Numbers 34-36; Mark 10:32-52

Selected Verses

Moreover, you shall accept no ransom for the life of a murderer,
who is guilty of death, but he shall be put to death.

Num. 35:31

For even the Son of Man came not to be served but
to serve, and to give his life as a ransom for many.

Mark 10:45

Reflections

Under the Mosaic Law, a manslayer had protection and a right to a trial to determine whether he murdered intentionally or killed unintentionally. Life was precious, both the life of the one who died and the life of the one who killed him. Under Moses, the Israelites applied capital punishment very carefully after due process of law.

The guilty murderer, duly convicted, could not be ransomed. There could be no deal-making. No plea bargaining. No offering of an animal sacrifice to take the place of the convict. He must die under the law.

What a contrast with the grace of God in Jesus Christ! Jesus came to give His life as a ransom for guilty people—many, very guilty people. I suspect that some of those guilty people had already died under the Mosaic Law, guilty of murder, but repentant and believing and saved by the grace of God and for the glory of God.

Think about It

The guilty in this world still have to serve their sentences even on Death Row. But they may be saved by grace alone, through faith alone, in Christ alone to know God as Father in the eternal state to come.

How many, who could not be ransomed from their guilt under the Law of Moses, found redemption through faith in the coming Messiah who would give His life a ransom for many? Only eternity will reveal this.

But Jesus Christ, God's Son, purchased life for all who come to Him in faith. That is the contrast between law and grace. May He be praised for serving and saving all of us who believe in Him. And all who are still to believe in Him.

The Grace of God to All Nations

Today's Reading: Deuteronomy 1-2; Mark 11:1-19

Selected Verses

Turn northward and command the people, "You are about to pass through the territory of your brothers, the people of Esau, who live in Seir; and they will be afraid of you. So be very careful. Do not contend with them, for I will not give you any of their land, no, not so much as for the sole of the foot to tread on, because I have given Mount Seir to Esau as a possession.

Deut. 2:3b-5

And he was teaching them and saying to them, "Is it not written, 'My house shall be called a house of prayer for all the nations'? But you have made it a den of robbers."

Mark 11:17

Reflections

Throughout the Old Testament, God indicates that He has other nations in view as He brings salvation through Israel. How instructive to discover that God provided and protected lands for the descendants of Esau who was not the chosen son of Isaac! The Lord also provided lands for Lot's heirs, the Ammonites and the Moabites. He even restricted those lands from Israelite takeover.

Jesus clearly understood and taught this global perspective as indicated in today's selected verse from Mark. The temple was to be a house of prayer for all the nations. Even before Jesus' day, Judaism had degenerated into a very inward focused religion, and the Lord quotes from the prophets Isaiah and Jeremiah in His rebuke of the money changers (Isaiah 56:7; Jer. 7:11). But Jesus was making disciples who were going to go to the Gentiles in the entire world with His gospel.

Think about It

Unless you can trace your ancestry back to Jews, you are, like me, a Gentile. You are, like me, a beneficiary of God's grace to Israel, whereby came the Scriptures and our Lord Jesus Christ. Should we not be humbled by His amazing grace to all the nations? Praise God that He has seen fit to call to Himself a people for His glory from all the tribes and tongues of the earth.

Keeping Your Soul

Today's Reading: Deuteronomy 3-4; Mark 11:20-33

Selected Verses

> *Only take care, and keep your soul diligently, lest you forget the things that your eyes have seen, and lest they depart from your heart all the days of your life. Make them known to your children and your children's children.*

Deut. 4:9

> *And whenever you stand praying, forgive, if you have anything against anyone, so that your Father also who is in heaven may forgive you your trespasses.*

Mark 11:25

Reflections

Moses, in his final instructions to the Israelites, reminded them of God's great power and deliverance on their behalf, beginning in Egypt right up to the end of Moses' life on the threshold of the Promised Land. He warned them to keep their souls diligently, not forgetting all that God had done for them. He told them to pass these lessons on to their children and grandchildren. This was no idle command because their faithfulness to the Lord would be tested soon and often.

Jesus' gave instructions to His disciples near the end of His earthly life and ministry. He told them to take care to resolve interpersonal conflicts. They were even to interrupt their prayers to forgive others, lest God not hear their requests for forgiveness.

Think about It

Here are two ways God's people in all ages need to keep their souls diligently. One, we need to give thanks for God's power which He displays before us for good every day in countless ways. That same power may be unleashed against us for discipline when we forget Him and follow after other gods. Two, we need to beware of the danger of holding grudges against others for real or imagined offenses. Don't forget. We need God's mercy and forgiveness continually no less than they.

Keep your soul diligently. Remember God's power. Cultivate gratefulness. Praise God for His mercy. Show the same to others.

Warning! Dangerous Road Ahead

Today's Reading: Deuteronomy 5-7; Mark 12:1-27

Selected Verses

Oh that they had such a heart as this always, to fear me and to keep all my commandments, that it might go well with them and with their descendants forever!

Deut. 5:29

Jesus said to them, "Is this not the reason you are wrong, because you know neither the Scriptures nor the power of God?"

Mark 12:24

Reflections

The Lord took delight in the initial enthusiasm of the Israelites for His law. They indicated a commitment to be faithful and obedient, but God knew their resolve would not last. They would be drawn away by false gods and pagan people. Their hearts would not remain steadfast to fear Yahweh and to keep all His commandments. They would risk deprivation rather than believe God.

The Sadducees in Jesus' day went off track for two reasons. They didn't know the Scriptures, and they didn't know the power of God. Why did they not know the Scriptures? The Sadducees disregarded any supernatural incidents in the Old Testament. They did not count on God's power or intervention in human history. Since they assumed nothing supernatural was possible, they also assumed that the resurrection was impossible. They plotted to ridicule the idea of a resurrection by creating a dilemma for Jesus.

We know how that ended. The Sadducees came out looking foolish because Jesus used the Pentateuch (which they held to) to prove their position untenable. God is God of the living. To the Lord those who have died physically in this world are still alive to Him and always will be. The resurrection is true. Jesus Himself would prove it.

Think about It

The ancient Israelites veered off from obedience to God. Why? They replaced the fear of the Lord with fascination for other gods. The Sadducees erred because they did not know God's Word well and they did not believe in the power of God. They trusted their own minds and their own five senses to arrive at truth.

These sorts of spiritual maladies abound today. Beware of the dangerous roads ahead. Let it not be said of us that our hearts were not wholly the Lord's or that we failed to know His Word and His power.

Not Far from the Kingdom of God

Today's Reading: Deuteronomy 8-10; Mark 12:28-44

Selected Verses

Circumcise therefore the foreskin of your heart, and be no longer stubborn.

Deut. 10:16

And when Jesus saw that he answered wisely, he said to him, "You are not far from the kingdom of God." And after that no one dared to ask him any more questions.

Mark 12:34

Reflections

In yesterday's reading in Mark, wily questioners came to Jesus attempting to trick Him or trap Him in His words. In today's reading, however, a scribe who came appears to have been sincere. He wanted to know "Which commandment is the most important of all?" He heard Jesus' answer, repeated it, and affirmed it. Jesus found the man's response to reflect wisdom and commended him as being "not far from the kingdom of God."

What indicated that this scribe was near the kingdom? He seems to have recognized Jesus' authority. He showed receptivity to Jesus' teaching. His response to the Lord revealed a hunger to know the truth. He was ready to obey the truth once it was clear to him.

Perhaps he had what Moses called a circumcised heart.

Moses told the Israelites to circumcise the foreskin of their hearts, and to stop being stubborn. Their hearts were in danger of becoming insensitive. They were at risk of becoming unreceptive. Moses knew that even though Israel had God's law, they might ignore it, growing callous to its commands.

Think about It

What is the condition of your heart before God's word? Are you wise and receptive, hungry to know and grow, like the scribe? Beware of an uncircumcised heart that knows the truth but is insensitive to it. Those who love God's word are close to the kingdom of God.

Worship: True and Biblical

Today's Reading: Deuteronomy 11-13; Mark 13:1-13

Selected Verses

You shall not do according to all that we are doing here today, everyone doing whatever is right in his own eyes, for you have not as yet come to the rest and to the inheritance that the Lord your God is giving you.

Deut. 12:8-9

And Jesus said to him, "Do you see these great buildings? There will not be left here one stone upon another that will not be thrown down."

Mark 13:2

Reflections

The true worship of God must be offered according to His word, not based on the whims of the worshipers. This is called the "regulative principle." Moses laid down these laws before the Israelites entered the Promised Land. They would find worship sites all over the land where the previous occupants made offerings to false gods. God wanted those worship sites obliterated. He required that true worship be done according to His law and in the place He would designate.

That place was first Shiloh and later Jerusalem, where Solomon would build a temple according to God's law. Later the invading army of Nebuchadnezzar destroyed it. Faithful Jews under Ezra rebuilt it. But Jesus told His disciples that second temple would not last. Sure enough, history tells us that in 70 AD, the armies of Rome under Titus destroyed that temple in Jerusalem. It has never been rebuilt.

Old Testament worship pointed to the Messiah, the Lord Jesus Christ, who fulfills all the symbols of the temple and the priesthood. Paul wrote that God's temple now is His people. They gather around the world in all kinds of places and structures (1 Cor. 3:16-17). He may be worshiped in truth without the need for a physical temple, but Christ must be central and God must be worshiped in Spirit and in truth (John 4:23,24; Matt. 18:20).

Think about It

Yes, the regulative principle still applies to our worship, but sincere believers differ as to exactly how that looks. We ought to exercise humility and patience with one another as we differ on some aspects of corporate worship. Meanwhile, let us worship Him daily in our homes and weekly in our congregations with due reverence and awe.

Watchfulness: Good and Bad

Today's Reading: Deuteronomy 14-16; Mark 13:14-37

Selected Verses

Take care lest there be an unworthy thought in your heart and you say, "The seventh year, the year of release is near," and your eye look grudgingly on your poor brother, and you give him nothing, and he cry to the Lord against you, and you be guilty of sin.

Deut. 15:9

And then they will see the Son of Man coming in clouds with great power and glory. And then he will send out the angels and gather his elect from the four winds, from the ends of the earth to the ends of heaven.

Mark 13:26-27

Reflections

One of the functions of God's word is to warn His people to obey Him and not look for creative ways to avoid doing right.

In ancient Israel, God instructed His people in how they were to manage their economy so that there would be no poverty among them. God made provisions for addressing those in need. But the Lord knew their hearts. He warned them against trying to evade their responsibilities. If the year of release were near, a loan would be almost an outright gift.[2] He warned them not to take into account the coming year of release, as they were considering the needs of their poor brother. One might be tempted to ignore the appeal of the needy, but the Lord would hear his cry and bring judgment on the neglectful, unresponsive relative.

In Jesus' teaching about the coming time of tribulation, He also warned people to be watchful, but for a different reason. The coming of the Son of Man in power and glory is certain but the time is unknown. In contrast, the years of release or of Jubilee came predictably every seven years or every 49 years. There is a godly watchfulness and an unrighteous watchfulness.

Think about It

Believers should live each day as if the Lord could come. We ought not to think that today does not matter because final judgment seems to be delayed. Neither ought we to neglect our duties in this world because we are convinced the Lord will be here within hours. We are called to be watchful in a good way not calculating so as to disobey.

Do the things God has called you to do today. When He comes you will be glad you did.

---

[2] See note in *The Reformation Study Bible*, page 275.

The Three Offices of Jesus

Today's Reading: Deuteronomy 17-19; Mark 14:1-25

Selected Verses

I will raise up for them a prophet like you from among their brothers. And I will put my words in his mouth, and he shall speak to them all that I command him. And whoever will not listen to my words that he shall speak in my name, I myself will require it of him.

Deut. 18:18-19

And as they were eating, he took bread, and after blessing it broke it and gave it to them, and said, "Take; this is my body." And he took a cup, and when he had given thanks he gave it to them, and they all drank of it. And he said to them, "This is my blood of the covenant, which is poured out for many."

Mark 14:22-24

Reflections

In Deuteronomy Moses laid out principles for the offices of prophet, priest, and king in Israel. Certainly, the law spoke much about the priesthood, but now Moses also addresses the matter of prophets and kings, too.

In all three of these offices, God alone would designate the occupants. No one was to assume the role of priest, prophet or king. Warnings were given to those who might seek the role of prophet and use that office to lead the nation astray to other gods. Kings were not to use their authority to lead the nation away from the Lord. The law regulated the work of the priesthood.

The people of Israel were under obligation to respect those in authority, duly chosen and installed by God. They must not disregard those anointed by the Lord.

The culmination of rebellion against the Lord's anointed came when Christ Jesus appeared. He fulfilled the promise of God to raise up a prophet like Moses. Jesus inherited the throne of David to reign forever over God's elect people. He was the great High Priest above the Aaronic priesthood after the order of Melchizedek (Heb. 5:9,10).

Think about It

Jesus Christ fulfilled all these offices perfectly, yet His people rejected Him. Judas betrayed Him. The Sanhedrin condemned Him. Pilate turned Him over for crucifixion. All seemed lost, but His broken body and poured out blood brought a new covenant of salvation to all who believe in Him.

No words can adequately express the immense wisdom and grace of God toward us in Christ, our prophet, priest, and king. Praise Him, though your words be feeble. Never lose the wonder of who He is and what He has done for us.

God's Grace for Every Battle and Failure

Today's Reading: Deuteronomy 20-22; Mark 14:26-50

Selected Verses

And when you draw near to the battle, the priest shall come forward and speak to the people and shall say to them, "Hear, O Israel, today you are drawing near for battle against your enemies: let not your heart faint. Do not fear or panic or be in dread of them, for the Lord your God is he who goes with you to fight for you against your enemies, to give you the victory."

Deut. 20:2-4

And Jesus said to them, "You will all fall away, for it is written, 'I will strike the shepherd, and the sheep will be scattered.' But after I am raised up, I will go before you to Galilee."

Mark 14:27-28

Reflections

Moses instructed the people of Israel about the proper sense of confidence in the Lord as they prepared to go into the Promised Land and face entrenched enemies. He did not tell them that they were the greatest army ever fielded nor that their enemies were a bunch of wimps. He promised that the Lord their God would go with them to fight for them and to give them the victory.

Jesus' disciples also faced a daunting enemy, those opponents of the Lord who had conspired together to arrest Him and put Him to death. Jesus forewarned the disciples that they would fall away. He said their desertion would fulfill Scripture. They objected. Peter asserted that he would die with Jesus, if necessary. All the other disciples gave a hearty "amen."

Of course, these were empty promises. But Jesus also pointed them beyond their failure - to His resurrection, He would meet them in Galilee.

Think about It

The key to remaining faithful under extreme pressure is to focus on God, His presence, His power, and His faithfulness. He will be with us in the worst of trials. He will never leave us or forsake us. We may waver. We may fall away, like the disciples. But He will never fail us. He is gracious to His fearful sheep.

What scary trial do you face now? Are you confident of His presence? If you have failed to trust Him do you know that He welcomes back His frightened sheep and defeated children? Paul wrote to Timothy, "You then, my child, be strengthened by the grace that is in Christ Jesus" (2 Tim. 2:1). Be confident in Him. In Christ, there is grace to face your toughest battles and grace to cover your greatest failures.

Handling Overwhelming Guilt

Today's Reading: Deuteronomy 23-25; Mark 14:51-72

Selected Verses

If you make a vow to the Lord your God, you shall not delay fulfilling it, for the Lord your God will surely require it of you, and you will be guilty of sin. But if you refrain from vowing, you will not be guilty of sin. You shall be careful to do what has passed your lips, for you have voluntarily vowed to the Lord your God what you have promised with your mouth.

Deut. 23:21-23

And immediately the rooster crowed a second time. And Peter remembered how Jesus had said to him, "Before the rooster crows twice, you will deny me three times." And he broke down and wept.

Mark 14:72

Reflections

The Mosaic Law held the Israelites up to high and noble standards of integrity and social concern. There were numerous laws protecting the needy from exploitation by the wealthy. Here we see a law concerning the making and keeping of vows. Vows were made freely, before God, but once made they had to be kept. People were not to swear casually, but to take seriously their commitments. No cheap talk. A man's word was his bond.

Peter broke his vow to Jesus, to stand by Him even if it cost him his life. He shamelessly denied the Lord. Peter was not the only one, but Mark gives us a close up of Peter's cowardice and remorse. The grief Peter felt when he heard the rooster and remembered Jesus' words is palpable.

Think about It

Certainly, we see the breakdown of vow-keeping in our society. We can't trust each other. It's easy to break commitments. We are quick to file suits but slow to keep promises. Married couples divorce as if no binding vow had been made.

Who of us has not broken a solemn vow of some kind? Who of us cannot identify with Peter's rash vow and thoughtless lying to save his skin? Peter could not keep his vow, not even for one night. He needed an innocent Lamb to die for his sin, the broken vow and a million other transgressions. So do we. Jesus did that on the cross.

Do not get stuck in endless remorse and weeping. Trust Christ, who bore our sins in His body on the cross. In Him we become forgiven vow-breakers. We even become the righteousness of God (2 Cor. 5:21).

The Crucifixion: Were You There?

Today's Reading: Deuteronomy 26-27; Mark 15:1-26

Selected Verses

Cursed be anyone who takes a bribe to shed innocent blood. And all the people shall say, "Amen."

Deut. 27:25

And Pilate again said to them, "Then what shall I do with the man you call the King of the Jews?" And they cried out again, "Crucify him." AndPilate said to them, "Why, what evil has he done?" But they shouted all the more, "Crucify him." So Pilate, wishing to satisfy the crowd, released for them Barabbas, and having scourged Jesus, he delivered him to be crucified.

Mark 15:12-15

Reflections

Moses instructed the Israelites to bind themselves to the law by swearing curses on themselves should they disobey it. This they were to do upon entering the land and arriving at Mount Ebal and Mount Gerizim. One of the laws they swore to uphold was the law to administer justice and not to accept a bribe to shed innocent blood. Judges could be bought off by wealthy parties and the poor, innocent person would suffer even death. What a great offense to the God who made mankind in His own image!

The ultimate violation of this law was committed when Jesus was falsely charged by the chief priests, the scribes, the elders, and the whole council. Then they turned Him over to Pilate for execution. Pilate saw what an injustice this was. He knew it was pure envy that drove the Jewish leaders to accuse Jesus. But Pilate wished to satisfy the crowd. So he released the criminal Barabbas, whipped Jesus, and sent Him off to crucifixion.

In all of human history, there had never before been another perfectly innocent man, only Jesus. In all of human history, there has never been a greater miscarriage of justice. The Jewish leaders, the crowds in Jerusalem for the Passover, the Roman governor, the Roman soldiers, all supported this evil action. Even the disciples contributed by their absence

Think about It

The old spiritual asks: "Were you there when they crucified my Lord?" The correct answer is, "Yes, I was there. I was part of sinful humanity that brought down the Son of God for my sins."

"Oh Lord, sometimes it causes me to tremble, tremble, tremble." Does it cause you to tremble? If so, thank God that you grasp what He did that day. Trust Him that though your sins are as scarlet, in Christ, you stand cleansed before Him (Isaiah 1:18; 53:11).

The Father's Delight in the Son's Death

Today's Reading: Deuteronomy 28; Mark 15:27-47

Selected Verses

And as the Lord took delight in doing you good and multiplying you, so the Lord will take delight in bringing ruin upon you and destroying you. And you shall be plucked off the land that you are entering to take possession of it.

Deut. 28:63

And Jesus uttered a loud cry and breathed his last. And the curtain of the temple was torn in two, from top to bottom. And when the centurion, who stood facing him, saw that in this way he breathed his last, he said, "Truly this man was the Son of God!"

Mark 15:37-39

Reflections

Moses described the seemingly endless ways Israel would suffer if they disobeyed God's law, if they were not careful to obey it all, and if they did not "serve the Lord [their] God with joyfulness and gladness of heart" (Deut. 28:47). Their suffering would be through loss of crops, famine, mental anguish of all kinds, national humiliation, family breakdown, and (shudder) cannibalism.

Israel did fail to obey God. Israel did suffer the consequences predicted. But the ultimate suffering came not upon the nation but upon the Messiah, God's own Son Jesus Christ. He bore the full weight of God's wrath for His people. Jesus suffered for their sin. God the Father willed that His Son should bear this. It is accurate, although shocking, to say that God the Father delighted to bring ruin upon His Son thus vindicating His holiness and just wrath.

Think about It

So fully did Jesus' death satisfy the wrath of God that the temple curtain separating the people from the Holy of Holies, wherein was the mercy seat, was torn in two. In Christ God made the way for all His people to come into His presence and to receive mercy.

What a great salvation Jesus' death purchased for us! How delighted was God to open a way for His people to come into His presence! Let these truths grip you afresh today.

Where Does Sin Come From?

Today's Reading: Deuteronomy 29-30; Mark 16

Selected Verses

But if your heart turns away, and you will not hear, but are drawn away to worship other gods and serve them, I declare to you today, that you shall surely perish. You shall not live long in the land that you are going over the Jordan to enter and possess.

Deut. 30:17

Afterward he appeared to the eleven themselves as they were reclining at table, and he rebuked them for their unbelief and hardness of heart, because they had not believed those who saw him after he had risen.

Mark 16:14

Reflections

Moses warned the Israelites that their problem would not be that God's law was too hard to understand. It was not too far above them to grasp. Their problem with keeping the law would be a problem of the heart not the head. Their hearts would turn away from God's word. They would not love His law and that would result in their shutting their ears to it. This would not result in mere agnosticism or neglect of worship. They would begin to worship other gods and not Yahweh their true and living God who had delivered them by His powerful hand out of slavery in Egypt. "Beware of your heart," Moses was saying.

On the first day of the week, after Jesus was buried, several women went to the tomb with spices to anoint His body. They worried about how to get the big stone away from the opening. The women did not expect to find the stone rolled away, much less Jesus resurrected and gone. But that is what happened. They saw a young man dressed in white. They were afraid, but they didn't doubt what they had seen. They told the disciples what had happened, but they got a disbelieving response. Later there was another sighting of Jesus by two disciples. Their report also fell on deaf ears.

Then Jesus appeared to the eleven disciples (twelve minus Judas). He rebuked them for their "unbelief and hardness of heart." Again, it was a heart problem that accompanied their refusal to believe.

Think about It

Where does sin come from? It's a heart problem. God's truth is not irrational nor hard to grasp with the mind. But to believe we need hearts inclined toward God. Pray that your heart will never be hardened or turned away from God's word. Beware of heart problems.

A Serving of Grace with a Dose of Reality

Today's Reading: Deuteronomy 31-32; Luke 1:1-23

Selected Verses

For I know how rebellious and stubborn you are. Behold, even today while I am yet alive with you, you have been rebellious against the Lord. How much more after my death!

Deut. 31:27

And behold, you will be silent and unable to speak until the day that these things take place, because you did not believe my words, which will be fulfilled in their time.

Luke 1:20

Reflections

The Bible never sugarcoats the reality of fallen human nature. People, even God's people, are not viewed through rose-colored glasses but rather are shown to be sinners who never seem to learn from their mistakes and have a hard time believing God's plain and clear word.

Moses had reassured the Israelites that God would be with them as they entered the Promised Land, but he also told them that he knew their hearts. They would forsake the Lord and go after other gods. Moses knew that they already showed this tendency during his lifetime and they would not improve after his death.

Of course, all that Moses predicted came true. The people abandoned their Lord to worship other gods. Nevertheless, God showed enormous mercy and grace to them in the midst of all their failures and rebellion.

We come to the incident with Zechariah, the elderly childless priest who was assigned the duty of entering the Holy of Holies in the temple. He was greeted by the angel Gabriel. It must have been a terrifying moment. The announcement that he and Elizabeth would have a son had to be beyond startling. Yet Zechariah dared to question the truthfulness of the angel's words. He showed shameless disbelief and was struck dumb for his obtuseness. The Lord disciplined him but still blessed him in his old age with an outstanding son, John the Baptist.

Think about It

Throughout the Scriptures, God gives His people a dose of reality, but He also shows His mercy, grace, and patience toward us. He will not abandon those He has chosen for Himself. He is faithful, although we show stubbornness and unbelief far too often.

Praise God for never leaving or forsaking us redeemed sinners. How desperately we need a huge serving of grace with a dose of reality!

The Everlasting Arms

Today's Reading: Deuteronomy 33-34; Luke 1:24-56

Selected Verses

There is none likeGod, O Jeshurun,
who rides through the heavens to your help,
through the skies in his majesty.
The eternal God is your dwelling place,
and underneath are the everlasting arms.
And he thrust out the enemy before you
and said, "Destroy."

Deut. 33:26-27

He has shown strength with his arm;
he has scattered the proud in the thoughts of their hearts.

Luke 1:51

Reflections

Both Moses and Mary express awe and reverence for the power and faithfulness of God.

Moses, in today's reading, pronounces blessings on the tribes of Israel as he knows the time of his death is drawing near. Rather than express anger and disappointment that he has been denied entrance into the Promised Land, Moses takes the opportunity to give glory to God. His words of praise are both true and inspiring.

Moses could speak with the perspective of a man who for 120 years had seen the power of God in his life. God saved him at birth, protected him from prosecution for murder, watched over him during his exile, called him at a burning bush, gave him victory over the Egyptians, and guided him through the wilderness to the border of the Promised Land. Moses knew God. God had been faithful, and God had been powerful on Moses' behalf. What better way for Moses to say goodbye than to lift words of praise to God?

Mary, the young virgin engaged to Joseph, faced a completely unexpected life. Suddenly, the angel Gabriel broke into her world announcing what was to become of her. She would be the mother of the Son of God. Mary's response is one of bewilderment which turns to submission and praise to God. She, like Moses, revels in thoughts of the powerful arm of God. God is able to do the impossible. God is going to do all His will. He turns the world right side up.

Think about It

How have you already seen God's power and faithfulness in your life? How do you need to remember God's power today? "Do not be afraid," the angel said to Mary (Luke 1:30). He is the God whose arm is strong and everlasting. Trust Him today. The everlasting arms are underneath you.

Fear: Is It Good or Bad?

Today's Reading: Joshua 1-3; Luke 1:57-80

Selected Verses

*Before the men lay down, she came up to them on the roof and said to the men,
"I know that the Lord has given you the land, and that the fear of you has
fallen upon us, and that all the inhabitants of the land melt away before you."*

Josh. 2:8-9

That we, being delivered from the hand of our enemies, might serve him without fear.

Luke 1:74

Reflections

Rahab, the prostitute of Jericho, makes a most eloquent statement about the Lord, the God of Israel whom the people of her land have come to fear. They know how God has led the people for forty years out of Egypt and through the wilderness. The Israelites have had successful military confrontations. In vivid terms she describes the inhabitants of the land as "melting away" before Israel and their God.

When Zechariah and Elizabeth's baby boy was born, Elizabeth announced that his name was John. Her decision contradicted the custom stipulating that babies were always named for family members. Zechariah, still mute, wrote his agreement to the name on a tablet. Immediately, he was able to speak, but the people were overcome by fear. They saw the hand of God in this.

Zechariah, with his regained ability to talk, began giving praise to God. He prophesied about the ministry of his son in glowing but not exaggerated terms. God's purposes were to deliver His people from their enemies so that they might serve Him without fear, that is, without fear of their enemies.

Think about It

What place does fear have in your life? There is a proper fear of God which is "clean, enduring forever" and brings true wisdom (Ps. 19:9; Prov. 9:10). God's people fear Him in a reverent, healthy way, but they are not to be afraid of their enemies whom He has defeated. After all, God has already decreed victory for those who are His. The places where the sole of Joshua's foot was going to tread had already been given to him (Josh. 1:3). Fear God. Do not fear His and your enemies. The land is already yours. Serve Him today confident of His ultimate victory.

Whose Side Is God On?

Today's Reading: Joshua 4-6; Luke 2:1-24

Selected Verses

*And Joshua went to him and said to him, "Are you for us, or for our
adversaries?" And he said, "No; but I am the commander of the army
of the Lord. Now I have come." And Joshua fell on his face to the earth
and worshiped and said to him, "What does my lord say to his servant?"*

Josh. 5:13b-14

*And the shepherds returned, glorifying and praising God
for all they had heard and seen, as it had been told them.*

Luke 2:20

Reflections

Joshua meets the commander of the army of the Lord, very possibly a pre-
incarnate appearance of the Son of God. Joshua has war on his mind as he and
the Israelites encamp in the plains of Jericho about to face their first military test
in the land. Naturally, Joshua wonders who this Warrior supports. "Us or them?"
he asks, somewhat crudely. "No," says the commander bluntly, ruling the
question out of order. Joshua needed to learn that God's army is independent of
all earthly powers and rules over all other forces. God's army advances God's
glory and purposes. Earthly rulers and captains cannot marshal His forces for
their own goals.

In the Luke reading today, there is a curious irony. Jesus' birth is set in the
historical context of the reign of the Roman emperor, Caesar Augustus, and the
Syrian governor, Quirinius. But the angels make the advent announcement to
shepherds in the field who are watching their sheep. Shepherds in Bible times
were low on the socio-economic scale. They were considered so unreliable that
their testimony in a court of law was inadmissible.

Think about It

God works in and through human history and earthly powers, but He is
subject to none of them, not Caesar Augustus, not Quirinius, not even Joshua,
the leader of the Israelites, and certainly not any of the nations in existence
today. God is on His own side, but He calls people to join Him on His side to
serve and glorify Him.

May we be faithful to the Lord's calling to serve Him for His glory and
submit our needs and goals to Him today and always. God can use a shepherd or
an emperor for His purposes, but those He uses worship Him alone and ask,
"What does my lord say to his servant?"

Two Men Who Saw the Light

Today's Reading: Joshua 7-8; Luke 2:25-52

Selected Verses

*And afterward he read all the words of the law, the blessing and the curse, according
to all that is written in the Book of the Law. There was not a word of all that
Moses commanded that Joshua did not read before all the assembly of Israel,
and the women, and the little ones, and the sojourners who lived among them.*

Josh. 8:34-35

*Lord, now you are letting your servant depart in peace,
according to your word;
for my eyes have seen your salvation
that you have prepared in the presence of all peoples,
a light for revelation to the Gentiles,
and for glory to your people Israel.*

Luke 2:29-32

Reflections

God's focus, as we have seen before, includes not only the Israelites or the Jews, but all the peoples of the earth.

Joshua renews the covenant of God with Israel by reading the entire Book of the Law of Moses. The congregation included all Israel: the men, the women, the children, and the sojourners who lived among them. Those sojourners were not related physically to Israel, but merely living among them perhaps as servants. How important that Joshua included them in the reading of the law and the renewal of the covenant!

Simeon, who had waited all his life for the coming of the Messiah, met the infant Jesus in the temple. His long-awaited moment had come. He had seen the salvation of the Lord. That salvation was prepared in the presence of all peoples and would be a light for revelation to the Gentiles as well as a glory to God's people Israel. Certainly, Simeon understood the universal offer of salvation that was being extended to the entire world.

Think about It

God deserves our praise for sending His Son, Jesus, to save all who believe in Him from every nation, tribe, and tongue. Thank Him that Joshua granted the sojourners among the Israelites the privilege of hearing the Word of God. Praise God for His grace to old Simeon, who saw his dream of a lifetime fulfilled. He also gave us wise words about the work of Jesus Christ whose ministry extends to all peoples even you and me.

God's Intervention in Human History

Today's Reading: Joshua 9-10; Luke 3

Selected Verses

And Joshua captured all these kings and their land at one time, because the Lord God of Israel fought for Israel.

Josh. 10:42

And all flesh shall see the salvation of God.

Luke 3:6

Reflections

In today's reading in Joshua, God was at work defeating the enemies of Israel. Certainly, the twelve tribes saw the salvation of God from those who had defiled the land with pagan worship. God blessed them with much victory, using even hailstones and a suspended sunset to accomplish His purposes.

Luke quotes from Isaiah in introducing the ministry of John the Baptist. John was preparing the people for the coming of the Lord Jesus Christ. Isaiah described one who cried in the wilderness, calling the people to prepare the way of the Lord. That prophecy was fulfilled as John literally preached in the wilderness proclaiming a baptism of repentance for the forgiveness of sins.

Crowds came to John and sought baptism. He did not soft pedal his message but warned them of the wrath to come and the need to make changes in their lives that reflected true repentance. Two groups were specifically mentioned: the tax collectors and the soldiers. John's ministry was blessed by God so much that people thought perhaps he was the Christ, but later he clarified that Jesus was the One whose worth was far above his own and that Jesus would take away the sins of the world (John 1:29). Isaiah's words came true that all flesh would see the salvation of God.

Think about It

God intervenes in human history for the salvation of His people whether through dramatic or mundane means. Whether we see signs of miraculous intervention or not, He has promised to save those who come to Him through Christ. None of our enemies can stand before Him. He overcomes the sinful hearts of tax collectors and soldiers. He destroys the unrepentant but saves His own. Look for His presence as you pray and walk with Him today.

The Kingdoms Vs. *The* Kingdom

Today's Reading: Joshua 11-13; Luke 4:1-32

Selected Verses

And Joshua turned back at that time and captured Hazor and struck its king with the sword, for Hazor formerly was the head of all those kingdoms.

Josh. 11:10

And the devil took him up and showed him all the kingdoms of the world in a moment of time, and said to him, "To you I will give all this authority and their glory, for it has been delivered to me, and I give it to whom I will. If you, then, will worship me, it will all be yours."

Luke 4:5-7

Reflections

"The Only Thing That Is Constant Is Change" is a statement attributed to the Greek philosopher, Heraclitus. Christian theology disagrees because God is constant and unchanging. Nevertheless, to a large degree everything in our experience seems to be constantly changing, like the kingdoms of this world.

In Joshua's day, Hazor was head of several kingdoms. With God's leading and power, Joshua conquered Hazor and all the kingdoms of Canaan. The scripture tells us that God hardened the hearts of those kings so that they would fight against Israel and lose (Josh. 11:20). Hazor's kingdoms came under the dominion of Israel until the Assyrian captivity in 722 BC.

Clearly the devil has some control in this world, but only what God allows him. He tempts certain people with power and authority in exchange for allegiance to his evil causes and purposes.

Which people does Satan personally approach? We have at least a partial list in the Bible where we are told that the devil went after Eve, Job, Peter, and Jesus (Gen. 3:1-7; Job 1-2; Luke 22:31-34; Luke 4:1).

Hazor ruled a number of kingdoms. Later, Israel possessed those lands. When the devil approached Jesus to tempt him, Satan claimed to have authority over all the kingdoms of the earth. In the final analysis, these earthly kingdoms rightfully belong to God the Creator and He providentially controls them. But the ultimate kingdom is not an earthly temporal one. Jesus proclaimed the coming of the kingdom of God.

Think about It

Do you serve a changing kingdom or the Kingdom that belongs to our unchanging God? Seek His Kingdom and serve the King who is eternal. He hardens hearts of proud rulers and turns hearts of all at His will (Exod. 7:3; Prov. 21:1). Pray that His Kingdom may come in ultimate triumph soon and that we will be found in it.

God's Authority against Formidable Forces

Today's Reading: Joshua 14-15; Luke 4:33-44

Selected Verses

So now give me this hill country of which the Lord spoke on that day, for you heard on that day how the Anakim were there, with great fortified cities. It may be that the Lord will be with me, and I shall drive them out just as the Lord said.

Josh. 14:12

And they were all amazed and said to one another, "What is this word? For with authority and power he commands the unclean spirits, and they come out!"

Luke 4:36

Reflections

Remember Caleb? Along with Joshua, he was one of two adult survivors of the exodus from Egypt. He's back appealing to Joshua to grant him the hill country of Hebron as his inheritance in the land. Caleb, demonstrated not doubt but humility and an unassuming air, in expressing his dependence on the Lord to be with him as he cleared the enemy Anakim out of the territory he desired. The Anakim were a tall and frightening group of warriors whom the spies had met 40 years earlier when they did reconnaissance in the land. Joshua granted Caleb his request and blessed his old friend. The effort was successful because the Lord had authority over the Anakim and all the other great pretenders of this world.

Jesus controlled every kind of disease. He healed Simon's mother of a fever so quickly and completely that she immediately resumed her duties as hostess and homemaker as if nothing had occurred. The townspeople lined up to have Jesus heal them, too. Whatever sickness they had, he graciously healed. But his power over unclean spirits stunned them. A demonic man made a scene in the synagogue, screaming out his fear of destruction at the hands of Jesus. He even accurately identified Jesus as the "Holy One of God." The demon threw the man down, but Jesus commanded him to be silent and come out of him. The demon obeyed. The crowd was amazed at this demonstration of authority.

Think about It

Do you have confidence in God's control over this world? The triune God has revealed Himself, Father, Son, and Holy Spirit, one God in three persons who rules over the entire universe. Through the grace of Jesus His Son, the Father gives His Spirit to live in His children. All power and authority belong to Him. In Christ, you belong to Him who has power and authority over everyone and everything. Fear not. Trust Him who reigns over all.

Leadership Lessons from Jesus and Joshua

Today's Reading: Joshua 16-18; Luke 5:1-16

Selected Verses

So the men arose and went, and Joshua charged those who went to write the description of the land, saying, "Go up and down in the land and write a description and return to me. And I will cast lots for you here before the Lord in Shiloh.".

Josh. 18:8

But now even more the report about him went abroad, and great crowds gathered to hear him and to be healed of their infirmities. But he would withdraw to desolate places and pray.

Luke 5:15-16

Reflections

Both Jesus and Joshua model how effective leaders handle high-stress situations and high-maintenance people. There are two important guidelines here for effective leaders:

1. Effective leaders empower people to solve their own problems, as much as possible. Joshua gave the responsibility to the seven landless tribes to survey the territory, to write a description of the remaining land, dividing it in seven portions, and to report back to him for allotments. Earlier, Joshua told the tribe of Joseph (Manasseh and Ephraim) to clear their land rather than asking for more territory (Josh. 17:14ff).

2. Effective leaders take time for prayer even during high-stress times. Jesus' ministry was becoming more widely known and the crowds came with endless needs for healing and teaching. It was not a bad thing that they saw Jesus as the one who could both heal them and teach them, but there were limits to what one person, even Jesus, could do. Jesus modeled for us the need to take time alone in prayer.

Think about It

In whatever leadership roles you fill, are you following these two guidelines as you face pressure and the expectations of others? A mother recently told me how much joy she has seeing her young son assume more responsibility for getting himself ready for bed. In our church, we train and empower gifted people to teach Sunday school classes. This process adds quality to our classes and their members.

The biggest danger is the tendency to operate purely on human wisdom and to fail to take time alone for prayer. Evaluate your life today. Make the needed changes so that you handle high-stress situations and high-maintenance people in wise and godly ways.

Old Wine, New Wine, and the Problem of Receptivity

Today's Reading: Joshua 19-20; Luke 5:17-39

Selected Verses

These were the cities designated for all the people of Israel and for the stranger sojourning among them, that anyone who killed a person without intent could flee there, so that he might not die by the hand of the avenger of blood, till he stood before the congregation.

Josh. 20:9

And no one after drinking old wine desires new, for he says, "The old is good."

Luke 5:39

Reflections

In ancient Israel, the law of Moses included strict borders for each tribe and designated cities of refuge to protect people from retaliation for involuntary manslaughter. There was law and order as there should be in any peaceful society.

In Jesus' day, the Pharisees taught and demonstrated careful adherence to the law as they understood it. The problem was the Pharisees found it easier to stick with tradition than to consider the possibility of some new element being introduced into their world. They accused Jesus of blasphemy when He forgave a man his sins. These religious leaders grumbled when Jesus ate and drank with tax collectors and sinners. They questioned the piety of Jesus' disciples because of their failure to fast often and offer prayers.

Jesus responded to their criticisms with explanations that showed He did not violate the law but did go beyond their traditional understanding of lawfulness. He had power to forgive sin. He came to call sinners to repentance. His presence in the world was like a wedding, not a funeral, and it changed everything.

Jesus told the scribes and Pharisees that resistance to the new is natural and comfortable, but it is not always acceptable. Law and order are good, but sometimes receptivity and flexibility are needed because God was doing a new thing in sending the Son of Man. The law had only revealed the sinfulness of Man. Jesus brought the new wine of the gospel, forgiveness of sin for all who believe in Him.

Think about It

Beware of the error of the Pharisees who extended faithfulness to the law beyond its intended limits and turned it into rigid resistance to the gospel and rejection of the Messiah, Jesus Christ. But we could also be in danger of being receptive to the latest trends of our culture that says what Jesus claimed and did is outmoded. Faithfulness to Him and His gospel is the key.

Hated, Excluded, Reviled, Spurned, Blessed

Today's Reading: Joshua 21-22; Luke 6:1-26

Selected Verses

No, but we did it from fear that in time to come your children might say to our children, "What have you to do with the Lord, the God of Israel?"

Josh. 22:24

Blessed are you when people hate you and when they exclude you and revile you and spurn your name as evil, on account of the Son of Man! Rejoice in that day, and leap for joy, for behold, your reward is great in heaven; for so their fathers did to the prophets.

Luke 6:22-23

Reflections

In the book of Joshua, we come to the end of the conquest of the land. The war was over, and occupation had begun. It was now time for the eastern tribes (Reuben, Gad, and the half-tribe of Manasseh) to return to their territories across the Jordan River. They nearly set off a civil war by building an imposing altar on the western banks of the river without explaining what they were doing or what they meant by it.

Driven by fear of future exclusion from the rest of Israel and from the worship of God, the eastern tribes erected what was suspected to be an unauthorized worship site potentially leading to apostasy and the wrath and judgment of God. The whole nation was still smarting from the wickedness of Achan that had brought God's judgment on them (Josh._7). Fear on both sides of the Jordan almost resulted in war. Diplomatic talks clarified the issue and reduced everyone's fears. War was averted.

In Luke today we find Jesus experiencing hatred and rejection by the religious authorities of His day. The plotting against Him has begun. He knows opposition will ramp up and He will soon die. So will some who follow Him, but He does not tell them how to avoid opposition that comes on His account. He tells them, "when people hate you and when they exclude you and revile you and spurn your name as evil" to welcome it, because as they experience it, they are blessed and their reward will be great in heaven.

Think about It

Do not fear persecution on the account of Jesus Christ. Stay calm if they accuse you of being evil. This is nothing new. In ancient days, the prophets suffered and sometimes died for being faithful to God. Be faithful to the Lord and the gospel. God will bless any suffering and reward you both now and in eternity.

Note: please consult your physician before attempting to leap for joy.

Loving God and Enemies

Today's Reading: Joshua 23-24; Luke 6:27-49

Selected Verses

Be very careful, therefore, to love the Lord your God.

Josh. 23:11

But love your enemies, and do good, and lend, expecting nothing in return, and your reward will be great, and you will be sons of the Most High, for he is kind to the ungrateful and the evil. Be merciful, even as your Father is merciful.

Luke 6:35,36

Reflections

Joshua urged the Israelites to love the Lord their God and to flee marriage entanglements with their enemies, the pagan natives of Canaan. He knew that if they intermarried with pagans, they would be drawn away from faithful and sincere service to God. At the same time, there were notable examples of Gentiles coming into the covenant people of God. Rahab and her family were protected from destruction in Jericho and admitted into the lineage of Judah and Jesus (Matt. 1:5). So the intention of Joshua's command was not to deprive Gentiles of blessing and salvation, but to protect the Israelites from apostasy.

Jesus taught His disciples to love their enemies, demonstrating godliness reflective of the Father who is merciful and kind even to the ungrateful and evil. Jesus was not teaching a relativistic view of morality in which everything that is good to you is good. He specifically showed that there is good and evil and that these are not the same. Good and evil fruits come from good and evil trees. But Jesus sent His disciples to show mercy to their enemies, the ungrateful and the evil.

Think about It

Why does God patiently pour out blessings on those who rebel against Him? Paul wrote to the Christians in Rome: "Or do you presume on the riches of his kindness and forbearance and patience, not knowing that God's kindness is meant to lead you to repentance?" (Rom. 2:4). In due time, the evil will face the judgment of God, but meanwhile, we who believe in Jesus show our faith by an obedient, godly life including loving our enemies.

The prohibition of believers marrying unbelievers continues (2 Cor. 6:14). Marriage is not one of the ways believers show love to unbelievers. This may be misunderstood by them, but that is the risk we must take to live a life of obedience. Of course, unbelievers are not prohibited from marrying one another. In fact, they should marry if so inclined.

Love God. Love your enemies but love them as God does by doing them good and telling them of the gospel of Jesus Christ.

The Kingdom that Cannot Fail

Today's Reading: Judges 1-2; Luke 7:1-30

Selected Verses

They abandoned the Lord and served the Baals and the Ashtaroth.
So the anger of the Lord was kindled against Israel, and
he gave them over to plunderers, who plundered them.

Judg. 2:13-14a

I tell you, among those born of women none is greater than John.
Yet the one who is least in the kingdom of God is greater than he.

Luke 7:28

Reflections

Jesus came announcing the arrival of the kingdom of God. He demonstrated His power by healing a Gentile servant of a Roman centurion and raising a dead man (just to take the examples in today's reading). Word spread about Jesus, and the people were both fearful and joyful. God was visiting His people.

The disciples of John the Baptist came asking for clarification. Was Jesus the Messiah? Jesus' answer gave no doubt that He was and is. So, what are we to make of the ministry of John the Baptist?

Jesus said that John was unsurpassed among all mankind. His ministry marked the end of the era of the old covenant kingdom with its symbolic priesthood, earthly temple, feast days, and sacrifices. Something new had come: the kingdom of God and the new covenant. So new and different are these that Jesus could say that the one who is least in the kingdom of God is greater than the one who was greatest under the old covenant and kingdom.

Our reading in Judges underscores the failure of Israel under the old covenant. The nation started badly and continued with more downs than ups. They ignored God's commands and mixed with the pagans who had been marked for extermination. The people worshiped false gods, abandoning the true and living God, Yahweh, who had delivered them from Egypt and opened the Promised Land to them.

Think about It

The old covenant and kingdom fell far short of perfection, yet it did point to the need for something that only Jesus could bring—the kingdom of God. We must enter that kingdom by faith in Him. Charles Wesley's great hymn "Rejoice, the Lord is King" says it well:

His kingdom cannot fail,
He rules o'er earth and Heav'n,
The keys of death and hell are to our Jesus giv'n;
Lift up your heart, lift up your voice;
Rejoice, again I say, rejoice!

Are you in?

Women of Faith and Action

Today's Reading: Judges 3-5; Luke 7:31-50

Selected Verses

And she said, "I will surely go with you. Nevertheless, the road on which you are going will not lead to your glory, for the Lord will sell Sisera into the hand of a woman."

Judg. 4:9

And he said to the woman, "Your faith has saved you; go in peace."

Luke 7:50

Reflections

In today's readings we meet two women of faith (not counting a third, Deborah) from whom we can learn much. Deborah as a prophetess and judge in Israel recruits Barak to lead an army against the Canaanites who have been cruelly oppressing the nation for twenty years. Barak accepts the job on the condition that Deborah accompany him to the battle. She agrees but warns him that the glory for the victory will not go to him but to a woman. At that point the first-time reader guesses that the glory will go to Deborah, but not so. It is Jael, a Kenite woman, who in God's providence takes advantage of the opportunity to murder the Canaanite commander, Sisera, while he is sleeping peacefully in her tent.

During a meal at the home of a Pharisee named Simon, a notoriously sinful woman slips in and begins to wash, kiss, and anoint Jesus' feet showing great love and respect for Him. Simon judges Jesus for His acceptance of attention from such a woman. Simon's reasoning is: "Either, Jesus doesn't know who she is, in which case, He is not a true prophet, or He knows who she is and accepts a rank sinner again revealing Himself to be no prophet." Neither of these options is true. Jesus does know who she is and welcomes her because of her faith. She is a sinner whom God has called to Himself and whose sin is forgiven because she believes in God's Son who would take upon Himself the punishment for sinners such as her. Jesus rebukes Simon but exonerates and reassures the woman. "Go in peace," He says. She is saved by faith.

Think about It

Faith drives both of these women to act. God's word honors their faith although both went against the tide of society in doing God's will. The glory for the victory goes to Jael who is not even an Israelite. The peace and assurance of salvation goes to the sinful but believing woman who is roundly rejected by a Pharisee.

Barak and Simon, the men in these two stories, leave much to be desired, although reluctant Barak did come around (Heb. 11:32). We know nothing of the outcome of Simon the Pharisee's life. Learn from the women of faith who understood that "faith apart from works is dead" (James 2:26).

Facing the Truth

Today's Reading: Judges 6-7; Luke 8:1-21

Selected Verses

But Joash said to all who stood against him, "Will you contend for Baal? Or will you save him? Whoever contends for him shall be put to death by morning. If he is a god, let him contend for himself, because his altar has been broken down."

Judg. 6:31

For nothing is hidden that will not be made manifest, nor is anything secret that will not be known and come to light. Take care then how you hear, for to the one who has, more will be given, and from the one who has not, even what he thinks that he has will be taken away.

Luke 8:17

Reflections

The moment of truth had come in Israel. The angel of the Lord sent Gideon to tear down the altar of Baal that his father had erected. The local folks cried out in rage, but Joash, Gideon's father, showing a complete change of heart, stood up against the mob. He astutely observed that if Baal were a god, he would be able to take vengeance on the perpetrators himself. Thus, in one moment the light of truth shone on the lie of Baal. That false god was a mere invention of men, not a god with power to do anything for himself or against others.

Jesus in a more general statement announced that all hidden things would be made known and every secret was going to come to light. One of the secrets is that those who disregard God and His Word and who trust in other gods believe lies. They delude themselves. This is why Jesus warned His hearers to "take care" how they hear.

Think about It

Hearing God's Word and believing it have long been a problem. It began with the fall of Adam and Eve in the Garden of Eden. It is crucial to hear and believe God's instructions and commands. Those who don't hear or who hear and ignore what they have heard will stand before God's judgment and lose what they thought they had.

Are you an eager hearer and careful doer of God's Word? Check your attitude and be sure you are. Better to face the truth now and follow it than to suffer exposure as a fool on that day when God uncovers every lie and makes manifest every hidden thing.

Darkness or Light?

Today's Reading: Judges 8-9; Luke 8:22-56

Selected Verses

Thus God returned the evil of Abimelech, which he committed against his father in killing his seventy brothers. And God also made all the evil of the men of Shechem return on their heads, and upon them came the curse of Jotham the son of Jerubbaal.

Judg. 9:56-57

Then all the people of the surrounding country of the Gerasenes asked him to depart from them, for they were seized with great fear. So he got into the boat and returned.

Luke 8:37

Reflections

Fallen mankind, darkened by sin, flees from the light of God and from that which brings peace. Today we find two examples of this principle: the reaction to the healing of the demoniac man and the case of Abimelech and the people of Shechem.

The people of Shechem chose Abimelech, the violent, renegade illegitimate son of their former judge, Gideon, over one of his other seventy sons, like Jotham who showed considerable wisdom and leadership skills. In the end Abimelech brought destruction on himself and all who supported him. The logical path of peace and an orderly transition of power from the late Gideon to Jotham did not appeal to the society.

Jesus, in a dramatic encounter, delivered a man possessed by innumerable demons. His symptoms included a lifestyle of homelessness, nakedness, and violent behavior. They guarded him in chains, but even that was ineffective. Jesus healed the man so completely that when people saw him, clothed and sane, they were frightened.

Why did the people react with fear to the healing of this pathetic man? They saw that Jesus had power over demons. They saw a herd of pigs drown. A human being previously held in bondage to Satan found peace and sanity. But they did not find joy and expectancy of more good things to come. Instead, they asked Jesus to leave them. Sin-darkened minds prefer the dark to the light, chaos and violence to order and peace.

Think about It

Beware of loving darkness rather than light. John wrote, "For everyone who does wicked things hates the light and does not come to the light, lest his works should be exposed. But whoever does what is true comes to the light, so that it may be clearly seen that his works have been carried out in God" (John 3:20-21). Apart from the grace of God, we flee from the light straight into the darkness and the arms of the enemy. Walk, by God's grace, in the light (1 John 1:7).

The Power and Authority of God

Today's Reading: Judges 10-11; Luke 9:1-36

Selected Verses

Will you not possess what Chemosh your god gives you to possess?
And all that the Lord our God has dispossessed before us, we will possess.

Judg. 11:24

And he called the Twelve together and gave them power and authority over all demons
and to cure diseases, and he sent them out to proclaim the kingdom of God and to heal.

Luke 9:1-2

Reflections

God has power and authority over all things. This is shown throughout the Bible beginning on the first page of Genesis and it is demonstrated in today's readings.

Jephthah was a mighty warrior and also a powerful statesman able to argue from history and theology with his enemies, the Ammonites. He made a foolish vow, true, but he is still remembered for his faith in Heb. 11:32. He was acclaimed because he showed an understanding and confidence in God's power and authority over all the earth, the peoples, and the nations. With the king of the Ammonites, he argued that God had granted the land to Israel. Since they did not believe in the God of Abraham, Isaac, and Jacob, but trusted in Chemosh, they would get what he could give them. History and theology were on Jephthah's side.

Jesus always was in harmony with the power and authority of His Father. This is obvious as Luke mentions several times that Jesus took time alone to pray. He also gave His disciples the power and authority to preach the gospel and to heal. He sent them out to the villages. They obeyed and reported back to Him.

Israel under God's authority and power took the Promised Land. Jesus Christ under His Father's authority was beginning to take Jerusalem, Judea, Samaria, and the end of the earth for the Kingdom of God (Acts 1:8).

Think about It

Christians today may feel oppressed by those who follow other gods, but the God of the Bible is the true and rightful Creator and Lord of all. His power and authority rule over all things. Walk in faith and confidence in Him today. Your faith will soon be made sight when He comes or calls you home.

How God Uses Evil for Good

Today's Reading: Judges 12-14; Luke 9:37-62

Selected Verses

His father and mother did not know that it was from the Lord, for he was seeking an opportunity against the Philistines. At that time the Philistines ruled over Israel.

Judg. 14:4

But while they were all marveling at everything he was doing, Jesus said to his disciples, "Let these words sink into your ears: The Son of Man is about to be delivered into the hands of men."

Luke 9:43-44

Reflections

Samson had a promising beginning. The angel of the Lord foretold his birth. The Spirit of God came upon him. He had godly parents. But his character proved to be deeply flawed. Many of his failures had to do with his weakness for women.

Ignoring God's law and his parents' warning, Samson chose a wife from the Philistines. It grieved his father and mother. How could they foresee the victory over the Philistines his decision would bring about? Indeed, Samson would pay dearly for his foolishness, but God accomplished His will and defeated the enemy of Israel.

In Luke 9 we see Jesus at one of the high points of His earthly ministry. He delivered a demon-possessed boy, and the crowd voiced amazement at the majesty of God (vs. 43). As they marveled at Jesus' power, He turned to His disciples telling them of His imminent arrest.

Think about It

As incredible as it seems, Jesus' arrest, trial, and crucifixion were not examples of history going wild and the world out of control. Luke reports the words of Peter in Acts 2:22-23: "Men of Israel, hear these words: Jesus of Nazareth, a man attested to you by God with mighty works and wonders and signs that God did through him in your midst, as you yourselves know—this Jesus, delivered up according to the definite plan and foreknowledge of God, you crucified and killed by the hands of lawless men."

The most horrific and evil deed in all of human history, the crucifixion of the Son of God, resulted in salvation for all time, for all His people. While God commands us to be obedient to Him, He uses even our sin for good ends. Many know Romans 8:28, but too often forget it: "And we know that for those who love God all things work together for good, for those who are called according to his purpose."

We know it. Now, praise God that it's true.

Why Do Only Little Children See?

Today's Reading: Judges 15-17; Luke 10:1-24

Selected Verses

Now the lords of the Philistines gathered to offer a great sacrifice to Dagon their god and to rejoice, and they said, "Our god has given Samson our enemy into our hand."

Judg. 16:23

In that same hour he rejoiced in the Holy Spirit and said, "I thank you, Father, Lord of heaven and earth, that you have hidden these things from the wise and understanding and revealed them to little children; yes, Father, for such was your gracious will.

Luke 10:21

Reflections

God sovereignly reveals or hides truth according to His will. The effect is that two parties see the same things but draw opposite conclusions.

After Samson's repeated foolish decisions, the Lord abandoned him, and Samson fell into the hands of the Philistines. They were sure that their god, Dagon, had been responsible for this victory. They did not take into account that it was the God of Israel who gave Samson his power and that Yahweh was using the Philistines to discipline His wayward servant. The Dagon worshipers misinterpreted the meaning of their victory and failed to see the glory of the true and living God.

When Jesus sent out His disciples to preach and heal in His name, He issued a warning to the surrounding towns that had shown resistance to the display of the coming of the kingdom of God. They saw great miracles, but they understood nothing. They failed to draw correct and true conclusions of what was plainly happening in their times.

Think about It

It was not the worldly wise or the politically powerful that understood the times but the "little children" who got it. So it is today. Do you see the hand of God in both the advances of the gospel as well as the setbacks to Christ's Church? He reigns and all His will is being fulfilled.

Rejoice in Him no matter how the outward circumstances seem to be going. Look for His hand in all that happens. Pray for a childlike spirit and clear vision. Flee from spiritual blindness to the light of God's truth.

The Cost of Loving Your Neighbor

Today's Reading: Judges 18-19; Luke 10:25-42

Selected Verses

But the men would not listen to him. So the man seized his concubine and made her go out to them. And they knew her and abused her all night until the morning. And as the dawn began to break, they let her go.

Judg. 19:25

Which of these three, do you think, proved to be a neighbor to the man who fell among the robbers?" He said, "The one who showed him mercy." And Jesus said to him, "You go, and do likewise."

Luke 10:36-37

Reflections

The value of human life is emphasized throughout the Bible. When asked about how to obtain eternal life, Jesus showed that loving God and loving our neighbor are the two key elements of a righteous life. The first two chapters of the Bible show that humanity was specially created by God, male and female, in His image and according to His likeness and given life by His Spirit.

The fall soon introduced alienation from God and between the first humans. Their son was the first murderer, his victim being his own brother (Gen. 3,4).

God in the Bible holds all people responsible for how they treat one another. The command is simple, but it is not easy. Alas! Loving your neighbor as yourself can mean standing up against some serious opposition in society.

The old man in Judges 19 tried to protect the traveler in his village from the abusive men, but his neighbors stormed his house. He foolishly tried to placate their evil desires by offering them his daughter and the visitor's concubine. In the end, it cost a woman's life and started a civil war in Israel. The Samaritan in Jesus' parable reached across a huge racial divide to care for a wounded man. It's fairly easy in theory to say, "We should all love our neighbors as ourselves," but it is quite another thing to actually act consistently with that concept.

Think about It

Those who read the Bible and profess belief in it should be among the most caring of all people, willing and ready to pay a price, if necessary, to preserve and value life.

Look for opportunities to show mercy and kindness toward others today, but know that you may not be appreciated for it. It could even cost you more than you thought.

What to Do while Longing for the Kingdom

Today's Reading: Judges 20-21; Luke 11:1-28)

Selected Verses

In those days there was no king in Israel. Everyone did what was right in his own eyes.

Judg. 21:25

And he said to them, "When you pray, say:
"Father, hallowed be your name. Your kingdom come."

Luke 11:2

Reflections

The theme of the book of Judges is "there was no king in Israel [so] everyone did what was right in his own eyes." Especially the final chapters of the book show selected incidents which illustrate this same theme. People disregarded the law. Their worship of God was corrupted. Their marriages were in disarray. There was sexual immorality reminiscent of Sodom and Gomorrah. It is not hard to see that public opinion in Israel would soon favor installing a king. That would happen soon. But would a king in Israel solve the problems that existed under the Judges?

Hold that question for a bit and fast forward to the Gospel of Luke where Jesus' disciples observe His prayer life. They ask for instruction about prayer. Jesus gives them the prayer we usually call "The Lord's Prayer" with its assortment of sample petitions. After addressing God as Father and praying that His name be held as holy, the Lord gives them this petition, "Your kingdom come."

Now, back to the earlier question. The kingdom of Israel would not solve the problems of their society, much less the problems of the world. But Jesus came announcing the first stages of the arrival of the kingdom of God. He also gave His disciples the assignment of praying for the kingdom to come in its fullness.

Think about It

We have a responsibility to the secular governments or kingdoms we live in now. However, the only government that will last forever is the kingdom of God ruled by the Prince of Peace and the King of Kings, the Lord Jesus Christ.

Are you longing for that kingdom to fully come? Isn't it hard to wait for the eternal reign of our Lord, where peace will be permanent, sin will be unknown, love and justice will be the norm, and there will be no more sickness, sorrow, and death? We know from Scripture that this is God's ultimate will. It is right to be longing for the kingdom, but Jesus told us to pray that it may come soon. This is a prayer God is going to answer.

Something Greater

Today's Reading: Ruth 1-4; Luke 11:29-54

Selected Verses

Remain tonight, and in the morning, if he will redeem you, good;
let him do it. But if he is not willing to redeem you, then, as
the Lord lives, I will redeem you. Lie down until the morning.

Ruth 3:13

The queen of the South will rise up at the judgment with the men of this generation
and condemn them, for she came from the ends of the earth to hear the wisdom of
Solomon, and behold, something greater than Solomon is here. The men of Nineveh
will rise up at the judgment with this generation and condemn it, for they repented
at the preaching of Jonah, and behold, something greater than Jonah is here.

Luke 11:31-32

Reflections

Those who focus on material things and the passing values of this world are liable to miss the most important things. They choose short range benefits over eternal ones.

Jesus condemned the people of His day for demanding additional signs that would prove that He was the Messiah while ignoring the evidence which His words and life amply provided. He said that the Old Testament gave examples of Gentiles (the Queen of the South and the people of Nineveh) who believed with less evidence than the people of Capernaum. The contemporaries of Jesus' day chose to ignore the light they had and to overlook something greater than Solomon and Jonah. It was not politically correct or socially fashionable to believe in the Teacher from Nazareth.

In the Book of Ruth, Boaz showed himself to be faithful to God's law. Although it cost him, he agreed to redeem Ruth, that is, to marry her and provide an heir for Ruth's deceased husband. There was another, closer relative who should have been the kinsman-redeemer, but he declined to do so, choosing instead the material benefit of having an heir. As it turned out Boaz fathered a son by Ruth who entered into the royal lineage of David that eventually brought Jesus Christ. The unnamed shoeless relative is only remembered by his negligence while Boaz stands in the Old Testament as a type of Christ.

Think about It

Beware of choosing the things that only last in this world. By faith in God, choose something greater. Choose that which will last for eternity: the Word of God, the glory of God, and the Church of Jesus Christ.

Fear: When Is it Good and When Is it Not?

Today's Reading: First Samuel 1-3; Luke 12:1-34

Selected Verses

*Therefore the Lord, the God of Israel, declares: "I promised that your house
and the house of your father should go in and out before me forever," but
now the Lord declares: "Far be it from me, for those who honor me
I will honor, and those who despise me shall be lightly esteemed."*

1 Sam. 2:30

*But I will warn you whom to fear: fear him who, after he has killed, has authority
to cast into hell. Yes, I tell you, fear him! Are not five sparrows sold for two pennies?
And not one of them is forgotten before God. Why, even the hairs of your head
are all numbered. Fear not; you are of more value than many sparrows.*

Luke 12:5-7

Reflections

Contrary to popular opinion, what matters in life is how you are valued by God and how you are valued by God depends on whether you fear Him properly.

As high priest, Eli held a distinguished position in ancient Israel as he ministered in the tabernacle. Eli knew the law of God and the rituals associated with sacrifices and intercession before God. But he was an indulgent father. He allowed his sons to misuse their positions to satisfy their physical appetites for food and promiscuous sex. God held Eli responsible for dishonoring Him. Judgment was about to come upon him, his sons, and his posterity. He showed more fear of his sons than he did of God.

Jesus warned His disciples about the right and wrong kinds of fear. You should not fear anyone whose greatest power is to kill your body, He told them. You should fear the One who has authority to send you to hell. God deserves to be feared above all others. Yet He is the One who watches over sparrows. He is the One who numbers the hairs of your head. You are of much greater value than a sparrow.

Think about It

What are you afraid of? Do you fear being forgotten? Overlooked? Having a meaningless existence then dying in obscurity? If you are God's child, He will not forget or overlook you. Are you afraid of being caught, tortured, and executed for your faith? Fear not. God has power over your eternal destiny. All your enemy can do is kill you and inadvertently send you into the bosom of Abraham.

Fear God, but also trust God if you know Him.

The Importance of Being Faithful and Responsible

Today's Reading: First Samuel 4-6; Luke 12:35-59

Selected Verses

And he struck some of the men of Beth-shemesh, because they looked upon the ark of the Lord. He struck seventy men of them, and the people mourned because the Lord had struck the people with a great blow. Then the men of Beth-shemesh said, "Who is able to stand before the Lord, this holy God? And to whom shall he go up away from us?"

1 Sam. 6:19-20

Everyone to whom much was given, of him much will be required, and from him to whom they entrusted much, they will demand the more.

Luke 12:48b

Reflections

God holds people responsible according to what they have received from Him. We are to be stewards of God's truth and God's gifts.

The Israelites had entered into a covenant with God in which they were His unique people in all the earth (Exod. 19:1-6). God revealed His law to them which included instructions about the priesthood, the tabernacle, its furnishings, and the offering of sacrifices. The Ark of the Covenant was to be kept in the most holy place in the tabernacle where God met with the high priest on the Day of Atonement each year.

But in the days of the judges everyone did what was right in his own eyes. In that spirit, the priests allowed the ark to be carried onto the battlefield as they fought against their enemies, the Philistines. The plan backfired. The Philistines won the battle and stole the ark. God would not allow Himself to be manipulated or what He declared sacred to be desecrated. Rather, God held His people responsible for what they had been given.

Peter asked Jesus who He was targeting with the parable about the servants waiting for their master. "Was it for the Twelve or for the crowds?", he queried. In His typical fashion, Jesus redirects Peter's mind to his own responsibility and away from that of others. In essence, Jesus tells him "everyone is responsible for what they have been given, so be concerned about what you have and what you do with what you have."

Think about It

Jesus has promised to return. Meanwhile, God has given us truth to apply, gifts to use, and opportunities to serve Him as we wait. Be faithful and responsible today with what you have for His glory.

When Suffering Doesn't Make Sense

Today's Reading: First Samuel 7-9; Luke 13:1-21

Selected Verses

As Samuel was offering up the burnt offering, the Philistines drew near to attack Israel. But the Lord thundered with a mighty sound that day against the Philistines and threw them into confusion, and they were defeated before Israel.

1 Sam. 7:10

There were some present at that very time who told him about the Galileans whose blood Pilate had mingled with their sacrifices. And he answered them, "Do you think that these Galileans were worse sinners than all the other Galileans, because they suffered in this way? No, I tell you; but unless you repent, you will all likewise perish.

Luke 13:1-3

Reflections

While cause and effect relationships exist in our experience, it is not always possible to draw perfectly correct conclusions about those relationships because God intervenes in ways we sometimes do not understand. Suffering doesn't always come as punishment for some failure. In fact, it can come when we feel we are walking closely to the Lord.

The Israelites suffered for years under oppression by the Philistines. Finally, they cried out to the Lord for deliverance. Samuel called them together for prayer and repentance. Immediately, the Philistines were suspicious of this gathering and mounted an attack which intimidated the Israelites. The national prayer meeting seemed to actually make things worse. But then God intervened and sent thunder so deafening that the army of Philistea was thrown into confusion and defeat. The men of Israel chased them and struck them down.

In Jesus' day some Galileans were killed by Herod while attempting to offer sacrifices to God. A tower fell on some people at Siloam causing their deaths. Were those people merely reaping the consequences of their sins? Jesus denied that those victims were any worse sinners than their neighbors. He warned His hearers to repent or they would also perish.

Think about It

There can be an apparent disconnect, at least in the short term, between a person's spiritual life and their outward circumstances. Sometimes evil people prosper while godly people may face enormous suffering (Ps. 73). Turning to the Lord is not a quick fix for all our difficulties. It may bring on greater difficulties. Ultimately, the Lord promises that His people will "dwell in the house of the Lord forever" (Ps. 23:6). Are you suffering despite your obedience to God? Plod on in faith. May God give you grace as you await your eternal home.

What Does it Mean to Die Well?

Today's Reading: First Samuel 10-12; Luke 13:22-35

Selected Verses

Moreover, as for me, far be it from me that I should sin against the Lord by ceasing to pray for you, and I will instruct you in the good and the right way.

1 Sam. 12:23

And he said to them, "Go and tell that fox, 'Behold, I cast out demons and perform cures today and tomorrow, and the third day I finish my course.'"

Luke 13:32

Reflections

There is a point in the life of every person that his time on earth comes to an end. Both Jesus and Samuel were looking at that point in their lives in today's readings. We can learn something about the art of dying well from both of these passages.

In what the ESV Bible calls "Samuel's Farewell Address," the prophet closes with the words above. He promises to pray for the people of Israel and to instruct them in the good and right way. This is a fitting summary of the work of all those called to shepherd God's people: prayer and the ministry of the word (Acts 6:4). For Samuel, dying well means continuing to pray for God's people and to teach them about godly living until his last breath.

Jesus' ministry was characterized by teaching and prayer. In verse 22 we read, "He went on his way through towns and villages, teaching and journeying toward Jerusalem." Luke frequently reports on Jesus' prayer life (Luke 5:16; 9:18, 28-29; 11:1; 22:32, 39-46). The Lord is aware that He is about to finish His course. Meanwhile, He teaches His way to Jerusalem where He will be crucified and made an offering for the sins of His people.

Think about It

As disciples of Jesus Christ, we are called to follow in His steps (1 Pet. 2:21). That would certainly mean a life of prayer, obedience to God's word, and selfless service to others. If that is the best way to live, it is also the best way to die. Make every effort to live faithfully and practice a lifestyle worthy of maintaining until your final day. Seek to die well.

The Importance of Humility, or Who's on Your Guest List?

Today's Reading: First Samuel 13-14; Luke 14:1-24

Selected Verses

But now your kingdom shall not continue. The Lord has sought out a man after his own heart, and the Lord has commanded him to be prince over his people, because you have not kept what the Lord commanded you.

1 Sam. 13:14

For everyone who exalts himself will be humbled, and he who humbles himself will be exalted.

Luke 14:11

Reflections

Humility is a quality which God looks for in a person who is "after his own heart." Saul was a negative example of this truth which Jesus emphasized in His teaching.

Saul had early success as king and military commander, but it did not last long. He knew he was supposed to wait for Samuel to meet him on the battlefield. Saul was not to offer sacrifices, a responsibility reserved for priests. He knew, but he rationalized that it was more important to take matters in his own hands and avert a loss in battle than to trust God to work despite the circumstances.

It cost Saul his kingdom to offer the sacrifices. His days were numbered and he would not have a son sitting on the throne. God had a man after His own heart who would sit on Saul's throne. Saul lacked humility and trust in God and paid dearly for his arrogance. In a short while he had gone from a frightened, self-deprecating nobody to a proud, self-righteous tyrant. Promotion can be disastrous to one's humility.

Jesus made a number of observations at the dinner he attended (Luke 14). These observations served to provide a context for His teaching. He saw the pride and jockeying of the guests for the best seats at the meal. The Lord told them to take the lowest seats to avoid possible embarrassment later on when more distinguished guests arrived. He also told them to apply humility in inviting guests, not seeking repayment for their invitation. They should be concerned about their standing at the resurrection of the just (Luke 14:14). Here is the point. God invited people to His banquet and some rejected Him. The Lord then invites those who were sick or even non-Jews because God does not honor those who exalt themselves but those who humble themselves and have nothing to offer.

Think about It

If we would be godly, we must seek to grow in humility. Seek not the status and honors afforded by society, but instead seek to walk humbly before God and to be after His heart. Who's on your guest list?

Mercy for Limping Cross Bearers

Today's Reading: First Samuel 15-16; Luke 14:25-35

Selected Verses

And Samuel said to Saul, "I will not return with you. For you have rejected the word of the Lord, and the Lord has rejected you from being king over Israel."

1 Sam. 15:26

Whoever does not bear his own cross and come after me cannot be my disciple.

Luke 14:27

Reflections

God is merciful, but that quality must not be allowed to eclipse His holiness.

Saul persisted in disregarding the commands of God. In the battle with the Amalekites, he spared the king and the better animals rather than carry out the orders given by God through Samuel. When confronted by Samuel, Saul shifted the blame to the people, making his sin even worse by failure to own up to his responsibility. He showed his lack of heart toward God by referring to the Lord as "your" (Samuel's) God.

Jesus called people to follow Him and to be His disciples, but He was not so desperate for followers that they could come on their own terms. He told them they must hate their relatives and even their own lives if they would follow Him.[3] Those who follow Christ carry their cross, ready to die for Him at any time. This would not be an easy road and one ought to count the cost before setting out.

Think about It

But is there no mercy and grace for our failure and sin? Yes, of course there is. Jesus showed mercy and grace to Peter who denied Him at the time of His arrest. Are disciples of Jesus in danger of rejection with no appeal for forgiveness? No. The Lord is forgiving and His mercies are new every morning (Lam. 3:22-23). But remember Whom you serve. He is perfectly holy and we need to take seriously our walk with Him.

Christian brother or sister, learn from Saul who barely confessed his sin after repeated promptings by Samuel. Confess sin fully. Receive mercy and grace to go on. You get a fresh start each day. Jesus paid for your sins. Believe Him and keep limping on carrying your cross.

---

[3] "[Jesus] teaches that being His disciple means loving Him so unreservedly that all other loves seem to be hatred by comparison." *The Reformation Study Bible* (Sanford, FL: Reformation Trust, 2015), p. 1818.

People who Please God and Rock the Boat

Today's Reading: First Samuel 17-18; Luke 15:1-10

Selected Verses

And David had success in all his undertakings, for the Lord was with him. And when Saul saw that he had great success, he stood in fearful awe of him. But all Israel and Judah loved David, for he went out and came in before them.

1 Sam. 18:14-16

Now the tax collectors and sinners were all drawing near to hear him. And the Pharisees and the scribes grumbled, saying, "This man receives sinners and eats with them."

Luke 15:1-2

Reflections

He who faithfully does the will of God is likely to attract the attention and animosity of the vested elite of society. David and Jesus turned the course of history by doing God's will. They were both beloved by the rank and file people of their day but drew scorn and hostility from those whose positions of power were threatened.

David distinguished himself early by his passion for the glory of the living God who Goliath and the Philistines disrespected (17:26). So vocal was he that he irritated some and attracted others, even King Saul (17:31). But David's success with Goliath and in subsequent battles eventually unsettled Saul who was increasingly fearful of him. Saul began to look for ways to eliminate David. Saul sought his own glory and completely misunderstood the glory of God that David so passionately defended.

Jesus brought division to His society. The outcasts loved Him. He brought them hope of forgiveness and redemption. The Pharisees and scribes grumbled because of the Lord's acceptance of sinners. They sought to justify themselves before God and completely misunderstood the holiness of God and His mercy toward sinners.

Think about It

Those who know God well and proclaim His name faithfully are liable to upset the powers that be. Seek to know God well. Seek to lift up His name faithfully. Accept the consequences. God's approval is all that matters. Go ahead, rock the boat if God is glorified.

Ugly Ungratefulness

Today's Reading: First Samuel 19-21; Luke 15:11-32

Selected Verses

And Jonathan spoke well of David to Saul his father and said to him,
"Let not the king sin against his servant David, because he has not
sinned against you, and because his deeds have brought good to you."

1 Sam. 19:4

And he said to him, "Son, you are always with me, and all that
is mine is yours. It was fitting to celebrate and be glad, for this
your brother was dead, and is alive; he was lost, and is found."

Luke 15:31,32

Reflections

Ingratitude brings irrational behavior and hatefulness toward others.

Saul was so blinded by jealousy and fear of David that he could not see that the man he wanted to kill was his most loyal and beneficial ally. Saul was king of Israel, but the history of his reign is overshadowed by his senseless rivalry with a man who (as we shall see in subsequent readings) would not hurt him even when he could have easily assassinated him. Jonathan attempted to reason with his father and to point out how David had brought success to Saul but he could not keep this perspective clearly in mind. Saul would momentarily relent but then renew his pursuit of the man he feared. Instead of thanking God for David, Saul spent most of his energy trying to destroy David.

A similar attitude can be seen in the parable of the prodigal son whose older brother resisted attending the welcome home party. The father begged him to join in the feast, but he was offended by the graciousness and mercy of his father toward his returned son. He complained about not getting such glorious treatment himself. He resented the father's generosity because he felt entitled to more than his brother.

Think about It

Jesus does not tell us how the story ends. We leave them with the party going on. The father and older brother are standing outside discussing whether or not he will join the celebration. Does the brother continue to mope and pout, or does he enter into the food and festivities? We aren't told.

How would you respond? Would you rejoice in the goodness and grace of the father or would you feel short-changed, deserving of much more? Are you grateful for God's mercy or resentful that others who have sinned greatly have been blessed with forgiveness? Ingratitude is ugly, but, worse than that, it reveals a hardened, lost heart. If you are standing outside of the celebration, pray for a humble and grateful heart to enter in.

Who's Your Master?

Today's Reading: First Samuel 22-24; Luke 16:1-18

Selected Verses

He said to his men, "The Lord forbid that I should do this thing to my lord, the Lord's anointed, to put out my hand against him, seeing he is the Lord's anointed." So David persuaded his men with these words and did not permit them to attack Saul.

1 Sam. 24:6-7a

No servant can serve two masters, for either he will hate the one and love the other, or he will be devoted to the one and despise the other. You cannot serve God and money.

Luke 16:13

Reflections

A single-minded person knows whom he serves. She will be clear-sighted enough to make wise split second decisions in a crisis.

David was such a man. He knew what he believed, and he held to it when he had to make the choice between a popular, logical option and a wise, godly one. He and his men had been fleeing from Saul for some time. There were close calls when they barely escaped capture and sure death. They must have been weary of this kind of constant pressure. It was not fun.

Then, all of a sudden, their enemy was in their hands. He was helpless before them. David's men urged him to finish him off and end the madness. David did not flinch. He knew immediately what to do and not do. He spared the king's life but took the opportunity to prove to Saul that he was not against him. His men must have been incredulous. Saul showed temporary remorse for his treatment of David, but the pursuit would go on.

David did not serve two masters. He knew God well and served Him completely. David knew he would be king someday but in God's time. He would not compromise his principles of trusting God to work in His way and on His schedule. Thus, when the opportunity came to kill the king, David knew instantly the right course to take.

Jesus taught that one must be clear about whom he serves. No one can truly serve two masters. A day will come when loyalty will be tested. Which master will you serve? Only One deserves our complete devotion. He is the Triune God revealed in the Bible. Any other master is a rival, a counterfeit god.

Think about It

Prepare yourself for the test that will come. Who's your master? Make the right choice and keep that clear always.

Heeding a Timely Warning

Today's Reading: First Samuel 25-26; Luke 16:19-31

Selected Verses

And David said to Abigail, "Blessed be the Lord, the God of Israel, who sent you this day to meet me! Blessed be your discretion, and blessed be you, who have kept me this day from bloodguilt and from working salvation with my own hand!"

1 Sam. 25:32-33

If they do not hear Moses and the Prophets, neither will they be convinced if someone should rise from the dead.

Luke 16:31

Reflections

Abigail interceded for her husband and household, warning David that he would regret taking revenge for Nabal's insult. David saw the big picture: God was his protector and judge to whom he would answer. David was quick to hear (James 1:19). He heard Abigail's message and called off the attack.

Yet God's judgment fell on Nabal and he died within days of this incident. What David had planned to do, God did. The result was the same, but by leaving the matter in God's hands David did not incur guilt.

In the case of the rich man and Lazarus, the former had no concern for his soul or his eternal destiny until it was too late. He realized that his five brothers were similarly oblivious to what awaited them at death. He requested that Abraham send Lazarus back from the dead to warn his siblings to avoid the torment of Hades. Abraham told him that his brothers had sufficient information in the Scriptures, Moses and the Prophets, to escape torment and that if they did not heed the warnings already given, they would not heed the warnings of a resurrected man.

Indeed, many have heard that Jesus rose from the dead but ignore His words to their own destruction. They have been warned to flee the wrath to come but continue in complacency and unbelief (Luke 3:7; 13:1-5). Their attitude parallels that of Nabal, the fool, who thought himself safe from punishment. They assume the stance of the rich man who felt safe in his wealth.

Think about It

Have you heeded the timely warning? We cannot hold on to this life. David knew that his soul belonged to God and that his actions in this world were either pleasing to Him or worthy of punishment. He chose to heed the warning and please God. But David was not saved by his own works. Nor are we. Ultimately, only Jesus Christ, who died for the sins of His people and came back from the dead, can make us who believe in Him worthy of eternal life. We must believe His timely warning. Do not delay. Believe Him now.

The Danger of Presumption

Today's Reading: First Samuel 27-29; Luke 17:1-19

Selected Verses

Then Samuel said to Saul, "Why have you disturbed me by bringing me up?" Saul answered, "I am in great distress, for the Philistines are warring against me, and God has turned away from me and answers me no more, either by prophets or by dreams. Therefore I have summoned you to tell me what I shall do."

1 Sam. 28:15

So you also, when you have done all that you were commanded, say, "We are unworthy servants; we have only done what was our duty."

Luke 17:10

Reflections

Presumption may not be a word you hear or use every day, so let's start with a definition. The Google dictionary says that presumption is "behavior perceived as arrogant, disrespectful, and transgressing the limits of what is permitted or appropriate." A person with presumption is presumptuous. Here we meet some presumptuous people and learn an important lesson.

Saul was facing a military crisis. He had failed in all his attempts to find and kill his perceived rival, David. Now the Philistine army was amassing on his border, ready to strike. Saul had a long history of presumption. He took matters in his own hands ignoring God's law and Samuel's instructions. God had left him, but Saul presumptuously continued to seek God's help and direction. When he could not get an answer from God, he turned to a medium and sought the departed Samuel for guidance. Samuel merely reiterated the judgment that he had already pronounced on the king, that he would lose his kingdom. Samuel now added a timeline onto this verdict. Saul would die, with his sons, the next day. Saul was foolish to the end. His foolishness showed itself in presumption.

Jesus told a story about a hypothetical servant whose master waited on him rather than observing the normal division of labor. If that were to occur, we would charge the servant with being presumptuous, arrogantly accepting service from his master instead of respectfully offering service to him.

In another incident, Jesus healed ten lepers, an unheard of miracle. Yet only one of the ten thought to return and thank the Lord for His mercy to him. The nine were presumptuous.

Think about It

Presumption shows itself in our expectations, as if God owed us something. It shows itself when we fail to be grateful for all our undeserved blessings. It shows itself in failure to confess our sin and repent before God, asking for forgiveness of our presumption. Let presumption not be common in your life.

His Kingdom is Forever

Today's Reading: First Samuel 30-31; Luke 17:20-37

Selected Verses

Thus Saul died, and his three sons, and his armor-bearer, and all his men, on the same day together.

1 Sam. 31:6

Being asked by the Pharisees when the kingdom of God would come, he answered them, "The kingdom of God is not coming in ways that can be observed, nor will they say, 'Look, here it is!' or 'There!' for behold, the kingdom of God is in the midst of you."

Luke 17:20-21

Reflections

The king is dead! Long live the king! The cry goes out from the subjects who are either grieved or relieved depending on the nature of the king's reign. It happened in Israel on the day of Saul's death.

Saul, the first king of Israel, had a miserable reign thanks to his own foolishness. He failed to obey God, to trust God, and to recognize his sin. He never sought forgiveness. God's Spirit departed from him. He became paranoid and obsessively chased David around for years trying to kill him. His reign wreaked with his foolish decisions and dissolved in defeat and shame.

What are we to make of this? The then-new kingdom that had started out with some optimism and hope that Israel would be stable and successful ended in failure. A better king was desperately needed if a better realm was to be established. A kingdom will never be better than its king.

God raised up a new king and a new dynasty under David as we shall see in Second Samuel. The kingdom of God would come with the Messiah, the Lord Jesus Christ of the line of David. That is the true and final kingdom, but it would not come immediately during Jesus' earthly ministry which ended in His crucifixion, death, and resurrection.

Think about It

We still await the culmination of the kingdom. But we already know the identity of the King. We know that He is the perfect Son of God. We know much about His kingdom. His rule will be perfect. The people of His realm have been forgiven and will be made perfect when that kingdom comes in its fullness. His kingdom will be eternal.

Let us live for that day, announcing the true King Jesus Christ. His Kingdom is forever!

April 21 / Day 111
Prayer in the Face of Injustice

Today's Reading: Second Samuel 1-3; Luke 18:1-17

Selected Verses

And the king said to his servants, "Do you not know that a prince and a great man has fallen this day in Israel? And I was gentle today, though anointed king. These men, the sons of Zeruiah, are more severe than I. The Lord repay the evildoer according to his wickedness!"

2 Sam. 3:38-39

And will not God give justice to his elect, who cry to him day and night? Will he delay long over them? I tell you, he will give justice to them speedily. Nevertheless, when the Son of Man comes, will he find faith on earth?

Luke 18:7-8

Reflections

David gradually gained power to rule all Israel. He welcomed his repentant former enemy, Abner, but Joab, David's military commander, soon assassinated him. David showed mercy; Joab took revenge. The unity of the kingdom under David was jeopardized by Joab's action. David mourned for Abner and the people recognized that Joab had committed an injustice.

Jesus taught His disciples a parable so that they would pray rather than lose heart. It seems that they were in danger of getting discouraged about the injustice they saw in the world. They were about to see the greatest injustice ever perpetrated in human history, the arrest, trial, sentencing, and crucifixion of the Son of God. Jesus told them that even an irreverent, hard-hearted judge would not be able to resist the constant pleading of a widow.

But God is much more gracious to His elect than the judge was to the insistent widow. He will respond and bring swift justice to those who call on Him. Jesus was telling them, "Pray. Don't lose heart."

Think about It

Certainly, injustice abounds in human governments and societies. The powerful impose their wills on the weak. Shrewd and unprincipled people take advantage of the ignorant and trusting. Of course, it can be disheartening. Yet Jesus tells His disciples not to lose heart. Instead pray. He promises that God will give justice to His elect who cry to Him day and night.

Why do we not see more justice from God? The fault is in our lack of faith evidenced by lack of prayer. Do we cry to God or merely wring our hands and worry? Do we cry to Him in faith day and night, or merely send up an occasional perfunctory prayer and go back to whining about all the evils in the world? Think about that. Better yet, pray now that He may give justice to His elect.

The Cost of Following Christ

Today's Reading: Second Samuel 4-6; Luke 18:18-43

Selected Verses

As the ark of the Lord came into the city of David, Michal the daughter of Saul looked out of the window and saw King David leaping and dancing before the Lord, and she despised him in her heart.

2 Sam. 6:16

And he said to them, "Truly, I say to you, there is no one who has left house or wife or brothers or parents or children, for the sake of the kingdom of God, who will not receive many times more in this time, and in the age to come eternal life."

Luke 18:29-30

Reflections

David knew the cost of obeying God over pleasing his wife. Michal, growing up in Saul's household, must have imbibed some of her father's disregard for God's commands. When David began to worship God publicly, she found his enthusiasm disgusting. She ridiculed David, but David did not waver in his commitment to worship God and give due honor to the One to whom he owed his life and his throne.

Jesus' encounter with a rich ruler led to an insightful exchange between Peter and Jesus. Jesus' command that he sell all that he had and follow Him had offended the ruler. Peter reflected on the reality that he and his fellow disciples had left all to follow Christ. Jesus promises him and them that everyone who leaves his house and family for the kingdom of God would receive many times more in this world and then eternal life in the next age.

Think about It

Sometimes faithfulness to Christ comes down to a permanent rift with close family members. Have you determined to sell all and go follow Jesus? Do not make the fatal error of the rich ruler who could not part with his stuff in order to gain eternal life. In the words of the old gospel song:

> *I'd rather have Jesus than silver or gold;*
> *I'd rather be His than have riches untold;*
> *I'd rather have Jesus than houses or lands;*
> *I'd rather be led by His nail-pierced hand*

(Refrain)

> *Than to be the king of a vast domain*
> *or be held in sin's dread sway;*
> *I'd rather have Jesus than anything,*
> *this world affords today.*

131

The God Who Surprises Us

Today's Reading: Second Samuel 7-9; Luke 19:1-28

Selected Verses

> *You have spoken also of your servant's house for a great while to come, and this is instruction for mankind, O Lord God!*
>
> 2 Sam. 7:19b

> *And Jesus said to him, "Today salvation has come to this house, since he also is a son of Abraham. For the Son of Man came to seek and to save the lost."*
>
> Luke 19:9-10

Reflections

David experienced great military success as king of Israel. He reached the point of being able to rest from the continual battles he had experienced most of his life. His thoughts turned to building a house or temple for the Ark of God. Nathan, the prophet, initially saw this as a good thing until the Lord revealed another plan for David and his dynasty.

David would not build a house for God, but God would build a house for David—not an earthly house but an eternal throne with an eternal ruler, not a throne over Israel but over all mankind. From the New Testament, we understand that covenant pointed to the Lord Jesus Christ who has been exalted to the right hand of God the Father and rules forever. God's plan for David was far greater than a mere earthly temple. Is it too much to say that David was stunned by the gracious covenant which God made with him?

Our Lord surprised many of His contemporaries by His welcoming outcast sinners like the tax collector, Zacchaeus. Jesus Christ came as the fulfillment of the covenants with Abraham and with David, and He came to seek and save lost people both within and without the nation of Israel.

Think about It

What a surprise that a holy God would take on human flesh and live among us not to reject and condemn us but to seek and to save us! God surprises us and the gospel tells us how good He is to all who believe in His Son. Are you surprised by His love and mercy to you? Isn't His grace truly amazing?

Give praise to Him. As the psalmist wrote: "He does not deal with us according to our sins, nor repay us according to our iniquities" (Ps. 103: 10). That more than surprises me. It blows my mind.

The Hidden Consequences of Sin

Today's Reading: Second Samuel 10-12; Luke 19:29-48

Selected Verses

And the Lord afflicted the child that Uriah's wife bore to David, and he became sick. David therefore sought God on behalf of the child. And David fasted and went in and lay all night on the ground.

2 Sam. 12:15b-16

And when he drew near and saw the city, he wept over it.

Luke 19:41

Reflections

The biblical historian lays out David's sin here in great detail. We are able to trace his downfall and learn how one bad decision led to another until he had committed adultery, impregnated another man's wife, and had the innocent party murdered in the cover up. It is a repugnant series of events, but it shows how easily a man after God's heart can go astray.

To his credit David is prompt to repent, but there will be ongoing consequences of his sin. He is driven to fast and pray seeking God's mercy on his dying baby. The sin which brought him short term pleasure came with an enormous price tag that continued for the rest of his life.

Luke describes Jesus' arrival at Jerusalem where He knows He will die, rejected by the leaders of His people. But in the passage, Jesus weeps, not for His own suffering but, for the suffering of the people of Jerusalem. He wept because they could have known peace, but instead they would experience destruction. Even children would see the tearing down of their city.

Some, like David, see their sin and heed the call to repent. Others, like the residents of Jerusalem, fail to repent of their sin and go on in it as if nothing were wrong. Jesus, the sinless Son of God, wept over the sin of those who would not repent and find peace because their eyes were closed to it. He wept for the suffering that was going to come.

Think about It

Do you repent promptly? Do you weep over the consequences of sin like Jesus did? We are never more Christlike than when we weep and pray for those whose eyes are closed to the coming pain of judgment for sin. Let us take sin seriously, our own and that of others, and proclaim "the things that make for peace" to those who will hear.

Authority: Rejected and Abused

Today's Reading: Second Samuel 13-14; Luke 20:1-26

Selected Verses

> *Now therefore let me go into the presence of the king, and if there is guilt in me, let him put me to death. Then Joab went to the king and told him, and he summoned Absalom. So he came to the king and bowed himself on his face to the ground before the king, and the king kissed Absalom.*

2 Sam. 14:32b-33

> *But he looked directly at them and said, "What then is this that is written: 'The stone that the builders rejected has become the cornerstone'? Everyone who falls on that stone will be broken to pieces, and when it falls on anyone, it will crush him."*

Luke 20:17-18

Reflections

David ruled as the duly anointed king of Israel. He had authority to apply the Law of God in the land, to bring justice. However David failed to take any action after the rape of his daughter, Tamar, by his son (her half-brother) Amnon. He was angry, but he did nothing. Absalom plotted the murder of Amnon. David took no action against Absalom and eventually reinstated him.

As we shall see tomorrow, Absalom exploited the desire for a king that would act justly in the land to mount an insurrection against his father (2 Sam. 15:4-6). David had raised sons similar to himself, an adulterer and a murderer, and he apparently found it hard to be consistent as a ruler and as a father.

Jesus assumed authority to teach and preach and heal. His popularity threatened those in power. They attempted to trap Him into some chargeable offense that would end His influence. In this passage they asked Him directly the basis of His authority. We know how that turned out. Then Jesus taught a parable showing that their rejection of Him and His authority would end in their own destruction. Rather than take to heart His warning, they re-doubled their efforts to arrest Him.

But Jesus is the rightful King of kings and Lord of lords (Rev. 19:11-16). He is not blinded by any sin of His own. He executes justice perfectly. Those who reject His authority will suffer the consequences.

Think about It

Let us submit to the One who sits at the right hand of the throne of God and give Him our worship and obedience (Phil. 2:5-10).

Manipulative Leaders

Today's Reading: Second Samuel 15-16; Luke 20:27-47

Selected Verses

So Absalom stole the hearts of the men of Israel.

2 Sam. 15:6b

And in the hearing of all the people he said to his disciples, "Beware of the scribes."

Luke 20:45-46a

Reflections

How easily impressive, charismatic leaders with seeming power and wisdom lead people astray!

Absalom carefully mounted a campaign that would rival that of any of our current crop of politicians. He spent money to equip himself with a chariot and horses and a company of men to run before him. Then he made it a practice to station himself where he could talk to people who had legal problems. He worked the crowds doing the grassroots campaign thing. He made promises about the great improvements he would bring if he were in formal leadership.

In short, he stole the hearts of the people.

Then the day came when he made his move. David's support collapsed like a house of cards, and Israel followed Absalom as their new king. It almost worked, and except for the providence of God it would have worked. The point is people are fickle and can easily be won over by a powerful person making compelling promises of a better life.

In Jesus' day, the scribes were viewed with awe. They were dignified, seemed to be spiritual, disciplined in piety. Everyone recognized them. At the same time, they used their knowledge of the law to take financial advantage of unsuspecting widows. Jesus warned His disciples to beware of them.

Think about It

The problem of devious religious and political leaders is not new. Certainly, both the Church and our nation need leaders of character and integrity, but those who rise to high positions are not always to be trusted and never to be trusted blindly.

Pray for our leaders both in the Church and in society. Beware of those who veer off from God's truth. Do not be led astray. Study the Scriptures and seek God's wisdom. And remember: we are not home yet. Jesus Christ is the only true leader who is never manipulative. Someday His Kingdom will come in full and He alone will be our truly wise and powerful and beneficent leader.

The Providence of God

Today's Reading: Second Samuel 17-18; Luke 21:1-19

Selected Verses

And Absalom and all the men of Israel said, "The counsel of Hushai the Archite is better than the counsel of Ahithophel." For the Lord had ordained to defeat the good counsel of Ahithophel, so that the Lord might bring harm upon Absalom.

2 Sam. 17:14

By your endurance you will gain your lives.

Luke 21:19

Reflections

As we saw yesterday, Absalom put together a foolproof plan to overthrow his father's throne and make himself king. Well, it was not really foolproof, was it? God gave David wisdom to send the loyal Hushai back as a mole in Absalom's cabinet. The Lord gave Hushai an amazing ability to paint a picture of the consequences of following the advice of Ahithophel and to make a compelling argument for delaying the pursuit of David. God turned the heart of Absalom toward Hushai's advice so that the Lord could carry out His will to bring harm to David's mutinous son (Prov. 21:1).

The outcome? Absalom was defeated and killed, and David's throne was saved.

Jesus foretells things yet to come in the lives of the apostles. He describes the destruction of the temple, the false "christs" that would appear, wars, tumults, national uprisings, earthquakes, famines, pestilences, terrors, and great signs from heaven. These things would occur after the disciples had suffered arrest, persecution, imprisonment, and inquisitions by religious and political authorities. They would be turned in by close relatives. Some would be killed. All would be hated.

Could this be God's will? Yes, and it had a purpose. "This will be your opportunity to bear witness," Jesus told them. Furthermore, God would be with them through all their trials. He told them not to concern themselves about what to say. He would give them the wisdom and words when the time came. No one would refute their statements. He promised that not a hair of their heads would perish. He would save their lives.

Think about It

Do you know that God by His providence preserves you? Do you know that you are safe to do His will and nothing can harm you? Can you trust Him no matter what forces mount up against you? Will you stand up and bear witness with the wisdom and words He gives you in that day? Stand firm in Him. He rules the universe. He will keep you down to the last hair on your head. Fear nothing. Fear no one. Trust God alone.

Chaos: The Old Normal

Today's Reading: Second Samuel 19-20; Luke 21:20-38

Selected Verses

So all the men of Israel withdrew from David and followed Sheba the son of Bichri. But the men of Judah followed their king steadfastly from the Jordan to Jerusalem.

2 Sam. 20:2

But watch yourselves lest your hearts be weighed down with dissipation and drunkenness and cares of this life, and that day come upon you suddenly like a trap. For it will come upon all who dwell on the face of the whole earth. But stay awake at all times, praying that you may have strength to escape all these things that are going to take place, and to stand before the Son of Man.

Luke 21:34-36

Reflections

After Absalom was overthrown, the kingdom of Israel did not simply pick up where it left off. David created a problem immediately by going into such grief over the death of his son that Joab had to sternly exhort him lest the nation reject his return to the throne. David wisely responded and warded off a dangerous situation. But then there was a conflict between Judah and the other tribes over who should reinstate the king. That resulted in another civil war. David named Amasa as a commander and Joab promptly assassinated him. The kingdom was coming unglued on every level. Chaos reigned. David seems to have held steady through all of this until his kingdom was restored.

That would not be the last time the world would see such turmoil. Jesus prophesied that there would be a time of destruction of the temple. This occurred in 70 AD. He further indicated that there would be worldwide terror that would come upon all people. No one would escape the distress of nations, the cosmic upheavals. This is yet to come.

Think about It

Chaos is really the old normal. It has always been with us. How can we handle it? We can learn from what happened in the past, and we can learn from what Jesus taught us. He said, "Watch yourselves. Stay awake. Pray for strength." He promised that if we did we will stand before the Son of Man. Jesus said, "Watch your hearts." Take comfort in God's Word. Get guidance from His Word. Hold to the Lord who promised that we who do will stand before Him. To the extent that faithful men and women know and believe the Word of God they are prepared for whatever may come their way.

God's Timing: Does He Schedule Things?

Today's Reading: Second Samuel 21-22; Luke 22:1-30

Selected Verses

Now there was a famine in the days of David for three years, year after year.
And David sought the face of the Lord. And the Lord said, "There is bloodguilt
on Saul and on his house, because he put the Gibeonites to death."

2 Sam. 21:1

For the Son of Man goes as it has been determined,
but woe to that man by whom he is betrayed!

Luke 22:22

Reflections

A famine came upon Israel. David understood that it was not due to bad luck or some unfortunate coincidence. He knew that God ruled over the harvest whether it be light or heavy. David turned to the Lord for answers and guidance. The Lord revealed to Him the reason for the famine. It had to do with the guilt incurred by Saul over the breaking of a treaty with the Gibeonites and the attempt to annihilate them. Though the treaty itself was foolish and based on deception, God held Israel responsible to maintain their integrity and honor the treaty perpetually (Josh. 9). Seven of Saul's descendants were executed to satisfy the demand for justice. The famine ended.

In Jesus' final days before His arrest, trial, and crucifixion we are allowed to see all the forces at work to bring Him down. The chief priests and scribes were plotting to kill Him. Satan was entering into Judas. The disciples were preparing for the Passover and arguing about which one of them was the greatest. Jesus was serving and teaching them the meaning of His death.

In a matter of a few hours all these protagonists would converge in the Garden of Gethsemane, and the final act would begin on Jesus' earthly ministry. Was it a coincidence? No, not at all. It was by God's decree that all this would come about at that precise moment for the salvation of the nations.

Think about It

Are the random incidents in your life really random or are they carefully sent by God according to His plan? Do you ask "why this?" or "why now?" How would it change your attitude to have a clearer conviction about the providence of God? Yes, God does schedule things—all things. We may not always understand God's actions and timing, but we can always be sure it is Him who is doing it. Furthermore, He has a purpose and plan for our good and His glory.

Rulers Remembered: The Just and the Unjust

Today's Reading: Second Samuel 23-24; Luke 22:31-53

Selected Verses

The God of Israel has spoken;
the Rock of Israel has said to me:
When one rules justly over men,
ruling in the fear of God,
he dawns on them like the morning light,
like the sun shining forth on a cloudless morning,
like rain that makes grass to sprout from the earth.

2 Sam. 23:3-4

But this is your hour, and the power of darkness.

Luke 22:53b

Reflections

As David neared the end of his life, God reassured him. Just governance would not be overlooked. The Lord blesses the king who rules justly, that is, in the fear of God. The despot is a law to himself. The tyrant recognizes no higher authority than himself. He rules without fear of a final judgment day before a completely informed Eternal Deity (Rom. 2:16).

The Lord's blessing on the god-fearing leader is described in terms analogous to beautiful weather and an abundant harvest. There is sun and rain in just the right amount resulting in lush crops. Human hearts fill with energy and joy in the anticipation of a good day and a good future as they live under just leadership.

By contrast, in the darkest moment of human history, hard-hearted, treacherous rulers surrounded the Son of God in the Garden of Gethsemane. They came to escort Him to His death. They epitomized unjust rulers, lacking any fear of God.

Unsurprised Jesus awaited them. He spoke directly and fearlessly showing them that their actions were cowardly, done under cloak of night, away from the crowds of attentive listeners who sought His teaching. He made it clear that they operated only by permission of God the Father Who allowed them their hour to act and freedom to carry out the dark deeds they had contrived.

Think about It

Unjust rulers have their day, but God will bring justice on them and blessing on those who have ruled justly. Woe to the ruler who ignores his date with the Judge of the whole earth.

Give thanks. God remembers just rulers and punishes unjust ones. Their hour and power will end. Whatever your role in this world exercise your authority in the fear of God.

God's Wisdom and Sovereignty

Today's Reading: 1 Kings 1-2; Luke 22:54-71

Selected Verses

So the kingdom was established in the hand of Solomon.

1 Kings 2:46b

And the Lord turned and looked at Peter. And Peter remembered the saying of the Lord, how he had said to him, "Before the rooster crows today, you will deny me three times." And he went out and wept bitterly.

Luke 22:61-62

Reflections

Human history is filled with foolishness and wickedness, but God rules over all and uses even the wrath of man to praise Him (Ps. 76:10).

Adonijah was yet another spoiled son of David. Adonijah like his brother Absalom attempted to grasp the throne his elderly father had promised to Solomon. Joab and Abiathar, David's commander and the high priest, supported Adonijah. David acted quickly and successfully to set up Solomon as the new king. Solomon suspended the execution of Adonijah putting him on probation instead. However, it wasn't long before Adonijah made his move. He asked permission to marry Abishag, the beautiful Shunnamite woman who had cared for David on his death bed. Solomon saw where Adonijah was going with that request. The young king applied the death sentence to his devious brother immediately.

Adonijah's death led to Joab's. Within three years, Solomon had cause to execute Shimei for his violation of probation. What was the result of all this? The kingdom was established in the hand of Solomon. God used the evil of people to bring about His purpose for the kingdom.

In another instance centuries later, Peter's denial removed the potential obstacle of armed resistance by the disciples to the crucifixion of Christ. Christ's death had to occur to obtain the salvation for all God's elect people. On a personal level, Peter's notorious failure taught him how great his need for mercy and salvation was. Peter had boasted of his commitment and determination a few hours earlier (Luke 22:33). But he had to learn the depth of his sin and the greater depth of God's grace toward him. God again used evil to bring about His good purposes both for Peter and for all His chosen people.

Think about It

Do you despair when confronted by evil in yourself and in the world? Remember that God is wise and sovereign. He will do all that He decrees. He will be glorified even in the evil that goes on day in and day out. His kingdom is far greater than Solomon's and it will be established forever.

The Backdrop of God's Glory

Today's Reading: 1 Kings 3-5; Luke 23:1-25

Selected Verses

And God gave Solomon wisdom and understanding beyond measure, and breadth of mind like the sand on the seashore, so that Solomon's wisdom surpassed the wisdom of all the people of the east and all the wisdom of Egypt. For he was wiser than all other men.

1 Kings 4:29-31a

So Pilate decided that their demand should be granted. He released the man who had been thrown into prison for insurrection and murder, for whom they asked, but he delivered Jesus over to their will.

Luke 23:24-25

Reflections

Solomon is said to have "loved the Lord" and was walking in the statutes of his father, David (3:3). God came to him in a dream and offered to answer his prayer for whatever he desired. Solomon asked for an understanding mind to govern the people God had given him. God was pleased with the request. He granted it and much more to Solomon. Solomon was known for his wisdom both within the kingdom and internationally.

Under this wise king, Israel reached the pinnacle of its glory. Never before and never again would there be such a wise king and a prosperous kingdom. This golden age of Israel would continue until Solomon himself stopped obeying God and followed other gods (1 Kings 11:1-13).

By stark contrast, at Jesus' trials (before the Jewish Sanhedrin and then before Pilate and Herod) the depth of foolishness is seen. The Sanhedrin found Him guilty on trumped up charges and spun those to imply some sort of revolutionary terrorist status to Jesus. Neither Pilate nor Herod found him guilty, but Pilate succumbed to the pressure of the crowd and sentenced Him to death by crucifixion.

Think about It

We will see that Solomon's reign demonstrates that even gifted, promising leaders who disobey God will fail. But the foolish and evil rulings of the Jews and the Romans that seemed to destroy Jesus' life and ministry became a crucial element in God's plan of redemption for all mankind. The Church of Jesus Christ has spread to every corner of the earth. Praise God that He is glorified in the crucifixion, resurrection, and ascension of our Lord. He is glorified in the ongoing proclamation of the gospel throughout the world. He has shown His glory against the backdrop of human foolishness. Praise God for His glory, power, and wisdom that has reached to you and me.

Two Kings; Two Offerings

Today's Reading: First Kings 6-7; Luke 23:26-38

Selected Verses

Thus all the work that King Solomon did on the house of the Lord was finished. And Solomon brought in the things that David his father had dedicated, the silver, the gold, and the vessels, and stored them in the treasuries of the house of the Lord.

1 Kings 7:51

There was also an inscription over him, "This is the King of the Jews."

Luke 23:38

Reflections

Solomon spared no expense in building and furnishing the temple of God in Jerusalem. As you read the details of the construction, the quality of the materials, and the description of the workmanship, you have to marvel at the care that was taken. The building was not for common use nor for a common person. It was to be for the God of glory and majesty. It was to be the permanent site of the sacrifices offered to Him and the home of the Ark of the Covenant where God would meet the high priest on the Day of Atonement.

The dedication of the completed temple was undoubtedly the finest hour in the golden age of the United Kingdom of Israel. So it comes as a jolt to turn to Luke and read about the crucifixion of the King of the Jews, Jesus Christ. It also occurred in Jerusalem, not far from the second temple (Solomon's temple was burned during the Babylonian captivity 2 Kings 25:9).

The sinfulness of mankind and the mercy of God stand here side by side in stark contrast. On that most awful day, the crowd gawked at Jesus. The rulers scoffed at Him. The soldiers mocked Him. Meanwhile, He prayed, "Father, forgive them for they know not what they do." Above His head, they hung a sign, "This is the King of the Jews."

Solomon and his temple had not failed. That building met all expectations. But it wasn't enough. The offerings in the temples pointed to the true Offering that would be made not *by* a king but *of* the King, Jesus, the perfect Lamb of God, the perfect offering for sin.

Think about It

If you are a believer, your King offered Himself that day in your place. Be amazed.

Paradise: Who Gets In?

Today's Reading: First Kings 8-9; Luke 23:39-56

Selected Verses

And this house will become a heap of ruins. Everyone passing by it will be astonished and will hiss, and they will say, "Why has the Lord done thus to this land and to this house?" Then they will say, "Because they abandoned the Lord their God who brought their fathers out of the land of Egypt and laid hold on other gods and worshiped them and served them. Therefore the Lord has brought all this disaster on them."

1 Kings 9:8-9

And he said, "Jesus, remember me when you come into your kingdom." And he said to him, "Truly, I say to you, today you will be with me in Paradise."

Luke 23:42

Reflections

Above the euphoria of celebrating the completion of the Temple and the installation of the Ark of the Covenant, there was a certain ominous cloud, the possibility that the people of Israel might not be faithful to their God. There still existed the allurement of other gods. There was no guarantee that the nation would not abandon the God who had delivered their fathers from the land of Egypt and thus incur judgment. That beautiful temple could end up a heap of ruins.

In fact, it did.

The kingdom would be divided; the kings and the people would incorporate pagan worship either in place of or alongside their worship of the Lord. God would turn them over to foreign powers. We will come to that later in our reading. You see where this story is going. We may as well rain on the parade.

Then we turn to Luke. Jesus the Messiah has been officially rejected by the rulers, tried before them and the Roman governor, and crucified beside two criminals. One of them calls out for mercy. Jesus assures him, in those famous words, "Truly, I say to you, today you will be with me in Paradise."

Indeed, the initial excitement of the temple dedication would not last. Israel made a mess of their worship and executed their Savior. But God is able to do far above what we ask or think (Eph. 3:20-21) and He made their greatest evil the ground for their salvation beginning with the repentant criminal.

Think about It

Who gets into paradise? Not one who puts hope and confidence in his own ability to be perfectly faithful to God. The one who will enter paradise trusts in the only One who was perfectly faithful, the Lord Jesus Christ. He ushered a guilty criminal into Paradise, and He can usher you in, too, by grace alone through faith alone (Eph. 2:8,9).

The Heart of the Problem

Today's Reading: 1 Kings 10-11; Luke 24:1-35

Selected Verses

And the Lord was angry with Solomon, because his heart had turned away from the Lord, the God of Israel, who had appeared to him twice and had commanded him concerning this thing, that he should not go after other gods. But he did not keep what the Lord commanded.

1 Kings 11:9,10

And he said to them, "O foolish ones, and slow of heart to believe all that the prophets have spoken! Was it not necessary that the Christ should suffer these things and enter into his glory?" And beginning with Moses and all the Prophets, he interpreted to them in all the Scriptures the things concerning himself.

Luke 24:25-27

Reflections

J C Ryle wrote: "True faith does not depend merely on the state of man's head and understanding, but on the state of his heart. His mind may be convinced. His conscience may be pierced. But so long as there is anything the man is secretly loving more than God, there will be no true faith."

Solomon's heart "had turned away from the Lord" and he had gone after other gods. Did all those pagan wives and concubines have anything to do with this? Of course (1 Kings 11:3-4). But no one forced Solomon to marry all those unbelievers. He did it because his heart was either already turned away from the Lord or he was willing for it to be turned away. As a result, God diminished his legacy.

The disciples walking to Emmaus had lost hope that Jesus whom they believed to be dead would redeem Israel. Jesus told them they were foolish and "slow of heart to believe all that the prophets have spoken." How many times had He told them He would rise on the third day? So Jesus spent the rest of the evening explaining to them how the Scriptures pointed to Him and to the things that had happened. Nothing had gone wrong except the hearts of the disciples that were slow to believe the truth of the resurrection.

Think about It

God promised to give His people changed hearts—of flesh, not stone (Ezek. 36:26). He did give new hearts to the disciples as Jesus opened the Scriptures to them. Has God given you a new heart, one that is turned toward the Lord and that is quick to believe? If not, call upon Him for mercy and grace to receive new life and a new heart that loves Him and believes Him. The heart is the problem, but God can give you a new one.

Default Position Reset

Today's Reading: First Kings 12-13; Luke 24:36-53

Selected Verses

*And when the prophet who had brought him back from the way heard
of it, he said, "It is the man of God who disobeyed the word of the Lord;
therefore the Lord has given him to the lion, which has torn him and
killed him, according to the word that the Lord spoke to him."*

1 Kings 13:26

Then he opened their minds to understand the Scriptures,

Luke 24:45

Reflections

Our readings today demonstrate that the natural, human, default position on faith and truth is to hold it loosely, discard it easily, and trust in our own reasoning.

The bold prophet from Judah went in obedience to God to Bethel and confronted the King of Israel, Jeroboam. He refused Jeroboam's invitation to come to his home based on God's command to leave Bethel and return home without eating or drinking there. So far so good.

But then another old prophet told the bold one that God had given him new instructions, to come to the old prophet's home and eat bread and drink water. It was a lie. The bold prophet gave in and accepted the invitation. Then the old prophet told him he would die for his disobedience. That happened. Apparently, despite his bold stance before Jeroboam, his default position on the truth was to question what God had said to him clearly and trust another man.

In the case of the disciples, Jesus graciously corrected their misunderstanding of the Scriptures. He opened their minds to understand, and He promised them the Holy Spirit. He also gave them a mandate, commonly called "the Great Commission," to be His witnesses proclaiming repentance and forgiveness of sins in His name to all nations. Without the Lord's correction they would have muddled on in doubt and disbelief, in their default position on the truth.

Think about It

How desperate and needy we are for God to enable us to understand, believe, and obey His Word! But praise God He does not leave us in confusion. If we are His own, He resets the default position of our human hearts and minds. Pray that you will not doubt nor second guess what He clearly says. Study His word diligently to believe and obey it.

Born of God

Today's Reading: First Kings 14-15; John 1:1-28

Selected Verses

*They did according to all the abominations of the nations
that the Lord drove out before the people of Israel.*

1 Kings 14:24

He came to his own, and his own people did not receive him. But to all who did receive him, who believed in his name, he gave the right to become children of God, who were born, not of blood nor of the will of the flesh nor of the will of man, but of God.

John 1:11-13

Reflections

Solomon's apostasy led to the division of the kingdom under Rehoboam and Jeroboam. Neither of them was humble or repentant, but they continued in the path taken by Solomon. The divided kingdom stayed at war during the lifetimes of these two kings. They continued to worship other gods. Their practices mirrored those of the peoples that God had evicted from the land when Israel entered.

When Jesus came, fulfilling the promise of a Messiah, He was not universally received. The gospel records show that as His ministry unfolded official opposition increased culminating in His crucifixion. Jesus came revealing the glory of the Father, full of grace and truth. Those who were sent to arrest Him said, "No one ever spoke like this man!" (John 7:46).

But despite Jesus' powerful words, the nation officially rejected Him. Why? They were not born of God. Those who are born of God are children of God who manifest this reality by receiving Christ and believing in His name. Everyone is God's creature, made by Him, but not all who owe Him their existence are His children (John 1:3,10).

Neither severe hardship such as decades of war, nor mighty works like the incarnation of God the Son automatically results in faith and repentance in people. It takes a new birth, a birth brought about by God, to turn the hearts of sinners to Himself and to make them His children.

Think about It

If you have been born of God, then you are His child. Your home is with Him, not here. But you and I will be there soon. Rejoice and be faithful as you await that day.

Stop Limping and Follow Christ

Today's Reading: First Kings 16-18; John 1:29-51

Selected Verses

And Elijah came near to all the people and said, "How long will you go limping between two different opinions? If the Lord is God, follow him; but if Baal, then follow him." And the people did not answer him a word.

1 Kings 18:21

The next day again John was standing with two of his disciples and he looked at Jesus as he walked by and said, "Behold, the Lamb of God!" The two disciples heard him say this, and they followed Jesus.

John 1:35-37

Reflections

Israel under King Ahab continued in the rebellious ways of Jeroboam. God sent a prophet, Elijah, to proclaim a drought as a means of getting their attention. This went on for three years, but the nation did not cry out to God. They continued to put hope in the false god Baal. Elijah called for a showdown, a battle of the gods on Mount Carmel. As this definitive demonstration of the truth began, Elijah described the people as limping between two different opinions. They tried to use the Lord and Baal to solve their problems, but the Lord would not allow this kind of syncretism.

We know from our reading how this turned out. The Lord God of heaven and earth was shown to be the only one who could act. Baal and his prophets were exposed as frauds. Any reasonable person would give up following Baal and fully follow the Lord.

In Jesus' early ministry, John the Baptist introduced Him to his disciples as "the Lamb of God who takes away the sin of the world" (vs. 29). The next day, as Jesus walked by, two of John's disciples heard him say, "Behold, the Lamb of God!" Maybe these two had thought about John's comment overnight. Maybe they had tossed and turned pondering what they should do. Their teacher, John, was saying that this Jesus was greater than he was, One who would baptize with the Holy Spirit. They must have thought, "It's time to follow Jesus" because follow Him they did.

Think about It

God will not allow us to go limping between two opinions. Are you following Him or the god of our culture? Are you following the One who came as the Lamb of God to take away the sin of the world? Only He is more powerful than Baal. Only He takes away sin. Stop limping and follow Jesus Christ wherever He leads.

Foolish Views of God

Today's Reading: First Kings 19-20; John 2

Selected Verses

And a man of God came near and said to the king of Israel, "Thus says the Lord, 'Because the Syrians have said, "The Lord is a god of the hills but he is not a god of the valleys," therefore I will give all this great multitude into your hand, and you shall know that I am the Lord.'"

1 Kings 20:28

Now when he was in Jerusalem at the Passover Feast, many believed in his name when they saw the signs that he was doing. But Jesus on his part did not entrust himself to them, because he knew all people and needed no one to bear witness about man, for he himself knew what was in man.

John 2:23-25

Reflections

The Syrians under King Benhadad suffered a defeat by King Ahab and the army of Israel. Behadad's advisers told him that the power of the God of Israel was limited to the hills and that He could do nothing if they fought Israel in the plains. God sent a prophet to tell Ahab that He would give them victory over Syria in the valleys to show His power. Although Israel's army is described as "two little flocks of goats" and the Syrian invaders "filled the country," God did give Israel the victory and King Benhadad was captured (1 Kings 20:26, 29).

When Jesus came to Jerusalem, He demonstrated His authority by cleansing the temple. Perhaps the people had heard that He turned water to wine previously. They professed to believe in Him, but Jesus saw through them. He knew that they only believed superficially. They wanted signs, bread, and healing, but they would not truly commit themselves to Him. To them Jesus was a source of power and provision but not their Lord and Master.

Think about It

It is futile to try to manipulate God for personal advantage. We may not defy Him, believing that He is in any way limited. He is God, omniscient and omnipotent. Paul warned "Do not be deceived: God is not mocked, for whatever one sows, that will he also reap" (Gal. 6:7).

To those who believe in Him, God is loving and He has given His Son as an offering for our sins. But He calls us to show our faith by submitting ourselves joyfully and gratefully to Him in worship and obedience. Serve God and flee all erroneous thoughts of Him.

Seeking Darkness or Light

Today's Reading: First Kings 21-22; John 3:1-21

Selected Verses

There was none who sold himself to do what was evil in the sight of the Lord like Ahab, whom Jezebel his wife incited. He acted very abominably in going after idols, as the Amorites had done, whom the Lord cast out before the people of Israel.

1 Kings 21:25-26

Jesus answered him, "Truly, truly, I say to you, unless one is born again he cannot see the kingdom of God."

John 3:3

Reflections

Those who do evil avoid the light. They are not concerned about entering the Kingdom of God. They run from God, rather than seek Him.

Ahab exemplified a man who "sold himself to do what was evil in the sight of the Lord." On a whim, he ordered Naboth executed on trumped up charges because he had property that Ahab wanted. He worshiped idols. He was completely self-centered. Whenever he didn't get his way he was "vexed and sullen." His conniving wife, the evil Jezebel, urged him on. Ahab's death came by God's providence even though he had disguised himself in battle. As prophesied, the dogs licked up his blood in the vineyard he had taken from Naboth.

Jesus gave the Pharisee Nicodemus a stern warning. No one can see the kingdom of God without being born again, being born of the Spirit. Yet, Jesus goes on to say, it is not as if there are people who are desperately seeking to enter the kingdom and cannot find a way. The fact is that people love darkness, not light, because their deeds are evil. They hate the light. If they did what was true they would come to the light.

Ahab sought the darkness. All those who are not born of the Spirit seek the darkness. None of them are concerned about entering the kingdom of God.

Think about It

How about you? Have you been born again? If so, you will do what is true. You will flee the darkness and come to the light. You will love the light not the darkness. If you are not sure, but are concerned about making sure that is a good sign the rebirth has taken place or is taking place in you. Pray for God to do His work of bringing new spiritual birth to your soul. I'll see you in His kingdom.

Life or Wrath: Which Will It Be?

Today's Reading: Second Kings 1-3; John 3:22-36

Selected Verses

But the angel of the Lord said to Elijah the Tishbite, "Arise, go up to meet the messengers of the king of Samaria, and say to them, 'Is it because there is no God in Israel that you are going to inquire of Baal-zebub, the god of Ekron? Now therefore thus says the Lord, You shall not come down from the bed to which you have gone up, but you shall surely die.'" So Elijah went.

2 Kings 1:3-4

For he whom God has sent utters the words of God, for he gives the Spirit without measure. The Father loves the Son and has given all things into his hand. Whoever believes in the Son has eternal life; whoever does not obey the Son shall not see life, but the wrath of God remains on him.

John 3:34-36

Reflections

God does not overlook unbelief and the rejection of His messengers who reveal His truth to mankind. More than that, to reject God's prophets and His Son is to incur eternal wrath.

Ahaziah, the king of Israel, attempted to turn to the pagan god, Baal-zebub, to learn whether or not he would recover from his injury. God intervened and sent Elijah to rebuke him and to tell him he would not recover because of his unbelief.

John's gospel warns us of the danger that comes if we do not believe in the One whom God has sent to utter His words. Those who heard Jesus were divided right down to the moment of His crucifixion. Some believed and some did not. The benefits or consequences were and are dramatic. Whoever believes in the Son has eternal life. Whoever does not obey the Son shall not see life, and furthermore, the wrath of God remains on him.

Think about It

It is no small matter to disbelieve in God's revelation of Himself. What will keep us from having eternal life is not only our many sins, but our great sin of unbelief in the One whom God sent so that whoever believes in Him should not perish but have eternal life (John 3:16).

If you believe in the Son, praise God for His mercy. If you are like Ahaziah, seeking answers about your destiny from other gods or authorities, repent and believe in Christ. There is a God who knows all and controls all. He is not the god of this world but the triune God revealed to us by the Son.

Two Unlikely Converts

Today's Reading: Second Kings 4-5; John 4:1-30

Selected Verses

*Then he returned to the man of God, he and all his company, and he came
and stood before him. And he said, "Behold, I know that there is no God
in all the earth but in Israel; so accept now a present from your servant."*

2 Kings 5:15

*So the woman left her water jar and went away into town and said to
the people, "Come, see a man who told me all that I ever did. Can this
be the Christ?" They went out of the town and were coming to him.*

John 4:28-30

Reflections

Naaman, a Syrian general who came down with leprosy, learned from his
Israelite servant girl that there was a prophet in Israel who was known to perform
miracles. Certainly Elisha's record is comparable to that of the Lord Jesus Christ
Himself. Among other things, Elisha raised a dead boy and fed a large crowd
with a small portion of food. The details are interesting, but, suffice it to say,
Naaman was healed and learned that there was not merely a miracle-working
prophet in Israel, there was a God in Israel, One who is uniquely God in all the
earth. Naaman was not just healed of a deadly disease. He became a believer in
the God of Abraham, Isaac, and Jacob.

Jesus encountered a Samaritan woman at a well in Sychar. The conversation
is fascinating and reveals so much of the love and wisdom of Christ. At the
conclusion of the discussion, the woman leaves her water pot and heads off to
town to tell everyone about the Jewish man whom she suspects to truly be the
Messiah. The whole town turns out to meet Him.

Think about It

God saves the most unlikely people, a Syrian general and a Samaritan
woman with a bad track record for marriage. Are you another unlikely convert?
If so, give thanks for His mercy to you. Do you know anyone who needs Christ
but seems to be a hopeless candidate for salvation? Do not lose heart or stop
praying. God is able to save whomever He calls to Himself.

Authority and Faith

Today's Reading: Second Kings 6-8; John 4:31-54

Selected Verses

And the king rose in the night and said to his servants, "I will tell you what the Syrians have done to us. They know that we are hungry. Therefore they have gone out of the camp to hide themselves in the open country, thinking, 'When they come out of the city, we shall take them alive and get into the city.'"

1 Kings 7:12

The father knew that was the hour when Jesus had said to him, "Your son will live." And he himself believed, and all his household.

John 4:53

Reflections

The king of Israel heard that the Syrian army had fled, leaving their equipment and food behind. Even though Elisha had already prophesied that there would be abundance of food within a day, the king suspected a trick. He assumed that Elisha was wrong, so he was not expecting some kind of miraculous intervention. But the prophet was right and the king was wrong. Did his position as king cause him to be more self-confident and less willing to believe God's word through His prophet? It seems that those who have the most power and wealth sense the least need for divine assistance.

But this is not always the case. When Jesus arrived at Cana, an official of King Herod the Tetrarch went to Jesus requesting healing for his son. The official hoped that Jesus would come to his home and heal the boy, but Jesus rebuked him for seeking signs and wonders as a basis for faith. The man implored him again and Jesus sent him on his way with a promise that his son would be well. The healing occurred at the hour Jesus had spoken. Jesus was being constantly tested by the people who requested signs, but, in the case of the official, Jesus tested him to see if he believed enough to return home with only the assurance of the Lord's word. He passed the test and believed, as did his whole household.

Think about It

Having power and wealth does not help a person to believe the truth. It may even hinder faith. What makes a person believe is the regenerating work of the Holy Spirit in his or her heart. No one comes to Christ without the drawing of the Father (John 6:44).

If you believe God, it is not because you have some inherent wisdom to do so. It is His doing completely. You believe because He drew you. He drew you because He wanted to. You responded because He gave you a heart to believe. For that He deserves all your praise.

Reconciliation with God Brings Joy that Lasts

Today's Reading: Second Kings 9-11; John 5:1-24

Selected Verses

So all the people of the land rejoiced, and the city was quiet after Athaliah had been put to death with the sword at the king's house.

2 Kings 11:20

Truly, truly, I say to you, whoever hears my word and believes him who sent me has eternal life. He does not come into judgment, but has passed from death to life.

John 5:24

Reflections

When Jehoash was crowned king at age seven, Jehoiada the priest, led the nation to renew their covenant with God to be His people. Certainly, Jehoiada was the real leader of Judah and he led well. The wicked queen Athaliah had been executed and the rightful heir to David's throne, Jehoash, was inaugurated. There was joy in the land as long as Jehoiada lived.

Jesus ministry brought division and conflict in Jerusalem. He healed a man who had been an invalid for 38 years, but the Jews criticized Him for healing on the Sabbath, calling God His Father, and "making himself equal with God" (John 5:18). Jesus made stupendous claims about Himself in this passage. He said He only did what the Father was doing. The Son was perfectly in sync with His Father. Jesus was giving life to whomever He would. He said the Father had given Him all authority to judge. Jesus said His word, if heard and believed, imparted eternal life and freedom from judgment and death.

Think about It

Jehoiada's leadership brought joy to the land of Judah until his death. But neither the priest nor the revival he led would last forever. Someone greater was needed to lead the people to a permanent solution for the problem of guilt and sin. That One was Jesus. His word brings life. Do you have it? Trust Him. He and the Father give life to those who believe His word because through Him, and only through Him, we are reconciled to God. That is a basis for joy that lasts forever.

The Trap of Popular Opinion

Today's Reading: Second Kings 12-14; John 5:25-47

Selected Verses

*You have indeed struck down Edom, and your heart has lifted you up.
Be content with your glory, and stay at home, for why should you
provoke trouble so that you fall, you and Judah with you?"*

2 Kings 14:10

*How can you believe, when you receive glory from one another
and do not seek the glory that comes from the only God?*

John 5:44

Reflections

Amaziah, king of Judah, defeated Edom. Then he called on Jehoash, king of Israel, for a face off on the battlefield. Jehoash called his bluff and told him to "be content with [his] glory." Good advice, but Amaziah wasn't buying it. They fought and Amaziah lost badly, not only the battle but all the gold and silver in the temple and the palace. He would die in a conspiracy. He foolishly started and lost a war that was about his own glory, not God's.

Jesus confronted the Jews who were increasingly opposed to Him and His teaching. He unmasked their motives. They sought glory from one another and not from God. No wonder they could not see that God had sent Jesus, His Son, and that there was overwhelming support for His claims. John the Baptist, Jesus' own works, the Father's approval, and the Scriptures all pointed to Him as the Messiah. Those who sought public approval and acclaim were too blinded by their pursuit to see and accept the obvious truth.

Think about It

Amaziah, though a king, fell into the trap of popular opinion. The Jews who rejected Jesus were also guilty of seeking glory from their peers. Our sin nature has an insatiable desire for glory. Nothing will suffice.

How much does popular opinion affect your decisions and your viewpoints? Jesus calls us to follow Him, the One who did not seek glory from people. We will never follow Christ until we rid ourselves of the desire to please others. Follow Him alone and be free from the tyranny of the fear and praise of men. You will be glad in that hour when the dead are called to the resurrection of life and judgment.

A Humble King

Today's Reading: Second Kings 15-17; John 6:1-21

Selected Verses

Shallum the son of Jabesh conspired against him and struck him down at Ibleam and put him to death and reigned in his place.

2 Kings 15:10

When the people saw the sign that he had done, they said, "This is indeed the Prophet who is to come into the world!" Perceiving then that they were about to come and take him by force to make him king, Jesus withdrew again to the mountain by himself.

John 6:14-15

Reflections

Shallum held one in a line of short-lived reigns on the throne of Israel. He came to the throne through conspiracy and the assassination of Zechariah. But his reign lasted only a month before he, too, was assassinated. The prophet Hosea would later indict Israel for their failure to seek God's direction for their kingdom which contributed to all that instability (Hos. 8:4).

What a contrast to Jesus! He relinquished the glories of His heavenly status and came to earth. He began announcing the kingdom of God, healing the sick, and feeding the hungry. The fickle crowds wanted to make Him king, but they had the wrong reasons and the wrong methods. So Jesus disappeared to avoid that happening. He knew their hearts. They were only responding to the signs He did and wanted a king who could take care of their health and their hunger (John 2:23-25; 6:2). They thought of an earthly kingdom, but His kingdom was not of this world (John 18:36).

Although Jesus was the rightful king of all Creation, His goal was not to be merely a king in this world. He would redeem His people and be established as the Lord of lords and King of kings at the right hand of God the Father in His eternal kingdom (Phil. 2:5-11; Rev. 19:16).

Think about It

See how glorious and worthy is our King, the Lord Jesus Christ whose every action and decision showed love, grace, humility, and justice! Give Him, the humble King, the praise He deserves and love Him with all your heart, soul, mind, and strength today.

What Pleases God

Today's Reading: Second Kings 18-19; John 6:22-44

Selected Verses

He trusted in the Lord, the God of Israel, so that there was none like him among all the kings of Judah after him, nor among those who were before him. For he held fast to the Lord. He did not depart from following him, but kept the commandments that the Lord commanded Moses. And the Lord was with him; wherever he went out, he prospered.

2 Kings 18:5-7a

Then they said to him, "What must we do, to be doing the works of God?" Jesus answered them, "This is the work of God, that you believe in him whom he has sent."

John 6:28-29

Reflections

Hezekiah came to the throne in Jerusalem at a most difficult time. Assyria was the dominant nation and was putting pressure on both Israel and Judah. Israel fell and Assyria prepared to finish off Judah as well. But Hezekiah trusted the Lord. Taunting came and threats of Assyrian victory, but Hezekiah prayed and sought the Lord. He turned to the prophet Isaiah for advice. God delivered them and turned sure defeat into a time of freedom and prosperity.

The Jews asked Jesus what they needed to be doing in order to do the works of God. Their question implied that they wanted to please God and that they assumed that God could be pleased by some actions, some works on their part. Jesus corrected them by saying that the work of God for them was to believe in the One whom God had sent to them. They stumbled over His plain teaching, looking for some way of getting on the right side of God, but they were missing the most basic quality of the godly person: faith.

Think about It

The writer to the Hebrews said, "And without faith it is impossible to please him, for whoever would draw near to God must believe that he exists and that he rewards those who seek him" (Heb. 11:6).

How about you? Do you trust God or, when life is unbearable, do you frantically try to be "good enough" to merit God's favor? God looks for the believing heart and is pleased. Trust Him even if the Assyrians are at your doorstep. The same God who was with Hezekiah is able to see you through and to graciously deliver you from your worst nightmare. Faith is what pleases God. Always was and always will be.

Why We Choose Belief or Unbelief

Today's Reading: Second Kings 20-22; John 6:45-71

Selected Verses

But they did not listen, and Manasseh led them astray to do more evil than the nations had done whom the Lord destroyed before the people of Israel.

2 Kings 21:9

And he said, "This is why I told you that no one can come to me unless it is granted him by the Father." After this many of his disciples turned back and no longer walked with him. So Jesus said to the Twelve, "Do you want to go away as well?"

John 6:65-67

Reflections

People choose to believe or not believe, but without the work of the Spirit in a person's heart there will be no inclination to believe.

Today's reading demonstrates the ups and downs of the kings of Israel and Judah. Hezekiah had led Judah in a period of faithfulness like none before him. We also read about Josiah who repaired the temple, rediscovered the book of the law, and led the nation to revival. But in between these two godly kings was Manasseh who had the longest and worst reign in the history of Judah. He led the people to do more evil than the Canaanite nations that God had judged and destroyed under Joshua. How do these things happen? Why would a great and godly king (Hezekiah) have such a wicked son (Manasseh)? How does such a wicked king (Manasseh) father such a godly son (Josiah)?

Clearly, something is at work in these fathers and sons besides mere heredity or environmental influence. The difference, we discover, is God the Father who draws people to Himself (John 6:44). It is the Spirit who gives life (John 6:63). It is Jesus whose body and blood gives eternal life to the one who believes in Him. Those who heard Jesus either responded with disbelief and even disgust, or they drew near to Him concluding like Peter did when he said, "Lord, to whom shall we go? You have the words of eternal life, and we have believed, and have come to know, that you are the Holy One of God." (John 6:68-69).

Think about It

To whom will you go? Jesus' words either comfort or repel you. If you believe, you may be sure it is the drawing of the Father and the life-giving ministry of the Spirit. If you do not believe, but are troubled by your unbelief, that, too, is the work of God in you. Call to Him for faith to believe and grace to repent of your sins and come to the Bread of Life. You are not controlled by your family history or outward circumstances either for good or bad. Your choice reflects your heart. May God give us His Spirit so that we can believe!

Be Careful What You Don't Wish For

Today's Reading: Second Kings 23-25; John 7:1-31

Selected Verses

*Before him there was no king like him, who turned to the Lord with
all his heart and with all his soul and with all his might, according
to all the Law of Moses, nor did any like him arise after him.*

2 Kings 23:25

*If anyone's will is to do God's will, he will know whether the teaching
is from God or whether I am speaking on my own authority.*

John 7:17

Reflections

Yesterday we saw that we choose unbelief because that is the natural
inclination of our hearts. By the regenerating work of the Holy Spirit, we are
born again with hearts inclined toward God. Today we see that another obstacle
to believing, besides being spiritually dead and unable and unwilling to believe, is
that as unbelievers we do not really want to do God's will.

Jesus told the crowds, who were astounded by His teaching despite His
apparent lack of formal education, that His teaching came from the One who
sent Him. What He taught was not His own but His Father's teaching. God the
Father's authority was behind the Son's words. How can you know this? Jesus
said, if anyone's will is to do God's will, that person will know whose the
teaching is. People around Jesus all heard Him, but they responded in a wide
variety of ways. Some sort-of believed. Some seriously doubted. Others
wondered. But Jesus said the confusion would clear up immediately for that
person who was seeking to do God's will.

Josiah, although living some six centuries before Jesus, was certainly a man
whose will was to do God's will. When the Book of the Covenant was found,
Josiah devoured it. He then gathered all the people together and read it to them
in its entirety. He wanted to do God's will, and he wanted the people in his
kingdom to do so, too.

Think about It

It is a dangerous thing to be indifferent or averse to the will of God. Be
careful what you don't wish for. Make it your greatest desire to do God's will.
Seek to know it through His Word. One thing we know He wills for us is our
sanctification, that we grow to be more like His Son (I Thessalonians 4:3;Rom.
8:29). Eventually, if we believe, we will be like Him for we will see Him as He is
(1 John 3:2).

The Spirit of God: The Water of Life

Today's Reading: First Chronicles 1-2; John 7:32-53

Selected Verses

These are the kings who reigned in the land of Edom before any king reigned over
the people of Israel: Bela the son of Beor, the name of his city being Dinhabah.
Bela died, and Jobab the son of Zerah of Bozrah reigned in his place.

1 Chron. 1:43-44

On the last day of the feast, the great day, Jesus stood up and cried out,
"If anyone thirsts, let him come to me and drink. Whoever believes in me, as
the Scripture has said, 'Out of his heart will flow rivers of living water.'" Now
this he said about the Spirit, whom those who believed in him were to receive,
for as yet the Spirit had not been given, because Jesus was not yet glorified.

John 7:37-39

Reflections

In our reading today, we find a long list of those who lived, ruled, and died. Some, like the kings of Edom, ruled for a time, but they died and someone stepped up to rule in their place. One after another, they ruled, died, and were replaced. You might wonder, "Is this all there is to life?" You and I may be less significant in our time than these Edomite kings were in theirs. Will we leave anything for future generations? Will our life really have long term significance?

Jesus called His disciples to come to Him, to believe in Him, to receive the Spirit, and to know the living water that flows out of the believer's heart. He has been promising eternal life for those who eat His flesh and drink His blood. He calls us not to live and die and be forgotten, but to live, believe, and live forever.

Think about It

The history leading up to Christ's coming is important because it shows the need for something more than ruling for a time in this world. It points to the fallen state of man and the need for a savior. My fellow believer, do not think your life is of no lasting importance. You have God's Spirit, the living water that wells up to eternal life (John 4:14). Rejoice in His mercy and goodness to you. No wonder the officers who failed in their attempt to arrest Him said, "No one ever spoke like this man!"

Light or Darkness—Which Will You Choose?

Today's Reading: First Chronicles 3-5; John 8:1-20

Selected Verses

But they broke faith with the God of their fathers, and whored after the gods of the peoples of the land, whom God had destroyed before them. So the God of Israel stirred up the spirit of Pul king of Assyria, the spirit of Tiglath-pileser king of Assyria, and he took them into exile, namely, the Reubenites, the Gadites, and the half-tribe of Manasseh, and brought them to Halah, Habor, Hara, and the river Gozan, to this day.

1 Chron. 5:25-26

Again Jesus spoke to them, saying, "I am the light of the world. Whoever follows me will not walk in darkness, but will have the light of life."

John 8:12

Reflections

The half-tribe of Manasseh included a large population, mighty warriors, famous men, and heads of their fathers' houses (1 Chron. 5:23-24). But they did not walk in the light of the truth of God. They served other gods who had shown their inability to deliver the nations that served them in the past. Despite the long list of accolades mentioned about this half-tribe they failed in the most important matter, to remain faithful to the God of Israel. They were in "Who's Who" as far as their contemporary society was concerned, but they got only scorn and judgment from the Lord.

Jesus proclaimed Himself to be the Light of the world. Those who follow Him have the light of life. Those who do not must walk in darkness, like the half-tribe of Manasseh.

Think about It

The fame and acclaim of this world can contribute nothing to one who is walking in darkness. Have you determined to walk in the light? Better to walk in the light and be in societal obscurity than the reverse. The Apostle John wrote: "But if we walk in the light, as he is in the light, we have fellowship with one another, and the blood of Jesus his Son cleanses us from all sin" (1 John 1:7). Seek to walk in the light of Christ today. Your steps may not be easy, but they will be sure. You will walk in freedom from guilt and in the great fellowship of all those who walk in the light.

None so Blind

Today's Reading: First Chronicles 6-7; John 8:21-36

Selected Verses

But Aaron and his sons made offerings on the altar of burnt offering and on the altar of incense for all the work of the Most Holy Place, and to make atonement for Israel, according to all that Moses the servant of God had commanded.

1 Chron. 6:49

He said to them, "You are from below; I am from above. You are of this world; I am not of this world. I told you that you would die in your sins, for unless you believe that I am he you will die in your sins."

John 8:23-24

Reflections

Ever since the nation of Israel was constituted with the Law of Moses, the priesthood had been established with the system of sacrifices for atonement for sin as the central element. It was such a significant part of the religious culture of the nation that one tribe, the Levites, were ordained to exclusively tend to the matters surrounding worship and sacrifices. One family within the tribe of Levi, the descendants of Aaron, was eligible for the priesthood.

God designed the sacrificial system to show the heinousness of sin and the need for atonement, an offering to God for offenses made against Him. But when Jesus Christ, the promised Messiah, came who would be the One to bear the sins of His people, many displayed caution, skepticism, rejection, and hostility toward Him. As we see throughout the Gospel of John, His origin was debated. His words were parsed and doubted. His explanations were questioned and re-questioned. The evidence of His authenticity was dismissed.

Now He plainly tells them that they will die in their sins if they do not believe in Him. His whole purpose in life is to save His people from their sins (Matt. 1: 21). He is "the Lamb of God who takes away the sin of the world" (John 1:29). Faith in Him is a matter of life and death.

Think about It

Yet many refused to see. The problem of sin has existed since the Fall of Man. God has presented His Son to be the atonement. Is it not plain? Is it not clear? Why persist in unbelief? Why remain blind? The old saying, attributed to the Puritan Pastor and Commentator Matthew Henry, is true, "None so deaf as those that will not hear. None so blind as those that will not see." If your unbelief troubles you, call to Him for faith and the ability to repent. If you see, give Him praise for His great mercy to you.

The Consequences of Not Hearing

Today's Reading: First Chronicles 8-10; John 8:37-59

Selected Verses

So Saul died for his breach of faith. He broke faith with the Lord in that he did not keep the command of the Lord, and also consulted a medium, seeking guidance. He did not seek guidance from the Lord. Therefore the Lord put him to death and turned the kingdom over to David the son of Jesse.

1 Chron. 10:13-14

Whoever is of God hears the words of God. The reason why you do not hear them is that you are not of God.

John 8:47

Reflections

The Book of First Chronicles opens with a meticulous genealogy of Israel as we have been seeing. There are not many details about all those individuals until we come to Saul. Then the writer zooms in on the final hours of Saul's life. His life ended the same way he lived it during the long years of his reign. He disregarded God's commands. For example, he sought guidance from a medium. He led the nation to defeat and died in agony by suicide. Three of his sons died at the same time. The threat of imminent defeat and death did not serve to awaken Saul to his need to repent and turn to the Lord for mercy and deliverance.

The Jews listening to Jesus reacted negatively to His every claim. They hid behind their status as descendants of Abraham. They were sure that God was their father. Yet they were already plotting to kill their Messiah. They considered Jesus to be the one who was illegitimate, not themselves. They drip with self-righteousness. As the Apostle Paul would later write, "And even if our gospel is veiled, it is veiled to those who are perishing. In their case the god of this world has blinded the minds of the unbelievers, to keep them from seeing the light of the gospel of the glory of Christ, who is the image of God" (2 Cor. 4:3-4).

Think about It

Privilege and status did not make Saul faithful or obedient. He grew harder as his life unfolded and he left a shameful legacy to his nation. Many of the Jews in Jesus' day did not believe the Truth when He lived among them. We can learn from these examples of foolishness and blindness, but will we? Let us learn and humble ourselves to hear and do what God has said.

Free to Lead like Jesus

Today's Reading: First Chronicles 11-13; John 9:1-23

Selected Verses

In times past, even when Saul was king, it was you who led out and brought
in Israel. And the Lord your God said to you, "You shall be shepherd
of my people Israel, and you shall be prince over my people Israel."

1 Chron. 11:2

His parents said these things because they feared the Jews, for
the Jews had already agreed that if anyone should confess that
Jesus to be the Christ, he was to be put out of the synagogue.

John 9:22

Reflections

Godly leaders seek to do His will, and therefore are free to act with courage and give clear direction to their followers.

Saul, the first king of Israel, failed on many levels in his leadership. He failed to encourage faithfulness to the Lord and obedience to the Law of God. Worship of God seems to have been neglected under Saul (1 Chron. 13:3). Even while Saul was the king, it was David who gave real leadership to the nation.

Although David was loyal to him, Saul did not trust David and wasted much of his time and energy trying to assassinate him. In the end, David became king in a joyous coronation that reunited the kingdom of Israel (1 Chron. 12:38-40).

In Jesus' day, the Jews showed some of the same leadership weaknesses as Saul. Jesus' power and popularity threatened them. They adamantly resisted the mounting evidence that pointed to His identity as the Messiah. These leaders used their authority to squelch discussion and intimidate the citizenry. They ruled that "if anyone should confess Jesus to be the Christ, he was to be put out of the synagogue." Just as Saul demanded that everyone side with him against David, so the Jewish authorities also drew a line insisting that the people choose between them and Jesus.

Think about It

Godly leaders encourage those they lead to seek the Lord, to know His Word, and to follow Christ. A godly leader, like King David, knows that God is the real King of His people. They recognize that human leaders never exceed the position of princes. Are you free from the slavery of pleasing people or the jealousy of holding on to your position? Are you able to use whatever leadership authority you have to encourage faithfulness to God? Consider how you can facilitate godliness in those the Lord has allowed you to lead.

No Drama; Simple Trust

Today's Reading: First Chronicles 14-16; John 9:24-41

Selected Verses

Now the Philistines had come and made a raid in the Valley of Rephaim. And David inquired of God, "Shall I go up against the Philistines? Will you give them into my hand?" And the Lord said to him, "Go up, and I will give them into your hand."

1 Chron. 14:9-10

Jesus heard that they had cast him out, and having found him he said, "Do you believe in the Son of Man?" He answered, "And who is he, sir, that I may believe in him?"

John 9:35-36

Reflections

David was off to a good start in his reign (except for all the wives). When the Philistines heard that he was on the throne they wasted no time in coming against him in battle. Perhaps their utter defeat of Saul, a few years earlier, had left them overconfident. Maybe they thought the new king would be distracted with all the matters of the kingdom and be an easy push over. But David was a seasoned military commander. He could have relied on his extensive experience, but he consulted the Lord for direction about how to respond to the approaching army. David was not presumptuous but desired to know what God wanted him to do. David showed simple trust in the Lord.

That simple trust paid off. David was victorious.

Jesus had a second encounter with the man who had been born blind. The now-seeing man had held his ground in the repeated interviews with the Jewish authorities. Now Jesus asks him if he believes in the "Son of Man." Of course, the man does not know what Jesus means, but he is quick to express simple trust in the Lord. "And who is he, sir, that I may believe in him?" he asks without hesitation. Jesus introduces himself to the man as that One to whom He had referred.

And the man worshiped him. That healed man got more than he bargained for that day: physical sight and spiritual sight. His simple trust was well-placed.

Think about It

What is your attitude toward God and His Word? Does your faith express itself in simple trust? No drama, just a readiness to accept whatever the Lord puts in front of you today? Seek to be a person who believes without delay and without excuses, one who trusts simply.

A Different Kind of Shepherd

Today's Reading: First Chronicles 17-19; John 10:1-21

Selected Verses

Now, therefore, thus shall you say to my servant David, 'Thus says the Lord of hosts, I took you from the pasture, from following the sheep, to be prince over my people Israel, and I have been with you wherever you have gone and have cut off all your enemies from before you. And I will make for you a name, like the name of the great ones of the earth.

1 Chron. 17:7-8

I am the good shepherd. I know my own and my own know me, just as the Father knows me and I know the Father; and I lay down my life for the sheep.

John 10:14-15

Reflections

David's life started out very simply. He was the youngest son of his family. He was assigned the unenviable task of taking care of the sheep, dirty, dumb sheep who could not take care of themselves, nor be left alone. His work meant hot days and cold nights. We wouldn't have imagined that he would one day sit on the throne of Israel. Much less, would we have imagined that his dynasty would be guaranteed by God Himself through the prophet Nathan. The Messiah, the Lord Jesus Christ, would be of David's lineage.

As Jesus revealed Who He is through His teaching, He presented Himself as the Good Shepherd. He is good because, unlike mere hired shepherds He would pay the ultimate price of death to save His sheep. The relationship He has with His sheep is intimate and unique. He knows His sheep and they know Him. They flee from a stranger. They do not recognize the stranger's voice.

Sure enough, the people who heard Him make these claims and promises revealed their identity as either trusting Him or doubting Him. You could tell who His sheep were by their response to His voice.

Think about It

How amazing the beauty and intricacy of God's plan is! He painted a picture in the Old Testament through the history of Israel, and He fulfilled it in the advent of the Son of David, Jesus Christ, who will reign forever and ever. Flee other voices. Trust Him, my fellow sheep, we need Him who died and rose for us, dirty, dumb, and unworthy as we are.

Why We Must Stay with God's Word

Today's Reading: First Chronicles 20-22; John 10:22-42

Selected Verses

Only, may the Lord grant you discretion and understanding, that when he gives you charge over Israel you may keep the law of the Lord your God. Then you will prosper if you are careful to observe the statutes and the rules that the Lord commanded Moses for Israel. Be strong and courageous. Fear not; do not be dismayed.

1 Chron. 22:12-13

Jesus answered them, "Is it not written in your Law, 'I said, you are gods'? If he called them gods to whom the word of God came—and Scripture cannot be broken—do you say of him whom the Father consecrated and sent into the world, 'You are blaspheming,' because I said, 'I am the Son of God'?"

John 10:34-36

Reflections

David advised his son, Solomon, who would succeed him as king. He told him that the Lord would be the One giving him charge over Israel. Solomon needed to understand that he was a vassal, a steward of the kingdom of God's people, not his own autonomous boss. Furthermore, David emphasized the need for discretion and understanding to keep and to observe carefully God's law if Solomon were to prosper. Solomon did not hold to the Law of God fully to the end of his life and the consequences were devastating.

The Jews continually questioned and criticized Jesus during His years of earthly ministry. It only got worse, and, of course, concluded with the arrest, trial, and crucifixion. In the incident mentioned in John 10, He used Scripture to defend His reference to God as His Father and His claim to be the Son of God. In a parenthetical comment, He says, "Scripture cannot be broken." He frequently showed His trust in the veracity of the Bible. Here the Lord makes a strong and clear claim about the nature of God's Word—that it cannot be broken. He knew the Word, used the Word, and applied the Word to real life situations and questions.

Think about It

Jesus said, "Heaven and earth will pass away, but my words will not pass away" (Matt. 24:35). Do you hold God's Word in high esteem? Are you convinced that Scripture cannot be broken? Do not consider it wasted time that you invest in the careful reading, studying, and obeying of the Bible. Stay with it.

Your Assignment from God

Today's Reading: First Chronicles 23-25; John 11:1-17

Selected Verses

*And they cast lots for their duties, small and great, teacher
and pupil alike. The first lot fell for Asaph to Joseph.*

1 Chronicles 25:8,9a

*So the sisters sent to him, saying, "Lord, he whom you love is ill." But
when Jesus heard it he said, "This illness does not lead to death. It is for
the glory of God, so that the Son of God may be glorified through it."*

John 11:3-4

Reflections

Under David's reign, God's people were given assignments for His glory. In today's reading, there are long lists of people who had responsibilities in the service of worship, such as playing musical instruments. Maybe you find the lists of names tedious to read, but if your name were on that list you would not. Those listed there had positions, an assignment, a specific job to do, and a time and place to do it.

In John 11, we learn about two benefits from the illness and subsequent death of Lazarus. First, it was for the glory of God and so that the Son of God would be glorified through it (John 11:4). Jesus would show His power in this incident and the disciples would learn more about His glory. Second, it was so that those disciples might believe (John 11:14-15). Jesus was all about teaching His disciples so that they might believe in Him.

Death is universal. No mere human has ever solved the problem of death. But Jesus, the Son of God, came to give eternal life to all who hear His word and believe God (John 5:24). Lazarus had the assignment of getting sick and dying so that the glory of God would be seen and the disciples would believe.

Think about It

It is thrilling to know we too have an assignment in God's great cosmic plan. It may be through suffering and death or it may be through playing beautiful music or through innumerable other ways. Seek to glorify Him whether you are clearly conscious of your role or not. Just think, the story of the raising of Lazarus has been preached from pulpits and discussed around supper tables for centuries. Though this God is always glorified and His people are strengthened in faith. Lazarus completed his assignment. May you complete yours, too.

Learning to Trust the Love of God

Today's Reading: First Chronicles 26-27; John 11:18-46

Selected Verses

*And Obed-edom had sons: Shemaiah the firstborn, Jehozabad the second,
Joah the third, Sachar the fourth, Nethanel the fifth, Ammiel the sixth,
Issachar the seventh, Peullethai the eighth, for God blessed him.*

1 Chron. 26:4

*When Jesus saw her weeping, and the Jews who had come with her also weeping, he was
deeply moved in his spirit and greatly troubled. And he said, "Where have you laid him?"
They said to him, "Lord, come and see." Jesus wept. So the Jews said, "See how he loved him!"*

John 11:33-36

Reflections

Today's reading in First Chronicles includes long lists of names, yet, as we have seen before, there are treasures to be found in these lists. One example is the comment about Obed-edom, "God blessed him." The note in my Reformation Study Bible (page 626) helped me remember that Obed-edom was the man who took care of the ark of the covenant for three months after a mishandling of it had resulted in death (1 Chron. 13:13-14; 2 Sam. 6:10-11). Now we pick up with this same Obed-edom and learn that God's blessing included eight sons who served as gatekeepers.

What image do you have of the Man Jesus? Is He too cool and calm to ever show grief or sadness? Is He always upbeat, joyful, and in total control? Think again. John 11 does not give us that picture. When Jesus arrived at Bethany, the home of Martha and Mary, He was deeply moved and troubled by what He saw there: a distraught family, friends seeking to console them, and everyone grieving. His love and compassion for the sisters and the friends of Lazarus expressed itself in tears that flowed. Isn't it curious that Jesus knew He would raise Lazarus from the dead in a few minutes, but for the moment He entered into the agony of the bereaved family and felt their suffering?

Think about It

God's plan for the lives of Obed-edom and Lazarus took them in different paths centuries apart from each other but always under the providential care of the Lord who reigns over all things. Praise Him who does not overlook the loving and careful service of Obed-edom. Neither will He forget your service for Him. Take comfort in this. The Lord who cared for Lazarus' family knows and cares for you who are His. He is the resurrection and the life. Fear not. His plan is good and ends with His victory. Meanwhile, walk on by faith and keep learning to trust the love of God.

Why Mercy Triumphs over Judgment

Today's Reading: First Chronicles 28-29; John 11:47-57

Selected Verses

*And you, Solomon my son, know the God of your father and serve him
with a whole heart and with a willing mind, for the Lord searches all
hearts and understands every plan and thought. If you seek him, he will
be found by you, but if you forsake him, he will cast you off forever.*

1 Chron. 28:9

*But one of them, Caiaphas, who was high priest that year, said to them, "You
know nothing at all. Nor do you understand that it is better for you that one man
should die for the people, not that the whole nation should perish." He did not
say this of his own accord, but being high priest that year he prophesied
that Jesus would die for the nation, and not for the nation only, but
also to gather into one the children of God who are scattered abroad.*

John 11:49-52

Reflections

David, in turning over the kingdom to his son, Solomon, charged him to know and serve God. This was not merely good advice but an urgent mandate. Solomon would rule over people, but they were God's people not his. His leadership would affect the population and be either a credit or discredit to their God. The God that Solomon needed to know and serve is One who "searches all hearts and understands every plan and thought." He cannot be manipulated or fooled. He knows not only the actions of all people but their hearts and thoughts as well. To fail in this mandate is to incur eternal judgment.

Caiaphas was high priest of Israel in the final days of Jesus' earthly ministry. He stood as the highest authority among the Jews who lived under a Roman governor in that day. Like Solomon, Caiaphas held an obligation to know and serve God, but he failed to see that the Son of God was among them making the Father known (John 1:18). So the high priest proposed Jesus' execution and unwittingly decreed the offering of the true Passover Lamb who would die for God's elect people both in Israel and throughout the earth. His words had one meaning to him but another in reality.

Think about It

Solomon did fail to fully serve God and so have we. We all deserve to die. But "God so loved the world, that he gave his only Son, that whoever believes in him should not perish but have eternal life" (John 3:16). God gives the promise of eternal life to all who believe in Him. Praise Him for the promise of mercy that triumphs over the warning of judgment because Jesus died in our place (James 2:13).

Lessons from Mount Moriah

Today's Reading: Second Chronicles 1-3; John 12:1-19

Selected Verses

*Then Solomon began to build the house of the Lord in Jerusalem on
Mount Moriah, where the Lord had appeared to David his father, at the
place that David had appointed, on the threshing floor of Ornan the Jebusite.*

2 Chron. 3:1

*The crowd that had been with him when he called Lazarus out of the tomb
and raised him from the dead continued to bear witness. The reason why
the crowd went to meet him was that they heard he had done this sign.*

John 12:17-18

Reflections

Mount Moriah is significant in biblical history. We hear about it first when Abraham went to that location to offer his son, Isaac, in response to God's command (Gen. 22:2). A thousand years later, David buys property from a Jebusite named Araunah in order to make an offering there to avert the plague, he had brought upon the nation by taking a census. The location of that property is none other than Mt. Moriah. It would become the location of the temple which Solomon built.

Long before Jesus' time, the first temple (Solomon's) had been destroyed by Nebuchadnezzar in the Babylonian invasion. After the captivity the temple was rebuilt. That second temple is the one which is mentioned in the gospels and which Jesus cleansed (John 2:13-17), but it was in the same location, Mt. Moriah. That temple would later be destroyed by the Roman general Titus in 70 AD.

After Jesus raised Lazarus from the dead, He rode into Jerusalem as the crowds hailed Him as King of Israel (John 12:13). John points out that it was because of the resurrection of Lazarus that the crowds came to see and welcome Jesus. All this is occurring in the vicinity of Mt. Moriah and the second temple which would soon to be destroyed.

Think about It

On Mt. Moriah God told Abraham He would provide His own sacrifice for sin, and David learned that the punishment for his sin demanded an offering. Near Mt. Moriah Jesus gave Himself as the ultimate offering, referring to it when He cleansed the temple of money changers and sellers of sheep, oxen, and pigeons. "Destroy this temple," He told the Jews, "and in three days, I will raise it up." He was, of course, referring to His body, His crucifixion, and His resurrection (John 2:18-22).

Don't miss the important lessons of Mt. Moriah where God's mercy met mankind's desperate need and our Lord Jesus Christ reconciled His people to God forever.

Choosing which Glory to Seek

Today's Reading: Second Chronicles 4-6; John 12:20-50

Selected Verses

When the song was raised, with trumpets and cymbals and other musical instruments, in praise to the Lord, "For he is good, for his steadfast love endures forever," the house, the house of the Lord, was filled with a cloud, so that the priests could not stand to minister because of the cloud, for the glory of the Lord filled the house of God."

2 Chron. 5:13-14

Isaiah said these things because he saw his glory and spoke of him. Nevertheless, many even of the authorities believed in him, but for fear of the Pharisees they did not confess it, so that they would not be put out of the synagogue; for they loved the glory that comes from man more than the glory that comes from God.

John 12:41-43

Reflections

In our reading in Second Chronicles Solomon inaugurates the temple with the placement of the Ark of the Covenant in the Holy of Holies. The celebration was accompanied by a host of musicians and singers who lifted praise to God for His goodness and His steadfast love that endures forever. The Lord showed His acceptance of their worship by a cloud that filled the house. That was no normal cloud but the very glory of God Himself. Even the priests could not stand to minister before this display of God's majesty.

In John we find Jesus proclaiming that the hour has come for Him to be glorified (vs. 23). He prays for the Father's name to be glorified (vs. 28), and the Father audibly responds that He has glorified it and will glorify it. On a related note, John comments that many of the authorities believed in Jesus but would not confess this for fear of the Pharisees and of being put out of the synagogue. John concludes with these telling words, "for they loved the glory that comes from man more than the glory that comes from God."

Think about It

Scripture from start to finish, from creation to final judgment, reveals the glory of God. The universe itself does the same. "The heavens declare the glory of God," wrote David (Ps. 19:1). But never has the glory of God been seen more powerfully than in the person of Jesus Christ. "For God, who said, 'Let light shine out of darkness,' has shone in our hearts to give the light of the knowledge of the glory of God in the face of Jesus Christ" (2 Cor. 4:6).

Which glory do you seek, the glory from God or the glory from people? The choice is clear. We were made in His image for His glory. Flee the empty glory of man. Seek His glory alone.

171

Two Kings in Contrast

Today's Reading: Second Chronicles 7-9; John 13:1-17

Selected Verses

Thus King Solomon excelled all the kings of the earth in riches and in wisdom. And all the kings of the earth sought the presence of Solomon to hear his wisdom, which God had put into his mind.

2 Chron. 9:22

When he had washed their feet and put on his outer garments and resumed his place, he said to them, "Do you understand what I have done to you? You call me Teacher and Lord, and you are right, for so I am. If I then, your Lord and Teacher, have washed your feet, you also ought to wash one another's feet.

John 13:12-14

Reflections

Solomon was endowed by God with great wisdom. With that came the honor of being consulted by all the other kings and queens of the earth, and of gathering wealth beyond comparison. Although the writer of Chronicles does not focus on it, Solomon was a victim of his own earthly success, being tripped up by the paganism of his many wives and concubines (1 Kings 11:1-40). We read that he died and was buried quietly with his forefathers. Humanly speaking, his reign was successful and peaceful.

Jesus had just been received in Jerusalem and acclaimed king of Israel (John 12:12-15). But where do we find Jesus on the night of the Passover? Washing the disciples' feet and wiping them with a towel. He had no recognized earthly power or position. He was not wealthy. Jesus was hunted by the elite, not sought by them for advice. He was merely Teacher and Lord for twelve disciples. Did He die quietly after a long reign? No. He died in agony on a cross. Unlike Solomon, He would not be buried with his fathers but in a borrowed tomb. Yet, most importantly, neither would Christ Jesus rot in a grave, but rise triumphantly to life as the Conqueror of death and the Savior of His people.

Think about It

Truly Solomon's reign is antithetical to Jesus' life and ministry at His first coming, and only a pale reflection of the glory of the Kingdom of God which Jesus proclaimed and which is still to come completely. Jesus is the King of Israel, the chosen people of God from all the earth who are blessed to be His. Pray that His kingdom may come in fullness soon. Meanwhile, let us follow our Teacher and Lord in humble obedience and loving service.

Setting our Hearts to Seek the Lord

Today's Reading: Second Chronicles 10-12; John 13:18-38

Selected Verses

And he did evil, for he did not set his heart to seek the Lord.

2 Chron. 12:14

I am not speaking of all of you; I know whom I have chosen. But the Scripture will be fulfilled, "He who ate my bread has lifted his heel against me." I am telling you this now, before it takes place, that when it does take place you may believe that I am he.

John 13:18-19

Reflections

The arrogance of mortal man is often astounding. Rehoboam grew up as a grandson of David and prince under his father, Solomon, during the glory days of the old united kingdom of Israel. For him it was easy to assume that nothing would change unless it was for the better. When he took the throne, Rehoboam rejected the wise counsel of his elders and followed the foolish advice of his peers. As a result, he lost control of the ten tribes of Israel and was left with only Judah and Benjamin. He failed to be a good king or a good spiritual leader to the nation. The Chronicler says, "He did evil, for he did not set his heart to seek the Lord."

Judas accompanied Jesus and the disciples. Outwardly, he appeared to be one of them. When Jesus sent him out, no one thought it was unusual. No one suspected him. But what was in his heart was about to come out. He gave place to Satan and Satan entered into him. He, like Rehoboam, did not set his heart to seek the Lord. Like Rehoboam, God called his number. Judas died by suicide (Matt. 27:3-10; Acts 1:18-19).

Think about It

Whatever we do during our lifetimes, we do with God's resources. We breath His air, we walk on His earth, and we depend on His sustenance and providence to keep us going. Then, like everyone else from kings to paupers, we die. What did we do and what did we stand for? Eventually the truth comes out.

Is it time for a heart check? Let us set our hearts to seek the Lord and pray for grace to keep that focus all the days of our lives. The heart that is set to seek the Lord will not be easily moved or inhabited by Satan. Are you in?

Who, Me? God's Fellow Worker?

Today's Reading: Second Chronicles 13-16; John 14

Selected Verses

*For the eyes of the Lord run to and fro throughout the whole earth,
to give strong support to those whose heart is blameless toward him.*

2 Chron. 16:9

*Truly, truly, I say to you, whoever believes in me will also do the works that I
do; and greater works than these will he do, because I am going to the Father.*

John 14:12

Reflections

King Asa had some good years but, sadly, he veered off course by trusting in the power of a foreign ruler instead of maintaining confidence in the God who had delivered him in former times. Why did he veer off? Perhaps, he thought he was strong enough to handle the situation without the Lord. Perhaps, he forgot that he was merely a steward of God's people and that God would not abandon him if he was faithful and believing. Maybe it was all of the above. At any rate, his heart was not blameless toward the Lord and he paid for his unfaithfulness dearly with continual wars for the rest of his life.

In John 14, there is a long list of ways that Jesus shows His love for His disciples. He is concerned to bring comfort to their troubled hearts. The Lord wants them to be with Him and He reassures them that He is the way to the Father. He promises to send them a Helper, the Holy Spirit, and He tells them the Father, Son, and Holy Spirit will be with them.

There is another promise, however, that parallels my thoughts on Asa. That is, Jesus promised that His disciples would do the works that He did, and even greater works than He had done, because He was going to the Father. His going to the Father coincided with His sending the Holy Spirit and the beginning of the disciples doing those promised greater works. Indeed, those unlikely and unlearned men would soon be changing history with the gospel (Acts 4:13).

Think about It

Here we have two ways to approach our work and responsibility before God. We may rely on our own resources or the resources we can scrounge up from others, like Asa did. Or we may rely on God, maintain a clear understanding that we work with Him and that He will "give strong support to those whose heart is blameless toward him." Today, be neither overconfident nor overwhelmed, but walk blamelessly before God by Christ's mercy and be His fellow worker.

Dangerous Alliances with God-Haters

Today's Reading: Second Chronicles 17-19; John 15

Selected Verses

Jehoshaphat the king of Judah returned in safety to his house in Jerusalem. But Jehu the son of Hanani the seer went out to meet him and said to King Jehoshaphat, "Should you help the wicked and love those who hate the Lord? Because of this, wrath has gone out against you from the Lord."

2 Chron. 19:1-2

If the world hates you, know that it has hated me before it hated you. If you were of the world, the world would love you as its own; but because you are not of the world, but I chose you out of the world, therefore the world hates you.

John 15:18-19

Reflections

Jehoshaphat had a great reign going until he went astray making a marriage alliance with Ahab, king of Israel. Ahab was described as one who hated the Lord. Why did the king who had taken such care to seek the Lord and walk in His commandments (2 Chron. 17:4) abruptly throw in his lot with the rebellious king Ahab? Maybe he hoped to reunify the nation. Maybe he hoped to move Israel back to faithfulness to God. Neither of those goals was bad in itself. But in allying with Ahab, Jehoshaphat became a participant in that king's disobedience. He ignored the wise counsel of Micaiah who stood up to the 400 lying prophets. He entered a battle that God had not sanctioned and nearly lost his life. In the end he was rebuked for his foolishness.

Jesus warned His disciples to expect hatred from the world. They had been chosen out of the world and would receive the same treatment that their master had received, for "a servant is not greater than his master" (vs. 20). One who abides in Christ will be fruitful but will also be persecuted.

Think about It

It may seem extreme but there are people who hate God. It was true in Jehoshaphat's day, in Jesus' day, and in our day. Jehoshaphat paid a price for ignoring this reality. The disciples received the Lord's advice to look for opposition from those who hated Him.

Two lessons are clear. One, beware of alliances with those who hate God. Marriage and business partnerships between believers and unbelievers are out of bounds. Two, be prepared to experience rejection, opposition, and even hatred for your identification with Jesus Christ. We are not to withdraw from the world, but rather hold forth the truth in a dark society. Walk in His steps. Proclaim the gospel without compromise. But flee dangerous alliances.

The Army that Self-Destructed

Today's Reading: Second Chronicles 20-22; John 16:1-15

Selected Verses

And when he had taken counsel with the people, he appointed those who were to sing to the Lord and praise him in holy attire, as they went before the army, and say,

> *"Give thanks to the Lord,*
> *for his steadfast love endures forever."*

And when they began to sing and praise, the Lord set an ambush against the men of Ammon, Moab, and Mount Seir, who had come against Judah, so that they were routed. For the men of Ammon and Moab rose against the inhabitants of Mount Seir, devoting them to destruction, and when they had made an end of the inhabitants of Seir, they all helped to destroy one another.

2 Chron. 20:21-23

The ruler of this world is judged.

John 16:11

Reflections

Here we have one of the most bizarre battles in all of history. Three armies were drawn up against Judah and King Jehoshaphat. The king was terrified, but he wisely turned to God for direction and wisdom. Reassured by the Lord, Jehoshaphat appointed a choir and marching band to go ahead of the army praising God. The Lord intervened on their behalf so that the three enemy armies began to kill each other. The praise band played while the opposition forces self-destructed. Jehoshaphat's army watched. God was glorified.

Jesus spoke solemnly to His disciples on the night before His crucifixion. He told them they would suffer hatred, ejection from the synagogues, and even martyrdom, but He promised them the Holy Spirit. He assured them they would be at an advantage since the Helper would be with them unlimited by the confines of a human body. The ministry of the Spirit would be to convict the world of sin, righteousness, and judgment. The Lord told them "...the ruler of this world is judged."

Think about It

Do you believe that what seems like the hopeless situation of the Church of Jesus Christ today is completely under God's control? Do you trust Him to bring ultimate victory over the forces of the ruler of this world? Can you, like Jehoshaphat's praise band, give thanks to the Lord, knowing that his steadfast love endures forever? Might we suffer? Of course, but our hope is in the Lord.

Take heart. The ruler of this world is judged and his armies will self-destruct. Praise God in advance.

Forgiveness for the Fickle

Today's Reading: Second Chronicles 23-25; John 16:16-33

Selected Verses

Now after the death of Jehoiada the princes of Judah came and paid homage to the king. Then the king listened to them. And they abandoned the house of the Lord, the God of their fathers, and served the Asherim and the idols. And wrath came upon Judah and Jerusalem for this guilt of theirs. Yet he sent prophets among them to bring them back to the Lord. These testified against them, but they would not pay attention.

2 Chron. 24:17-19

Behold, the hour is coming, indeed it has come, when you will be scattered, each to his own home, and will leave me alone. Yet I am not alone, for the Father is with me. I have said these things to you, that in me you may have peace. In the world you will have tribulation. But take heart; I have overcome the world.

John 16:32-33

Reflections

We humans are fickle creatures, easily swayed from apparently firm convictions by the changing circumstances of the world around us. But Jesus, unlike us, did not waver in the face of enormous opposition. He overcame the world.

King Joash of Judah barely survived the assassinations committed by the wicked Athaliah. At age seven, after being hidden almost his entire life, the priest Jehoiada made an elaborate plan to install the rightful king. Jehoiada was a good and wise counselor to Joash, and Joash held to the priest's advice. Then Jehoiada died. Joash did an about-face and abandoned the Lord for idolatry. He even killed Jehoiada's son for attempting to correct his decisions.

Jesus told His disciples that there was trouble ahead. They continued to profess their allegiance, but He warned them that they would fall away and abandon Him. That would not be the end of the story for Jesus would remain steadfast and overcome the world not only for Himself but for all His elect people, flaky disciples and all.

Think about It

Do you struggle with falling prey to the circumstances of life, either being seduced by the glory of this world like Joash or terrified by powerful forces that threaten your life, like the disciples? There is forgiveness for the fickle, struggling believer in Jesus Christ. He overcame the world for you.

Means of Grace in a Hostile Place

Today's Reading: Second Chronicles 26-28; John 17

Selected Verses

In the time of his distress he became yet more faithless to the Lord—this same King Ahaz. For he sacrificed to the gods of Damascus that had defeated him and said, "Because the gods of the kings of Syria helped them, I will sacrifice to them that they may help me." But they were the ruin of him and of all Israel.

2 Chron. 28:22-23

I do not ask that you take them out of the world, but that you keep them from the evil one. They are not of the world, just as I am not of the world. Sanctify them in the truth; your word is truth.

John 17:15-17

Reflections

King Ahaz rebelled against the Lord which led to defeat in battle and distress. Did he learn to turn to God through His failure? No. He took his disobedience to the next level and began worshiping the god of the Syrians. Some of the kings we have studied were corrupted by success. Others were corrupted by failure. In some cases, they turned to God in defeat and were delivered. The circumstances seem to be neutral factors. What is the difference? It is the work of God in the hearts of those kings that either turned them toward Himself or let them go on in apostasy and error.

Jesus knew the kind of world into which He was sending His disciples. He prayed for them and gave them God's word. They were not perfect. But in the end they succeeded in proclaiming the gospel far and wide and laying the foundations for the Church.

Think about It

What do we need in order to stand firm in the faith in a hostile world? Like the Apostles, we need God's word and we need God's power sustaining us in the midst of adversity and spiritual danger. Do we have that? Yes, Jesus is at the right hand of God interceding for us (Heb. 7:25). He has given us His Spirit (Rom. 8:1-17). We have the completed revelation of God in the Scriptures to equip us for every work He calls us to do (2 Tim. 3:16-17). We also need God's people, those who identify with Christ and fellowship with Him through the Sacraments.

Do not fear the world, but do be vigilant of your heart that your distresses or your successes not turn you away from the Lord who keeps His own. Do not make a bad thing worse. Trust Him and make diligent use of the means of grace.

What to Do When Obedience Brings Ridicule

Today's Reading: Second Chronicles 29-31; John 18:1-23

Selected Verses

So the couriers went from city to city through the country of Ephraim and Manasseh, and as far as Zebulun, but they laughed them to scorn and mocked them. However, some men of Asher, of Manasseh, and of Zebulun humbled themselves and came to Jerusalem. The hand of God was also on Judah to give them one heart to do what the king and the princes commanded by the word of the Lord.

2 Chron. 30:10-12

When he had said these things, one of the officers standing by struck Jesus with his hand, saying, "Is that how you answer the high priest?" Jesus answered him, "If what I said is wrong, bear witness about the wrong; but if what I said is right, why do you strike me?"

John 18:22-23

Reflections

Hezekiah set out to turn Judah and Israel back to the Lord. After cleansing the temple and consecrating the priests, his next step was to celebrate the long-neglected Passover. The king sent out couriers to the northern kingdom inviting them to join in the feast, but it seems the typical response was to laugh them to scorn.

There were exceptions, of course, as "some men of Asher, of Manasseh, and of Zebulun humbled themselves and came to Jerusalem." Why did these few respond? The next verse says it was the hand of God which "was also on Judah to give them one heart to do what the king and the princes commanded by the word of the Lord." It is God Who works in human hearts to bring about obedience and faith. Otherwise, people mock and scorn the Lord's messengers as they did the couriers of the king.

Jesus' obedience was the most costly of anyone in all of human history. In His trial before Annas, He was questioned about matters of public knowledge as they searched for grounds on which to charge Him. Jesus spoke the truth but was struck for it. This was only the beginning of the sufferings, mocking, and abuse He would receive.

Think about It

When you obey God and suffer for it, are you tempted to second-guess your action? Do you expect to have your obedience to God instantly rewarded? Neither Hezekiah's couriers nor Jesus did. Obey by faith and be ready to follow the steps of your Savior who suffered for you. His reward was not instant, but it was great and it was eternal. Your reward may be delayed, too, but it will come in God's time.

A Basis for Confidence

Today's Reading: Second Chronicles 32-33; John 18:24-40

Selected Verses

"Be strong and courageous. Do not be afraid or dismayed before the king of Assyria and all the horde that is with him, for there are more with us than with him. With him is an arm of flesh, but with us is the Lord our God, to help us and to fight our battles." And the people took confidence from the words of Hezekiah king of Judah.

2 Chron. 32:7-8

Jesus answered, "My kingdom is not of this world. If my kingdom were of this world, my servants would have been fighting, that I might not be delivered over to the Jews. But my kingdom is not from the world."

John 18:36

Reflections

Pilate, the Roman governor, was presented with Jesus to be tried, yet no charges were filed against Him. Rightly, Pilate wanted clarification as to the offenses of the prisoner. It finally came out that Jesus was claiming to be a king although His kingdom was not an earthly one. Nor were His followers mounting any kind of attack against the powers of Rome. It was a bizarre exchange in which Pilate looks confused and perplexed. He tries to release Jesus but finally succumbs to mob pressure. So much for the so-called rule of law! But since Jesus' kingdom was not of this world, it could not be defeated by any force in this world, not even the misapplication of law in the Roman Empire.

By contrast, the kingdom of Judah in Old Testament times was a kingdom of this world. Like every aspect of the culture of Israel in those days (the priesthood, the religious ceremonies, and the political structure) life in the kingdom revealed the instability of mankind and the need for a greater kingdom with a Perfect King. That King was and is Jesus Christ. Hezekiah had some good days and saw temporary victory over the Assyrians. Manasseh was famously evil during most of his life, but in the end he repented. Amon reverted to the worst days of his father. Stability eluded them. Nothing lasted long.

Think about It

The Kingdom of God is a Kingdom based on truth and governed by a Perfect Eternal King. We wait for it, but we should not be idle in our waiting. What has God given you to do today to hasten the day when our faith shall be sight? Do it with all your heart and with confidence. The King is coming and His Kingdom is spiritual and eternal.

Fleeing to Satan? Really?

Today's Reading: Second Chronicles 34-36; John 19:1-22

Selected Verses

*And they burned the house of God and broke down the wall of Jerusalem and
burned all its palaces with fire and destroyed all its precious vessels. He took into
exile in Babylon those who had escaped from the sword, and they became servants
to him and to his sons until the establishment of the kingdom of Persia, to fulfill
the word of the Lord by the mouth of Jeremiah, until the land had enjoyed its
Sabbaths. All the days that it lay desolate it kept Sabbath, to fulfill seventy years.*

2 Chron. 36:19-21

*They cried out, "Away with him, away with him, crucify him!" Pilate said
to them, "Shall I crucify your King?" The chief priests answered, "We have
no king but Caesar." So he delivered him over to them to be crucified.*

John 19:15-16

Reflections

When people attempt to flee from God, they always flee to something else.

The margin notes in the Reformation Study Bible helpfully point out that at
Jesus' trial the chief priests in their eagerness to rid themselves of Jesus Christ
confessed to being loyal to Caesar. In other words, they forsook their professed
allegiance to the Lord God as their ruler (Ps. 24; 47). God alone is ruler over all
the nations and peoples of the earth. He alone is worthy of worship and praise.
But the chief priests, in rejecting Christ, enthroned Caesar in their hearts and
minds. Such was the level of their sin.

The people of Judah had also forsaken their God, despite the brief return to
some level of faithfulness under the reign of Josiah. In fleeing from God, even by
failing to honor one of His laws like the keeping of the Sabbath, they turned to
other gods and other laws. God through Jeremiah told them they would pay for
their negligence of the Sabbaths. They would have forced Sabbath-keeping
during their seventy years of exile. This was the indictment against Judah that
resulted in their captivity in Babylon.

Think about It

Keep your heart with all vigilance (Prov. 4:23) for those who abandon the
Lord do not move to a neutral position spiritually and theologically, but they
actually flee into the arms of Satan.

God's Sovereignty in Human History

Today's Reading: Ezra 1-2; John 19:23-42

Selected Verses

In the first year of Cyrus king of Persia, that the word of the Lord by the mouth of Jeremiah might be fulfilled, the Lord stirred up the spirit of Cyrus king of Persia, so that he made a proclamation throughout all his kingdom and also put it in writing: "Thus says Cyrus king of Persia: The Lord, the God of heaven, has given me all the kingdoms of the earth, and he has charged me to build him a house at Jerusalem, which is in Judah."

Ezra 1:1,2

For these things took place that the Scripture might be fulfilled: "Not one of his bones will be broken." And again another Scripture says, "They will look on him whom they have pierced."

John 19:36-37

Reflections

Ezra records God's sovereign moving by His Spirit in Cyrus the king of Persia to make a decree to send Jewish exiles back to Judah to rebuild the temple. Ezra knows this is the Lord's doing, but Cyrus in his written decree shows that he, too, recognizes that he is doing God's work. Cyrus makes his own decree to the Jewish exiles to gather resources and to go and do the work. God further moved in the exiles to want to do this project. God works at every level here.

The details surrounding Jesus' crucifixion, death, and burial all reveal that Scripture is being fulfilled while the participants seem to be unconscious of that fact. The soldiers cast lots for His garment. They forgo breaking His legs to hasten His death but thrust a spear in His side. John relates all of these actions to earlier prophecy which is fulfilled precisely. Yet there is no indication that the soldiers have either knowledge of the Scripture or awareness of the importance of their seemingly inconsequential actions.

Think about It

Are you aware that the events of this day, whether in Washington, DC, or Moscow, Russia, or Moscow, Idaho are all under God's providence? He does hold the whole world in His hands while we go about often oblivious to this truth. Are we robots? No, we act freely, but God engineers the outcomes and purposes so that His will is perfectly executed. We may choose to obey Him or not. In the end He will be glorified and His purposes will come to pass.

Do not fret that the world is out of control and going to hell in a hand basket. God is still on the throne. Be confident in Him and grateful to Him, and, like Cyrus, do what He gives you to do.

Life in Christ: More than a Temple

Today's Reading: Ezra 3-5; John 20

Selected Verses

But many of the priests and Levites and heads of fathers' houses, old men who had seen the first house, wept with a loud voice when they saw the foundation of this house being laid, though many shouted aloud for joy, so that the people could not distinguish the sound of the joyful shout from the sound of the people's weeping, for the people shouted with a great shout, and the sound was heard far away.

Ezra 3:12-13

Now Jesus did many other signs in the presence of the disciples, which are not written in this book; but these are written so that you may believe that Jesus is the Christ, the Son of God, and that by believing you may have life in his name.

John 20:30-31

Reflections

The presence of God among His people, Israel, in Old Testament times was symbolized by the tabernacle and later the temple. Because of persistent, unrepentant sin, God sent Nebuchadnezzar and the Babylonian army to conquer Judah, capture the king, and destroy the temple. Now, in our reading, God allows the returned Jewish exiles to rebuild the temple in Jerusalem under a grant by Cyrus, king of Persia, but their joy is mixed with bitter sorrow when the elders see how small the new temple is going to be.

When Jesus rose from the dead, He fulfilled His prophecy to do so and to do so in three days. "Destroy this temple, and in three days I will raise it up," He told the Jews (John 2:19). He showed Himself again and again to the bewildered disciples and they began to understand and to believe. "Have you believed because you have seen me? Blessed are those who have not seen and yet have believed," He said to Thomas, the famous doubter. John says to all the world that he wrote his gospel so that we "may believe that Jesus is the Christ, the Son of God, and that by believing [we] may have life in his name."

Think about It

The temple brought temporary joy mixed with disappointment. But it was never meant to be more than a symbol of God's dwelling place with us. God took on flesh and dwelt among us in His Son, Jesus (John 1:14). In Him, we have life by faith. It is real life that lasts forever because He finished the work of atoning for the sins of His people. Believe and live! We are nearing home.

Following Christ without Distraction

Today's Reading: Ezra 6-8; John 21

Selected Verses

For Ezra had set his heart to study the Law of the Lord,
and to do it and to teach his statutes and rules in Israel.

Ezra 7:10

When Peter saw him, he said to Jesus, "Lord, what about this man?" Jesus said to him,
"If it is my will that he remain until I come, what is that to you? You follow me!"

John 21:21-22

Reflections

Peter was by nature an impulsive and fickle person. This is obvious from the various stories we read about him in the gospels. Remember his nervous response to the transfiguration of Jesus? On another occasion, He confessed Jesus as the Son of God, but moments later Jesus rebuked him for contradicting the Lord's prophecy about His death and resurrection. Peter promised to be loyal to Jesus to death, if necessary, and followed that up with multiple denials that he knew Him.

Now Jesus speaks to him personally giving him the opportunity to confess three times his love for Christ. Jesus charges Peter three times: "Feed my lambs, tend my sheep, and feed my sheep." Jesus then makes a reference to Peter's future martyrdom and says, "Follow me." But Peter, true to form, notices another disciple nearby (John) and asks what will come of him. Jesus gently tells him it's none of his business and repeats His earlier command, "You follow me."

Peter needed to take a lesson from Ezra, who "set his heart" to study, do, and teach the Law of God. Ezra focused on what God had given him to do and would not be distracted from it. Peter did indeed learn this lesson as we can tell from accounts of his later life in the New Testament about his service for Christ in the gospel.

Think about It

How about you? Have you set your heart to study, do, and teach God's word? Are you single-mindedly following Christ? We can all improve in this. But the Lord who was gracious, merciful, and patient with the Apostle Peter is the same toward us who struggle to be faithful to Him. Pray that you will be undistracted in your devotion to the Lord and His word.

To the End of the Earth

Today's Reading: Ezra 9-10; Acts 1

Selected Verses

While Ezra prayed and made confession, weeping and casting himself down before the house of God, a very great assembly of men, women, and children, gathered to him out of Israel, for the people wept bitterly. And Shecaniah the son of Jehiel, of the sons of Elam, addressed Ezra: "We have broken faith with our God and have married foreign women from the peoples of the land, but even now there is hope for Israel in spite of this."

Ezra 10:1-2

But you will receive power when the Holy Spirit has come upon you, and you will be my witnesses in Jerusalem and in all Judea and Samaria, and to the end of the earth.

Acts 1:8

Reflections

God promised in His covenant with Abraham that in him all the families of the earth would be blessed (Gen. 12:3). Meanwhile, God told His people entering the Promised Land to destroy the heathen nations and not to intermarry with them. Whenever they disregarded this command, they suffered for it and brought problems on the nation. Yet there were clear exceptions where foreigners joined themselves to Israel and worshiped Yahweh. Some examples are: Tamar, Rahab, and Ruth, all who entered into the royal lineage of David and Jesus Christ. The arrogant disregard for God's law appalled Ezra as he witnessed those marriages. The kingdom had just experienced severe judgment, being ejected from their land and taken captive, in part, for their mixing in marriage and in worship with unbelievers.

Yet it was always God's plan to save people from all the nations. Jesus announced the imminent coming of the Holy Spirit to His Apostles. They would receive power and they would be His witnesses in Jerusalem, Judea, Samaria, and to the end of the earth. Their mission would not be fruitless. The result? The Church exploded throughout the entire known world within a few generations.

Think about It

God calls the Church is to be holy and evangelistic. Naturally, this creates tension as we seek to live and witness among lost people without adopting their beliefs and sinful lifestyles. Rely on the Holy Spirit, not your own power, and be a witness to Jesus. He is the only hope of the world. In Him all the families to the end of the earth will be blessed as they hear the gospel and believe in Jesus Christ.

Today's Reading: Nehemiah 1-3; Acts 2:1-13

Selected Verses

> *O Lord, let your ear be attentive to the prayer of your servant, and to the*
> *prayer of your servants who delight to fear your name, and give success*
> *to your servant today, and grant him mercy in the sight of this man."*

Neh. 1:11

> *And at this sound the multitude came together, and they were bewildered,*
> *because each one was hearing them speak in his own language. And they were*
> *amazed and astonished, saying, "Are not all these who are speaking Galileans?"*

Acts 2:6-7

Reflections

News of the ruined walls of his beloved Jerusalem devastated Nehemiah. True, Cyrus had ordered the rebuilding of the temple. Exiles had been allowed to return to do that work. Now, decades later, Nehemiah learns that the city is defenseless. He goes to God in prayer, a prayer that reveals his deep knowledge of the Lord. Nehemiah mentions a fascinating characteristic of God's servants that they delight to fear His name.

When the Holy Spirit comes upon the disciples gathered together on the day of Pentecost, suddenly they begin to preach to the crowds in various languages. And the people are able to understand them perfectly. God was manifesting Himself at that time and place through His apostles. The work of God, so dramatically revealed, stirred up all kinds of emotions in these devout men: bewilderment, amazement, astonishment, and perplexity.

Think about It

Do you think of a committed Christian as one who is cold and stoic? We see in Scripture that believers most certainly feel deeply the power and presence of God. Do you think of fear as being antithetical to delight? "How can someone delight to fear God's name?" you may ask. Yet the knowledge of Almighty God brings a proper fear and awe to the heart of the believer that is joyful. The fear comes because we know Him to be Almighty, but that knowledge is also accompanied by joy in knowing that He can and will fulfill His Word and keep us safe until He gets us home to glory. Fear God. Delight in the fear of Him. Be amazed. Enjoy emotional engagement with God. Just don't be cold.

Generosity and Contentment:
How We Know We're Saved

Today's Reading: Nehemiah 4-6; Acts 2:14-47

Selected Verses

*Then they said, "We will restore these and require nothing from them. We will do as you say."
And I called the priests and made them swear to do as they had promised. I also shook out the
fold of my garment and said, "So may God shake out every man from his house and from his
labor who does not keep this promise. So may he be shaken out and emptied." And all the
assembly said "Amen" and praised the Lord. And the people did as they had promised.*

Neh. 5:12-13

*And all who believed were together and had all things in common. And they were selling
their possessions and belongings and distributing the proceeds to all, as any had need.*

Acts 2:44-45

Reflections

The Reformation restored focus on justification by faith alone—faith that
expresses itself in good works and good attitudes. In today's reading we have
examples from Nehemiah's day and from the times of the early Church.

The Jews had suffered greatly through the captivity. When the exiles returned
to Judah, some were destitute. Others had managed to accumulate some wealth.
The poor had to sell their children into slavery to other Jews just to pay their taxes.

When Nehemiah learned about this he was furious. He called the people
together and immediately rebuked those who had engaged in this abusive
practice. The response was good because the loan sharks recognized that they had
violated God's law and they stood in fear of Him. Nehemiah's bold and swift
leadership averted the crisis. The wall building resumed amidst joy and unity.

In the early Church, members differed widely in their material wealth. Yet
the power of the gospel and presence of the Holy Spirit so moved them that they
voluntarily looked out for one another. There seemed to be no need to exhort
them to share with one another, at least not at this point.

Think about It

John Calvin wrote that we are saved by faith alone, but the faith that saves is
never alone, i.e. it is accompanied by good works like generosity and good
attitudes, like contentment. Does your use of material resources reflect trust in
God and love for others? Are you generous with what you have? If you have less
than others, do you resent your lack or are you content with food and clothing (1
Tim. 6:6-10)? Flee from the love of money. Be as generous as you are able. Learn
contentment. Saving faith bears fruit in generosity and contentment.

The Importance of Expository Preaching

Today's Reading: Nehemiah 7-8; Acts 3

Selected Verses

They read from the book, from the Law of God, clearly, and they gave the sense, so that the people understood the reading.

Neh. 8:8

But what God foretold by the mouth of all the prophets, that his Christ would suffer, he thus fulfilled. Repent therefore, and turn back, that your sins may be blotted out, that times of refreshing may come from the presence of the Lord, and that he may send the Christ appointed for you, Jesus, whom heaven must receive until the time for restoring all the things about which God spoke by the mouth of his holy prophets long ago.

Acts 3:18-21

Reflections

In both Old and New Testaments, the importance of clear preaching is demonstrated. Expository preaching includes both the reading of Scripture and the explanation of the meaning of it.

In Nehemiah's day there had been a lack of reading and teaching the Scriptures. When the people heard the Word, they were grieved by what they heard and understood. They wept. It was natural that they should feel the weight of their failure and sin, but then the preacher (whether Ezra or Nehemiah, is not clear) exhorts them, "Go your way. Eat the fat and drink sweet wine and send portions to anyone who has nothing ready, for this day is holy to our Lord. And do not be grieved, for the joy of the Lord is your strength" (8:10).

In Acts, another preacher stands proclaiming God's Word, also in Jerusalem but centuries after Ezra and Nehemiah's day. Peter takes the opportunity, afforded by the crowd attracted by the healing of a lame man, to proclaim the good news of the risen Christ. The bad news precedes the good news, they have killed the Author of life, Jesus, but Peter tells them they may repent, turn back, and have their sins blotted out. God will hear their prayer and send times of refreshing from His presence. Then they may wait expectantly for Christ, who promised to come back for His people.

Think about It

The gospel teaches us of our sin, but it doesn't end there. It takes us to the mercy and grace of God who saves His repentant people, restores us to Himself, and gives us joy. Are you both grieved by your sin and relieved by God's joy? Good expository preaching is a means of grace that takes us to both repentant grieving and unspeakable joy. Be sure you hear God's word from faithful expository preachers.

God or Government? Choosing Whom to Obey

Today's Reading: Nehemiah 9-11; Acts 4:1-22

Selected Verses

Behold, we are slaves this day; in the land that you gave to our fathers to enjoy its fruit and its good gifts, behold, we are slaves. And its rich yield goes to the kings whom you have set over us because of our sins. They rule over our bodies and over our livestock as they please, and we are in great distress.

Neh. 9:36-37

But Peter and John answered them, "Whether it is right in the sight of God to listen to you rather than to God, you must judge, for we cannot but speak of what we have seen and heard." And when they had further threatened them, they let them go, finding no way to punish them, because of the people, for all were praising God for what had happened.

Acts 4:19-21

Reflections

Nehemiah, the governor of Judah under King Artaxerxes, gives an eloquent analysis of the history of Israel from Abraham to the return from captivity. He sees how God has been gracious and good to them giving commands that, if obeyed, would bring them prosperity and security. Even after repeated episodes of rebellion, God showed mercy to them. Nehemiah reflects on their status in his day and sees that the people, although living back in Judah, are virtual slaves in their own land. They are not free to enjoy the fruit of their labor. They are controlled by a foreign power due to their disobedience. He calls the people back to faithful worship of the Lord and they make a covenant to respect the law. This is a wonderful example of a political leader proclaiming spiritual truth and actually facilitating the population's obedience to God.

Fast forward to the time of Peter and John who in Jesus' name heal a lame man in the temple. They face opposition from the authorities who prohibit their preaching in the Savior's name. Peter says that they will obey God. Peter understands that the chief priests are under God's authority and they will suffer if they prohibit what God commands or command what God prohibits.

Think about It

Are you aware that the powers of governments are granted by God? Officials must answer to Him as we all must. Are you ready to obey God rather than be complicit in disobedience if it comes to that? Be prepared with knowledge of His Word and trust in Him. God can give us wise leaders who fear Him, like Nehemiah. But, if He doesn't, we will obey God rather than man.

Praying to a Big God for Big Things

Today's Reading: Nehemiah 12-13; Acts 4:23-37

Selected Verses

Remember this also in my favor, O my God, and spare
me according to the greatness of your steadfast love.

Neh. 13:22

When they were released, they went to their friends and reported what
the chief priests and the elders had said to them. And when they heard it,
they lifted their voices together to God and said, "Sovereign Lord, who
made the heaven and the earth and the sea and everything in them."

Acts 4:23-24

Reflections

A notable feature of the book of Nehemiah is his prayer life. On a number of occasions, he asks God to "remember him" (Neh. 5:19; 13:14, 22, 31). It appears that Nehemiah is comfortable turning to God in the midst of his writing. He shows recognition of God's holiness and his own need for forgiveness despite his many works of obedience. At times, it seems like he is offering his works as a basis for his acceptance before God, but we should probably not judge him too severely if he did not grasp as fully as we can the grace of God through the atonement for sin made by the Lord Jesus Christ. Certainly, in the verse quoted above, he shows an awareness of and dependence on the love of God.

In Acts, Peter and John have been released from arrest by the chief priests after being warned not to preach in the name of Christ. What do they do? They look for their friends, their fellow believers, they make a report as to what had occurred, and then they begin to pray. How do they address God? They address Him as the "Sovereign Lord, who made the heaven and the earth and the sea and everything in them." But notice what they do not request. Do they ask for safety? No! Nor do they pray for the destruction of their enemies. They pray for boldness to keep speaking God's Word. And God hears their prayer, fills them with His Holy Spirit, and gives them continued boldness.

Think about It

What can you learn from the examples of prayer in the lives of Nehemiah, Peter, and John? Be sure you remember who God is and what He wants of us. Pray to a big God. Pray for big things—things that you know He wants. After all, He is the Sovereign Lord, who made the heaven and the earth and the sea and everything in them, isn't He?

The Faithful Church Impacts Culture

Today's Reading: Esther 1-3; Acts 5:1-16

Selected Verses

The couriers went out hurriedly by order of the king, and the decree was issued in Susa the citadel. And the king and Haman sat down to drink, but the city of Susa was thrown into confusion.

Esther 3:15

And great fear came upon the whole church and upon all who heard of these things. Now many signs and wonders were regularly done among the people by the hands of the apostles. And they were all together in Solomon's Portico. None of the rest dared join them, but the people held them in high esteem.

Acts 5:11-13

Reflections

Through fascinating circumstances, Esther, a Jew in captivity, becomes the queen of the Persian king. About this time, a pompous man named Haman becomes second to the king. Mordecai, Esther's cousin and guardian, causes proud Haman to become infuriated by his refusal to show him homage. Haman, learning that Mordecai is a Jew but unaware of his relationship to Queen Esther, decides to use his newly acquired power to exterminate, not only Mordecai but, all the Jews in the empire. With the decision announced, the king and Haman relax with a cool drink while the capital city turns chaotic. Tomorrow we will learn how the faithful believer Mordecai fared.

In Acts, the early church was alive with passion for the gospel and with love for its members. Enter two hypocrites, Ananias and Sapphira, who pretend to give all their wealth to the apostles. Their truth comes out and they die for their lie. The news spread and fear gripped everyone both inside and outside of the church. The word was out: don't trifle with these Christians! No one dared to join them, but, on the other hand, "The people held them in high esteem. And more than ever believers were added to the Lord, multitudes of both men and women" (vs. 13-14). No one joined them unless they truly believed. Who would enter a group where you might die if you were a phony?

Think about It

Do you, like me, long for a revival in the Church of Jesus Christ, where the level of commitment to God and His people is such that hypocrisy would melt away? If we are steadfast, like Mordecai, we may yet see that. Be ready. The obedient church wins. Ananias loses. The faithful church impacts culture. God is glorified.

Obedience by Faith

Today's Reading: Esther 4-6; Acts 5:17-42

Selected Verses

Then I will go to the king, though it is against the law, and if I perish, I perish.

Esther 4:16

But the high priest rose up, and all who were with him (that is, the party
of the Sadducees), and filled with jealousy they arrested the apostles and
put them in the public prison. But during the night an angel of the
Lord opened the prison doors and brought them out, and said, "Go and
stand in the temple and speak to the people all the words of this Life."

Acts 5:17-20

Reflections

Obedience to God must be by faith, because it does not always bring pleasant results immediately and, sometimes, it can even cost you your life. Yet for the Christian, his obedience always has a positive outcome because even loss of life brings him into the glorious presence of God.

Esther was queen, but she and all the Jews were under a death sentence because of Haman's instigation of the king's decree. Mordecai challenged her to go to the king and plead for a reprieve from the law. After some back and forth, Esther agreed, knowing that, if the king did not hold out the golden scepter to her, she would be executed. She uttered her famous words, "if I perish, I perish."

Of course, in her case the king received her and heard her plea. She did not have to wait long for the reward of her obedience.

The apostles continued to preach the gospel of the risen Christ, and the high priest and the Sadducees had them thrown back into prison. This time the angel of the Lord opened the door of the prison and sent the apostles back to the temple to preach. The officials looked like fools when they sent to the prison and could not find them. Finally, a report came in that they were preaching in the temple again. At their hearing they maintained that they "must obey God rather than men."

Think about It

There really is no downside to obedience by faith to God for even if we perish, we win the victor's crown (2 Tim. 4:6-8). Be ready to obey by faith today, no matter what the outcome. If you are persecuted for your obedience, you may go straight to glory. But, if not, you will be able to rejoice "that you were counted worthy to suffer dishonor for the name."

June 23 / Day 174
Nobodies Made Famous by God

Today's Reading: Esther 7-10; Acts 6

Selected Verses

And the king took off his signet ring, which he had taken from Haman, and gave it to Mordecai. And Esther set Mordecai over the house of Haman.

Esther 8:2

And the twelve summoned the full number of the disciples and said, "It is not right that we should give up preaching the word of God to serve tables. Therefore, brothers, pick out from among you seven men of good repute, full of the Spirit and of wisdom, whom we will appoint to this duty."

Acts 6:2-3

Reflections

Mordecai is an example of a man who was faithful in the small things. He stepped up when his uncle and aunt died leaving a young daughter, Esther, becoming her guardian and raising her. He reported a plot against the emperor, Ahasuerus, which may have saved him from assassination. Mordecai played a key role in saving the Jews from extermination throughout the Persian Empire when he urged Queen Esther to appeal to the king for relief. He took all of these actions without holding any power or position. He just did the right thing when he had opportunity. Yes, he was eventually recognized. His enemy was hanged on the gallows meant for Mordecai, and he took over that villain's property and authority. All this was by God's providence.

The apostles assigned Stephen to a group of seven servants whose task was to serve tables and wait on the widows of the Hellenists. God had an even bigger role for Stephen. He filled him with grace to do great wonders and signs and to be an invincible debater for the gospel (Acts 6:8-10). He was faithful in the position he had, and God allowed him to rise to greater prominence and effectiveness.

Think about It

In my college days at home basketball games, our student body would taunt the players of opposing teams as they were introduced. After the announcer gave a name, one side of the coliseum would shout, "Who's he?" and the other side would respond, "Nobody!" Mordecai was nobody. Stephen was nobody. Yet God used them mightily for His purposes in the plan of redemption. He still does this. Be faithful where you are, even though you may be considered nobody. You do not need a high profile position to do the work He has for you.

193

Everyone's a Theologian

Today's Reading: Job 1-3; Acts 7:1-19

Selected Verses

Then his wife said to him, "Do you still hold fast your integrity? Curse God and die."
But he said to her, "You speak as one of the foolish women would speak. Shall we receive
good from God, and shall we not receive evil?" In all this Job did not sin with his lips.

Job 2:9-10

And the high priest said, "Are these things so?" And Stephen said:
"Brothers and fathers, hear me. The God of glory appeared to our father
Abraham when he was in Mesopotamia, before he lived in Haran.

Acts 7:1,2

Reflections

Job was an upright man. In every way, his life was exemplary. He was chosen by God for a special task, although he did not consent to it nor did he know what it was. He suffered every imaginable loss: his wealth, his children, and his health. Even his wife urged him to "curse God and die." But he would not. He clung to his belief that God had given him good things and it was only right to accept "evil" from Him. Job was not in denial as we see throughout the book, and he certainly lamented his situation. He wished he had never been born. But he never sinned with his lips. He knew God and determined to keep trusting Him even when his pain-wracked life made no sense.

Stephen spoke so powerfully about Christ that the authorities concocted a plan to eliminate him through a mock trial with false witnesses. They charged that he blasphemed Moses and God and that he stated that Jesus would destroy the temple and change the customs of the Mosaic law. At his trial Stephen gave a brilliant and God-honoring review of the history of Israel. Clearly he understood how God is the One working in the world and showing grace, mercy, and power to His people. Here he had common ground with the Jews, so they listened. Stephen was no blasphemer. He told the story of the great Jehovah who guided Israel and still wisely and sovereignly works to bring about His purposes.

Think about It

What does your speech say about your theology? Does it reveal an awareness of the presence and power of God in both your personal life as well as the world around you? Rewind today's tape. What would your hearers say is your view of God? Be a good theologian, and honor God in your speech.

The Danger of Forsaking
the Fear of the Almighty

Today's Reading: Job 4-6; Acts 7:20-43

Selected Verses

He who withholds kindness from a friend forsakes the fear of the Almighty.

Job 6:14

This is the Moses who said to the Israelites, "God will raise up for you a prophet like me from your brothers."

Acts 7:37

Reflections

Job's friends sat quietly with him. They listened when he finally broke his silence. Then Eliphaz spoke. He lectured about God's discipline of His children assuming that Job deserved to be corrected. He missed the truth and failed to comfort his suffering friend. Job responded with continued lament for his condition but then complained about the lack of support from his friends. He considered that Eliphaz had withheld kindness from a friend.

How can anyone cold-heartedly turn his back on a loved one in his moment of extreme anguish? Why wouldn't common decency make a person feel sympathy towards even a complete stranger in dire straits? Job says these attitudes are proof of having forsaken the fear of the Almighty. It takes extreme arrogance to think that the Omnipotent God of Creation and Providence could never bring him to the same condition. One has to be overly self-assured and proud to feel immune from God's powerful hand.

The authorities that examined Stephen in Acts 7 seem to have a similar problem. They accuse him falsely and demand an explanation, but they are about to get more than they bargained for. Stephen is giving them a summary of the history of Israel, tracing the theme of their rebellion against Moses, God's chosen leader. Moses, whom they accuse Stephen of blaspheming, foretold that a prophet like himself would be sent to them. But these leaders continue the policies of their forefathers, rejecting the ones whom God sends to deliver them. They, like Eliphaz, have forsaken the fear of God.

Think about It

What part does the fear of God play in your life? Does fear of God drive you to confession of sin, of eager obedience, and of love for others? Fear of God is not an outdated, Old Testament concept, but is part of the mindset that has been renewed by God. Peter wrote, "Live as people who are free, not using your freedom as a cover-up for evil, but living as servants of God. Honor everyone. Love the brotherhood. Fear God. Honor the emperor." (1 Peter 2:16-17). Practice those things and never forsake the fear of the Almighty.

Wanted: Celestial Mediator

Today's Reading: Job 7-9; Acts 7:44-60

Selected Verses

Then Job answered and said: "Truly I know that it is so: But how can a man be in the right before God? If one wished to contend with him, one could not answer him once in a thousand times."

Job 9:1-3

Which of the prophets did your fathers not persecute? And they killed those who announced beforehand the coming of the Righteous One, whom you have now betrayed and murdered, you who received the law as delivered by angels and did not keep it.

Acts 7:52-53

Reflections

Job struggles with the reason for his suffering while his would-be comforters heap accusations on him in an effort to explain the frowning providence of God in his life. Job does not claim to be perfect, but he does not understand how his suffering is punishment that fits the crime. He recognizes that a man cannot be right before God on his own terms. But destitution, poverty, bereavement, and relentless pain seems over the top. "There is no arbiter between us, who might lay his hand on us both," moans Job (9:33). So here God is showing us through Job that there must be a mediator between God and man in order for reconciliation to take place. That can only be God Himself, His Son, the Lord Jesus Christ, God Incarnate.

As Stephen closes his defense, which could also be called a sermon, he indicts the Jewish authorities for their killing of that Mediator. They have continued in the footsteps of their forebears, resisting the Holy Spirit, persecuting the prophets, and, now, executing the Righteous One, the arbiter that Job longed for. They prove Stephen's point by immediately stoning him to death.

Think about It

Two men, Stephen and Job, suffer for their faith. One is delivered by death almost immediately and the other is made to stagger on in suffering a while longer before experiencing relief.

God has different paths for each of His children to trod, but in the end, those who are His trust Him, do not justify themselves but seek the Arbiter whom the Lord has appointed, Jesus, the Righteous One, who alone can mediate between God and man (1 Tim. 2:5; Acts 4:12). Walk on trusting Him, my fellow disciple.

When Believers Suffer

Today's Reading: Job 10-12; Acts 8:1-25

Selected Verses

I will say to God, Do not condemn me; let me know why you contend against me.

Job 10:2

Now those who were scattered went about preaching the word. Philip went down to the city of Samaria and proclaimed to them the Christ. So there was much joy in that city.

Acts 8:4, 5, 8

Reflections

To Job, his suffering seemed like condemnation from God. It felt like God was punishing him and he wondered why. His assumption was wrong. God was not punishing him, so the question why could not be answered by some failure in Job. He was truly left in the dark for quite some time. His friends did not help with their comments and mixed-up analyses. Some of what they said was true, but they certainly had less insight into what God was doing than even Job.

Job says some wise things in the midst of his pain. For example, "In the thought of one who is at ease there is contempt for misfortune; it is ready for those whose feet slip." (12:5) In other words, suffering is ready to pounce on you when you slip, but those who have no suffering look with disdain on those who do. We are truly sustained by God's mercy and grace. Our heart beats and our lungs breathe at His will.

Some who suffer for their faith get a glimpse of why it is. The disciples were scattered from Jerusalem due to the severe persecution that began with the stoning of Stephen. They naturally told the good news of Christ and the hope of the resurrection wherever they went. Philip, one of the seven men chosen with Stephen to wait on tables, saw powerful results from his preaching in Samaria so "there was much joy in that city." Ask one of those Samaritans why they thought God allowed a persecution against the believers in Jerusalem. You would probably get an enthusiastic answer to the effect that the persecution brought them the gospel and life eternal.

Think about It

God is free to do with us what He will. He is also free to reveal His reasons or not. He calls us to walk by faith, even in the dark. But He has promised to never leave us or forsake us (Heb. 13:5-6). Walk on in pain, if that is your lot today. He had a purpose for Job and the disciples in Jerusalem. He knows what He is doing with you, too.

God's Ambassadors

Today's Reading: Job 13-15; Acts 8:26-40

Selected Verses

You would call, and I would answer you;
  you would long for the work of your hands.
For then you would number my steps;
  you would not keep watch over my sin;
my transgression would be sealed up in a bag,
  and you would cover over my iniquity.

Job 14:15-17

Then Philip opened his mouth, and beginning with
this Scripture he told him the good news about Jesus.

Acts 8:35

Reflections

Scholars believe that Job lived about the same time as Abraham. Before his call from God, Abraham was a polytheist (believing in many gods). Job on the other hand, seems to grasp a theology of a single sovereign and holy God. But Job has no clear understanding of the resurrection or of life after death. Yet Job does show a longing for reconciliation with God through some kind of covering for his sin. He seems to have an inkling of hope of a resurrection, perhaps like a tree that is cut down but grows back up from its roots (14:7-17). It's just not very clear. He longs to know more and, soon, God will tell him more.

In the period following the stoning of Stephen and the subsequent persecution, God sends Philip to speak with an Ethiopian eunuch, the queen's treasurer, who had been in Jerusalem to worship. Philip is able to explain to him the meaning of Isaiah's writing and the good news about Jesus Christ. This results in the official's baptism. In these touching words, Luke records that the eunuch, after this one-on-one Bible study with Philip, "went on his way rejoicing." We can only imagine the impact of this man's testimony before the court officials of Ethiopia.

Think about It

God knows the hearts of those who seek Him, Job, the Ethiopian, and everyone else. He may directly intervene, as He will do with Job later on in our reading, or He may send someone to explain the gospel as He did in the case of Philip and the queen's treasurer. Did He send someone to you? Has He sent you to be a light to someone else? Give thanks for His providence in sending those who can help us understand His truth and in sending us to pass on the good news of Jesus. If you belong to Christ, God has appointed you His ambassador because the gospel goes out powerfully by word of mouth (2 Cor. 5:11-21).

Surprise! Role Reversals from God

Today's Reading: Job 16-18; Acts 9:1-22

Selected Verses

I also could speak as you do, if you were in my place; I could join words together against you and shake my head at you. I could strengthen you with my mouth, and the solace of my lips would assuage your pain.

Job 16:4-5

But Ananias answered, "Lord, I have heard from many about this man, how much evil he has done to your saints at Jerusalem. And here he has authority from the chief priests to bind all who call on your name." But the Lord said to him, "Go, for he is a chosen instrument of mine to carry my name before the Gentiles and kings and the children of Israel. For I will show him how much he must suffer for the sake of my name."

Acts 9:13-16

Reflections

Job is weary of his trials which have only been increased by the harsh and hurtful criticisms of his friends. For a moment he imagines switching places with them. He says essentially that if he were in their shoes he could either be critical (as they have been) or he could use his words to strengthen and comfort them. It seems Job is claiming that if given the chance he would not do what they do, but seek to be encouraging to them. Later in Job's story, we will learn that he does switch places with his friends and he has the opportunity to bless them.

Saul, who supported the stoning of Stephen and helped launch the persecution against the Church, had obtained arrest warrants for the believers in Damascus. On his way to bind others, he himself is stopped and bound in blindness by Jesus Christ. Saul changes immediately and follows the instructions the Lord has given him. Ananias in Damascus seems to know that Saul is coming to arrest them, but God tells him to look up Saul at a certain address and lay hands on him so that he may regain his sight. Ananias is understandably nervous and hesitant. But the Lord assures him that Saul is His chosen instrument to carry His name before the Gentiles, kings, and Israel. Ironically, the man who was going to lay hands on Ananias to arrest him, had Ananias' hands laid on him. What a reversal of roles that was!

Think about It

God's Providence may have peculiar turns, but all is under His wise and sovereign will. You may get a surprise so be ready to trust and glorify God no matter how unexpected and bizarre those role reversals seem to be.

Strength for Today; Hope for Tomorrow

Today's Reading: Job 19-20; Acts 9:23-43

Selected Verses

For I know that my Redeemer lives,
and at the last he will stand upon the earth.
And after my skin has been thus destroyed,
yet in my flesh I shall see God,
whom I shall see for myself,
and my eyes shall behold, and not another.
My heart faints within me!

Job 19:25-27

So the church throughout all Judea and Galilee and Samaria
had peace and was being built up. And walking in the fear of
the Lord and in the comfort of the Holy Spirit, it multiplied.

Acts 9:31

Reflections

Job continues his complaint against God in vivid terms. He has been abandoned by everyone he knows. But suddenly he seems to recall that he has a Redeemer, One who will save him. That Redeemer is alive and will reveal Himself after Job has finally died. God has stripped poor Job of every comfort and dignity of this life, but there will come a meeting. Job will see his Redeemer.

The church had been devastated with persecution, but God had turned it to good by sending out His people to proclaim the good news of Jesus throughout the nearby nations. Saul went after them but found Jesus himself. He then became a preacher of the gospel he had been seeking to silence. He had to flee for his life from his former allies. Meanwhile a measure of peace came to the church in Judea, Galilee, and Samaria. The church grew spiritually and numerically. The disciples were "walking in the fear of the Lord and in the comfort of the Holy Spirit."

Think about It

No matter what your situation today, seek to walk in the fear of the Lord and the comfort of the Holy Spirit. If you are suffering, like Job, remember that your Redeemer is alive. He awaits you when this life is over. As the old hymn goes,

Strength for today and bright hope for tomorrow,
Blessings all mine, with ten thousand beside!

(from "Great is Thy Faithfulness" by T.O.Chisholm 1866-1960)

The Christian and Personal Piety

Today's Reading: Job 21-22; Acts 10:1-23

Selected Verses

They say to God, "Depart from us! We do not desire the knowledge of your ways. What is the Almighty, that we should serve him? And what profit do we get if we pray to him?"

Job 21:14-15

At Caesarea there was a man named Cornelius, a centurion of what was known as the Italian Cohort, a devout man who feared God with all his household, gave alms generously to the people, and prayed continually to God.

Acts 10:1-2

Reflections

Job describes the wicked who prosper as those who tell God to "get lost," have no passion to know Him or His ways, and won't serve God or pray to Him. Instead they ask, "What's in it for me?" If we want to know what the godly man or woman looks like, we can just reverse these descriptions. The godly seek God's presence. They draw near to God and find that He draws near to them (James 4:8). They want to know Him and His ways. God's people serve Him and pray to Him without hesitation and know that it is a privilege to serve Him and pray to Him. Nothing else is needed or desired but to know Him.

Cornelius, a Roman military officer, would seem to be an unlikely candidate for the roll call of faith. Not so. He was "a devout man who feared God with all his household, gave alms generously to the people, and prayed continually to God." Undoubtedly, his understanding of the gospel of Jesus Christ was lacking, but God saw his heart and sent Peter to him to proclaim the good news. Cornelius was not saved by his piety, but it did show his passion to know the Lord and God heard him. He led his family toward the Lord and had a soldier who was devout (Acts 10:7). It would seem that Cornelius' fear of the Lord impacted his personal life, his family, and his professional life. By the way, we see included here the virtue of the fear of God, a quality notably lacking among people today.

Think about It

How do you view your devotional life? Is it a joy? Do you anticipate being in the Lord's presence? Is prayer merely for personal benefit or is it communion with your Savior? Is reverent fear of God a characteristic you seek to develop? Think about it. Make attitude adjustments as needed.

Two Truths in Focus

Today's Reading: Job 23-25; Acts 10:24-48

Selected Verses

How then can man be in the right before God?
How can he who is born of woman be pure?

Job 25:4

And he commanded us to preach to the people and to testify that he is the one appointed
by God to be judge of the living and the dead. To him all the prophets bear witness
that everyone who believes in him receives forgiveness of sins through his name.

Acts 10:42-43

Reflections

Bildad sees some things very clearly. God is holy, and man is sinful. But he misses the mercy and grace of God, so he asks, "How then can man be in the right before God?" This pessimistic view is not common in western society today. We are apt to hear more words extolling the greatness of humankind. "How enlightened we are! How noble are our works! God? Who's that?" We pray to whomever, but only in times of extreme desperation. Then we revert to faith in ourselves and "confidence in confidence alone," as Julie Andrews sang in "The Sound of Music." (Although to be fair, I suspect that the real Maria Von Trapp would have sung "I have confidence in God.")

Peter's message to Cornelius and his company shows this accurate understanding of the holiness of God and the promise of forgiveness through faith in Christ. Cornelius had been a devout man, but devout men are depraved like all others, corrupted by sin in every part. He sought God and God provided for the centurion to hear the gospel from Peter himself. Not only that, but God sent His Holy Spirit on that group as they listened to the Apostle. Peter was getting the picture. God had sent him to preach to Gentiles. They believed. God sent the Holy Spirit upon them, and Peter immediately baptized them. The Gentiles were being saved. Jesus did die for the world.

Think about It

An accurate understanding of the gospel will keep in focus both the holiness of God that will result in Jesus' judging the living and the dead, and the grace of God which manifests itself in Christ's redemption of all who believe in Him.

Be sure you keep a clear vision of the holiness of God and the grace of God. By so doing, you will not lose sight of both the need of humanity and the power of the gospel for salvation to everyone who believes, to the Jew and to the Gentile. Remember: Jesus is both Judge and Redeemer.

Can We Have a Barnabas or Two?

Today's Reading: Job 26-28; Acts 11

Selected Verses

> *Then Job answered and said:*
> *"How you have helped him who has no power!*
> *"How you have saved the arm that has no strength!*
> *"How you have counseled him who has no wisdom,*
> *and plentifully declared sound knowledge!"*

Job 26:1-3

They sent Barnabas to Antioch. When he came and saw the grace of God, he was glad, and he exhorted them all to remain faithful to the Lord with steadfast purpose, for he was a good man, full of the Holy Spirit and of faith. And a great many people were added to the Lord.

Acts 11:22-24

Reflections

Job complains again about the ineffectiveness of his friends' counsel and advice in the face of his great and obvious need. He has no power or strength and no answers as to why he is suffering. He needs to hear truth, but they accuse him and ply simplistic views based on "recrimination theology" that God judges without mercy and grace giving to each his just desserts, no more, no less. Wisdom is a treasure not found in this conversation. He ends today's reading with the observation, " Behold, the fear of the Lord, that is wisdom, and to turn away from evil is understanding" (28:28).

Barnabas goes to Antioch to check out a report that Hellenists (Greek-speaking, uncircumcised Gentiles) were being converted. They had heard and believed the gospel from the refugees who had been scattered by the persecution. In contrast to Job's friends, Barnabas, full of the Holy Spirit, exhorts and encourages them "to remain faithful to the Lord with steadfast purpose." As a result, "a great many people were added to the Lord." Despite Peter's testimony to God's work among the gentiles, the church is in uncharted territory with this spiritual awakening among non-Jews. They want to understand how God is at work in new ways. Barnabas is a man who had shown, by his openness to the converted Saul, that he is a good man full of the Holy Spirit and of faith. His mission to Antioch is eminently successful, blessing the church there and bringing glory to God.

Think about It

If we are to be used by God with our words, we need to be filled with the Holy Spirit and with faith. We need to be people who fear God, holding Him in awe and reverence. Pray that you will be a "Barnabas" for the world in which you live. Job needed one and so do we.

Glory Stealing Can Be Fatal

Today's Reading: Job 29-30; Acts 12

Selected Verses

> *I chose their way and sat as chief,*
> *and I lived like a king among his troops,*
> *like one who comforts mourners.*
> *But now they laugh at me,*
> *men who are younger than I,*
> *whose fathers I would have disdained*
> *to set with the dogs of my flock.*

Job 29:25-30:1

And the people were shouting, "The voice of a god, and not of a man!" Immediately an angel of the Lord struck him down, because he did not give God the glory, and he was eaten by worms and breathed his last. But the word of God increased and multiplied.

Acts 12:22-24

Reflections

Job remembered a time when he had been at the top of the food chain. Everyone was in awe of him. No one questioned his decisions. He had the final word. Now that has all gone. He is the laughingstock of his former kingdom. Now the people of low status look down on him.

King Herod played to the crowds but lacked any reverence for God. He found that executing James brought him popularity, so he arrested Peter. The Lord sent an angel to release Peter, but Herod just blamed the disappearance on the sentries and had them put to death. He left town for Caesarea. Meanwhile, the people of Tyre and Sidon sought reconciliation with Herod. His accepting their praise of him as a "god, and not a man" brought God's wrath and his immediate death.

The difference between Herod and Job is that the latter attributed his prosperity and success to God. His losses were, to him, evidence that God had withdrawn His favor from him. Job never stopped seeking God. Herod never began to seek God. Death was the last chapter in Herod's life. Suffering was only the mid-point of Job's life.

Jesus asked the disbelieving Jews, "How can you believe, when you receive glory from one another and do not seek the glory that comes from the only God?" (John 5:44). God spoke through the prophet Isaiah saying, "For my own sake, for my own sake, I do it, for how should my name be profaned? My glory I will not give to another" (Isaiah 48:11).

Think about It

Don't be clueless like the egotistical Herod or the faithless Jews who basked in the glory of man. Job knew that God was the source of all blessing, and he would learn that God's ways and wisdom may not be questioned. Walk humbly giving Him all the glory, because glory stealing can be fatal.

Holy Desires Amidst Trying Times

Today's Reading: Job 31-32; Acts 13:1-25

Selected Verses

For I was in terror of calamity from God,
and I could not have faced his majesty.

Job 31:23

Now Paul and his companions set sail from Paphos and came to
Perga in Pamphylia. And John left them and returned to Jerusalem,
but they went on from Perga and came to Antioch in Pisidia.

Acts 13:13-14

Reflections

Job recited his claims to a righteous life. He lists many sins but swears before God that he is innocent of them. What motivated him to live such an upright life? He was in awe of God. He thought of the majesty of God and what it would be like to be in His glorious presence. Job still has much to learn about God, but on this point he is right. God deserves all obedience and reverence.

When Saul (now Paul) and Barnabas were sent out by the Holy Spirit and the church in Antioch as missionaries they invited John, also called Mark or John Mark, to assist them. John saw how God had led in the decision to send these men out to preach. He had been on Cyprus when Paul confronted an evil magician named Elymas whom God had struck blind. John had been there when the proconsul, Sergius Paulus, had sought to hear the word of God and had been transformed by it. Despite all this, John quit the mission midway and went home to Jerusalem.

Why did he do this? We are not told, but certainly Paul and Barnabas must have known something about John's decision-making process. The two missionaries later disagreed so sharply about taking John on another missionary journey that they parted ways (Acts 15:37-39). John had failed them. Barnabas, known for compassion, wanted to restore John. Paul did not. John may have demonstrated a lack of fear of displeasing God or no passion to glorify Him. There was no doubt about his failure to follow through. The question was whether or not to give him a second chance.

Think about It

A desire to please God and a longing to glorify Him will keep us steady and faithful when our service for Him leads through times of trials. Job had it. John did not, although he would later show he matured over time (2 Tim. 4:11). You will not perform perfectly, but in the final analysis you will stand before God's majesty accepted, not for your performance, but for Christ's on your behalf.

God's Providence vs. Man's Autonomy

Today's Reading: Job 33-34; Acts 13:26-52

Selected Verses

Behold, God does all these things,
twice, three times, with a man,
to bring back his soul from the pit,
that he may be lighted with the light of life.

Job 33:29-30

And when the Gentiles heard this, they began rejoicing and glorifying the word
of the Lord, and as many as were appointed to eternal life believed. And the word
of the Lord was spreading throughout the whole region. But the Jews incited
the devout women of high standing and the leading men of the city, stirred up
persecution against Paul and Barnabas, and drove them out of their district.

Acts 13:48-50

Reflections

Elihu sets about correcting the faulty statements of Job and his three counselors. Elihu correctly emphasizes the justice of God in all His dealings and the way of God to use trials and difficulties to correct His children. This point has been mostly ignored by the three counselors with the exception of a brief comment by Eliphaz (Job 5:17).

In his account of the first missionary journey of Paul and Barnabas, Luke reports that "as many as were appointed to eternal life believed." Apostles proclaimed the gospel. Some believed. Why? God had appointed them to eternal life. Others rejected because they were not appointed for eternal life. The difference is not in the words of the preacher. It is in the response of the hearer. That is the result of the sovereign work of grace in the heart of the hearer.

Think about It

Personal autonomy is an idol of our times, maybe the greatest idol. The doctrines of the sovereignty and providence of God thunder against that false god. Do you believe in the Lord Almighty Who rules over all things, even the hearts of people? If so, that would be a likely indicator that He has appointed you for salvation. If not, you are still called to repent and believe the gospel, but you cannot and will not in yourself, without His powerful working in you to bring a new birth (Mark 1:15; John 3:3).

Does all this stir in you sense of desperation? Call on God to "be merciful" to you, a sinner (Luke 18:13). God has promised that He is "near to all who call upon Him, to all who call upon Him in truth" and "Everyone who calls on the name of the Lord will be saved" (Ps. 145:18; Rom. 10:13).

Stop and Consider

Today's Reading: Job 35-37; Acts 14

Selected Verses

> *Hear this, O Job;*
> *stop and consider the wondrous works of God.*
>
> Job 37:14

> *In past generations he allowed all the nations to walk in their own ways. Yet*
> *he did not leave himself without witness, for he did good by giving you rains*
> *from heaven and fruitful seasons, satisfying your hearts with food and gladness.*
>
> Acts 14:16-17

Reflections

God's glory is set forth in splendor in His creation. The Psalmist wrote, "The heavens declare the glory of God, and the sky above proclaims his handiwork. Day to day pours out speech, and night to night reveals knowledge" (Ps. 19:1-2). This is a truth as old as time and hard to ignore. Yet Paul wrote that the unrighteous suppress the obvious truth of God and exchange the truth for a lie (Rom. 1:18-25).

Elihu, in his monologue before Job, calls on him to "stop and consider the wondrous works of God." Elihu spoke truth displayed in the earliest event of biblical history: Creation. He may have lacked love and compassion for his suffering friend, but we cannot accuse him of a falsehood at this point.

Paul brings up a similar declaration in his speech to the crowd at Lystra. He credits God with all the blessings that they had experienced of rains and fruitful seasons, of food and gladness which brought satisfaction to their hearts. He starts where they are human beings, just like himself, who have received far more than they deserve.

Think about It

God's power and deity in the things He has made and the blessings He sends is clearly evident. Yet those who refuse to acknowledge Him as God are only angered or irritated by these reminders. Fallen mankind, apart from God, likes to think that he is the captain of his soul and the master of his fate. The claims of the Bible refute that view. But stop and consider that, "In Him we live and move and have our being" (Acts 17:28). If you believe, be sure your praises go to Him often. He is worthy of all our adoration, all day, every day. If you doubt this, stop and consider.

Silence before God

Today's Reading: Job 38-39; Acts 15:1-21

Selected Verses

> Then the Lord answered Job out of the whirlwind and said: "Who
> is this that darkens counsel by words without knowledge? Dress for
> action like a man; I will question you, and you make it known to me."

Job 38:1-3

> But we believe that we will be saved through the grace of the Lord Jesus, just as they
> will. And all the assembly fell silent, and they listened to Barnabas and Paul as they
> related what signs and wonders God had done through them among the Gentiles.

Acts 15:11-12

Reflections

Job and his friends have ranted on for thirty-five of the first thirty-seven chapters of the book. The complaining of Job did not relieve him nor vindicate him before his friends. His would-be counselors' opinions and lectures did not strike home to either help Job or indict him. At last God interrupts the futile discussion and answers Job out of the whirlwind as he seems unable to hear anything soft and gentle. God hurls questions at Job to show him his weakness and ignorance. He can only be silent for he has no answers. He is stilled before the Almighty Creator Who not only knows all things but has made all things.

God was also doing a great work in the days of the Apostles. Persecution sent the disciples everywhere proclaiming the gospel of the resurrected Christ. Even Gentiles heard and believed. Peter had seen this first. Paul and Barnabas were seeing amazing conversions of Gentiles, too.

What should have been great news, however, was disturbing to some of the Jewish believers in Jerusalem. They could accept Gentile believers but not uncircumcised Gentile believers. The apostles called a counsel to discuss the question and to determine their policy on how Gentile believers should be treated in light of the Law of Moses. Peter was helpful in clarifying the truth of the doctrine of salvation by grace alone for all who believe whether Jews or Gentiles. Paul and Barnabas' report of the work of God made all the assembly fall silent. Like Job, they learned to be quiet, to listen, to think, and to observe what God had done.

Think about It

As we saw yesterday, there is a time to "stop and consider." Stop the endless babble of personal opinion and pomposity. Consider what God has done in Creation and in Salvation. As the prophet wrote: "But the Lord is in his holy temple; let all the earth keep silence before him" ((Hab. 2:20).

God Uses People, Warts and All
Today's Reading: Job 40-42; Acts 15:22-41

Selected Verses

So Eliphaz the Temanite and Bildad the Shuhite and Zophar the Naamathite
went and did what the Lord had told them, and the Lord accepted Job's prayer.
And the Lord restored the fortunes of Job, when he had prayed for
his friends. And the Lord gave Job twice as much as he had before.

Job 42:9-10

Barnabas took Mark with him and sailed away to Cyprus, but Paul chose
Silas and departed, having been commended by the brothers to the grace of
the Lord. And he went through Syria and Cilicia, strengthening the churches.

Acts 15:39b-41

Reflections

The focus of the book of Job has been on his experience of tremendous affliction as evidence to Satan of how a redeemed man serves God whether he prospers or suffers. Job stood the test and we can all cheer at the end when God reveals Himself to that poor beleaguered man. God is vindicated by Job whose mouth is shut in humility. Job has been in our focus, but the three friends of Job were also under God's watchful eye. They were in line for some discipline. They had spoken foolishly and ignorantly. Job was exonerated, and they were rebuked. God told Eliphaz to make an offering for their sin and promised to hear Job's prayer on their behalf. Eliphaz obeyed and he, Zophar, and Bildad were restored to the Lord.

Paul and Barnabas left Jerusalem unified. They preached and taught the congregation in Antioch. Everything was going smoothly, but then they had a disagreement about taking John Mark on a second missionary journey. They split up going in different directions. How did they do? Both seemed to have fruitful ministries. Paul, we learn later, had a change of heart about John Mark (Col. 4:10; Philem. 24; 2 Tim. 4:11). Indeed, Peter later would refer to Mark as "his son" (1 Peter 5:13).

Think about It

God works through human instruments. He used Job, Paul, Barnabas, and Mark despite their imperfections. Others, named and unnamed, were blessed by their prayers, preaching, teaching and other service for God's glory. Can God use you? Yes, indeed. He uses all of His people for small and great purposes. Be alert to the service He has for you today.

Salvation Belongs to the LORD

Today's Reading: Psalms 1-3; Acts 16:1-15

Selected Verses

Salvation belongs to the Lord; your blessing be on your people!

Ps. 3:8

One who heard us was a woman named Lydia, from the city of Thyatira, a seller of purple goods, who was a worshiper of God. The Lord opened her heart to pay attention to what was said by Paul. And after she was baptized, and her household as well, she urged us, saying, "If you have judged me to be faithful to the Lord, come to my house and stay." And she prevailed upon us.

Acts 16:14-15

Reflections

The Psalmist was in dire straits. According to the title of Psalm 3, David wrote this during his exile from Jerusalem while his son, Absalom, briefly overthrew his father's kingdom. David turned to God in the crisis, recognizing that only the Lord could save him. "Salvation belongs to the LORD," he affirms. Absalom had skillfully won over the people of Israel to support him. David fled Jerusalem. But it seemed inevitable that David would be assassinated and Absalom would take firm control of the kingdom.

Yet, "salvation belongs to the LORD." David held to that truth, and, against all odds, Absalom listened to David's planted advisor, Hushai who purposely gave him bad advice. Absalom followed it, and died in the ensuing battle (2 Sam. 17-18). God saved David's life and kingdom. The odds set by probability cannot limit God.

Lydia was a worshiper of God, a Gentile woman who believed in the God of Israel and the moral law of Moses without adopting the dietary and ceremonial laws. Luke tells us that the Lord opened her heart to pay attention to what Paul said. Without the intervention of the Holy Spirit, neither a Lydia nor anyone else is able to hear and believe the gospel (Jer. 13:23; John 6:44, 65; Rom. 9:16; 1 Cor. 2:14; 2 Thessalonians 2:13-14; 2 Tim. 1:9-10). God saved Lydia spiritually.[4]

Think about It

God saves kings and Gentile women, like David and Lydia. How does the truth that "salvation belongs to the Lord" affect your prayer life and your daily confidence in Him? Can you lie down and sleep, knowing the Lord will sustain you? Trust Him when in danger for He saves. Proclaim the gospel to others knowing that God opens hearts as He wills and saves lost people.

---

[4] The Reformation Study Bible notes p. 1945

Midnight in a Roman Jail

Today's Reading: Psalms 4-6; Acts 16:16-40

Selected Verses

You have put more joy in my heart
than they have when their grain and wine abound.
In peace I will both lie down and sleep;
for you alone, O Lord, make me dwell in safety.

Ps. 4:7-8

About midnight Paul and Silas were praying and singing hymns to God, and the
prisoners were listening to them, and suddenly there was a great earthquake,
so that the foundations of the prison were shaken. And immediately
all the doors were opened, and everyone's bonds were unfastened.

Acts 16:25-26

Reflections

What do you do while you are held in stocks in a Roman jail at midnight? If you are Paul and Silas, you pray and sing hymns to God. Meanwhile, the other prisoners and, we may assume, the sentries and guards listen in. How can we account for such incongruous behavior? These Christian missionaries have what the Psalmist calls joy that the Lord has placed in their hearts. They have peace that allows them to trust God in a place that, for anyone else, could not be called safe. They pray and sing because that was what they normally did when they had time on their hands. Perhaps they were not comfortable enough to sleep, but they were peaceful and joyful enough to pray and sing.

God answered them in a dramatic way, with a great earthquake. The prison was rocked, the doors were opened, and everyone's bonds were unfastened. Who was running that place? The same One to Whom Paul and Silas prayed and sang. God is in control. He is always in control, at all times and in all places. He watches over His people down through the centuries, in David's time, in Paul's day, and right to us in this twenty-first century.

Think about It

Have you learned to have peace and joy no matter what adversity comes your way? Could you pray and sing in prison at midnight? Could you have joy when your grain and wine has run out? Can you lie down and sleep with an army encamped against you? David, Paul, and Silas could. Learn to trust in God, as they did.

The Importance of Seeking God

Today's Reading: Psalms 7-9; Acts 17:1-15

Selected Verses

The Lord is a stronghold for the oppressed,
A stronghold in times of trouble.
And those who know your name put their trust in you,
For you, O Lord, have not forsaken those who seek you.

Ps. 9:9-10

Now these Jews were more noble than those in Thessalonica; they received the word with all eagerness, examining the Scriptures daily to see if these things were so. Many of them therefore believed, with not a few Greek women of high standing as well as men.

Acts 17:11-12

Reflections

David knew suffering and difficulties throughout his life, but he also had learned to count on God no matter what came his way. He knew how to take refuge in God (Ps. 7:1). He knew that God would never abandon him or anyone else who was seeking Him. God was his rock and stronghold no matter whether circumstances were good or bad.

As Paul, Silas, and Timothy continued on their missionary journey through the towns of Macedonia, they preached about Jesus to the Jews and those Gentiles who adhered to Judaism. The response was mixed, not everyone believed and some became hostile, but they saw faith everywhere they went, too. The Jews in Berea who heard Paul were especially diligent in studying the Scriptures to see if what Paul was telling them was really true. These were people who, no doubt, had been seeking God in His word. God would not forsake them and He sent them none other than the Apostle Paul to proclaim to them the truth of Christ.

Think about It

How does your daily life reflect a seeking after God? Are you dependent on success in your activities and business in order to remain confident in the Lord or are you spiritually stable no matter what storm you are in? Seek the Lord through His word and prayer. Be alert to His providence in your circumstances. Let Him be your stronghold. This was the way of David, the Bereans, Paul, Silas, and Timothy. Seek Him for He will never forsake those who seek Him.

God's Righteous Judgment

Today's Reading: Psalms 10-12; Acts 17:16-34

Selected Verses

Why does the wicked renounce God
and say in his heart, "You will not call to account"?
But you do see, for you note mischief and vexation,
that you may take it into your hands;
to you the helpless commits himself;
you have been the helper of the fatherless.
Break the arm of the wicked and evildoer;
call his wickedness to account till you find none.

Ps. 10:13-15

The times of ignorance God overlooked, but now he commands all people everywhere to repent, because he has fixed a day on which he will judge the world in righteousness by a man whom he has appointed; and of this he has given assurance to all by raising him from the dead.

Acts 17:30-31

Reflections

The Psalmist analyzes the thought processes of the wicked who say, in essence, "God is not going to judge people." They assume that God doesn't know what is going on, but He does. They assume that He will not take action against their evil schemes, but He will. The idea of final judgment runs throughout the Bible. God is both holy and sovereign, so He must put right the injustice of mankind. God helps the fatherless and the weak and the poor. He hears their pleas and will bring full justice.

In Athens, Paul declares the existence of the God that they call the "unknown god." They had many idols, but, in case they had overlooked a god, they added this one for good measure. Paul tells them about the God who is Creator and Sustainer of life. This God cannot be contained in a temple because He is infinite. He is the God who needs nothing and depends on nothing for His existence. He is not distant and aloof but will judge the world in righteousness on the appointed day by a Man whom He has raised from the dead, namely Jesus Christ. Like the wicked of Psalm 10, some of the people of Athens mocked the idea of judgment. Some wanted to hear more.

Think about It

Many today dismiss the idea of final judgment. At the same time, they search desperately for a reason to live. Without a clear understanding of the judgment of God we will neither have a reason to live nor motivation to seek God's forgiveness and to live in holiness before Him. Be sure you are clear on the judgment of God and how Jesus said we may escape it (John 5:24).

The Authority of the Bible

Today's Reading: Psalms 13-16; Acts 18

Selected Verses

Therefore my heart is glad, and my whole being rejoices; my flesh also dwells secure. For you will not abandon my soul to Sheol, or let your holy one see corruption.

Ps. 16:9-10

And when he wished to cross to Achaia, the brothers encouraged him and wrote to the disciples to welcome him. When he arrived, he greatly helped those who through grace had believed, for he powerfully refuted the Jews is public, showing by the Scriptures that the Christ was Jesus.

Acts 18:27-28

Reflections

In the first century, the Apostles used the Scriptures of the Old Testament powerfully and effectively as they spread throughout the known world proclaiming that the promised Christ had come. Later the New Testament containing the Apostles' teaching would be added, completing our Bible.

The Messiah, Christ, was promised to Israel and sent to them. He lived out His life and ministry culminating in His death by crucifixion, His resurrection, and His commissioning of His Apostles to go into the entire world and make disciples of all nations. That work which Jesus commissioned still goes on today throughout the earth.

The Psalms are filled with references which had immediate relevance to their time but would later be more completely fulfilled by Jesus in His earthly life. Here we have a prophecy which both Peter and Paul understood to point clearly to His resurrection (Acts 2:25-28; 13:35). To see Christ in the Psalms and other Old Testament scriptures motivated the Apostles and fueled their boldness as they preached to the Jews.

One of those Jewish converts to Jesus Christ was a gifted man named Apollos. He displayed great eloquence in his speech and diligence in his study of the Word of God, but he received needed help from the mentoring of Paul's disciples, Aquila and Priscilla. Apollos went on to Achaia and had an effective ministry encouraging the believers and showing the Jews from the Scriptures that the Christ was Jesus.

Think about It

Do you rely on the Scriptures as the basis for your faith and in your presenting Jesus to others? We need to beware of relying on arguments based on mere human reasoning and logic and neglecting to point people to the claims of Christ made in God's Word. Let the Word of God be your authority for your life and your ministry. The Apostles modeled this, and we will be wise to follow their example. We may yet see amazing growth in Christ's Church.

God's Delight in Your Prayer

Today's Reading: Psalms 17-18; Acts 19:1-20

Selected Verses

They confronted me in the day of my calamity,
but the Lord was my support.
He brought me out into a broad place;
he rescued me, because he delighted in me.

Ps. 18:18-19

And fear fell upon them all, and the name of the Lord Jesus was extolled.

Acts 19:17

Reflections

The Psalms are filled with exclamations of praise to God for His power and goodness to His needy people. Psalm 18 lists many ways in which the Lord delivered David. Appropriate praise is offered, but then we see this curious line, "he rescued me, because he delighted in me." David grasped something about God that is often overlooked. God is not annoyed with us when we come to Him seeking help, strength, wisdom, deliverance, etc. God is not merely putting up with us. David understood that the Lord delighted in him. The Almighty is not bothered that one of His children should come incessantly asking for things. God delivered David because He "delighted" in him.

By contrast, there are several incidents in the book of Acts in which unscrupulous opponents of the gospel attempt to obtain the Holy Spirit for money or to invoke the name of Jesus for personal gain. In Ephesus, the seven sons of Sceva attempt to cast out a demon in Jesus' name. They fail as the demon overcomes and possesses them. The incident brought a wave of fear to the population. They realized that they may not trifle with the name of Jesus. God does not delight to hear the prayers of those who are not His.

Think about It

You know that God is all-powerful, omnipotent, and sovereign. He controls all things. You probably believe He can do whatever He wishes to do. You don't doubt that there is no problem too big for Him. Like the people of Ephesus, you grasp the sanctity and power of the name of Jesus. But do you believe that He delights to hear your prayer and rescue you? How confident are you in His loving kindness, His tender care, His infinite love, and His pleasure in responding to your requests? Think about God delighting in you the next time you ask Him for something you desperately need.

Cultural Collision Coming

Today's Reading: Psalms 19-21; Acts 19:21-41

Selected Verses

Be exalted, O Lord, in your strength!
We will sing and praise your power.

Ps. 21:13

"Men, you know that from this business we have our wealth. And you see and hear that not only in Ephesus but in almost all of Asia this Paul has persuaded and turned away a great many people, saying that gods made with hands are not gods. And there is danger not only that this trade of ours may come into disrepute but also that the temple of the great goddess Artemis may be counted as nothing, and that she may even be deposed from her magnificence, she whom all Asia and the world worship."

Acts 19:25-27

Reflections

The Psalmist exemplifies true worship as he praises God for all He is and has done. He thanks the Lord for His mercy, grace, and goodness to His people and prays for God to be exalted. He commits to sing and praise God's power. And he desires that God be pleased with his thoughts and words (Ps. 19:14).

On the other hand, Paul was preaching in Ephesus, a stronghold of false worship and idolatry. His message threatened the lucrative business of the silversmiths and others who profited from the cult of Artemis. One of the tradesmen, Demetrius, called a meeting to warn the community of the danger that would come to them if Paul should succeed in diminishing the worship of this false goddess. Chaos ensued. The crowd worked itself up to a frenzy until the town clerk quieted them.

Think about It

Jesus said, "No one comes to the Father, except through me" (John 14:6). We may not impose the gospel by force on unbelievers. But the secular culture convulses when we proclaim the truth and hearers believe. We cannot settle for some benign multicultural coexistence. Jesus calls His disciples to tell the good news of life in His name. They will teach, preach, explain, reason, debate, prove, and live by faith before the watching world. Force can silence them, but they will not shrink back in fear nor shut up.

Are you prepared for the impact of the gospel on a culture which is increasingly hostile to the exclusivity of the message? Prepare yourself. Remember it is enough to please God with the words of your mouth and the meditation of your heart.

The Best Encouragers

Today's Reading: Psalms 22-24; Acts 20:1-16

Selected Verses

I will tell of your name to my brothers;
in the midst of the congregation I will praise you:
You who fear the Lord, praise him!
All you offspring of Jacob, glorify him,
and stand in awe of him, all you offspring of Israel!
For he has not despised or abhorred
the affliction of the afflicted,
and he has not hidden his face from him,
but has heard, when he cried to him.

Ps. 22:22-24

After the uproar ceased, Paul sent for the disciples, and after encouraging
them, he said farewell and departed for Macedonia. When he had gone through
those regions and had given them much encouragement, he came to Greece.

Acts 20:1-2

Reflections

Sufferers make the best encouragers because they are more in touch with the realities of both earth and heaven than others whose lives are more comfortable and secure.

The writer of Psalm 22 expresses great agony and great trust in the Lord through all of his sufferings. He never loses sight of either his pain or his God but shows that godly perspective which sees the "here and now" and the "there and then." The words of this Psalm were on Jesus' lips on the cross and, no doubt, comforted Him as He suffered and died.

Paul was certainly a suffering encourager. He had just endured jail time in Philippi, ridicule in Athens, and the riot in Ephesus. The Jews were working on a plot to assassinate him (Acts 20:3), yet he went about encouraging the believers. What could stop the progress of the gospel ministry through Asia and Europe? Not riots; nor assassination plots; nor beatings and imprisonments. Nothing. Paul was in a unique position, as the lightning rod for the gospel, to reassure the saints that the preaching of the gospel could not be stopped. Adverse circumstances would not change the truth of the gospel nor the mandate of Jesus to go and make disciples of all nations (Matt. 28:19,20).

Think about It

If you would be an encourager, learn God's word and be ready to suffer. God is able to strengthen you for that ministry which is always in great demand.

Ready to Die; Ready to Live

Today's Reading: Psalms 25-27; Acts 20:17-38

Selected Verses

One thing have I asked of the Lord,
that will I seek after:
that I may dwell in the house of the Lord
all the days of my life,
to gaze upon the beauty of the Lord
and to inquire in his temple.

Ps. 27:4

But I do not account my life of any value nor as precious to myself,
if only I may finish my course and the ministry that I received
from the Lord Jesus, to testify to the gospel of the grace of God.

Acts 20:24

Reflections

David knew adversity and he knew how to turn to God for safety and refuge. But he also sought to know the Lord even more deeply, to be in His presence at all times not merely when he was facing danger. David loved the Lord. He found Him beautiful and wanted to gaze upon Him. He wanted to learn from Him in His temple. These desires did not indicate that David sought to escape the responsibilities of daily life and retreat into some monastery. He goes on to plead: "Teach me your way, O Lord, and lead me on a level path because of my enemies" Ps. 27:11.

He wanted to know God so he could walk in His ways in the midst of all the pressures of everyday life.

Paul understood that "imprisonments and afflictions" awaited him, but he resolved that his life was only valuable as he was able to finish the course God had set out for him and to fulfill the ministry the Lord Jesus Christ had assigned to him. Indeed, Paul would face years of imprisonment and, according to tradition, a martyr's death.

Think about It

Jesus said, "For whoever would save his life will lose it, but whoever loses his life for my sake will save it" (Luke 9:24). Have you settled this? Are you ready to die so you are ready to live? As Joshua told the Israelites, "Choose this day whom you will serve...But as for me and my house, we will serve the Lord" (Josh. 24:15). Be ready to die, so you are ready to live.

The Prayer that Never Fails

Today's Reading: Psalms 28-30; Acts 21:1-14

Selected Verses

The Lord sits enthroned over the flood;
the Lord sits enthroned as king forever.
May the Lord give strength to his people!
May the Lord bless his people with peace!

Ps. 29:10-11

When we heard this, we and the people there urged him not to go up to Jerusalem. Then
Paul answered, "What are you doing, weeping and breaking my heart? For I am ready not
only to be imprisoned but even to die in Jerusalem for the name of the Lord Jesus." And
since he would not be persuaded, we ceased and said, "Let the will of the Lord be done."

Acts 21:12-14

Reflections

The prayer that never fails, according to the fictional Father Tim of novelist Jan Karon's Mitford series, is "Thy will be done." This phrase was part of the prayer Jesus taught His disciples—the same words He prayed in the Garden of Gethsemane before His crucifixion. Here in Acts, Paul's friends prayed it also (see Matt. 6:10; 26:39-42).

In Tyre, concerned believers understood that Paul would suffer if he went to Jerusalem. Luke tells us that "Through the Spirit they were telling Paul not to go on to Jerusalem" (vs. 4). Agabus, a prophet, foretold Paul's imprisonment in Jerusalem. Others in Phoenicia urged him not to go. It was hard for Paul to hear this, and it hurt him because it was going to hurt them. Nevertheless, he was determined to go to Jerusalem though it cost him his life. He had settled that matter. He believed it was what God wanted him to do. They resigned themselves with the words, "Let the will of the Lord be done."

But the Lord whose will they sought is One who presides over the chaos and turmoil of human life on planet Earth (not to mention the entire universe). As the Psalmist says, He sits enthroned over the flood. His reign never ends. His will is always done. He is the One who gives strength to His people so they may endure the trials He sends. He grants peace so that even in the face of sure suffering His servants know quietness as they pray the prayer that never fails.

Think about It

Must you see bright skies every day in order to have peace? Do you frantically seek to avoid any discomforting situations, much less, life-threatening ones? Make it your aim to be content as long as His will is done.

The Limits of Wise Counsel

Today's Reading: Psalms 31-33; Acts 21:15-40

Selected Verses

> But I trust in you, O LORD;
> I say, "You are my God."
> My times are in your hand;
> rescue me from the hand of my enemies and from my persecutors!

Ps. 31:14-15

> After these days we got ready and went up to Jerusalem.

Acts 21:15

Reflections

Paul had heard from several wise fellow believers that he would suffer arrest and adversity in Jerusalem. He also heard them urge him not to go. They loved him, and they did not want him to suffer and possibly die. Paul was not foolhardy. There were certainly several instances when Paul avoided danger (e.g. Acts 9:23-25; 29-30; 13:50,51; 14:19-20; 17:13-14). Indeed, Luke comments that Paul and Barnabas "shook off the dust from their feet against [Antioch in Pisidia] and went to Iconium" (Acts 13:51) following the policy Jesus had given to His disciples when He sent them out to preach to unresponsive people (Matt. 10:14).

Paul probably remembered the words of Psalm 31 quoted above. His trust was in the Lord. He knew that he had been given a purpose and a ministry to complete. He believed it included going into the lions' den of Jerusalem where some believers had questions about him and where unbelieving Jews were out to get the former persecutor of the Church. Paul trusted God who had his times in His hands.

So he did not follow the advice of his many well-meaning friends. He got ready and went to Jerusalem. Luke doesn't tell us how Paul was so sure he needed to do this. He just went. As prophesied, he did begin to suffer almost immediately, but he would remain faithful and use that platform of suffering to glorify God and proclaim the gospel in some very unusual settings.

Think about It

God does not guarantee that His path for us will be easy and pleasant or even "sensible" at all times. Be ready for anything, so that someday you can say:

"Blessed be the Lord, for he has wondrously shown his steadfast love to me when I was in a besieged city. I had said in my alarm, 'I am cut off from your sight.' But you heard the voice of my pleas for mercy when I cried to you for help" (Ps. 31:21-22).

When the Righteous are Afflicted

Today's Reading: Psalms 34-35; Acts 22

Selected Verses

> *Many are the afflictions of the righteous,*
> *but the Lord delivers him out of them all.*
> *He keeps all his bones;*
> *not one of them is broken.*

Ps. 34:19-20

> *Up to this word they listened to him. Then they raised their voices and said,*
> *"Away with such a fellow from the earth! For he should not be allowed to live."*

Acts 22:22

Reflections

Righteousness does not exempt a person from afflictions, as the Psalmist's words and Paul's experience both affirm. Above all, the only perfect Righteous One, the Lord Jesus Christ, sustained the greatest afflictions ever known.

Nowhere in Scripture does God promise a life free from trials for His people. He does promise to be with His own and to deliver them out of all their adversities. But He does not give a time schedule. It could be soon or it could be after death. The specific promise of Psalm 34:20, we learn from the Apostle John (John 19:36), was made to Jesus and fulfilled at His crucifixion.

Paul's life became increasingly difficult. In Jerusalem, he faced angry mobs of Jews and nervous Roman authorities who wanted to maintain order. God was not displeased with Paul, His servant and messenger to the Gentiles, yet God assigned him some very great afflictions which Paul accepted and used as a platform from which to preach the good news of life in Christ.

Think about It

It may seem illogical that the righteous suffer many afflictions. Why wouldn't life be better by living in a godly way? Why wouldn't God see that those who honor Him the most suffer the least? Job certainly asked this question and waited in agony for an answer. He didn't know what the Bible tells us about his suffering, that it was to vindicate the name and glory of God before Satan. Yet Job had no complaints in the end. He stopped questioning God. He prayed for his friends. And God restored all his losses doubly (Job 42:9-10).

Believing reader, are you facing hard times which seem to have no relationship to any failure, foolishness, or sin in your life? Take rest in God who promises to be near to the brokenhearted and to save the crushed in spirit (Ps. 34:18). He will deliver you in His time because Jesus Christ suffered to purchase your redemption and promised to deliver you from all affliction in His presence forever.

Paul's Tweet

Today's Reading: Psalms 36-37; Acts 23:1-11

Selected Verses

> *How precious is your steadfast love, O God!*
> *The children of mankind take refuge in the shadow of your wings.*
> *They feast on the abundance of your house,*
> *and you give them drink from the river of your delights.*
> *For with you is the fountain of life;*
> *in your light do we see light.*

Ps. 36:7-9

It is with respect to the hope and the resurrection of the dead that I am on trial.

Acts 23:6

Reflections

The Psalms offer an antidote for the tendency to complain, to be bored, restless, overwhelmed, or impatient. This antidote is to meditate on the Lord, His Word, His steadfast love, and His constant providential care. On the flipside, the antidote includes a healthy dose of fear of the Lord knowing that He will destroy the wicked. Do not "flatter" yourself that He can't see you and bring you to account for your sin. Instead, run to Him for mercy. Fear Him. Praise Him. Love Him. Delight in Him.

Paul must have understood this as his difficulties grew more and more serious. He used wisdom, even shrewdness, in addressing the Sanhedrin, the Jewish court composed of members with severe theological differences. In what we would call today a "sound bite" or "tweet", he summarized the problem, "It is with respect to the hope and the resurrection of the dead that I am on trial." Paul, by this statement, showed that, despite his imprisonment and the constant threats to his life, his hope was undiminished and his focus on the gospel was undistracted. His trust in the historic resurrection of Jesus Christ was the basis for his life and ministry. His words set off an intense and disorderly debate in the court. He was no longer the focus of their attention, but the subject of hope and the resurrection of the dead took center stage.

Think about It

The chief end of man is to glorify God and enjoy Him forever.[5] Review this frequently when the circumstances of life are at best monotonous and at worst terrifying. Are you prepared for this day with its unforeseeable trials or, most likely, its predictable sameness? Whatever may come, seek to drink from the river of God's delights. You are given the task of enjoying Him, today and forever.

---

[5] Westminster Shorter Catechism, question 1.

God's Providential Care

Today's Reading: Psalms 38-40; Acts 23:12-35

Selected Verses

> Be pleased, O Lord, to deliver me!
> O Lord, make haste to help me!
> Let those be put to shame and disappointed altogether
> who seek to snatch away my life;
> let those be turned back and brought to dishonor
> who delight in my hurt!
> Let those be appalled because of their shame
> who say to me, "Aha, Aha!"

Ps. 40:13-15

> So the soldiers, according to their instructions, took
> Paul and brought him by night to Antipatris.

Acts 23:31

Reflections

The Psalmist endured much pain partly from his own sin and partly from the severe oppression that was mounted against him unjustly. There is a difference between suffering due to our own sin and suffering due to being God's servant (see 1 Pet. 2:18-25). But it is often not easy to separate our suffering into such neat, clean categories. The Psalmist was suffering and in these laments he mixes the two causes and appeals to the Lord for forgiveness and deliverance. Unlike Job, he recognizes some responsibility for what he is having to endure but also cries out for relief from those who plot against him unjustly (Ps. 38:3-4,11-12, 17-20; 40:12).

The events of Paul's life show the power of God working providentially to preserve him from unjust suffering and for further service. Forty men conspire to kill him. His nephew overhears the plot and reports it to Paul. Paul wisely asks the centurion to take his nephew to the tribune. The tribune takes immediate action and rescues Paul whom he then sends to the governor for trial, and, let us add, to witness to the gospel of Jesus Christ. Imagine how the conspirators were completely "put to shame and disappointed altogether"!

Think about It

Most of us do not suffer such opposition as Paul did, but we do suffer in smaller ways. Do you know that He watches over you? Do you know that while you may feel that your iniquities are more than the hairs of your head (40:12) God's care for you is such that He has the hairs of your head numbered and your iniquities covered by the blood of Christ (Luke 12:4-7; 24:44-47)? Trust His providential care. No one can thwart His plan for you. No, not even yourself.

Now or Never: The Procrastinator's Dilemma

Today's Reading: Psalms 41-43; Acts 24

Selected Verses

By this I know that you delight in me:
my enemy will not shout in triumph over me.
But you have upheld me because of my integrity,
and set me in your presence forever.

Ps. 41:11-12

After some days Felix came with his wife Drusilla, who was Jewish, and he sent for Paul and heard him speak about faith in Christ Jesus. And as he reasoned about righteousness and self-control and the coming judgment, Felix was alarmed and said, "Go away for the present. When I get an opportunity I will summon you."

Acts 24:24-25

Reflections

Procrastination is not only the thief of time, but also the handiest and flimsiest excuse of those who have no desire or intention of taking some needed and radical course of action or making a difficult and important decision. My father used to carry around in his pocket a small wooden disk with the inscription "TUIT." If I said to him, "I'll do that when I get around to it," he would smile, reach into his pocket, pull out the little disk and hand it to me saying, "Here, now you've got a round TUIT." He finally let me keep the round TUIT permanently as I always seemed to need it.

Felix, the governor, had power over Paul, his prisoner, but not over the God of judgment of whom Paul spoke. That topic alarmed him, but, like so many others today and down through history, he deluded himself with the thought that he would think about it later, when he got around to it.

Believers in Jesus Christ are not alarmed by the thought of standing before the God of judgment. Like the Psalmist, we know that the Lord delights in us and that, rather than be swept away in condemnation, we will stand accepted before Him forever. The true believer has a desire for God not unlike the desperate need for air and water, so we say, "As a deer pants for flowing streams, so pants my soul for you, O God. My soul thirsts for God, for the living God" (Ps. 42:1-2).

Think about It

Is that your mindset, that you must know more of God? Do you crave His presence, His Word, His will in your life? Beware of the Felix mentality of saying, "when I get around to it." Now is the time to seek the Lord, to study His word, to pray, to obey, to be in worship with His people, and to make diligent use of the means of grace.

God Will be Glorified

Today's Reading: Psalms 44-46; Acts 25

Selected Verses

"Be still, and know that I am God.
I will be exalted among the nations,
I will be exalted in the earth!"
The Lord of hosts is with us;
the God of Jacob is our fortress.

Ps. 46:10-11

To the Jews I have done no wrong, as you yourself know very well. If then I am a
wrongdoer and have committed anything for which I deserve to die, I do not seek
to escape death. But if there is nothing to their charges against me, no one can give
me up to them. I appeal to Caesar." Then Festus, when he had conferred with
his council, answered, "To Caesar you have appealed; to Caesar you shall go."

Acts 25:10-12

Reflections

Psalm 46 reminds us that whether there is chaos in the cosmos or bloodbaths on the battlefields, God still rules over all things. The believer is told not to fear but to be quiet and focus on the Lord who is over all the madness of men and the disintegration of the physical world. Nothing can stop Him, nor thwart His will, nor sever His people from Him.

Paul must have had a firm grasp on this truth as he was passed from one jurisdiction to another: from the Jews, to the Roman tribune, from Felix to Festus and from Festus to Agrippa and later to Caesar. The arrested Apostle had stated his position, "not guilty." The charges weren't sticking, but he was still in custody as a favor to the Jews. He sought to maintain a clear conscience (Acts 24:16) and clearly stated that he would accept any sentence which was just, even death. Festus shows confusion and ambivalence, offering to let Paul be tried in Jerusalem. Paul appeals to Caesar. The charges against him are not clear much less proven. But Paul remains steady, trusting that God is using his testimony to the gospel in this setting before governors and kings for His glory.

Think about It

Do not be intimidated by the apparent powers of this world's political systems. God still rules. Do not panic if it seems like the world may blow apart through some natural catastrophe. In the midst of these kinds of crises, God shows His power and sovereignty. Be still. Trust Him. He will be glorified.

The Pompous Dead

Today's Reading: Psalms 47-49; Acts 26

Selected Verses

Man in his pomp yet without understanding is like the beasts that perish.

Ps. 49:20

And Agrippa said to Paul, "In a short time would you persuade me to be a Christian?"
And Paul said, "Whether short or long, I would to God that not only you but also
all who hear me this day might become such as I am—except for these chains."

Acts 26:28-29

Reflections

The Psalmist exalts God at every turn and is not impressed with the things that society holds of great value: power, prestige, wealth, and knowledge. One does not need to read far in the Scripture before confronting this reality, but one may be far up the ladder of so-called success before discovering it is leaning against the wrong wall.

King Agrippa makes a perfect example of this truth. Luke's account shows that the society held him and his wife, Bernice, in high esteem. They entered the audience hall with great pomp (Acts 25:23). Paul is presented to them and he begins his defense describing his previous life and his conversion to Jesus Christ. Festus discounts the whole story as one of a mad man, deluded through too much education. Paul appeals to the king for confirmation of what he is saying. Agrippa, at least, does not call Paul crazy and admits that what he is saying is more than a mere defense. Agrippa understands that Paul is attempting to win him to Christ!

What makes Paul so bold as to turn his own trial into an opportunity to preach Christ to a king and queen? He was not intimidated by all the royal fanfare. Rather Paul was enthralled with the glories of his Lord Jesus Christ. Whether or not he was consciously thinking about Psalm 49, it is safe to say that he was mindful that "man in his pomp yet without understanding is like the beasts that perish." The king lacked understanding like a mere beast.

Think about It

Are you prepared to grasp even the difficult moments of your life to proclaim the good news of Jesus Christ? Remember kings, queens, and all pompous humans without understanding of the gospel will perish just like beasts. Be ready to warn them.

Sunless Days and Starless Nights

Today's Reading: Psalms 50-52; Acts 27:1-25

Selected Verses

> Offer to God a sacrifice of thanksgiving,
> and perform your vows to the Most High,
> and call upon me in the day of trouble;
> I will deliver you, and you shall glorify me.
>
> Ps. 50:14-15

> For this very night there stood before me an angel of the God to whom I belong and whom I worship, and he said, "Do not be afraid, Paul; you must stand before Caesar. And behold, God has granted you all those who sail with you." So take heart, men, for I have faith in God that it will be exactly as I have been told.
>
> Acts 27:23-25

Reflections

The Psalmist makes a powerful statement about God. He is the rightful owner of all people and all things, so we belong to Him and He deserves our thankful worship no matter how bleak our circumstances. God needs nothing from us. He lacks nothing because all things are already His. Humans may insult Him with their puny offerings given in an attitude of pride or duty. What does God want? "Offer to God a sacrifice of thanksgiving," says the Scripture.

Paul in his eventful voyage on a prison ship to Rome becomes the real leader despite his lowly status as a prisoner. His initial advice to winter over at Fair Havens was unheeded but was later proven to have been wise. As the ship is driven by a storm, the angel of God appears to Paul giving him a promise of deliverance. Paul identifies God as the One to whom he belongs and the One whom he worships. In the midst of a storm, which blocked out the sun and the stars day after day, Paul was clear on who God is and who he was before Him. "I belong to Him and I worship Him," Paul says.

Nothing that happened to Paul could diminish his convictions about the reality of God's existence and of His personal care for him. When trials increased his praise and thanksgiving did too.

Think about It

How can you tell your faith is unshaken in the storm? Check the level of your thanksgiving. Be sure your praise of God is on the rise. God is pleased with a sacrifice of thanksgiving. Nothing is more glorifying to Him than genuine praise and thanks especially on sunless days and starless nights. Besides that, it also proves your faith is firm.

Contagious Confidence

Today's Reading: Psalms 53-55; Acts 27:26-44

Selected Verses

Cast your burden on the Lord,
and he will sustain you;
he will never permit
the righteous to be moved.

Ps. 55:22

"Therefore I urge you to take some food. For it will give you strength, for not a hair is to perish from the head of any of you." And when [Paul] had said these things, he took bread, and giving thanks to God in the presence of all he broke it and began to eat. Then they all were encouraged and ate some food themselves.

Acts 27:34-36

Reflections

The Psalmist describes the pain of betrayal. His close friend has turned against him. The person whom he trusted and ate with is out to get him. The burden of this is enormous. It's as if the person you counted on to help you carry a load, quit carrying it, and jumped on your back and added to your load. David says to cast that burden on the Lord. The result is confidence in God's sustaining power. Nothing can occur without His permission, and He will not permit the righteous to be moved.

Jesus, too, knew betrayal by His close friend and disciple, Judas Iscariot (Matt. 26:45-56). This psalm sustained the Lord who was the only Righteous One who could legitimately claim the promise that He would never be moved. Who are we to claim this promise, struggling sinners that we are? But by His suffering all who believe in Him are made righteous. Thus, Paul and all the saints down through history can cast their burdens on God expecting to be sustained and kept even in a time of betrayal, shipwreck, or other calamity (2 Cor. 5:21).

Paul demonstrated his confidence in the Lord to sustain him through both his words and his actions. He reassured the crew and passengers, and he ate a meal in front of them. As a result, they responded to him and did as he urged them. Soon they gained strength for the impending shipwreck and the swim for shore. Every one of them survived the sea.

Think about It

Have you seen how the godly spread confidence to others by their trust in the Lord? Consider how God can use your words and actions to inspire others to trust Him and to cast their burdens on Him. Yes, be contagious. Spread the germs.

When Theory Becomes Reality

Today's Reading: Psalms 56-58; Acts 28:1-15

Selected Verses

> *This I know, that God is for me.*
> *In God, whose word I praise,*
> *in the Lord, whose word I praise,*
> *in God I trust; I shall not be afraid.*
> *What can man do to me?*

Ps. 56:9b-11

> *And so we came to Rome. And the brothers there, when they heard*
> *about us, came as far as the Forum of Appius and Three Taverns*
> *to meet us. On seeing them, Paul thanked God and took courage.*

Acts 28:14-15

Reflections

Throughout the Psalms we are told of the trials and afflictions that come to a believer. He may be unjustly treated, falsely accused, betrayed, ridiculed, and pursued by an army. The godly man or woman clings to the Lord, delights in His law, and trusts God no matter what. Through those trials the disciple learns that even when life is difficult, God is there. God is for me.

Paul went through months of trials as a prisoner. He endured shipwreck and even a snake bite. But everywhere he went the Lord was there keeping him and using his life to minister to others. Finally, he made it to Rome and, right away, he met brothers who were anticipating his arrival. All the stress of that trip melted away as, again, God showed that He had a purpose for Paul in Rome, a purpose which included service to the church in Rome.

Paul had written earlier to the Roman Christians telling them, "What then shall we say to these things? If God is for us, who can be against us? He who did not spare his own Son but gave him up for us all, how will he not also with him graciously give us all things?" (Rom. 8:31-32). Might this have been Paul's way of expressing the thought of Psalm 56? Paul was no novice when he wrote Romans 8, but God proved Himself in even more ways by the time he met the believers face to face in Rome.

Think about It

There is no substitute for real life experience in knowing God. Biblical truth may be perceived with the mind and believed but it becomes reality in the actual rough and tumble of life where God shows Himself to be faithful to His people.

Wherever you are in life, young, old, or in-between, seek to know God through His Word and to prove His promises through your experience of trusting Him. There is no way to learn how powerful and present God is other than daily faith and obedience.

Flee to the Banner

Today's Reading: Psalms 59-61; Acts 28:16-31

Selected Verses

You have set up a banner for those who fear you,
that they may flee to it from the bow.　　Selah
That your beloved ones may be delivered,
give salvation by your right hand and answer us!

Ps. 60:4-5

When they had appointed a day for him, they came to him at his lodging in greater numbers. From morning till evening he expounded to them, testifying to the kingdom of God and trying to convince them about Jesus both from the Law of Moses and from the Prophets. And some were convinced by what he said, but others disbelieved.

Acts 28:23-24

Reflections

David uses a military analogy to faith and salvation. The troops are scattered and about to die. The commander sets up a banner to rally them back. They see the banner and head for it. There they are saved from defeat and the tide of victory is turned in their favor. Would a soldier who is in dire straits not flee to the banner raised by his commander? Not likely.

Yet look what happened when Paul raised the banner of the gospel among the Jews in Rome. He used their Scriptures in his efforts to convince them. Some believed and some did not. Why not? It was not that Paul had failed to be clear. He diagnosed their condition from the prophet Isaiah. Their hearts were dull, ears nearly deaf. They closed their eyes. The banner was raised. They refused to flee to it.

They had their opportunity, but they did not grasp it. Paul told them he would take the message to the Gentiles, and they would listen.

Think about It

Those who fear God are His beloved. They show their true identity by fleeing to the banner He has raised, the gospel of Jesus Christ. There they find salvation. But dulled hearts do not respond to the message despite its clarity.

Have you fled to the banner? If not, Christ has sent out the command to all to repent and believe the gospel now. Pray that God would deliver you from a dull heart and grant you faith that leads to repentance.

If you are one of His disciples, your task and mine is to keep proclaiming the good news of life in Jesus Christ from the Bible, accurately and faithfully, as Paul modeled. Some will believe. Some will not. Take courage. Stay the course, because to everyone who flees to the banner, God will grant salvation.

Two Ways to Live—Your Choice

Today's Reading: Psalms 62-64; Romans 1

Selected Verses

My soul will be satisfied as with fat and rich food,
and my mouth will praise you with joyful lips,
when I remember you upon my bed,
and meditate on you in the watches of the night;
for you have been my help,
and in the shadow of your wings I will sing for joy.

Ps. 63:5-7

For although they knew God, they did not honor him as God or give thanks to him,
but they became futile in their thinking, and their foolish hearts were darkened.

Rom. 1:21

Reflections

David opens his heart again and again, showing us how much he longs for God. His attitude is like someone desperate for air and water—he simply cannot live without God. He finds his satisfaction in Him. The psalmist finds shelter and protection in Him. He praises God with joy as he sings of Him. To him, the worship of God is not a necessary and unpleasant chore for he finds delight in God.

By contrast, Paul describes people who take no interest in God. They have no time to praise Him nor give Him thanks. They presumptuously go on their merry way in foolishness. Their negligence is inexcusable because God's invisible attributes, His eternal power and divine nature are clearly perceived in creation (vs. 19-20). Rather than worship and thank God, they grow even more foolish and exchange the glory of God for images of animals. They worship creatures, not the Creator.

Think about It

We humans are united by the characteristic of being worshipful beings, but we are differentiated by the object of worship which we choose. Mankind was made to worship the true and living God and if he will not worship God he will worship something less than God for anything that is not God is less than Him. We must have an object of worship. It is common to call our celebrities "idols". Why not? We worship them and they encourage it. But they are fallen creatures, like us, not worthy of worship. God will call them and us to answer for our idolatry.

Find your satisfaction and joy in the eternal triune God: Father, Son, and Holy Spirit. He is magnificent. He is worthy of all our praise and worship. There is only one true object of worship and there are only two ways to live. The choice is clear.[6]

---

[6] For a simple presentation of the two ways to live, visit http://www.matthiasmedia.com.au/2wtl/.

When the Church is Full of Hypocrites

Today's Reading: Psalms 65-67; Romans 2

Selected Verses

> *May God be gracious to us and bless us*
> *and make his face to shine upon us,*   Selah
> *that your way may be known on earth,*
> *your saving power among all nations.*

Ps. 67:1-2

You who boast in the law dishonor God by breaking the law. For, as it is written,
"The name of God is blasphemed among the Gentiles because of you."

Rom. 2:23-24

Reflections

The Psalmist has a lofty view of the impact of God's blessing on His people spreading out to all the nations of the earth. Truly, God does rule over all the earth. He is the God of all flesh. Through His providence He rules over everyone and everything. Nothing escapes Him. All owe Him everything.

But, alas, this vision of a worldwide impact of blessing and worship dimmed due to the very people who had the Word of God. Paul says, "The name of God is blasphemed among the Gentiles because of [them]."

How did God deal with this? He judged His people for their unfaithfulness through the captivities of the Kingdoms of Israel and Judah. But He acted for the sake of His own name to restore them to the land (Ezek. 36:16-38).

In Jesus' lifetime, the Jews faced the question of whether or not to believe the Messiah, the Christ whom God had sent them. Most of them failed to believe, yet according to Paul they still maintained their spiritual pride and arrogance, looking down on the Gentile pagans. In Romans 2 he warns them not to be smug in their cultural superiority.

Think about It

Fellow Christian, have you considered how our hypocrisy as believers can cause the lost to blaspheme our God? Have you pondered how God's blessing on us is impacting the unbelieving world around us?

At the end of the age, God will bring His elect from every tribe and tongue (Rev. 7:9-10). In Abraham through whom came Jesus Christ, all the families of the earth will be blessed (Gen. 12:3). The Psalmist had it right. "God shall bless us; let all the ends of the earth fear him!" (67:7). And they shall. Pray for the fulfillment of this promise soon. Flee hypocrisy. Live in such a consistent, God-honoring way as to bring glory to Him.

Shut Mouths; Believing Hearts

Today's Reading: Psalms 68-69; Romans 3

Selected Verses

More in number than the hairs of my head
*   are those who hate me without cause;*
mighty are those who would destroy me,
*   those who attack me with lies.*
What I did not steal
*   must I now restore?*
O God, you know my folly;
*   the wrongs I have done are not hidden from you.*

Ps. 69:4-5

But now the righteousness of God has been manifested apart from
the law, although the Law and the Prophets bear witness to it—the
righteousness of God through faith in Jesus Christ for all who believe.

Rom. 3:21-22

Reflections

The Psalmist cries out in anguish for the injustice heaped on him, but, at the same time, he recognizes his own folly and wrongs. He knows that God knows them. He may have tried to hide them, but they are not hidden from the Lord. No one is completely righteous before God. True, some suffer great injustice, but such suffering does not blot out the record of sin committed and establish the sufferer as righteous before God. We are all both victims and perpetrators.

Paul tells the Romans that the law is given to shut our mouths and to hold the whole world accountable to God. Where can we turn? We can only turn to Jesus Christ through Whom the righteousness of God apart from the law is manifested. By God's grace, salvation from the condemnation of the law is through Him for all who believe. In Christ, there is justification (the declaration that all debts have been paid in full), redemption (the price paid to purchase freedom from slavery to sin and guilt), and propitiation (the offering made to satisfy the just wrath of God). It is a gift. So it cannot be earned but can only be received by faith.

Think about It

Beware of trusting in your own works for acceptance before God. A careful look at God's law and our own works will show that we cannot satisfy its demands. We can only shut our mouths and flee to Christ. In Him alone, we find the gift of salvation which encompasses everything we need to restore us as God's beloved children. Be sure you trust Him as the only basis for your justification, not your works or a life relatively better than someone else's. We should have shut mouths and believing hearts.

Praise and Faith When All Seems Lost

Today's Reading: Psalms 70-72; Romans 4

Selected Verses

> *My lips will shout for joy,*
> *when I sing praises to you;*
> *my soul also, which you have redeemed.*

Ps. 71:23

> *No unbelief made him waver concerning the promise of God, but he grew strong*
> *in his faith as he gave glory to God, fully convinced that God was able to do what*
> *he had promised. That is why his faith was "counted to him as righteousness."*

Rom. 4:20-22

Reflections

Much of the content of the Psalms is praise to God. But this praise is not isolated from the realities of life, the struggles, and the seemingly hopeless dilemmas that can come to the believer. In the midst of it all, the Psalmist frequently lifts up his voice in praise for deliverance experienced or expected.

Paul, in his letter to the Romans, shows that the greatest dilemma of all is the problem of our sin before a holy God. No one is righteous—not one (Rom. 1:18-3:20). Yet, God manifested His righteousness through faith in Jesus Christ who shed His blood for the redemption of all who believe in Him.

Paul anticipates a question about the role of Abraham in all of this and carefully lays out the case showing that Abraham himself was justified by faith not by the law of circumcision or any other law. Abraham believed that God would fulfill His promises to make him the father of many nations despite his and Sarah's advanced age, and that faith was counted to him as righteousness. In what might be considered an aside, Paul says, Abraham "grew strong in his faith as he gave glory to God."

Think about It

How can you cultivate faith especially in what appears to be a hopeless situation? Learn the lesson from Abraham. Try giving glory to God. Give glory to Him for what He has done in the past. Praise Him for what He is doing now. Give glory to Him for His wisdom in answering prayers according to His purposes and timing. Perhaps you will see the fulfillment of your prayers, but, if not, God will be glorified and your focus will be where it should be, on Him not on your problem.

When the Prosperity Gospel Goes Bankrupt

Today's Reading: Psalms 73-74; Romans 5

Selected Verses

Whom have I in heaven but you?
And there is nothing on earth that I desire besides you.
My flesh and my heart may fail,
but God is the strength of my heart and my portion forever.

Ps. 73:25-26

Therefore, since we have been justified by faith, we have peace with God through our Lord Jesus Christ. Through him we have also obtained access by faith into this grace in which we stand, and we rejoice in hope of the glory of God. Not only that, but we rejoice in our sufferings.

Rom. 5:1-3

Reflections

As Psalm 73 opens, the writer is not satisfied at all—not in God, not with life. He lays out a common complaint. "Why do the unrighteous prosper while good people suffer?" His observation is accurate in many cases. You'd think the opposite would always hold. But keep reading. The Psalm gives us two answers to that question.

The first, and most obvious, answer is that though the present life may be comfortable for them the end of the wicked is ruin, destruction, and terrors (vs.17-19). In light of this, the Psalmist's complaint turns into a confession of his ignorance and brutishness toward God (vs. 21-22).

Second, the righteous clings to the hope of a good final end, unfazed by the suffering of his present life. He has the Lord with Him and enjoys God's guidance. The godly anticipate the glory to come (vs. 23, 24). God is all he desires, all he needs. He has everything in Him. Why complain and compare?

Paul in Romans 5 expands this thought as he describes the relationship which the justified sinner has with God. That new relationship is one of peace, grace, joy, and hope all through faith in the Lord Jesus Christ. Are there sufferings? Yes! But even sufferings are a cause for joy, because they serve to build endurance, character, and hope. How is this possible? Because of the love God has "poured into our hearts through the Holy Spirit who has been given to us" (vs. 5).

Think about It

Even for us who know Christ, envy of the wicked and complaints about our lot in life will crop up from time to time in our hearts. Don't let them take root and flourish. Instead find joy in the hope of coming glory and be satisfied in God alone. As pastor and author Dr. John Piper, famously says "God is most glorified in us when we are most satisfied in Him." We will not learn to be satisfied in Him without a good portion of suffering after the prosperity gospel has gone bankrupt.

Why Did Christ Die?

Today's Reading: Psalms 75-77; Romans 6

Selected Verses

For not from the east or from the west
and not from the wilderness comes lifting up,
but it is God who executes judgment,
putting down one and lifting up another.
For in the hand of the Lord there is a cup
with foaming wine, well mixed,
and he pours out from it,
and all the wicked of the earth
shall drain it down to the dregs.

Ps. 75:6-8

We were buried therefore with him by baptism into death, in order that, just as Christ was raised from the dead by the glory of the Father, we too might walk in newness of life.

Rom. 6:4

Reflections

The Psalms frequently address the contrast between the wicked and the righteous. The wicked are under God's judgment although they may appear to be successful for a time (Ps. 73). God is the One who lifts up and puts down people on earth. He is a holy God Who will ultimately bring justice through His judgment. There can be no escape from justice.

Jesus Christ came to bring grace and truth (John 1:17). The truth is we are all sinners. We should drink to the dregs the cup of God's wrath. But the grace of Christ is that, instead of us drinking the cup, Jesus drank it for us (Matt. 26:36-46). Now we, who believe in Him, have been buried with Him by baptism into His death.

Paul anticipated some readers thinking that they may sin to the max since they had been freed from judgment by Christ's death. That is to miss the message entirely. Grace is given to us not so we may sin freely but so we may live in newness of life for God's glory. If we have died with Christ, His death is our death, and we are now freed from sin to live a life that reflects our belonging to Him.

Think about It

Are you learning to walk in newness of life as an obedient servant of righteousness? Does your life show you are His and that you are grateful for what He did? That is why He died, so take care how you live.

Wait Till You Hear This!

Today's Reading: Psalm 78; Romans 7

Selected Verses

We will not hide them from their children,
but tell to the coming generation
the glorious deeds of the Lord, and his might,
and the wonders that he has done.

Ps. 78:4

Likewise, my brothers, you also have died to the law through the body
of Christ, so that you may belong to another, to him who has been
raised from the dead, in order that we may bear fruit for God.

Rom. 7:4

Reflections

With the perspective of the New Testament and the life and ministry of the Lord Jesus Christ, we could say "Wait till you hear this!" to the Psalmist who reveled in God's mighty works to Israel. God had done for Israel something unthinkable, unimaginable. He brought ten plagues on Egypt, delivered an enslaved people from that world powerhouse, led them out of the land loaded with spoils, opened up the Red Sea for them to cross, and drowned the pursuing army in the water behind them. This is a story that needs to be told generation after generation. Pass it on!

But wait till you hear this!

In the New Testament we learn that God took on human flesh and lived on earth. We know Him as Jesus of Nazareth, who is the Christ, God's Anointed One, the Messiah. His people rejected Him and crucified Him, but His death bought redemption from the guilt of sin under the law. His death was not a terrible tragedy but the greatest victory ever accomplished.

How do we know? He rose again from the dead. Since that time millions have believed in Him. They trust Him, not their own good works, for the forgiveness of their sins and the gift of eternal life. These millions understand themselves to have died with Him so that His death for sin serves as their death for sin. They are free from any remaining condemnation because their debt was fully paid by Jesus. As a result, these believers from every nation and language in the world belong to Him and live to bear fruit for God.

Think about It

God delivered a nation of a million people out of Egypt, some 3500 years ago, but in the past 2000 years, right down to today, He has been delivering untold millions of people from spiritual death and slavery to become His fruitful people. Tell the coming generation the glorious deeds of the Lord, and His might, and the wonders that He is doing. Pass it on! Wait till they hear that!

More than Forgiven

Today's Reading: Psalms 79-81; Romans 8:1-17

Selected Verses

> *Do not remember against us our former iniquities;*
> *let your compassion come speedily to meet us,*
> *for we are brought very low.*
> *Help us, O God of our salvation,*
> *for the glory of your name;*
> *deliver us, and atone for our sins,*
> *for your name's sake!*

Ps. 79:8-9

> *For God has done what the law, weakened by the flesh, could not do. By*
> *sending his own Son in the likeness of sinful flesh and for sin, he condemned*
> *sin in the flesh, in order that the righteous requirement of the law might be*
> *fulfilled in us, who walk not according to the flesh but according to the Spirit.*

Rom. 8:3-4

Reflections

The Psalmist cries out for forgiveness for the sins of the nation that led to the fall of Jerusalem and the temple. He laments their suffering but, even more, the disgrace brought on the name of God. The writer does not look for excuses, nor does he make promises to do better. He pleads for God Himself to atone for their sins. Truly, he grasps the seriousness of sin. No one is able to justify himself by turning over a new leaf. No one is qualified to repay the debt of offending our holy Creator and Lord.

Paul explains to the Romans just how God has answered this prayer of the Psalmist from so many centuries earlier. The law could only show us our sin, never save us. The law was weakened by the flesh, because our flesh is inclined to use the law as a springboard to rebellion. We do what the law says not to do (Rom. 7:13-25). He has freed us from the law of sin and death, that is, the law that says "you sin, you die."

Think about It

As usual, God's answer goes far above what the Psalmist (or we) could ask or think (Eph. 3:20-21). He has given His Spirit to those who are in Christ. Through Him we have life, peace, and guidance. Through Him we are adopted as God's children and, so, we call Him, "Abba! Father!" (Rom. 8:14-17). Sure, we suffer with Christ in this world, but we know that the glory to come far exceeds these present afflictions.

Does your sin and guilt weigh you down? Trust in Christ for the complete forgiveness of your sins. Rejoice that the law of sin and death is overcome, but more than that, in Him you have His Spirit and are adopted as His own child.

Denial? No! Hope? Yes!

Today's Reading: Psalms 82-84; Romans 8:18-39

Selected Verses

> For the Lord God is a sun and shield;
>> the Lord bestows favor and honor.
> No good thing does he withhold
>> from those who walk uprightly.

Ps. 84:11

> He who did not spare his own Son but gave him up for us all,
> how will he not also with him graciously give us all things?

Rom. 8:32

Reflections

We, humans, are known for denying reality under certain circumstances. As a little boy I could put on a tough face after a nasty fall on the playground with my buddies watching. "I'm OK!" I could claim loudly while grimacing inwardly. (That would not be the case if my mom was nearby to comfort.)

The God of the Bible never encourages our denial of reality. While the psalms are filled with laments, the Psalmist never loses hope. He finds his complete fulfillment in God. Nothing but God's presence delights him. There he sings for joy (Ps. 84:2). One day in the courts of the Lord is better than a thousand anywhere else. Being a doorkeeper for the Lord is better than being in prominence in the "tents of wickedness" (Ps. 84:10).

In the same way, Paul in his letter to the Romans doesn't downplay the reality of pain and suffering in this world. We groan as we wait eagerly for adoption as sons, the redemption of our bodies. To help us, we have hope that gives us patience. We have the Holy Spirit to help us pray and to intercede for us. God promises that all things work together for good and that He has predestined us to be conformed to the image of His Son. We are called, justified, and glorified by God.

Think about It

We can be confident that all this is true because if God has given us His Son, and He has, He will certainly give us every other necessary thing with Him. God promises that those who are in Christ Jesus will never lack any good thing.

If you are in Christ, you know what the Psalmist and the Apostle Paul are saying. Your heart longs to be with the Lord. This world is not your final destination. Nothing here totally satisfies you. You are a citizen of heaven and you want to be home (Phil. 3:20-21). But you are not home. Not yet. Your way may be difficult, but the victory is sure. You are more than a conqueror "through Him who loved us." Be filled with hope because our God is the God of hope (Rom. 15:13).

When You Despair over the Lost

Today's Reading: Psalms 85-87; Romans 9

Selected Verses

> Will you not revive us again,
>   that your people may rejoice in you?
> Show us your steadfast love, O Lord,
>   and grant us your salvation.

Ps. 85:6-7

> I have great sorrow and unceasing anguish in my heart. For I could wish that I myself were accursed and cut off from Christ for the sake of my brothers, my kinsmen according to the flesh.

Rom. 9:2-3

Reflections

The Psalmist calls out to God for Israel to again experience His blessing. He remembers past days when they knew the Lord's forgiveness and enjoyed His favor in the land. Now, that favor has been withdrawn. God is indignant with them. What can be done? The writer calls on the Lord for restoration. Only He can bring revival to the people. The Psalmist calls on God and he is confident in Him. He recognizes their foolishness, but he knows that God's love and faithfulness are greater than the waywardness of His people.

Paul also agonizes over Israel. He sees them foolishly ignoring all that God had given them. Look at the list of blessings they have uniquely received:

"They are Israelites, and to them belong the adoption, the glory, the covenants, the giving of the law, the worship, and the promises. To them belong the patriarchs, and from their race, according to the flesh, is the Christ, who is God over all, blessed forever. Amen" (Rom. 9:4-5).

What had they done with what they received? They wasted it. They turned away from their Messiah, who is God. Indeed, they crucified Him! Paul's anguish is palpable. So much so that he even states that he would give up his own salvation if that would bring them to Christ. Of course, it would not, but we get the picture of the depth of his despair about the Jews.

Think about It

What believer has not felt at least some level of despair over his or her unsaved loved ones? What can we do? Paul prayed for Israel. Psalm 85 gives us the right approach in our prayer. Remember God's blessings in the past. Confess any sins that need confessing in the present. Ask God for mercy and to give life to those who are dead in their sins. Trust God to do what is right in His time. Praise Him for His righteousness. Wait on Him. Repeat daily, as needed.

God's Faithfulness and Wisdom

Today's Reading: Psalms 88-89; Romans 10

Selected Verses

If his children forsake my law
    and do not walk according to my rules,
if they violate my statutes
    and do not keep my commandments,
then I will punish their transgression with the rod
    and their iniquity with stripes,
but I will not remove from him my steadfast love
    or be false to my faithfulness.

Ps. 89:30-33

Then Isaiah is so bold as to say,
"I have been found by those who did not seek me;
    I have shown myself to those who did not ask for me."
But of Israel he says, "All day long I have held out
    my hands to a disobedient and contrary people."

Rom. 10:20-21

Reflections

The Psalmist laments deeply the loss to Israel of God's apparent abandonment of them. He reasons that God's covenant with David was to maintain his offspring on the throne forever, conditional on the obedience of his descendants. Clearly the conditions were not met. David's descendants were a sorry lot, for the most part. After Solomon, the kingdom was divided and Rehoboam ruled over Judah alone. Idolatry became the norm in both Judah and Israel. Eventually foreign powers conquer those kingdoms and take the people into captivity.

But God promised to keep the Davidic line alive while punishing the rebellion of the kings in that line. How would He do this? What did His promise really mean? We learn from the New Testament that God sent His Son through the Virgin Mary of the line of David to be the King forever. Jesus was also called the "Lamb of God" (John 1:29). He took away the sins of the world. He became the High Priest whose offering was perfect and removed forever the need for further sacrifices (Heb. 10:11-14).

Paul longs for Israel to recognize their Messiah as their King and High Priest. In another move showing God's wisdom, He sends the gospel to the Gentiles, and they believed it. Yet this move was, in part, to make Israel jealous of the blessing they were missing. Paul says that Isaiah had foretold this strategy. Ironically, those who sought to be righteous by their own efforts [the Jews] did not obtain it while those who did not seek God and His righteousness [the Gentiles] found justification before Him by faith in Jesus.

Think about It

In light of world events and apparent chaos, consider the wisdom and faithfulness of God. Praise Him that His ways are not our ways and that He has triumphed over sin and Satan. He has won the battle.

Lifelong Fruitfulness

Today's Reading: Psalms 90-92; Romans 11:1-24

Selected Verses

The righteous flourish like the palm tree
and grow like a cedar in Lebanon.
They are planted in the house of the Lord;
they flourish in the courts of our God.
They still bear fruit in old age;
they are ever full of sap and green,
to declare that the Lord is upright;
he is my rock, and there is no unrighteousness in him.

Ps. 92:12-15

Then you will say, "Branches were broken off so that I might be grafted in." That is true. They were broken off because of their unbelief, but you stand fast through faith. So do not become proud, but fear. For if God did not spare the natural branches, neither will he spare you.

Rom. 11:19-21

Reflections

Psalm 92 compares God's righteous people to a palm tree planted in the house of the Lord. What is the function of this tree? It is to flourish, grow, and bear fruit. What fruit does it bear? Not dates or coconuts, (it is an analogy, don't forget!), but the fruit of a clear declaration "that the Lord is upright; he is my rock, and there is no unrighteousness in him." This promise of fruitfulness is directed to the elderly. They will continue to bear spiritual fruit into old age despite the decline of their physical strength.

Paul addresses something that must have been bothering the Christians in Rome. There seems to have been an issue (or, at least, a potential issue) of Christian Gentiles looking down on unbelieving Jews for rejecting Christ. The Apostle explains that this rejection (anticipated in the Old Testament) benefited the Gentiles who were then coming to Christ. Ultimately, we can expect a positive reaction among the Jews when they turn to the Lord. "Be humble about your acceptance before God. He could cut you off and restore the natural branches," Paul warns the Gentile Christians.

Think about It

God has securely grafted us who believe in His Son into His olive tree whether young or elderly. But it is not our own doing. It is by grace through faith, not by any merit on our part. We ought to maintain a humble, grateful attitude. As part of the tree in the house of the Lord, He planted us to bear fruit. God's grace will sustain us all the days of our lives as we keep declaring God's righteousness. So expect fruitfulness and beware of arrogance.

God Is—The Challenge of Describing the Holy One

Today's Reading: Psalms 93-95; Romans 11:25-36

Selected Verses

Mightier than the thunders of many waters,
mightier than the waves of the sea,
the Lord on high is mighty!
Your decrees are very trustworthy;
holiness befits your house,
O Lord, forevermore.

Ps. 93:4-5

Oh, the depth of the riches and wisdom and knowledge of God!
How unsearchable are his judgments and how inscrutable his ways!
"For who has known the mind of the Lord,
or who has been his counselor?"
"Or who has given a gift to him
that he might be repaid?"
For from him and through him and to him are all things. To him be glory forever. Amen.

Rom. 11:33-36

Reflections

How do you describe God? Psalm 93 uses an analogy to the highest human authority, the king. Admittedly, that comparison falls far short because God is a king whose reign always was and always will be. He is eternal. He rules, not over some limited territory, but over the whole universe.

How do you describe God? The Psalmist draws from the most powerful forces in nature: a flood, mighty waters, the sea. The waters roar. They sweep away everything in their path. But that is not an adequate description of the power of God for He is mightier than the sea. He is on high above it all.

Paul compares God to the wisest counselor or the richest man on earth. They could add nothing to the Lord's knowledge nor contribute anything He lacks. The Apostle seems out of superlatives as he cries out, "Oh, the depth of the riches and wisdom and knowledge of God! To him be glory forever. Amen."

Think about It

How do you describe God? Human kings make decrees, but they cannot guarantee their fulfillment. Maybe the kingdom will be overthrown. Maybe the king will die suddenly. The king's decree is only a statement of his intention. But God's decrees are "very trustworthy." He is holy, set apart, completely other. Forever.

We cannot adequately describe God, but give it a try. He is worthy and accepting of all our feeble, but heartfelt, efforts to praise Him. There can be no higher use of our minds and tongues.

Love God; Hate Evil

Today's Reading: Psalms 96-98; Romans 12

Selected Verses

> *O you who love the Lord, hate evil!*
> *He preserves the lives of his saints;*
> *he delivers them from the hand of the wicked.*
>
> Ps. 97:10

> *Let love be genuine. Abhor what is evil; hold fast to what is good. Love one*
> *another with brotherly affection. Outdo one another in showing honor.*
>
> Rom. 12:9-10

Reflections

Our psalms for today are at the heart of a section in which God is worshiped and praised as King (Ps. 93; 95-100). We hear the exclamation, "The Lord reigns" several times. These psalms also portray God as the Judge of all the earth. His rule is absolute. His laws are perfectly just and His judgments are flawless. Obviously, the laws of human kings can be (and often are) biased. Their judicial rulings are not perfect, but our God is just in every way. His laws and judgments are infallible. So it is not only safe but right to love the Lord and to hate evil, as He defines it by His law.

The Psalmist exhorts us, who love the Lord, to hate evil. These are two sides of a coin, impossible to separate. If you love the Lord, you will hate evil. If you do not hate evil, your love for the Lord is in question. Can one's love for God be genuine, if he does not hate what God hates?

Paul makes an exhortation to the recipients of his letter in Rome which similarly includes the words "love" and "abhor." He raises the possibility and the danger of phony love. One may pretend to love but not truly love. Loving action can be counterfeit—a setup for later betrayal like Judas Iscariot. Check your love to be sure it is genuine, writes Paul. He then goes on to tell them to "Abhor what is evil."

Think about It

The Christian faith and life is not only a matter of correct theology, although that is essential, but also a matter of attitudes and actions—the involvement of the will and emotions. The one who presents himself to God as a living sacrifice seeking a renewed mind will be transformed in thoughts, attitudes, and actions. That renewal is a life-long process called sanctification which culminates when we see the Lord face to face (1 John 3:1-3).

Will you take one step forward in godliness today, by presenting yourself to Him as a living sacrifice out of genuine love for Him? Combine that with a hatred of evil, confessing the sin that lurks in your own heart. A renewed mind will bring a transformed heart to love God and hate evil.

The Role of Government

Today's Reading: Psalms 99-102; Romans 13

Selected Verses

I will look with favor on the faithful in the land,
that they may dwell with me;
he who walks in the way that is blameless
shall minister to me.
No one who practices deceit
shall dwell in my house;
no one who utters lies
shall continue before my eyes.

Ps. 101: 6-7

For rulers are not a terror to good conduct, but to bad. Would you have
no fear of the one who is in authority? Then do what is good, and
you will receive his approval, for he is God's servant for your good.

Rom. 13:3-4

Reflections

The authority of government comes from God, so those who govern are responsible to Him to punish bad behavior and encourage good and those who are governed are responsible to submit and obey as to God.

In Psalm 101 David sets high ideals for his reign. He says he will praise God, a necessary activity for one who could easily lose sight of the true King over all the earth. He acknowledges his need for the Lord's help and presence and vows to bring justice to those who do wrong. Instead, he will create a favorable climate for those who do right. David determined not to suffer deceivers in his cabinet. He promises to act quickly in dealing with crime. These noble goals describe a kingdom in which any upright person would love to live.

Paul continues addressing the Christians in Rome moving on to the issue of their relationship to the government. The Old Testament era of theocracy in Israel is no more. Since then and up to now, God's people live under secular authorities who are under God whether they recognize Him or not. Often, they do not. Yet Christians are commanded to submit to these officials, pay taxes, and show proper respect and honor. The government is to encourage those who do good and punish those who do not.

We know from other Bible passages that this general teaching of submission is limited to those situations in which the government does not command citizens to do what God prohibits or prohibits them from doing what God commands (Acts 4:18-20;5:29).

Think about It

What is your understanding of our responsibility to the government? Remember a ruler is "the servant of God, an avenger who carries out God's wrath on the wrongdoer." Pray for your leaders, those who govern, and seek to encourage them when they fulfill their roles properly before God (1 Tim. 2:1-4).

Purpose in Life: Unchanging and Unending

Today's Reading: Psalms 103-104; Romans 14

I will sing to the Lord as long as I live;
I will sing praise to my God while I have being.

Ps. 104:33

The one who observes the day, observes it in honor of the Lord. The one
who eats, eats in honor of the Lord, since he gives thanks to God, while
the one who abstains, abstains in honor of the Lord and gives thanks
to God. For none of us lives to himself, and none of us dies to himself.

Rom. 14:6-7

Reflections

For the believer, there is one clear lasting purpose around which everything revolves, to honor the Lord in life and in death. Circumstances change; that purpose never does.

The Psalmist's heart overflows in praise to God. God is due all honor for His being, His attributes, and His endless acts of kindness and love to His people. There is not enough time or words to express it all. As Fredrick Lehman put it in his hymn "The Love of God":

Could we with ink the ocean fill, And were the skies of parchment made,
Were every stalk on earth a quill, And every man a scribe by trade;
To write the love of God above would drain the ocean dry;
Nor could the scroll contain the whole, though stretched from sky to sky.

Paul addresses matters that were apparently causing divisions between believers in Rome: the keeping of Jewish feast days, and the eating of meat previously offered to idols. The Apostle points all of his readers to a place of common ground. They are all concerned about honoring the Lord, or, at least, they should be. That is the purpose of their lives. They have been redeemed to glorify God. The kingdom to which they have been called is not about what you eat but about "righteousness and peace and joy in the Holy Spirit" (vs. 17).

Think about It

Are you focused on what really matters, honoring God? We, who trust in Jesus Christ, can certainly agree that what matters most is His glory in and through our lives until He calls us home. That will help us get along even when we don't see eye to eye with each other on minor points. Let His glory keep you profitably occupied all the days of your life.

Do We Need the Old Testament?

Today's Reading: Psalms 105-106; Romans 15:1-21

Selected Verses

> Oh give thanks to the Lord; call upon his name;
> make known his deeds among the peoples!
> Sing to him, sing praises to him;
> tell of all his wondrous works!
> Glory in his holy name;
> let the hearts of those who seek the Lord rejoice!

Ps. 105:1-3

> *For whatever was written in former days was written for our instruction, that through endurance and through the encouragement of the Scriptures we might have hope.*

Rom. 16:3

Reflections

Psalm 105 gives us a good example of why we need the Old Testament if we are to fulfill our high calling to glorify God (Rom. 11:36; 1 Cor. 6:20; 10:31; Rev. 4:11). The psalm includes both a call to praise (vs. 1-6) and the content for praise (vs. 7-45). Like several other psalms, this one focuses on praising God for who He is and what He has done in history for the people of Israel. It is easy to see God's wisdom, faithfulness, power, and glory. Well, at least, it's easy to see when you read this psalm.

My experience personally and by observation of others is that it's not easy to think of words with which to praise God. It is easier to look at the problems of our lives and our world than to spend more than a few minutes giving praise to God. We need the Old Testament, in general, and the Psalms, in particular, to instruct us and encourage us to praise the Lord.

Paul makes his case to the Christians in Rome that the Scriptures that they had from the former days had a crucial place in their lives. It is hard to find a stronger passage in the New Testament urging the careful and continual study of the Old. After all, the Old Testament was the Bible that Jesus knew and frequently quoted. He relied on it when confronted by Satan and while dying on the cross (Matt. 4:1-11; 27:46; Ps. 22:1; Luke 23:46; Ps. 31:5). It was the Bible from which He taught the disciples about Himself (Luke 24:27). If Jesus and His disciples needed the Old Testament, don't we also?

Think about It

The Old Testament (just like the New) plays a key role in the life of believers in Jesus Christ giving them instruction leading to endurance, encouragement, and hope. Make it priority to know both Testaments. It's all God's word and will instruct you, sustain you, encourage you, and give you hope to finish the race.

How God Uses Means to Meet Needs

Today's Reading: Psalms 107-108; Romans 15:22-33

Selected Verses

Then they cried to the Lord in their trouble,
and he delivered them from their distress.
He led them by a straight way
till they reached a city to dwell in.
Let them thank the Lord for his steadfast love,
for his wondrous works to the children of man!

Ps. 107:6-8

At present, however, I am going to Jerusalem bringing aid to the saints. For Macedonia and Achaia have been pleased to make some contribution for the poor among the saints at Jerusalem.

Rom. 15:25-26

Reflections

Psalm 107 gives four vivid examples of how God worked to deliver people in need who called to Him in their distress. One group was homeless, others were imprisoned, some suffered for their sin, and still others were on the verge of shipwreck in a storm at sea. In each case, God heard their cries and delivered them. In each case, those who were delivered are admonished to give thanks to God for responding to their prayer and saving them. God is certainly due praise in these cases, but it would be naïve to assume that God never uses other people to answer the prayers of those who are helpless.

Take Paul, for example. He knew about the suffering of the believers in Jerusalem. As he traveled through Europe, he asked the churches there to help with this need. They responded and Paul was in the process of traveling to deliver the collection to the needy.

Think about It

God deserves all praise and thanks when He provides for those in need, but we ought not to sit back passively when we see a need assuming that He will intervene without the help of people like us.

Certainly, we are aware of more needs than any one of us can meet alone. We do need wisdom in choosing where to assist given the realities of our limited time and money. But beware of never responding to genuine needs thinking that God will intervene with no assistance from people. God uses means to meet needs that accomplish His purposes and you and I are some of the means He uses. Be ready to consider serving when you are called and able to do so.

The God of Wisdom and the Wisdom of God

Today's Reading: Psalms 109-111; Romans 16

Selected Verses

*The fear of the Lord is the beginning of wisdom;
all those who practice it have a good understanding.
His praise endures forever!*

Ps. 111:10

To the only wise God be glory forevermore through Jesus Christ! Amen.

Rom. 16:27

Reflections

Psalm 111 praises the works of God and tells us there is value in studying them. Scripture includes the work of scientists and historians here, not to mention educators who train students to do these kinds of work (vs. 2, 4). If God's glory is seen in what He has done in creation and in providence, then it stands to reason that He is glorified when His works are studied, remembered, and discussed.

The Christian need not hesitate to follow professions which can bring glory to God, but he must beware of careers which will likely force him to reject the very basis for wisdom, which is the fear of God. There can be tremendous pressure to conform to the status quo, the irrational assumption of a Godless universe self-created by a combination of time and chance. What would be the purpose or benefit of studying such a random cosmos? Can it even be done?

Here is where the godly man or woman, one who fears the Lord, has an advantage. The believer understands that God is wise, that is, He selects "the best and highest goal, together with the surest means of attaining it" as Dr. Packer tells us in his classic work "Knowing God". The Christian researcher can pray for wisdom, praise God for the order and beauty of His works, and (as Johannes Kepler is quoted as saying) "[think] God's thoughts after Him."

Think about It

In a day when many doubt the very existence of truth, how are we to find wisdom when we are not even sure there is truth upon which to base it? Believers will not be discouraged or give up all hope. We know there is a God. He has revealed truth to us and He teaches us wisdom as we consciously walk before Him.

We can be sure that all good and honest work done well glorifies God and benefits mankind. Keep walking in the fear of the Lord and seek to use whatever profession or vocation you have to serve Him wisely.

Unity for God's Glory

Today's Reading: Psalms 112-115; First Corinthians 1

Selected Verses

Not to us, O Lord, not to us, but to your name give glory,
for the sake of your steadfast love and your faithfulness!

Ps. 115:1

And because of him you are in Christ Jesus, who became to us wisdom
from God, righteousness and sanctification and redemption, so that,
as it is written, "Let the one who boasts, boast in the Lord."

1 Cor. 1:30-31

Reflections

The Psalmist prays a prayer that God loves to answer. He prays that all glory may go to the Lord and not to himself or his people. God does deserve all glory and those who give Him praise understand this.

Paul admonishes the Christians in Corinth who showed a total lack of passion for the glory of God. He points out their deep divisions over their loyalties to various pastors and apostles. It was popular for these believers to identify themselves with one leader or another, forming cliques. One group even said they were "of Christ" as if the others were not.

The Apostle disavows any intention of creating such parties within the congregation. He tells them that God's wisdom is contrary to the wisdom of this world which causes people to elevate themselves and seek their own glory—not God's. The divisions will stop when they renounce this false wisdom and find their identity in Christ. He is their wisdom, righteousness, sanctification, and redemption.

Think about It

What do you desire above everything else?

God blesses those who seek His glory, not their own, and God's blessings will not be found by those who seek their own glory. One of those blessings is unity with our brothers and sisters.

For us, believers, everything we need is in Christ. We ought to see ourselves as one in Him not divided in competing groups. Divisions often come from the desire for our own glory. Beware of ungodly affection that can grow in our hearts. There is but one way to the Father, through Jesus, and all of us who have come to Him are one with Him and with each other. Seek His glory, and unity will be a natural by-product. Boast in the Lord alone.

The Blessing of Being Simple

Today's Reading: Psalms 116-118; First Corinthians 2

Selected Verses

> *Gracious is the Lord, and righteous;*
> *our God is merciful.*
> *The Lord preserves the simple;*
> *when I was brought low, he saved me.*
> *Return, O my soul, to your rest;*
> *for the Lord has dealt bountifully with you.*

Ps. 116:5-7

> *Now we have received not the spirit of the world, but the Spirit who is*
> *from God, that we might understand the things freely given us by God.*

1 Cor. 2:12

Reflections

The generosity of the Lord to His people is beyond measure. It is worthy of a continual sacrifice of praise. In Psalm 116, the writer revels in God's blessings to him. He recognizes God's mercy and grace in the face of impending death, in a time of distress and anguish. He wonders how to make any kind of sufficient offering to the Lord for all he has received from His hand. "I will offer to you the sacrifice of thanksgiving," he promises in vs. 17.

Why has God so richly blessed him? One quality which the Lord looks for in those He blesses is simplicity. He preserves the simple, we read in vs. 6. The simple are receptive to God's Law. Psalm 19:7 tells us "the testimony of the LORD is sure, making wise the simple." The simple become wise because they pay attention to God's Word.

Paul continues with his message to the Corinthians showing them that it was not lofty speech that he used to win them to Christ, but rather the simple message of Jesus Christ who was crucified. Those who believe and are mature are able to receive wisdom from God revealed by His Spirit to His people. The spirit of the world is of no assistance in knowing God, but God's Spirit reveals the things that no one could even imagine, the things that God has freely given to His own.

Think about It

The disciple of Jesus Christ is one who has become like a child, simple and trusting in the One who came to make the Father known and to save His people from their sins (Matt. 18:1-4; 1:21; John 1:14-18). He leads us to wisdom and blessing from the Lord. Seek to always be found among the simple.

The Christian's Identity: God's Lowly Farmhand

Today's Reading: Psalm 119:1-48; First Corinthians 3

Selected Verses

> Lead me in the path of your commandments,
> for I delight in it.
> Incline my heart to your testimonies,
> and not to selfish gain!
> Turn my eyes from looking at worthless things;
> and give me life in your ways.

Ps. 119:35-37

So neither he who plants nor he who waters is anything, but only God who gives the growth. He who plants and he who waters are one, and each will receive his wages according to his labor. For we are God's fellow workers. You are God's field, God's building.

1 Cor. 3:7-9

Reflections

All progress in our personal lives and our ministry to others depends on God. He commands us to be diligent in our use of the means of grace and in our proclaiming the gospel to the world, but He is the One who ultimately changes hearts and brings about growth.

The Psalmist proclaims his delight in God's law, but, at the same time, prays to God for help in following that law. As committed as he is to God's word, his pleas to the Lord reveal an awareness of his dependence on God. Of course, delight in God's law is a good, admirable trait. It is just not constant enough to be a reliable basis for one's spiritual life. God will have to work because there are innumerable other distractions, like selfish gain and worthless things.

The writer of the longest chapter in the Bible knew his own heart. There were good moments when he could focus on the Lord and His Word with great exuberance. He is not being deceptive when he professes to love the law, but he also knows the weaknesses of his flesh. He can be drawn away by money and entertainment. Jesus warned His disciples against these sorts of things in His parable about the sower. He told them the good seed of the Word can be "choked by the cares and riches and pleasures of life, and their fruit does not mature" (Luke 8:14).

Paul, too, understands his dependence on God for fruitful ministry. The Corinthians needed to learn that they are indebted to God for their responsiveness to the gospel, not to Paul or Apollos. Their divisiveness was partly a result of their misplaced adulation of their mentors.

Think about It

Give all praise to God, if you are walking in His ways, maturing as a disciple and bearing fruit. He alone causes the growth. At most, our identity is that of unprofitable servants and God's lowly farmhands.

Preparing for Finals

Today's Reading: Psalm 119:49-104; First Corinthians 4

Selected Verses

Let the insolent be put to shame,
because they have wronged me with falsehood;
as for me, I will meditate on your precepts.
Let those who fear you turn to me,
that they may know your testimonies.
May my heart be blameless in your statutes,
that I may not be put to shame!

Ps. 119:78-80

It is the Lord who judges me. Therefore do not pronounce judgment before the time, before the Lord comes, who will bring to light the things now hidden in darkness and will disclose the purposes of the heart. Then each one will receive his commendation from God.

1 Cor. 4:4-5

Reflections

The Psalmist knew severe opposition because of his trust in God and obedience to His law. His life was a rebuke to those who had no regard for the Lord. He prayed that the insolent would be shamed and the God-fearers would be drawn to him so that they would know God's word even better. But he also prayed for a blameless heart with respect to the Law of God. He did not want to be put to shame before the Judge.

In a similar way, Paul sought to be found commendable before God. He had received both criticism and acclaim by people. Some identified themselves with him to such a degree that they went around saying, "I am of Paul." This was causing serious division in the church. Paul would not hear of this. He said, "It is the Lord who judges me." He did not want the approval of men, especially since it was a basis for division.

How should they look at Paul and others, like Apollos? They were mere servants of Christ and stewards of the mysteries of God (vs. 1). He already said that they could do nothing but plant or sow, but had no power to cause growth (1 Cor. 3:6). Paul served God with a continual awareness of the judgment to come. He sought only to be faithful. Like the Psalmist, he wanted to have a blameless heart on that day when "the Lord comes, who will bring to light the things now hidden in darkness and will disclose the purposes of the heart."

Think about It

I heard of a Sunday School teacher who had a class for senior citizens. He said they attended faithfully because, at their advanced age, "they were preparing for finals." Do you serve Christ with this mindset? Are you seeking only His commendation at the end of your life? Be preparing for finals today.

260

Church Discipline and Membership

Today's Reading: Psalm 119:105-176; First Corinthians 5

Selected Verses

> My eyes shed streams of tears,
> because people do not keep your law.
>
> Ps. 119:136

> Is it not those inside the church whom you are to judge? God
> judges those outside. "Purge the evil person from among you."
>
> 1 Cor. 5:12-13

Reflections

The subject of Psalm 119 is the Word of God, also referred to as His statutes, rules, commandments, testimonies, precepts, and law. The glories of God's Word are praised. The Psalmist tells of his delight in and commitment to the law. There is also an occasional reference to the failure of some to obey the law. For the author, this disobedience on the part of some brought him to tears, and, apparently, at times it brought him to disgust (vs. 158). He is on the alert for those rebels as they threaten his faithfulness (vs. 115).

When we go to the New Testament, the people of God, the Church of Jesus Christ, are in far different circumstances than Old Testament Israel. Now the Church is composed of Jews and Gentiles. There is no theocracy, but the Church exists under various kingdoms and governments. Still, there is a responsibility of the Church to discipline its own members.

Corinth was a particularly wicked city in the days of the Apostles. Paul instructed them in the proper handling of a case of incest that would not have been tolerated even in secular society. Apparently, the guilty party was unrepentant, so Paul told them to remove him from their congregation. This process is referred to as excommunication. It is not the first step of discipline and is applied only when there is a refusal to repent for the sin or sins that were committed (see Matt. 18:15-17).

Think about It

For Church discipline to exist there must be formal local church membership, the defining of who is and who isn't under the discipline of the body. Everyone is either in the fellowship or not. Members are held responsible for godly living and obedience to the Scriptures. Non-members have not committed to be responsible. If you are a believer, be sure you are a member of a Bible-believing church and accountable for your life and walk with God. If you are a member, seek to encourage and admonish others as needed and be receptive to godly correction.

Church discipline is to be exercised but always with the hope of restoring the penitent and never with any kind of joy or satisfaction. If you are a pastor or an elder, exercise discipline with care and tears.

Peace and Purity in the Church

Today's Reading: Psalms 120-123; First Corinthians 6

Selected Verses

> Too long have I had my dwelling
> among those who hate peace.
> I am for peace,
> but when I speak, they are for war!
>
> Ps. 120:6-7

> To have lawsuits at all with one another is already a defeat for you.
> Why not rather suffer wrong? Why not rather be defrauded? But
> you yourselves wrong and defraud—even your own brothers!
>
> 1 Cor. 6:7-8

Reflections

Christians are called to be committed to the peace and purity of the church. There ought never be occasions when professing believers war against and defraud one another. But there are. Fortunately, God's word denounces this and gives instruction on how to respond.

Psalm 120 introduces the section of fifteen psalms known as "The Songs of Ascents," traditionally believed to be songs sung by pilgrims on their way to Jerusalem for the feasts. It is easy to see in these psalms the longing to be in Jerusalem and in the temple where the Lord's presence was most keenly felt.

In this case the psalmist is weary of dealing with liars and deceivers. The locations of Meshech and Kedar may be mentioned to epitomize Gentile locales where one would expect to find liars and deceivers and a total disregard for the fear of God. It seems that the world's culture had moved into Israel.

Paul found a similar situation in Corinth where the members of the congregation were going to secular courts with complaints against one another. The Apostle is horrified by the thought of this kind of hostility in the church. He tells them there is no place for this among God's people, who should be willing to suffer wrong and be defrauded before going to a pagan court against a brother.

Think about It

Sadly, these things continue to exist. Despite church members taking vows to "study the peace and purity of the church," we hear of lawsuits, divorces with no biblical foundation, and other shameful behaviors taking place.[7] Seek to be a force in your local church for peace and purity that God may be glorified.

---

[7] One of the five questions asked of new members in the Presbyterian Church of America is "Do you submit yourselves to the government and discipline of the Church, and promise to study its purity and peace?" (*Book of Church Order*, Ch. 57 Section 5).

Security vs. Restlessness

Today's Reading: Psalms 124-127; First Corinthians 7:1-24

Selected Verses

> *Those who trust in the Lord are like Mount Zion,*
> *which cannot be moved, but abides forever.*
> *As the mountains surround Jerusalem,*
> *so the Lord surrounds his people,*
> *from this time forth and forevermore.*

Ps. 125:1-2

> *You were bought with a price; do not become bondservants of men. So, brothers,*
> *in whatever condition each was called, there let him remain with God.*

1 Cor. 7:23-24

Reflections

It is pleasant to picture the Jews of Ancient Israel trudging up the dusty roads to Jerusalem on Mount Zion singing the songs of ascents. They go with expectation of being in the holy city near the temple, and, most of all, in the Lord's presence. The mount looks solid, and feels immovable. The psalmist helps them picture their trusting relationship to God as one which keeps them as firm as the mount itself.

But they are not left on their own, merely clinging to Him in the hope that they do not let go and end up lost. The song goes on to point out the mountains which surround the city. These remind them that God surrounds His people. When? Sometimes? Off and on? No! "From this time forth and forevermore!" What comfort! What peace!

Paul addressed the subject of the marital and socioeconomic states in which the Corinthian believers might find themselves: single, married to a believer, married to an unbeliever, bond servitude, freedmen, etc. There seems to be restlessness in some to change one or more of these states. What is the best state to be in? Paul says (in essence), "the one the Lord called you in." There are advantages and disadvantages to any state in which they found themselves, but the important thing is to remember "you are bought with a price" and whatever you do "remain with God."

Think about It

We, Christians, are called to trust in the Lord and to recognize that we belong to Him by virtue of the purchase of our Redeemer, Jesus Christ. We owe no higher loyalty and no greater allegiance. As His disciples, we are first and foremost His servants, freed from sin and the restlessness that so often drives us to what appears desirable. Beware of enticements to flee the very situation in which God has placed you for His glory. Of course, we should flee any sinful situation, but being His disciple means trusting Him and being secure and fruitful wherever He has planted us. The grass is usually not greener on the other side of the fence. In Him, we have stability and security.

Wisdom: Making Sense of Apparent Contradictions

Today's Reading: Psalms 128-131; First Corinthians 7:25-40

Selected Verses

Your wife will be like a fruitful vine
within your house;
your children will be like olive shoots
around your table.
Behold, thus shall the man be blessed
who fears the Lord.

Ps. 128:3-4

This is what I mean, brothers: the appointed time has grown very short. From now on, let those who have wives live as though they had none, and those who mourn as though they were not mourning, and those who rejoice as though they were not rejoicing, and those who buy as though they had no goods, and those who deal with the world as though they had no dealings with it. For the present form of this world is passing away.

1 Cor. 7:29-31

Reflections

To understand the Bible properly, the reader needs to observe principles of interpretation, especially the principles of reading passages in context and seeking to let the whole Bible comment on specific passages.

The psalmist paints a lovely picture of the family life of a godly man where the husband fears God and God blesses him in every aspect of his life. His wife and children are an evidence of the goodness and blessing of God poured out on him. Who would not love to have a family like this or be a member of such a family?

In the first letter to the Corinthians, we seem to get a different message. Paul says that marriage brings concerns that occupy and distract people. It would be ideal, he says, for single or betrothed people to remain as they are and to give themselves in "undivided devotion to the Lord." Rather than holding up traditional family life as the epitome of God's blessing, Paul sees it as a potential obstacle to focused service for the Lord.

Think about It

So, which is it? Is marriage a blessing or a distraction to the believer? The answer is "it depends." Paul condemns the prohibition of marriage (1 Tim. 4:1-5). He honors marriage and teaches that it is an analogy of the relationship of Christ and the Church (Eph. 5:22-33). But neither does the Apostle suggest that marriage is the only way to personal fulfillment and fruitfulness (2 Tim. 2:3-4).

Marriage is for most but not everyone (Gen. 2:18-25; Matt. 19:10-12). The Scriptures advise the use of wisdom as we make decisions about marriage or other kinds of responsibilities that will impact our freedom to serve God. Seek the whole picture of what the Bible teaches on any matter before jumping to conclusions. Let's handle apparent contradictions in the Bible carefully. Truth matters.

The Care and Feeding of Recovering Idolaters

Today's Reading: Psalms 132-135; First Corinthians 8

Selected Verses

> *The idols of the nations are silver and gold,*
> *the work of human hands.*
> *They have mouths, but do not speak;*
> *they have eyes, but do not see;*
> *they have ears, but do not hear,*
> *nor is there any breath in their mouths.*
> *Those who make them become like them,*
> *so do all who trust in them.*
>
> Ps. 135:15-18

> *We know that "an idol has no real existence," and that "there is no God but one."*
>
> 1 Cor. 8:4

Reflections

Scripture tells us that there is One God, the Creator of all things, who made mankind in His own image and after His likeness (Gen. 1:26-27). But what happens when people reject their God? They replace Him with some other "god," one of their own imagination. The psalmist tells us that the impact on these idolaters is very negative. Worshipers start looking like the thing they worship. The worship of a non-existent god of one's own fabrication diminishes that worshiper to the level of that god.

Despite the apparent hopeless state of those reduced to less than humans, God's grace and sovereign election to salvation overcomes and redeems those sub-humans. Paul reports that this happened in the city of Corinth (1 Cor. 6:9-11). Praise God!

On the other hand, many new believers recovering from a vast host of sins populated the Corinthian church. More mature believers might inadvertently cause offense to these young disciples. Paul gives them some urgent advice about the care and feeding of recovering idolaters. Of course, idols don't exist but former idol worshipers could easily be offended by seeing their fellow Christians eating at pagan feasts or enjoying food previously offered to idols. The point is don't make your brother stumble even if what you are doing is not technically wrong.

Think about It

Although idol worshipers are reduced to less than human, they are not beyond the saving grace of God in Jesus Christ. When converted idolaters enter the church, more mature members must be sensitive to them as they grow in the knowledge of the Lord.

Do you need to limit your freedom in order to keep a brother or sister from stumbling? Do you need to grow in the conviction that there is but One God, so that you progress in your sanctification, fleeing the baggage of your sinful past? Let those who are mature lead the way in the care and feeding of recovering idolaters.

Being and Doing the Lord's Work

Today's Reading: Psalms 136-138; First Corinthians 9

Selected Verses

> *The Lord will fulfill his purpose for me;*
> *your steadfast love, O LORD, endures forever.*
> *Do not forsake the work of your hands.*

Ps. 138:8

> *Are not you my workmanship in the Lord?*

1 Cor. 9:1

Reflections

God's people are both the object of His Providences and the means to accomplishing them. God's people are used by Him in ministry and are changed by Him for His purposes.

David in Psalm 138 rejoices in God's steadfast love and faithfulness. He praises God for answered prayer, for strength in time of need. Now he experiences trouble, but his confidence is unwavering. God is firmly in control and will complete what He has begun. David knows he is God's workmanship. "Please," he prays, "don't stop working in and on me!"

Paul, too, understood how God works in and through people that He has saved by grace through faith. He wrote to the church in Ephesus, "For we are His workmanship, created in Christ Jesus for good works, which God prepared beforehand that we should walk in them" (Eph. 2:8-10).

In his letter to the Corinthians, Paul adds another layer to this concept. God uses people to work for Him in the lives of others. Paul saw himself as a workman and a gardener in the Lord's work. The believers in Corinth were his workmanship. He had "sown spiritual things" among them (vs. 11). He had proclaimed the gospel to them (vs. 14). Wherever he went he made himself a servant to all, adapting as much as possible to those he was seeking to win (vs. 19-23). He exercised self-control and disciplined his body in order to do what he was called to do, to complete the work assigned to him by the Lord.

Think about It

You are probably a product of someone else's work or ministry in you. Maybe you are still being discipled, mentored, and shepherded. Be sure you are an eager, appreciative learner. If you are serving others in the gospel, be careful to run so as to win the prize. After all, you are the work of the Lord's hands, and He also uses your hands to do His work. We *are* the Lord's work, and we *do* the Lord's work. May God be glorified in us and through us.

To Whom Do You Trust Your Life?

Today's Reading: Psalms 139-141; First Corinthians 10:1-13

Selected Verses

> *Search me, O God, and know my heart!*
> *Try me and know my thoughts!*
> *And see if there be any grievous way in me,*
> *and lead me in the way everlasting!*

Ps. 139:23-24

> *Therefore let anyone who thinks that he stands take heed lest he fall. No*
> *temptation has overtaken you that is not common to man. God is faithful,*
> *and he will not let you be tempted beyond your ability, but with the temptation*
> *he will also provide the way of escape, that you may be able to endure it.*

1 Cor. 10:12-13

Reflections

David in Psalm 139 writes some of the most eloquent statements ever penned about the glory and majesty of God: His omniscience, His omnipresence, and His goodness. That goodness is not only seen at a cosmic level but also on a personal level. God's thoughts toward David are beyond counting.

Then the author calls for the judgment of God against the wicked. Is that a result of all the reflection on God's holiness? It seems so. David hates sin. He doesn't want any part of those who are God's enemies. But he is not so foolish as to think he is incapable of sin himself. "Search me, O God, and know my heart! See if there be any grievous way in me," he prays. "Lead me in the way everlasting!"

Paul tells the Corinthians that the history of Israel was given to provide examples to them of the dangers that come, even to those who know God best, from giving in to their sinful natures. The Israelites knew more about the power and glory of God than anyone since Adam and Eve, yet they sinned grievously against God and were punished with death in the wilderness. "Don't think you could never do the same. Learn from their bad example," Paul tells them. Sin is not inevitable because God always provides a way of escape to the one who does not trust in himself.

Think about It

The slogans of western society "trust yourself" and "you can do it" are failing us. God tells us that He knows us and that we must trust in Him if we are to walk in the way everlasting, the way that leads to heaven. Face it. You can't do it. Trust God. He will open your spiritual eyes to the truth and lead you through temptations to victory, ultimately, in glory.

Guidance for Complex Decisions

Today's Reading: Psalms 142-144; First Corinthians 10:14-33

Selected Verses

Answer me quickly, O LORD!
My spirit fails!
Hide not your face from me,
lest I be like those who go down to the pit.
Let me hear in the morning of your steadfast love,
for in you I trust.
Make me know the way I should go,
for to you I lift up my soul.

Ps. 143:7-8

So, whether you eat or drink, or whatever you do, do all to the glory of God. Give no offense to Jews or to Greeks or to the church of God, just as I try to please everyone in everything I do, not seeking my own advantage, but that of many, that they may be saved.

1 Cor. 10:31-33

Reflections

The Christian is called to glorify God, to make sacrifices to build up others, and to avoid being offensive or selfish so that many may be saved. With those purposes in view, even complex ethical decisions become more obvious.

We aren't given the specific historical setting of Psalm 143, but it is clear that David is desperate. There is much honesty expressed in these Psalms. No room for denial here. The author feels he needs direction from God and he needs it fast. Apparently he had to make a decision by morning. This could be a prayer in the evening and David is praying that it will be clear to him by then as to which direction he should go.

The Corinthian believers also faced a dilemma. They wonder how to handle the touchy situation of food offered to idols. Some see it as a non-issue and have freedom to eat that food with no qualms. Others are troubled by the idea of eating this food that was offered to demons. Paul is clear that there is really no problem in eating the food, but there is a problem of causing a brother to stumble. He gives the readers of his letter some very simple, clear and practical guidelines as to when to eat and when not to eat.

Think about It

Let's put these guidelines into the form of questions to ask when making complex, ethical decisions: How can I best glorify God? How can I be helpful and build others up? How can I avoid offending so that an unbeliever is more able to find his way to salvation? Have I prayed to God for wisdom and waited for clarity on the matter? Consider how you can apply these questions to the difficult decisions you must make.

To My Dying Breath

Today's Reading: Psalms 145-147; First Corinthians 11:1-15

Selected Verses

Praise the Lord!
Praise the Lord, O my soul!
I will praise the Lord as long as I live;
I will sing praises to my God while I have my being.

Ps. 146:1-2

All things are from God.

1 Cor. 11:12

Reflections

Those who know God well never lose their focus on Him whether in the pressures of life at its prime or the pain of life at its end. God is always foremost in the hearts and minds of His people.

The psalmist praises God for a host of reasons, but, besides that, he commits himself to keep praising God as long as he lives, as long as he has his being. He could say, "to my dying breath." Even in a lifetime, one could never exhaust the things for which God deserves praise and adoration. There is no end to His works of creation and providence which reflect His glory. The psalms help us put words to our thoughts and thoughts to our observations. God in the psalms helps us see His hand in more things and proclaim His praise more clearly.

Paul deals with many difficult questions in his letter to the Corinthians. Now he turns to issues related to corporate worship in the church and the proper and distinct roles of men and women in the church. The passage raises as many questions as answers, but one thing is clear, "All things are from God." Paul has already set this idea before his readers earlier in the letter (1 Cor. 8:5-6). It is the principle around which he orients his thinking and instruction on the matters they are dealing with.

Think about It

The fact is that the purpose of our existence—as creatures made in God's image whether male or female—is His glory. We fulfill that purpose in our actions, attitudes, thoughts, and speech. I have been privileged to know a few fervent disciples of the Lord Jesus Christ who were using their final breath to give Him praise. That is my goal and desire, to praise Him while I have being, to my dying breath. How about you? This is our calling in Christ. Be sure you own it.

The Grand Finale of Victory

Today's Reading: Psalms 148-150; First Corinthians 11:16-34

Selected Verses

Kings of the earth and all peoples,
princes and all rulers of the earth!
Young men and maidens together,
old men and children!
Let them praise the name of the LORD,
for his name alone is exalted;
his majesty is above earth and heaven.

Ps. 148:11-13

For as often as you eat this bread and drink the cup,
you proclaim the Lord's death until he comes.

1 Cor. 11:26

Reflections

God is worthy of all praise from all people, whether rich or poor, old or young, men or women, for His Son died to redeem sinners and is coming again to reign forever.

The Book of Psalms ends with a grand finale of praise to God. The writers have taken us through the valley of the shadow of death, described unimaginable agonies of body and soul, and cried out to God, "How long?" But now in this last section of five psalms, we break through all the darkness and emerge into the unclouded day of God's majesty, power, and glory.

In this sense, the Psalter reflects our present life as well as our expectant hope for the joy that we will know when the Kingdom of God comes in all its fullness. Meanwhile, we walk by faith with our fellow believers in the Church Militant, that is, the Church here on earth awaiting the return of our Lord and King.

Paul admonishes the Corinthians in their practice of the sacrament of the Lord's Supper. They fail to observe it with reverence. In fact, he says, some have died already as a judgment of God on their sacrilege. The focus is to be upon His death which purchased our redemption and His promised return when we will be with Him forever.

Think about It

There are innumerable ways in which we may praise God every day: in the mundane responsibilities of domestic life, in our work, in our driving, in our kindness and courtesy to others. Praise Him today whether you are in formal, corporate worship with His people, or in the trenches of every day existence. Praise Him for the cross of Jesus Christ; praise Him for His promised coming in glory. It could be today, so be warmed up to sing His praise in the grand finale of victory.

The Importance of Seeking Wisdom

Today's Reading: Proverbs 1-2; First Corinthians 12

Selected Verses

If you seek it like silver
and search for it as for hidden treasures,
then you will understand the fear of the LORD
and find the knowledge of God.

Prov. 2:4-5

Therefore I want you to understand that no one speaking in the Spirit of God ever
says "Jesus is accursed!" and no one can say "Jesus is Lord" except in the Holy Spirit.

1 Cor. 12:3

Reflections

The book of Proverbs instructs God's people in wise living, but it is not a self-help book. Many self-help books assume that we are alone in the universe, answerable to no one but ourselves, and without any God to guide or assist us. But the Proverbs continually tell us to fear God as the key to wisdom and understanding (1:7). So fearing God leads to understanding, but understanding leads us back to the fear of God. Yes, this is circular reasoning, but it proves itself true in life. All reasoning is ultimately circular because one must presuppose one or more assumptions that cannot be proven. We assume that there is a God, the Eternal One who created all things and that He has revealed Himself in Scripture and in creation.

Proverbs reminds us that God controls all things and that He is just. His holiness is reflected here in a clear distinction between good and evil and right and wrong which shows the application of the moral law or Ten Commandments (Exod. 20; Deut. 5) to everyday life and relationships.

Paul urges the Corinthians to get informed and to gain understanding to help them in their lives and fractured relationships. He teaches them how to view themselves as a body with many members. Thus, they need to accept their own diverse gifts and to accept one another. They are members of the body of Christ called to glorify Him (1 Cor. 6:15-20). He has also taught them that their body is the temple of the Holy Spirit given to them by God. By the Spirit, they cannot but confess, "Jesus is Lord!" To curse Christ is clear evidence of not having that Spirit. On the contrary, all who have the Spirit of God will confess that Jesus is our wisdom from God, righteousness, sanctification, and redemption (1 Cor. 1:30).

Think about It

Wisdom and understanding which leads to the true knowledge of God and a proper fear of the Lord are keys to a blessed life. But we are not left to raise ourselves by our own bootstraps. It is the Holy Spirit who gives us this understanding and the ability to love and praise the Lord Jesus Christ. Seek Him and His wisdom, the One in Whom are found all the treasures of wisdom and knowledge (Col. 2:1-3).

The Practice of Love

Today's Reading: Proverbs 3-4; First Corinthians 13

Selected Verses

> *Do not withhold good from those to whom it is due,*
> *when it is in your power to do it.*
> *Do not say to your neighbor, "Go, and come again,*
> *tomorrow I will give it"—when you have it with you.*
> *Do not plan evil against your neighbor,*
> *who dwells trustingly beside you.*

Prov. 3:27-29

> *Love is patient and kind; love does not envy or boast; it is not arrogant or rude.*
> *It does not insist on its own way; it is not irritable or resentful; it does not*
> *rejoice at wrongdoing, but rejoices with the truth. Love bears all things,*
> *believes all things, hopes all things, endures all things. Love never ends.*

1 Cor. 13:4-8a

Reflections

The wisdom literature of the Bible has a recurring theme of the wicked man versus the godly man (e.g. Ps. 1, Prov. 1, etc). In Proverbs we see that the godly man is wise and that wisdom grows out of the fear of the Lord. This godly wisdom has both a vertical (God-ward) and horizontal (man-ward) dimension. In relationship to others, wise people are kind and loving. They are not stingy or selfish. Loving people give to others in need without delay or excuse. They never seek to trick their neighbor or take advantage of others.

Paul in his continuing instructions to the Corinthian church points them to the most important quality of a believer: love. He says that great accomplishments, even in the spiritual realm, have no importance if not accompanied by love. He describes it in terms of what it is not and what it is. The positive qualities include patience, kindness, and truthfulness. Love is unselfish and unending. This is the love that only Christ showed perfectly, but it is the essential virtue that He calls us to show to others if we would be known as His disciples (John 13:34, 35). The believers in Corinth needed to commit themselves to this kind of love, and so do I.

Think about It

How are you doing in showing Christlike love to others? Today is a good day to take stock. Make needed changes, either in attitudes, or in actions, or both.

The Mature Thinker

Today's Reading: Proverbs 5-6; First Corinthians 14:1-20

Selected Verses

There are six things that the Lord hates,
seven that are an abomination to him:
haughty eyes, a lying tongue,
and hands that shed innocent blood,
a heart that devises wicked plans,
feet that make haste to run to evil,
a false witness who breathes out lies,
and one who sows discord among brothers.

Prov. 6:16-19

Brothers, do not be children in your thinking. Be infants in evil, but in your thinking be mature.

1 Cor. 14:20

Reflections

In today's reading we come across the first of the numerical sayings in Proverbs (see also (Prov. 30:15-31). This list includes seven things that God hates. The first six are related to body parts, if you include breath which would imply the participation of the lungs. Certainly, the Scriptures leave no doubt about what is evil. Each of these vices has to do with personal relationships. Haughty eyes look down on other people. Lying may occur in our speech to others or in the formal setting of a false witness. Hands can murder after the heart has concocted the scheme. Feet and legs can carry one to do the wicked deed. God hates the creation of animosity between family members. How God's gift of life and healthy bodies can be abused for purposes which are an abomination to Him!

Paul calls the Corinthians to live in ways that build up, encourage, and console one another in the church (vs. 3). They seem to be concerned about themselves rather than one another. They use their gifts selfishly. The Apostle wants them to strengthen their ministry to one another. As it is, they show childish thinking and advanced levels of evil. This needs to be reversed.

Think about It

Hollywood offers entertainment for "mature audiences," but if the executives in the cinematographic industry believed their Bibles, they would change the designation to "immature audiences." Generally, they do not hate what God hates. As we read in Romans 12:1-2, present your body (eyes, tongue, hands, heart, feet) as a living sacrifice to Him. Be renewed in your mind so that you will be mature in thinking rather than experienced in evil. You will be likely to build up, encourage, and console those around you.

The Paths to Life and Death

Today's Reading: Proverbs 7-8; First Corinthians 14:21-40

Selected Verses

Blessed is the one who listens to me,
watching daily at my gates,
waiting beside my doors.
For whoever finds me finds life
and obtains favor from the Lord,
but he who fails to find me injures himself;
all who hate me love death.

Prov. 8:34-36

If anyone thinks that he is a prophet, or spiritual, he should acknowledge that the things I am writing to you are a command of the Lord. If anyone does not recognize this, he is not recognized.

1 Cor. 14:37-38

Reflections

The warnings of Proverbs are as needed and relevant today as they were thousands of years ago when they were penned. People of all ages are seduced by easily accessible online pornography. They assume anonymity, but millions learned otherwise when they signed up for a web service to facilitate relationships intended to lead to adultery. Fittingly, many of them were "busted" when the site was hacked and their identities were published openly for the world to see. Once again, the Scriptures prove true that ignoring the wisdom that leads to righteousness will end in death, either literally or figuratively.

This biblical wisdom does not merely lead us away from sin, but it also leads to a path of life and blessing only known to those who trust God. What can be more glorious and fulfilling than "favor from the Lord"? How is this obtained? By daily listening, watching, and waiting for His wisdom. That is why we read the Bible every day. We never outgrow our need for His wise guidance.

Paul tells the Corinthians that what he is writing to them is not mere personal opinion. He writes them commands from the Lord. If anyone disregards God's commands they are to be disregarded. Jesus promised to send His Spirit to reveal all the truth to His apostles and, certainly, what Paul and the others wrote in our New Testament is the result of that promise (John 14:26; 15:26; 16:12-15).

Think about It

Beware of those who reject (or even question) the authority of God's word. Instead, diligently seek God's wisdom in His word. You have no idea how it will save you from the path to death, but it will. Besides that, it will take you to life.

Choosing your Preacher

Today's Reading: Proverbs 9-10; First Corinthians 15:1-32

Selected Verses

Give instruction to a wise man, and he will be still wiser;
teach a righteous man, and he will increase in learning.
The fear of the Lord is the beginning of wisdom,
and the knowledge of the Holy One is insight.

Prov. 9:9-10

Now I would remind you, brothers, of the gospel I preached to you, which
you received, in which you stand, and by which you are being saved, if
you hold fast to the word I preached to you—unless you believed in vain.

1 Cor. 15:1-2

Reflections

The writer of Proverbs addresses the wise and the foolish. Like the sower in Jesus' parable, he puts out the truth and it falls on good soil and bears fruit or on rocky, thorny soil and produces nothing (Luke 8:4-15). The difference is not in the message taught, but in the receptivity of the hearer.

But are we to be receptive to every self-appointed expert, every professor of "truth"? How will we know who to trust? We will know if we fear the Lord. The true teacher fears the Lord and teaches the fear of the Lord. Anyone who teaches otherwise is certainly not from God.

Paul was a faithful teacher and apostle of Jesus Christ. In his letter to the Corinthians, he reminds them that he passed on to them what he had received, the gospel of Jesus Christ who died for our sins, was buried, rose again the third day, and was seen by Peter, the Twelve, and five hundred more. Paul was a reliable preacher of the truth. The Corinthians had been listening to fools masquerading as wise. Someone (or more than one) told them there was no resurrection. The Apostle quickly lists many strong arguments against this false doctrine. The historical reality of the resurrection of Christ is foundational to the gospel which is the basis for their faith and salvation.

Will Paul's readers respond positively to his corrections? They will if they are wise. They will if they fear the Lord.

Think about It

How do you assess the wisdom of those to whom you listen? Set your heart to fear God and to gain the knowledge of the Holy One. Choose your teachers and preachers carefully. Be sure they themselves qualify as wise, God-fearers before paying them any attention.

The Man of Dust; the Man of Heaven

Today's Reading: Proverbs 11-12; First Corinthians 15:33-58

Selected Verses

In the path of righteousness is life,
and in its pathway there is no death.

Prov. 12:28

The first man was from the earth, a man of dust; the second man is from heaven.
As was the man of dust, so also are those who are of the dust, and as is the man
of heaven, so also are those who are of heaven. Just as we have borne the image
of the man of dust, we shall also bear the image of the man of heaven.

1 Cor. 15:47-49

Reflections

Proverbs talks about life—but life in this world, for the most part. There are numerous keys to a joyful, peaceful, prosperous life. All things being equal, these maxims hold true, but all things are not equal. So the Proverbs will not "work" 100% of the time. There are exceptions. Sometimes good, industrious people suffer setbacks despite their best efforts. Righteousness leads to life rather than death, yet the only perfectly righteous Man who ever lived died a horrible death.

So Proverbs tell us how we ought to seek to live, being diligent in our work, kind toward others, speaking well of our neighbor, etc. These are good and right ways to live whether we get all the benefits promised or not. But in the gospel we learn that our good deeds are not sufficient to save us from eternal death. Jesus taught that "unless your righteousness exceeds that of the scribes and Pharisees, you will never enter the kingdom of heaven" (Matt. 5:20). Jesus shed His blood for the forgiveness of the sins of many, because there was no other way (Matt. 26:26-28).

Paul emphasizes the role of Jesus Christ, the second man, the One who, unlike the first man, did not come from the dust, but came down from heaven. He died and rose again. Now we, by faith, are promised a future in which we will bear the image of the Man of heaven. His resurrection gives us assurance that we too will be raised to have new spiritual bodies.

Think about It

Christ's disciples certainly seek to be righteous in this world, but they do so knowing they are not earning life but demonstrating that they already have it by the grace of the Lord and through faith in Him. If you know this hope of life, live righteously, but trust in the only Righteous One, Jesus. He will see us home and give us new spiritual bodies that cannot sin nor die. We will lose the image of the man of dust and bear the image of the Man of heaven.

The Importance of Giving to the Poor

Today's Reading: Proverbs 13-14; First Corinthians 16

Selected Verses

Whoever oppresses a poor man insults his Maker,
but he who is generous to the needy honors him.

Prov. 14:31

Now concerning the collection for the saints: as I directed the churches of Galatia, so you
also are to do. On the first day of every week, each of you is to put something aside and
store it up, as he may prosper, so that there will be no collecting when I come. And when
I arrive, I will send those whom you accredit by letter to carry your gift to Jerusalem.

1 Cor. 16:1-3

Reflections

Proverbs frequently commends the practice of giving to those who are poor. Here we see that one of the reasons, perhaps the most important reason, is the poor man was made by God. All who know their Bibles will recall that God made man in His own image and according to His likeness, male and female (Gen. 1:26-27). This teaching about the nature of all humans—that we are made in God's likeness—is a great equalizer. We vary in many ways—looks, intelligence, personalities, talents, preferences, etc.—but none of these differences (much less one's socioeconomic status) changes the reality of the image of God in us. Therefore, the writer of the proverb says our response to the needy either insults God or honors Him. Being generous to the needy is an act of worship to the Lord.

In Paul's day, there was significant poverty among the believers in Jerusalem. The Apostle organized a collection from several churches to assist these needy brothers and sisters. We learn a bit about some of Paul's administrative skills and convictions as we read today's passage. First, Paul wanted the people to save on a weekly basis, as they were able, for this collection. Second, Paul wanted them to select trustworthy representatives to take the fund to Jerusalem. Paul would write a letter commending the envoys to the church in Jerusalem and, possibly, accompany them himself. This seems to have been in order that the Corinthians would rest assured that the money would get to its intended destination and so that the people in Jerusalem would appreciate the intention of this action and the sacrificial efforts made to collect it.

Think about It

God's people are to be known for their care of the poor and needy. We, of all people, should be generous with those who are less fortunate. But we ought to be wise in the distribution of our resources, limited as they are. Become well-informed both about the identity of those who are truly in need and about reputable agencies through which you may assist them. It is an act that honors God as well as helps others. Make it count.

September 9 / Day 252

No Exceptions

Today's Reading: Proverbs 15-16; Second Corinthians 1

Selected Verses

Blessed is he who trusts in the Lord.

Prov. 16:20

*For we were so utterly burdened beyond our strength that we despaired of life itself.
Indeed, we felt that we had received the sentence of death. But that was to make us rely
not on ourselves but on God who raises the dead. He delivered us from such a deadly
peril, and he will deliver us. On him we have set our hope that he will deliver us again.*

2 Cor. 1:8b-10

Reflections

There are several Proverbs here that seem to emphatically state that if one does
right he will be blessed, and, if he does evil, he will suffer (Prov. 15:6, 10, 22, 24;
16:3, 4, 7, 20). Yet both in our personal experience and in other parts of the Bible,
we see the wicked enjoying success, at least temporarily. Conversely, godly people
may go through unspeakable trials. Paul himself was in this second category. So
was our Lord Jesus Christ as we already noted.[8]

The Apostle describes his suffering in terms of being on the verge of death.
He had no hope in this world, but his trust in God was strengthened. God raises
the dead. Maybe that was His plan. So Paul kept trusting God and was delivered.
He could look back on what he went through as a means of growing his faith
and trust.

Think about It

Who doesn't need to grow in trust in God? I'm sure I do.

If trust in God, such that He is glorified in whatever situation we are in, is
our goal (and it should be), what might He use to bring about the purifying of
our faith? In Job's case, it was bereavement, financial devastation, chronic
sickness and constant pain. His insensitive wife and badly misinformed friends
further compounded the problem. In Paul's case, it was some kind of near-death
experience.

I do not wish for you or me to go through anything remotely resembling
Job's or Paul's crises, but I am sure that the end result for us, like them, would be
wonderful. Pray for those who suffer today. Pray that you will be faithful and
that, whatever God chooses to send you, He will be with you and ultimately use
it for great good and for a ministry of comfort to others.

---

[8] See September 7 entry in this volume.

The Sniffable Christian

Today's Reading: Proverbs 17-18; Second Corinthians 2

Selected Verses

The crucible is for silver, and the furnace is for gold,
and the Lord tests hearts.

Prov. 17:3

But thanks be to God, who in Christ always leads us in triumphal procession,
and through us spreads the fragrance of the knowledge of him everywhere.
For we are the aroma of Christ to God among those who are being saved
and among those who are perishing, to one a fragrance from death to death,
to the other a fragrance from life to life. Who is sufficient for these things?

2 Cor. 2:14-16

Reflections

One of the themes in Proverbs is the dichotomy between fools and wise people, between the faithful and the slothful, between those who receive instruction and those who are wise in their own eyes. While it is not always evident to the observer the true state of another person's heart, God is able to test hearts and He does. Precious metal is purified by fire. The hearts of people are tested by God. So God's judgment will never be unjust. He is a Judge who truly has all the information (see Rom. 2:15-16).

Paul bares his thoughts and feelings about his ministry. He finds it painful to confront people on hard issues and when he does, he does it because he loves them. This does not mean that the responses he gets are always positive. He gets strong reactions to his mere presence because wherever he goes God "through us spreads the fragrance of the knowledge of him everywhere."

That fragrance will be either the scent of life or the stench of death depending on the heart condition of the one doing the sniffing. So God who tests hearts uses His people to reveal the state of hearts. This is not the only way God tests hearts, but it is certainly one way. And Paul exclaims, "Who is sufficient for these things?"

Think about It

Indeed, who wants to carry such a burden? Who wants to be the person who, when entering the room, causes the crowd to either flee from him or flock to him? But that is the role of the believer and, if we are such, we should assume this role with humility and submission.

No, *we* are not sufficient for these things. But it is not us. It is Christ in us. He "always leads us in triumphal procession." Trust Him. Follow Him. Expect to be sniffed.

By the way, if you find Christians abhorrent, be forewarned. You are probably perishing. May God give you grace to repent, believe, and find life in Him.

Slow Growth

Today's Reading: Proverbs 19-20; Second Corinthians 3

Selected Verses

Listen to advice and accept instruction,
that you may gain wisdom in the future.

Prov. 19:20

And we all, with unveiled face, beholding the glory of the Lord,
are being transformed into the same image from one degree of
glory to another. For this comes from the Lord who is the Spirit.

2 Cor. 3:18

Reflections

Many proverbs urge us to heed sound advice, to seek wisdom, to accept correction. Many promises are made to the one who is teachable and receptive. In vs. 20 above, there is an orientation toward the future. Various English translations differ as to whether the idea here is that instruction received now will result in your gaining wisdom *in* the future or gaining wisdom *for* the future. The difference is minor, and, either way, there is a certain dynamic going on. Time is a factor.

"Why do I need to learn this?" Teachers hear this question frequently. But children must learn information and skills for which they see no immediate or long-term purpose. Parents and other educators impart what they know will be useful to the child in later years. Children can whine and complain, but the failure to learn today's lessons is likely to turn into regret in future years. Growth is gradual, but God tells us to store up knowledge and wisdom for the time when we will need it.

Paul gives a defense of his ministry here. He calls the Corinthian believers his "letter of recommendation" to any who might require proof of the authenticity of his apostleship. From that thought he launches into some paragraphs showing the superior glory of the ministry of the new covenant over the old. Moses would veil his face after meeting with God to hide the fading glory, but in the new covenant our faces are unveiled, and the glory grows stronger rather than weaker. Again, time is a factor.

Think about It

Perhaps you find your spiritual growth imperceptible, like watching an oak tree grow. Seek wisdom today. Be receptive to instruction, even when it seems irrelevant. Praise God for sending His Spirit to write on our hearts His truth. He is at work in you, believing friend, but the distance between one degree of glory and the next may not be immediately evident.

The Best Is Yet to Be

Today's Reading: Proverbs 21-22; Second Corinthians 4

Selected Verses

The reward for humility and fear of the Lord
is riches and honor and life.

Prov. 22:4

Knowing that he who raised the Lord Jesus will raise us also with Jesus and bring
us with you into his presence. For it is all for your sake, so that as grace extends
to more and more people it may increase thanksgiving, to the glory of God.

2 Cor. 4:14-15

Reflections

In Old Testament times, much of the focus of God's commands and promises was on the way of wisdom and blessing in this life. Proverbs holds out much hope for reward for those who are humble and reverent before God. He has made a covenant with Israel to be their God, to keep them as His special people, to forgive their sins as they repent before Him and keep His law.

But behind these great covenant promises was an even greater ultimate end. God would send the Messiah. He would be the King in the lineage of David. He would also be the Suffering Servant, the Lamb of God, who would be pierced and crushed so that we might be healed and have peace (Isa. 53).

All this was still in the future at the time of Proverbs. Meanwhile, the faithful would heed the call to humility and the fear of the Lord. Many would see a reward in this life, but not all.

Then, came the Lord Jesus Christ proclaiming, "The time is fulfilled, and the kingdom of God is at hand; repent and believe in the gospel" (Mark 1:15). Alas, the old covenant kingdom of Israel was a mere shadow of the Kingdom of God.

Paul resisted it until he could resist no more, confronted as he was on the road to Damascus by Christ Himself (Acts 9:1-31). Now Paul tells the good news of the resurrection. God's grace was going out to more and more people. Thanksgiving shouts went up everywhere that grace went, and God was being glorified in places like Corinth, where darkness had ruled with an iron hand.

Think about It

Down through the centuries the gospel that promises life through the resurrected Christ has been proclaimed to the ends of the earth. Do not lose heart! Jesus told us to pray, "Thy Kingdom come" (Matt. 6:10). He is answering that prayer as the gospel goes forth and grace is received by millions in the most unlikely places. Most of all, God is glorified. If you are blessed with riches and honor and life in this world, rejoice! But remember, the best is yet to be when we enter into His kingdom and glory forever.

Aiming to Please God

Today's Reading: Proverbs 23-24; Second Corinthians 5

Selected Verses

Rescue those who are being taken away to death;
hold back those who are stumbling to the slaughter.
If you say, "Behold, we did not know this,"
does not he who weighs the heart perceive it?
Does not he who keeps watch over your soul know it,
and will he not repay man according to his work?

Prov. 24:11-12

So whether we are at home or away, we make it our aim to please him. For we must all appear before the judgment seat of Christ, so that each one may receive what is due for what he has done in the body, whether good or evil.

2 Cor. 5:9-10

Reflections

Today's reading in Proverbs points us to our responsibility for the lives of others who are dying, and we may assume, unjustly. Innocent people are killed by war, poverty, and abortion to name a few of the obvious causes. The media insures that we have a daily dose of the worst atrocities on the planet. We cannot say we know nothing about this. It is easy to be overwhelmed before breakfast seven days a week.

Paul reminded the Corinthians that this life is fleeting. Meanwhile, we should "make it our aim to please him." To begin with, we please Him when we recognize our utter depravity. We are not able to be righteous before Him, not in ourselves. We please Him when we trust in the One who died for us, that *in Him* we might become the righteousness of God (2 Cor. 5:21).

Think about It

Starting with Christ as our Redeemer, we may consider how we can further aim to please God. Clearly, no one of us can do everything to correct all the ills of our world and the culture of death. But we can do something. Edward Everett Hale, though a Unitarian, made this wise observation and resolution, "I am only one, but I am one. I can't do everything, but I can do something. The something I ought to do, I can do. And by the grace of God, I will."

So what can we do in our aim to please God? We can pray. We can proclaim the good news of life in Jesus Christ. We can give to ministries that serve hurting and dying people.

Life matters because there is judgment to come. Aim to please God. Begin by trusting in Christ alone for your righteousness.

Dangerous Alliances

Today's Reading: Proverbs 25-27; Second Corinthians 6

Selected Verses

*Crush a fool in a mortar with a pestle along with
crushed grain, yet his folly will not depart from him.*

Prov. 27:22

*Do not be unequally yoked with unbelievers. For what partnership has righteousness
with lawlessness? Or what fellowship has light with darkness? What accord has
Christ with Belial? Or what portion does a believer share with an unbeliever? What
agreement has the temple of God with idols? For we are the temple of the living God.*

2 Cor. 6:14-16

Reflections

The Proverbs sound many warnings about associating with fools. Here we see another reason why. You really cannot change a fool. You may take extreme measures similar to the process of crushing grain, but it will be futile. "His folly will not depart from him," we are told. Send him for advanced education, intensive therapy, military boot camp, wilderness survival training. You name it. It won't help. He is a fool and he remains a fool.

Are there no exceptions? Yes. We already saw that there are exceptions[9] to the Proverbs, that these maxims are general principles, but not ironclad promises that never fail. Nevertheless, you should not expect someone who has demonstrated a track record of folly to change even through much rehabilitation.

Paul on the other hand, tells the Corinthians to *never* be yoked unequally with unbelievers. No exceptions. This verse is often quoted in reference to choosing a marriage partner. Believers don't marry unbelievers. In the case of the Corinthians, Paul may have been intending for them to apply his command to those false prophets that had arisen among them or come to them (2 Cor. 11:12-14). The principle has wide application. Beware with whom you link up.

This does not mean we are not to seek to win unbelievers to Jesus Christ. On the contrary, we do build bridges of communication (1 Cor. 5:9-13). It is quite a different thing to seek to win a lost person (who, at some level, is going to be a fool for being an unbeliever) versus forming a binding partnership in marriage, business, or in the church with that non-Christian.

Think about It

Pray for the unbelieving fool, but beware that you do not form forbidden alliances with him or her. He is, by virtue of rejecting the gospel of Jesus Christ, the worst kind of fool. Give him the good news of salvation for even he is not too lost for Christ to save.

---

[9] See http://thistledewfarm.us/2015/09/09/no-exceptions/.

September 15 / Day 258

Two Sides of Godliness

Today's Reading: Proverbs 28-29; Second Corinthians 7

Selected Verses

> *A righteous man knows the rights of the poor;*
> *a wicked man does not understand such knowledge.*
>
> Prov. 29:7

> *Since we have these promises, beloved, let us cleanse ourselves from every*
> *defilement of body and spirit, bringing holiness to completion in the fear of God.*
>
> 2 Cor. 7:1

Reflections

The Proverbs continue contrasting the wise and the fool, the righteous and the wicked, the rich and the poor. The stereotypes don't always hold up, however. The poor are sometimes wise. The rich are sometimes foolish. But not always.[10]

The righteous man or woman "knows the rights of the poor." One who does not grasp the dignity and worth of every human being, by virtue of their being made in God's image, and thus entitled to rights, is classified with the wicked. This does not mean that the sluggard should be enabled to continue in his indolence. It does mean that a godly person will seek to be discerning, and to promote the well-being of the poor who have legitimate needs, perhaps because of health limitations, or the injustices of others, or "acts of God" like crop failures. The poor have rights, and the righteous will understand this. They will not ignore those in real need.

Paul urges the Corinthians to cleanse themselves from sin and to grow in holiness. This is God's purpose for His own people, that they should be godly, awaiting the appearing of our God and Savior Jesus Christ, and zealous for good works (Titus 2:11-13). They count this life as a transition period in which they can invest themselves in good works. One area of good works is care for the poor and suffering of this world. It is not enough to merely flee from sin, God's people are also called to do good to others.

Think about It

Sanctification, the process of growing in godliness, has both negative (don't do that) and positive (do this) aspects. Do you seek to grow both in fleeing from sin and fleeing to good works? Seek to glorify God in both those ways.

---

[10] See http://thistledewfarm.us/2016/07/21/warning-stereotyping-2/.

Poverty, Joy, and Generosity:
The Macedonians

Today's Reading: Proverbs 30-31; Second Corinthians 8

Selected Verses

She opens her hand to the poor
and reaches out her hands to the needy.

Prov. 31:20

We want you to know, brothers, about the grace of God that has been given among the churches of Macedonia, for in a severe test of affliction, their abundance of joy and their extreme poverty have overflowed in a wealth of generosity on their part.

2 Cor. 8:1-2

Reflections

Paul was concerned for the poor in Jerusalem. In an orderly way, he went about Macedonia and Achaia asking the churches to contribute to these needy brothers and sisters whom they had never met.[11] The Macedonian churches, those in Philippi, Thessalonica and Berea, were themselves suffering from affliction and extreme poverty.

There were two surprises here. One, Paul told them about the collection even though they were in need themselves. He did not want to rob them of the joy of doing what they could. Second, they gave far more than Paul expected. How were they able to do this? It was a result of the grace of God in their lives. Surely, they grasped "the grace of our Lord Jesus Christ, that though he was rich, yet for your sake he became poor, so that you by his poverty might become rich" (vs. 9).

Proverbs concludes with a picture of the godly woman, wife, and mother. We have met Lady Wisdom and her counterpart Ms. Folly in Proverbs 9. Now only the wise woman appears. One of her qualities is concern for the poor and needy. She gives to them and reaches out to them. She gives them resources and assists them in practical ways. Diligence, as exemplified by this woman, generally results in abundance. Abundance should result in generosity. Sadly, this is often not the case (Luke 12:13-21). One might think that poverty would squelch joy and generosity. In the Macedonian churches, the opposite was true. God's grace makes the difference.

Think about It

There is no greater evidence of the presence of God's grace than to have joy and generosity whether in need or in abundance. What glory that manifestation of grace brings to God! Look at Jesus, today, and learn joy and generosity whether you have much or little.

---

[11] See http://thistledewfarm.us/2017/09/08/importance-giving-poor/.

Why Life Is Not Vain

Today's Reading: Ecclesiastes 1-3; Second Corinthians 9

Selected Verses

All go to one place. All are from the dust, and to dust all return. Who knows whether the spirit of man goes upward and the spirit of the beast goes down into the earth? So I saw that there is nothing better than that a man should rejoice in his work, for that is his lot. Who can bring him to see what will be after him?

Eccl. 3:20-22

He who supplies seed to the sower and bread for food will supply and multiply your seed for sowing and increase the harvest of your righteousness. You will be enriched in every way to be generous in every way, which through us will produce thanksgiving to God. For the ministry of this service is not only supplying the needs of the saints but is also overflowing in many thanksgivings to God.

2 Cor. 9:10-12

Reflections

Solomon (who, we believe, wrote the book of Ecclesiastes) invested the time, money, and effort to pursue the meaning of life. But he came up with a rather bleak picture. After all his study and experimentation, he concluded that "All is vanity." The best humans can hope for, he wrote, is "To be joyful and to do good as long as they live; also that everyone should eat and drink and take pleasure in all his toil—this is God's gift to man" (Eccl. 3:12-13). Somehow it feels like something is missing, something that transcends this world. Certainly, Solomon grasps this too, as he says, "[God] has put eternity into man's heart, yet so that he cannot find out what God has done from the beginning to the end" (Eccl. 3:11).

But God's self-revelation continued with the coming of the Messiah, the Lord Jesus Christ, and the announcement of the Kingdom of God. Paul writes to those in Corinth who have heard this message and who are trusting in God's Son for salvation. He tells them that their faith expressed in generosity for the poor is actually sowing a harvest of righteousness that results in praise and thanksgiving to God.

Think about It

When God's people use the resources He supplies to serve others, this action produces win-win results for all. Blessing flows to the generous and to the needy. God is glorified. Far from being a vain, useless enterprise, generosity and good works produce lasting fruit. Take opportunities to give today. May the eternal, triune God be glorified, and may you be blessed! Life is not vain, and neither are good works done for Him.

Faithfulness Pleases God

Today's Reading: Ecclesiastes 4-6; Second Corinthians 10

Selected Verses

*When you vow a vow to God, do not delay paying it,
for he has no pleasure in fools. Pay what you vow.*

Eccl. 5:4

*For it is not the one who commends himself who is
approved, but the one whom the Lord commends.*

2 Cor. 10:18

Reflections

There is a common fallacy being foisted upon the unsuspecting public in our society today. It goes, "There is nothing you can do to make God love you more, and there is nothing you can do to make God love you less." As with all fallacies, there is some truth, but along with it is a dangerous, unbiblical implication. It is true we cannot by our actions manipulate God or change Him in any way, but this mantra seems to say, "What you do doesn't matter. God doesn't care about your personal behavior. Sin all you want. God still loves you. Neglect the means of grace. God still loves you. If you make an effort to serve Him, He won't even notice. He loves you just the same."

Solomon warned his readers about being casual in their relationship to God. The Lord "has no pleasure in fools," he told them. It does matter if you make a vow to God and then delay keeping it. God is not pleased with such foolishness. "God is the one you must fear," he declared (Eccl. 5:7).

Paul also was concerned about pleasing God. The Apostle had been denigrated by others who took pride in themselves. That gave him the context to propound his view of whose opinion matters. Clearly, all that ultimately matters is how the Lord views you. All the accolades or criticisms of the world do not affect God's evaluation. The commendation we should seek is God's and He knows what is really going on in our outward behavior and in our hearts.

Think about It

Does God care whether we are faithful or not? Yes, absolutely. We do not earn our forgiveness, but we do show evidence of it by the level of seriousness we give to our vows and spiritual disciplines. God is not a cruel taskmaster. He is no demanding tyrant. Yes, His love is secure, but He calls us to grow in holiness and to be faithful to the means of grace which He has provided. Seek the faithfulness that pleases God.

Wisdom: True and False

Today's Reading: Ecclesiastes 7-9; Second Corinthians 11:1-15

Selected Verses

But I say that wisdom is better than might, though the poor
man's wisdom is despised and his words are not heard.

Eccl. 9:16

For I feel a divine jealousy for you, since I betrothed you to one husband, to present
you as a pure virgin to Christ. But I am afraid that as the serpent deceived Eve by his
cunning, your thoughts will be led astray from a sincere and pure devotion to Christ.

2 Cor. 11:2-3

Reflections

Solomon, in reflecting on how wisdom works in the real world, relates a story of a small city attacked by a great army. Through the wisdom of an anonymous resident of the city, a poor man, the city overcame the attack. It is not hard to imagine the great party that the people held. But did they honor their benefactor? Did they erect a monument to the hero? No! No one remembered him. The presumptuous populace didn't bother to find out his identity or didn't care about the poor, wise man. How did the wise man respond to the slight? He was wise enough to create a successful strategy for victory in war, so he was probably wise enough to forgive the oversight and trust God for ultimate recognition. The city fathers failed to recognize the presence of greatness in their midst.

The members of the church in the ancient city of Corinth, on the other hand, did recognize and honor deceivers in their midst. False teachers came to them. They attempted to draw the church away from "a sincere and pure devotion to Christ." The Corinthians failed to see them for what they were—emissaries of Satan who "disguises himself as an angel of light" (2 Cor. 11:14). Foolishness never shows its hand. Satan never comes as a horned creature, dressed in red pajamas, and carrying a pitch fork. He comes showing what seems to be superior knowledge and wisdom.

Think about It

Aim to be well-informed of biblical truth and to never be drawn away from love for Jesus Christ. He is the Man who by His eternal wisdom delivered the city of His people from the army of Satan. Reject all counterfeit messengers and their phony gospel. Distinguish true wisdom from false. Things are not always the way they seem.

Escape the Vain Life

Today's Reading: Ecclesiastes 10-12; Second Corinthians 11:16-33

Selected Verses

The end of the matter; all has been heard. Fear God and keep his commandments, for this is the whole duty of man. For God will bring every deed into judgment, with every secret thing, whether good or evil.

Eccl. 12:13-14

For you gladly bear with fools, being wise yourselves! For you bear it if someone makes slaves of you, or devours you, or takes advantage of you, or puts on airs, or strikes you in the face. To my shame, I must say, we were too weak for that!

2 Cor. 11:19-21

Reflections

The book of Ecclesiastes closes with a final overarching statement about man's duty. Fear God and keep His commandments because you will face Him in judgment. It seems to contradict the oft-repeated phrase, "All is vanity." All does seem to be vain, at times. Hard work may not be fully rewarded, and crime may pay in the short run. But all is not really vanity, because, God is going to judge every deed, not only those which are easily observable but the secret ones, too. When we meet God, He will apply full justice.

Paul continues to admonish the Corinthians about their gullible trust in fools, those phony apostles who were doing Satan's work. He stoops to their level, in a sense, by defending himself and showing that his suffering demonstrates the authenticity of his calling by God.

The main reason people "gladly bear with fools" is that they desire to please them. They fear rejection by others, even those whose opinion clearly is of no consequence. They do not fear God, but fear man so they are easily manipulated, coerced, and led to foolishness. Proverbs 29:25 shows that the way to freedom from this malady is by replacing it with the trust in God.

Think about It

Do you suffer fools gladly? Turn away from this through faith in the Lord Jesus Christ. He died for this sin and gives His forgiven, Spirit-empowered disciples a proper fear of God. This is the duty we owe to Him, our Creator and Judge. Those who fear God may suffer for it in this world. But in the end God will approve them. He is the only One whose opinion matters. Escape the vain life.

Unstoppable Love

Today's Reading: Song of Solomon 1-3; Second Corinthians 12

Selected Verses

The voice of my beloved!
Behold, he comes,
leaping over the mountains,
bounding over the hills.

Song of Sol. 2:8

I will most gladly spend and be spent for your souls.

2 Cor. 12:15

Reflections

Over the centuries, Bible scholars have sought allegorical interpretations of the Song of Solomon attempting to minimize the obvious sensual language here. Yet today evangelical scholars hold widely that the poem speaks of the beauty of sexual love between a man and woman in the context of marriage. While sex has been and is abused by humanity the world over, when experienced within the boundaries set by God's law, it is honorable and God-glorifying (Heb. 13:4). Paul's comparison of the relationship of Christ and the Church to that of the relationship between a husband and wife does not denigrate the former relationship, but, rather, ennobles the latter (Eph. 5:22-33).

The poem poignantly describes the intense desire between a man and a woman in love. This attraction is not degraded or sinful but exalted and celebrated. The beloved revels in hearing her lover's voice. Her joy is palpable as she anticipates his arrival. He leaps over mountains and bounds over hills to get to her. Clearly, his love is unstoppable.

Paul is jealous for the Corinthian congregation as she seems to be on the verge of being seduced away from a "sincere and pure devotion to Christ" by "super-apostles" (2 Cor. 11:2-5). He has been making his case against these usurpers showing his own devotion to the Lord and to them. Though Paul is merely a messenger of Christ, he loves the Church on behalf of Christ. He loves whom the Lord loves, His elect people. So in showing that his ministry is authentic and reliable, he enumerates how he has paid and will pay a price to serve them in the gospel. "I will most gladly spend and be spent for your souls," he tells them. His love, like Jesus', is unstoppable.

Think about It

Are you married? Consider how well your marriage reflects the godly love and commitment of Christ to the Church. Can you say to your spouse, "I am glad to spend and be spent for your soul?" Whether you are a married or a single believer, think about the price Christ paid for your soul because of His unstoppable love for you.

The God of Peace and the Peace of God

Today's Reading: Song of Solomon 4-5; Second Corinthians 13

Selected Verses

> *I opened to my beloved,*
>> *but my beloved had turned and gone.*
> *My soul failed me when he spoke.*
> *I sought him, but found him not;*
>> *I called him, but he gave no answer.*

Song of Sol. 5:6

Finally, brothers, rejoice. Aim for restoration, comfort one another, agree with one another, live in peace; and the God of love and peace will be with you.

2 Cor. 13:11

Reflections

Romantic love has its ups and downs, and Solomon paints that picture in his Song. Anyone who has ever been in love can relate to this: the exhilaration of the first glimpse of the one who steals your heart completely (4:9) and the agony of possible loss of that relationship forever (5:6). With all the benefits and risks involved, we feel these are risks worth taking, because God said on the sixth day of creation, "It is not good that the man should be alone" (Gen. 2:18). So, most of us pursue a lifelong, loving relationship with a mate. Alas, it can be elusive. When found, it is never without difficulties and setbacks. But it is pleasing to the God of love to find it, and to nurture it.

In the church, Christians are called to live in love demonstrating true discipleship through a level of sacrificial love faintly reflecting that of Jesus Christ (John 13:34, 35). The Corinthian church of Paul's day had plenty of challenges. They were divided. Phony "super apostles" drew them away from the true faith. They were tolerant of gross sin in their midst. All this was unacceptable, but not fatal, to the fellowship. Paul instructed them in the two letters, which we still have, as to how to overcome these problems and be restored to a life of peace together. This is what God calls them to.

Think about It

All of us, believers, need one another in the context of the local church. We are called out to be His body and to work together for His glory. He is not glorified when sin is overlooked and tolerated and when there is division and competition that negates the message of reconciliation with God. That reconciliation with Him is the foundation for our reconciliation with one another. For us who are married in Christ, we also are called to model, on a human level, the relationship of Christ and His Church. The same commands and promises Paul gave the church in Corinth apply to us who are married. Seek to be such that the God of peace and the peace of God are always with you.

Reflections on God's Love

Today's Reading: Song of Solomon 6-8; Galatians 1

Selected Verses

I am my beloved's,
and his desire is for me.

Song of Sol. 7:10

But when he who had set me apart before I was born, and who called me by his grace,
was pleased to reveal his Son to me, in order that I might preach him among the Gentiles,
I did not immediately consult with anyone; nor did I go up to Jerusalem to those who
were apostles before me, but I went away into Arabia, and returned again to Damascus.

Gal. 1:15-17

Reflections

In Solomon's Song, he tells us of a beautiful and passionate love between a man and a woman. They describe each other with tenderness and awe. Each has found in the other all they could ever want in a spouse. No one or nothing could draw them away. They long to be together. They revel in being desired by each other.

In officiating weddings, I frequently use a famous prayer by Dr. Lewis Evans, the same one our pastor prayed for Mary and me. The next to last paragraph says, "May they never take each other for granted, but always experience that breathless wonder that exclaims, 'Out of all this world you have chosen me!'" Amen.

But there is an even greater love. It is the love of God—love which existed before time. It is love which planned our existence and, if God is pleased, chose us to be His own and to do His will. Paul marveled at the wonder of God's grace —His undeserved, unmerited favor. Paul never stopped exclaiming with breathless wonder, "Out of all this world, God has chosen me!"

Think about It

It is wonderful to know that the one you love so much, loves you just as much. How much more to know that the Eternal God knows, loves, and has set you apart for Himself before you were born!

Do you marvel that it pleased God to reveal His Son to you? No lack or longing obligated God to do it. He chose to do so because it pleased Him. Like the bride in the Song, never stop exclaiming, "I am My Beloved's and His desire is for me."

Legalism Dies Hard

Today's Reading: Isaiah 1-3; Galatians 2

Selected Verses

What to me is the multitude of your sacrifices?
says the Lord;
I have had enough of burnt offerings of rams
and the fat of well-fed beasts;
I do not delight in the blood of bulls,
or of lambs, or of goats.

Isa. 1:11

For through the law I died to the law, so that I might live to God. I have been crucified with Christ. It is no longer I who live, but Christ who lives in me. And the life I now live in the flesh I live by faith in the Son of God, who loved me and gave himself for me. I do not nullify the grace of God, for if righteousness were through the law, then Christ died for no purpose.

Gal. 2:19-21

Reflections

Isaiah spoke powerfully against the hypocrisy of the people of Judah. Their law-keeping was mere window-dressing. God was not pleased with their offerings and sacrifices. But wasn't this what God had commanded in the law given to Moses? Yes, but they were missing the essential part. The offerings and sacrifices were not intended to provide a cover-up for their sin. These should have been an outward expression of their repentance and contrition. God could see their hearts, and He was not impressed. He sent Isaiah to call them to act in ways that showed repentance and to seek His cleansing for even the most heinous sin (1:16-20).

In Galatia, a similar thing was occurring. The believers were abandoning the gospel of salvation by grace through faith in Jesus Christ and reverting to law-keeping as the basis for their reconciliation with God. Paul grieved deeply (Gal. 1:6-9). His letter aims to correct this grave and dangerous error. To make his point, Paul relates his own experience of receiving the gospel from Christ and, at one point, even having to confront Peter for wavering from that gospel.

Think about It

Why this tendency, of those who should know better, to revert to law-keeping for salvation? Perhaps, as justified people (but still not fully sanctified), we are prone to a prideful desire to merit our salvation, if just a little. Perhaps this error grows from a desire to cover-up our sin by appearing holy, instead of confessing our sin and trusting God's forgiveness. Beware of straying from the basis of our justification, the atoning sacrifice of Jesus Christ and not our faulty law keeping. Never rob God of His glory by reverting to trust in good works for your forgiveness. Legalism dies hard in Judah, in Galatia, and, I'm afraid, in our hearts today.

Heart Check Time

Today's Reading: Isaiah 4-6; Galatians 3

Selected Verses

Man is humbled, and each one is brought low,
and the eyes of the haughty are brought low.
But the Lord of hosts is exalted in justice,
and the Holy God shows himself holy in righteousness

Isa. 5:15-16

Christ redeemed us from the curse of the law by becoming a curse for us—for it is written,
"Cursed is everyone who is hanged on a tree"—so that in Christ Jesus the blessing of Abraham
might come to the Gentiles, so that we might receive the promised Spirit through faith.

Gal. 3:13-14

Reflections

Failure to see the holiness of God and the horror of sin is a problem which repeatedly crops up in human hearts. It happened in ancient Judah in Isaiah's day and it happened in Galatia in Paul's day. It continues to happen today.

Isaiah warned Judah of her sin and reminded them of the reality of death, the gaping mouth of Sheol consuming all humanity one by one. The people were living in denial. They presumed upon the grace and mercy of God as they relied on their own wisdom and ignored the perfect holiness of God. It would take a reawakening to the imminence of death and their utter failure to attain to God's purity to humble them. They needed to see Him "high and lifted up" (6:1). At the same time, they needed to see themselves as people of "unclean lips" (6:5). They needed to see how darkened their minds were as they reversed the definitions of good and evil (5:20). We do too.

The Galatians' situation is even more perplexing. Here were people who had heard and believed the gospel, repented of their sin, and had received the Holy Spirit by faith, but now through the influence of some false teachers were turning away from trusting Christ and returning to law keeping as the basis for their hope. Paul is astonished. Yet experience tells us that this is always a potential problem. It appeals to our pride to achieve our own acceptance before God. This attitude comes from either not seeing the holiness of God or not seeing the heinousness of our rebellion against Him. In our minds, we either dilute God's holiness or our sin. Usually both.

Think about It

God means for us to humble ourselves before Him, to see the awfulness of sin as reflected in the agony of Christ's death. He had to become a curse for us to free us from the curse upon us through the law. Do a heart check today. Beware of any creeping self-righteousness that diminishes your complete reliance on the Lord Jesus Christ for your standing before God.

Amazing Grace, Indeed!

Today's Reading: Isaiah 7-9; Galatians 4

Selected Verses

> *For to us a child is born,*
> > *to us a son is given;*
> *and the government shall be upon his shoulder,*
> > *and his name shall be called*
> *Wonderful Counselor, Mighty God,*
> > *Everlasting Father, Prince of Peace.*
> *Of the increase of his government and of peace*
> > *there will be no end,*
> *on the throne of David and over his kingdom,*
> > *to establish it and to uphold it*
> *with justice and with righteousness*
> > *from this time forth and forevermore.*
> *The zeal of the Lord of hosts will do this.*

Isa. 9:6-7

But when the fullness of time had come, God sent forth his Son, born of woman, born under the law, to redeem those who were under the law, so that we might receive adoption as sons. And because you are sons, God has sent the Spirit of his Son into our hearts, crying, "Abba! Father!"

Gal. 4:4-6

Reflections

King Ahaz was in a tizzy. He saw Israel joining with Syria against his kingdom, Judah. God sent Isaiah to him to reassure him that all would be well, that, in fact, Israel and Syria were the ones who would go down. Ahaz resisted the message and even turned down the offer of a God-sent sign. Isaiah gave him a sign from God anyway, and what a sign! The sign was "the virgin shall conceive and bear a son, and shall call his name Immanuel [God with us]" (7:14).

The sign had an immediate fulfillment, but it also pointed ultimately to the Incarnation of the Son of God, Jesus Christ, born of the virgin Mary. He would be Immanuel in every sense of the word. While the immediate fulfillment of the sign of the birth of a son to Ahaz would show assurance of deliverance of a short-term military threat, the ultimate fulfillment would bring deliverance from the guilt and curse of all those under the law. But not only that, this Son and Redeemer would bring adoption as sons of God, who would send His Spirit into the hearts of His people. Spirit-possessing sons would cry out "Abba, Father" and not live in fear of any army or any future legal process resulting in their conviction and sentencing.

Think about It

Let this truth sink deep in your heart. God sent His Son, a sign of His grace for guilty sinners. Amazing grace, indeed!

Unquenchable Joy

Today's Reading: Isaiah 10-12; Galatians 5

Selected Verses

You will say in that day:
"I will give thanks to you, O Lord,
for though you were angry with me,
your anger turned away,
that you might comfort me.
Behold, God is my salvation;
I will trust, and will not be afraid;
for the Lord God is my strength and my song,
and he has become my salvation."
With joy you will draw water from the wells of salvation.

Isa. 12:1-3

But the fruit of the Spirit is love, joy, peace, patience, kindness, goodness,
faithfulness, gentleness, self-control; against such things there is no law.

Gal. 5:22-23

Reflections

Judah and Israel were concerned about national security and relief from the oppressing nations. Isaiah came to them to speak of a Holy God Whom they had offended. He was justly angry with them. Assyria would defeat Israel. Judah was on probation. But Isaiah also gave them hope of a future in which they would know God's salvation. They would be comforted in the knowledge that His just anger was turned away.

The sweet promise "With joy you will draw water from the wells of salvation," brings to mind Jesus' words in John 7:38, "Whoever believes in me, as the Scripture has said, 'Out of his heart will flow rivers of living water.'" Jesus was describing the Spirit that all who believed in Him would receive.

Paul tells the Galatians that in Christ they have freedom: freedom from their sin, guilt, and condemnation under the law. They have the Spirit of God and He bears fruit in their lives: love, joy, peace, patience, kindness, goodness, faithfulness, gentleness, and self-control.

Think about It

There can be nothing to compare with the comfort which comes from being totally forgiven by God—that He holds no more anger against us. If the Spirit of God lives in us, how can we not have a deep joy that springs up like water from a well? Let the joy of your salvation fill you today. The joy He gives is unquenchable.

Judgment—Maybe Today?

Today's Reading: Isaiah 13-15; Galatians 6

Selected Verses

This is the purpose that is purposed
concerning the whole earth,
and this is the hand that is stretched out
over all the nations.
For the Lord of hosts has purposed,
and who will annul it?
His hand is stretched out,
and who will turn it back?

Isa. 14:26-27

Do not be deceived: God is not mocked, for whatever one sows, that will he also
reap. For the one who sows to his own flesh will from the flesh reap corruption,
but the one who sows to the Spirit will from the Spirit reap eternal life.

Gal. 6:7-8

Reflections

Isaiah saw a clear vision of God, Holy and lifted up. Now he proclaims oracles against various nations: Babylon, Assyria, Philistea, and Moab. All of these kingdoms were, at one time or other, a threat to Israel and Judah. God assures His people through Isaiah that all these nations are under His control. He will deal with their arrogance and pride and injustice.

Paul has admonished the Galatians to reject the false teaching of those who had come to bewitch and unsettle them (3:1; 5:12). Now he reminds them that God sits on the throne. He will act in judgment on those who are deceived—who think they can sow to their own flesh and get away with it. Two errors concerning sin are in view. One, that by keeping the law we can be justified before God. This is also called "works righteousness." Two, that sin is of no importance so we may sin all we please with no consequences. Only through the cross of Christ may we find forgiveness of sin. God will judge those who reject His Son, the only Savior and the only means of salvation.

Think about It

The nations of the Old Testament world have gone, removed from their proud perch. They failed to believe that God rules. Judgment is sure, and judgment is final.

We now face death and judgment. What do you believe will happen to you? Are you trusting your own good works to be acceptable before the Judge? Are you presuming that God is not really serious about our sin? Do not fall for those deceptions. Christ's death is the only way to salvation. Do not trust in your good works. Do not foolishly assume that God is not serious about our sin. Be ready to meet your God. It could be today.

301

God's Re-purpose Project

Today's Reading: Isaiah 16-18; Ephesians 1

Selected Verses

In that day man will look to his Maker, and his eyes will look on the Holy One of Israel. He will not look to the altars, the work of his hands, and he will not look on what his own fingers have made, either the Asherim or the altars of incense.

Isa. 17:7-8

In love he predestined us for adoption as sons through Jesus Christ, according to the purpose of his will, to the praise of his glorious grace, with which he has blessed us in the Beloved.

Eph. 1:4-6

Reflections

Isaiah speaks of a day when man would look to the true and living God, the Creator, who is the Holy One of Israel. In looking to Him, man would turn away from his own feeble religious offerings, his own efforts to commend himself to God, his false gods and blasphemous altars. Only by looking to God will anyone find forgiveness.

Paul elaborates on this in the first chapter of his letter to the church in Ephesus. In a tightly packed paragraph-sentence, the apostle lays out in soaring words the purpose of God for the world and His means of accomplishing it. At the heart of His purpose is His glory. He calls us to live for the praise of His glorious grace. But in ourselves, we are not able or qualified to fulfill that grand purpose. We need redeeming from our corruption. God has done that by giving His Son, the Lord Jesus Christ, to bear our sin and guilt. Through Him we have forgiveness of sin, are adopted as His sons (yes, male and female both enjoy the privileges of sons), and sealed with His Holy Spirit while we wait for all this to be completed.

Think about It

To re-purpose means to change something so that it can be employed for a new end. Although, to be precise, believers in Christ have recovered God's original purpose for us, it is not a stretch to say that we who were spiritually dead, and who were following the prince of the power of the air, have been re-purposed for God. What a glorious purpose! It is the only purpose worthy of all our life, all our strength, and all our love. May God give us grace to grow in fulfilling His every intention for our re-purposing.

Spiritual Desperation—Are You There?

Today's Reading: Isaiah 19-21; Ephesians 2

Selected Verses

Then they shall be dismayed and ashamed because of Cush their hope and of Egypt their boast. And the inhabitants of this coastland will say in that day, "Behold, this is what has happened to those in whom we hoped and to whom we fled for help to be delivered from the king of Assyria! And we, how shall we escape?"

Isa. 20:5-6

But God, being rich in mercy, because of the great love with which he loved us, even when we were dead in our trespasses, made us alive together with Christ—by grace you have been saved— and raised us up with him and seated us with him in the heavenly places in Christ Jesus.

Eph. 2:4-6

Reflections

God sent Isaiah to show Judah the folly of their trusting in Egypt and Cush for deliverance from the then-dominant power of Assyria. The prophet, under God's direction, went about barefooted and naked for three years to show them how destitute they really were. God would have Egypt and Cush barefoot and naked before it was over.

Paul paints a vivid picture of lost people. They are not merely weak in spirit, not just sick. Rather, they are stone cold dead in trespasses and sins. They may have been trusting that they were good enough to pass muster in a relative sense, that is, good enough to pass if graded on a curve instead of against the absolute perfect righteousness of God. In reality, they deserve hell, but instead God, who is rich in mercy and great in love, makes "them alive together with Christ" and saves them by grace alone.

Then what? Does He send them back into the world to try to improve their future record? No. He raises them up with Christ and seats them in the heavenly places in Christ Jesus. And these were previously dead, hopeless people. Spiritually bankrupt, they had nothing to offer God. They could not earn their acceptance nor pay their debt. All they could do was believe and receive what God did.

Think about It

Do you hold out some hope that you will eventually measure up to God's perfection? Or does desperation describe your spiritual state? Do you see your true condition apart from Christ: dead, alienated, condemned? It is not a good feeling to be desperate, but let us be desperate so that we can appreciate the great mercy and love of God for us.

The Purposes of God

Today's Reading: Isaiah 22-23; Ephesians 3

Selected Verses

Who has purposed this against Tyre,
the bestower of crowns,
whose merchants were princes,
whose traders were the honored of the earth?
The Lord of hosts has purposed it,
to defile the pompous pride of all glory,
to dishonor all the honored of the earth.

Isa. 23:8-9

This was according to the eternal purpose that he has realized in Christ Jesus our Lord,
in whom we have boldness and access with confidence through our faith in him.

Eph. 3:11-12

Reflections

It is not hard to see that the Bible reveals a God Who is over all the earth and all mankind. It is true that He chose Abraham and made a covenant with him and his descendants, but even that covenant included all the families of the earth (Gen. 12:3).

Through Isaiah (and other prophets) God gave warnings and instructions to the Gentile nations around Israel and Judah. Today we read about God's purposes to bring down the pomposity of Tyre and Sidon. They were proud in their successes, congratulating themselves for their victories and prosperity with no thought for God.

What concern did the God of Israel have for Tyre and Sidon? The same concern He had for all the families of the earth. Their prideful arrogance offended Him, but also drew His mercy and grace as He purposed that His Son would be the Savior of the world, including those from Tyre and Sidon and a thousand other tribes and nations that would come and go through human history.

The mystery of God's purpose was revealed to Paul and the other apostles and, through their writings, it was revealed to us. God was working out His plan for the fullness of time "to unite all things in him, things in heaven and things on earth" (Eph. 1:10). This was Paul's calling, to announce this mystery, the uniting of all in Christ. Jews and Gentiles in Christ are now one with God and with each other. Paul prays that his readers in Ephesus (and beyond) may grasp "the love of Christ that surpasses knowledge" and that they "may be filled with all the fullness of God" (Eph. 3:19).

Think about It

Press on to know God's glorious purposes through Jesus Christ. We have only scratched the surface on the eternal purposes of God.

October 2 / Day 275
God's Grand Narrative

Today's Reading: Isaiah 24-26; Ephesians 4

Selected Verses

O Lord, you are my God;
I will exalt you; I will praise your name,
for you have done wonderful things,
plans formed of old, faithful and sure.

Isa. 25:1

Rather, speaking the truth in love, we are to grow up in every way into
him who is the head, into Christ, from whom the whole body, joined
and held together by every joint with which it is equipped, when each part
is working properly, makes the body grow so that it builds itself up in love.

Eph. 4:15-16

Reflections

God planned the "grand narrative" of the Bible, as Sinclair Ferguson calls it, from eternity past.[12] We can summarize it by the terms: creation, corruption, conflict, and consummation. As Isaiah expressed it, these are "plans formed of old, faithful and sure." Nothing ever catches God by surprise. He wrote all of human history before it started. What He plans He completes.

Isaiah observes the chaos of the times and anticipates the coming judgment. But he also makes sweet promises. God will swallow up death forever and wipe away tears from all faces. The Lord will keep in perfect peace all who keep their minds on Him (Isa. 25: 8; 26:3). "Trust in the Lord forever," writes Isaiah, "for the Lord God is an everlasting rock" (26:4).

Paul, too, has the big picture in view as he exhorts the Ephesians to live in the unity of the Spirit of God. God has sent them apostles, prophets, evangelists, shepherds, and teachers to equip them for His service. Why? God wants them to grow in unity and maturity in Christ. These two objectives go together.

We live in the middle of the grand narrative which began with creation and continues with corruption (Gen. 3:1-13) and conflict (Gen. 3:15). But Jesus Christ has come announcing that "The time is fulfilled, and the kingdom of God is at hand; repent and believe in the gospel" (Mark 1:15). He told His disciples to pray that the Kingdom would come, so we know there is more to come (Matt. 6:10).

Think about It

In the daily chaos of this world, do you lose sight that God is completing His plans perfectly? Trust in the Lord, as Isaiah said. Seek unity and maturity as Paul admonished. God will fulfill His grand narrative.

---

[12] Sinclair Ferguson, *From the Mouth of God: Trusting, Reading, and Applying the Bible* (Edinburgh: The Banner of Truth Trust, 1982), 2014, p. 76.

October 3 / Day 276
To Spiritually Multi-Task

Today's Reading: Isaiah 27-28; Ephesians 5

Selected Verses

> *In days to come Jacob shall take root,*
> *Israel shall blossom and put forth shoots*
> *and fill the whole world with fruit.*

Isa. 27:6

> *Therefore be imitators of God, as beloved children. And walk in love, as Christ loved us and gave himself up for us, a fragrant offering and sacrifice to God.*

Eph. 5:1-2

Reflections

Paul has painted a glorious picture of the purposes of God in all the earth, uniting Jews and Gentiles in Christ. Christians are made alive in Him—made one with God and all other believers. He calls them to live in a way that is worthy of their high calling.

In today's reading the apostle uses the image of walking to describe the Christian life, that is, a life lived as imitators of God. That walk is to be characterized by love, reflecting the sacrificial love of Jesus for us. We are to walk as children of the light. That means fleeing impurity, and covetousness, and even talk that shows approval of such behavior. Wisdom should be evident in our way of life and in our use of time. This does not mean we live in joyless asceticism, but we exchange the artificially-induced peace and pleasure of drunkenness for the filling of the Spirit and God-glorifying, church-edifying singing.

Isaiah foretold of the time when Israel would fill the world with fruit. Certainly, it would be far more than he could have imagined. God planned to unite Jews and Gentiles in the Messiah everywhere from Jerusalem, to Judea and Samaria and to the ends of the earth (Acts 1:8).

Think about It

The kingdom has come in part and it will come fully when Christ returns for His bride, the Church. I can't wait, can you? Meanwhile, let's fill the world with fruit as we walk in love, light, and wisdom. By His grace, let us spiritually multi-task till He comes or calls us home.

Authenticity in Worship and Work

Today's Reading: Isaiah 29-30; Ephesians 6

Selected Verses

> *Ah, you who hide deep from the Lord your counsel,*
> > *whose deeds are in the dark,*
> > *and who say, "Who sees us? Who knows us?"*
> *You turn things upside down!*
> *Shall the potter be regarded as the clay,*
> *that the thing made should say of its maker,*
> > *"He did not make me";*
> *or the thing formed say of him who formed it,*
> > *"He has no understanding"?*

Isa. 29:15-16

> *Bondservants, obey your earthly masters with fear and trembling, with a sincere heart, as you would Christ, not by the way of eye-service, as people-pleasers, but as bondservants of Christ, doing the will of God from the heart, rendering service with a good will as to the Lord and not to man, knowing that whatever good anyone does, this he will receive back from the Lord, whether he is a bondservant or is free.*

Eph. 6:5-8

Reflections

Isaiah calls the people to worship with truth, not pretense, thinking that God cannot see their hearts and that He will be impressed by their phony professions of faith. Some think darkness is a safe cloak for their sin. These ideas are laughable. The prophet compares them to a lump of clay taking credit for its own existence and denying its own maker.

This arrogance is laughable, but very real and persistent. Jesus quoted Isaiah's words (from 29:13-14 in Matt. 15:8,9; Mark 7:6,7) as He indicted first century Judaism. It could easily be applied today. People trust in their own works, but even good religious works (like baptism, Bible reading, and church attendance) are not able to deliver us from God's wrath. Only the grace of God in Christ to those who repent of their sin and believe in Him is sufficient.

Paul addresses another kind of hypocrisy in his letter to the Ephesians. He tells bondservants to obey their masters as they would Christ. Their service is not for them but for Him. Some of these servants were only creating an appearance of work which the Apostle called "eye-service" and people pleasing. The Christian is always serving Christ, no matter who he works for.

Think about It

In the gospel, we learn that through faith we become Christ's own people. As His people, we are called to authenticity in our worship and in our work. Let it be so every Lord's Day and every work day.

Zion: The City Filled with Righteousness

Today's Reading: Isaiah 31-33; Philippians 1

Selected Verses

The Lord is exalted, for he dwells on high;
he will fill Zion with justice and righteousness,
and he will be the stability of your times,
abundance of salvation, wisdom, and knowledge;
the fear of the Lord is Zion's treasure.

Isa. 33:5-6

And it is my prayer that your love may abound more and more, with
knowledge and all discernment, so that you may approve what is excellent,
and so be pure and blameless for the day of Christ, filled with the fruit of
righteousness that comes through Jesus Christ, to the glory and praise of God.

Phil. 1:9-11

Reflections

The fall of Man in Genesis 3 touched off the millennia-long battle between the seed of the serpent and the seed of the woman, Jesus Christ. The enmity goes on, but never doubt the certainty of final victory through the resurrection of Jesus. He has already defeated Satan. Those in whom God has begun His work will be perfected at the day of Jesus Christ, the day of resurrection, the final judgment, and the glorification of the elect (Phil. 1:6).

The work of Christ in His people has already begun. It bears the fruit of righteousness through the Lord. That fruit brings God glory and praise and pleases Him. It is not to the credit of any human but to God. It fulfills the original purpose of mankind whom God made in His image and according to His likeness.

Isaiah makes a similar connection between the glory of God and the righteousness He produces in His people. "The Lord is exalted, for he dwells on high; he will fill Zion with justice and righteousness." God wants Zion filled with righteousness and He will do it.

Think about It

Meanwhile, we pray for growth in righteousness and eagerly await that day of completion. In a city filled with righteousness, God "will be the stability of your times, abundance of salvation, wisdom, and knowledge." Rather than trust in gold and silver, "the fear of the Lord [will be] Zion's treasure."

World leaders promise to bring about stability and prosperity, but which of them proclaims the need for the fear of the Lord who produces true stability and prosperity through righteousness? When Christ returns, there will be no more competition for dominance or for honor. Until then, pray that day may come soon when we shall dwell in Zion.

It's About God

Today's Reading: Isaiah 34-36; Philippians 2

Selected Verses

> *The wilderness and the dry land shall be glad;*
> *the desert shall rejoice and blossom like the crocus;*
> *it shall blossom abundantly*
> *and rejoice with joy and singing.*
> *The glory of Lebanon shall be given to it,*
> *the majesty of Carmel and Sharon.*
> *They shall see the glory of the LORD,*
> *the majesty of our God.*

Isa. 35:1-2

> *Therefore God has highly exalted him and bestowed on him the name*
> *that is above every name, so that at the name of Jesus every knee should*
> *bow, in heaven and on earth and under the earth, and every tongue*
> *confess that Jesus Christ is Lord, to the glory of God the Father.*

Phil. 2:9-11

Reflections

No matter where we open our Bibles and read, we are never far from the theme of the glory of God. His glory is proclaimed everywhere, but, between the fall of Man and the final judgment, humanity falls short of that glory. Contrary to popular culture, it's not about us. It's about God.

Isaiah prophesied of a day of restoration when deserts would blossom, and dry land would be refreshed. In that blessing of the earth, all would see God's glory.

At the time of this writing, the eastern United States had gone through ten days of rain. In Virginia, our joy at seeing rain after weeks of drought began to give way to gloom as the cloud cover remained day after day and steady rain saturated the ground. Floods arose taking out a hundred-year-old covered bridge. We prayed for relief and for safety from trees falling before expected high winds. Then on the eleventh day, we woke to cloudless, blue skies. The sun shone brightly, drying up the mud and restoring the beauty of early autumn. I praised God and I'm sure I was not alone.

Jesus knew the suffering of becoming a human, a servant, and a prisoner. He knew condemnation and the unspeakable pain of flogging and crucifixion. He bore that to save His people from their sin. God exalted Him and glorified Him. One day every knee will bow and recognize His Lordship. This will bring glory to God the Father.

Think about It

We live in a time characterized by fanatical self-worship. To be free, to be autonomous, to act however we please with no consequences, to be enraged that any one should call us to bow to God—these values rule our day. But it's not about us. It's about Him. Be sure you trust in Christ for forgiveness and life. Do not let the day of restoration be your day of condemnation. Your life and all of human history is about God.

No Confidence in the Flesh

Today's Reading: Isaiah 37-38; Philippians 3

Selected Verses

Truly, O Lord, the kings of Assyria have laid waste all the nations and their lands, and have cast their gods into the fire. For they were no gods, but the work of men's hands, wood and stone. Therefore they were destroyed. So now, O Lord our God, save us from his hand, that all the kingdoms of the earth may know that you alone are the Lord.

Isa. 37:18-20

Look out for the dogs, look out for the evildoers, look out for those who mutilate the flesh. For we are the circumcision, who worship by the Spirit of God and glory in Christ Jesus and put no confidence in the flesh.

Phil. 3:2-3

Reflections

In Isaiah's day, Sennacherib king of Assyria and his army romped across the world destroying kingdoms at will. He boasted that Judah would be next. After all—he reasoned—all the nations had their gods and none of them had been able to stand up to mighty Sennacherib. Hezekiah was intimidated, but he made the right response. He called on the prophet Isaiah for help and prayer. He prayed and repented himself. He asked God to intervene in such a way "that all the kingdoms of the earth may know that you alone are the Lord."

God heard and answered in a decisive way.

Sennacherib was diverted from Judah and then murdered by two of his own sons while he was worshipping his idols. How fitting! Sennacherib trusted in his flesh and in empty idols rather than seeking the true and living God of Israel. Meanwhile, Hezekiah and Judah were safe.

Paul warned the Philippians of the "Sennacheribs" that threatened them and elevated themselves as if they were perfect by their own law keeping. They trusted in their flesh. Paul said to look out for them. They seek their own righteousness and their own glory, but "we put no confidence in the flesh" wrote the Apostle.

Think about It

Beware of false teachers who diminish the need for faith in the Lord Jesus Christ, who say we are capable of attaining righteousness apart from Him. These do not glory in Him but, like Sennacherib, trust in themselves. Flee them. Put no confidence in your flesh or in those who tell you to do so.

Why Everything is Going Wrong

Today's Reading: Isaiah 39-40; Philippians 4

Selected Verses

> *To whom then will you liken God,*
> *or what likeness compare with him?*

Isa. 40:18

> *Rejoice in the Lord always; again I will say, rejoice. Let your*
> *reasonableness be known to everyone. The Lord is at hand.*

Phil. 4:4-5

Reflections

Where did we go off track? Easy question, if you believe the Bible. God made man (male and female) in His likeness (Gen. 1:26-31), but sin entered into man's experience when the woman succumbed to the temptation to be "like God, knowing good and evil." She then invited the man to join her, and he did.

Now Isaiah asks, "To whom then will you liken God, or what likeness compare with him?" The correct answer, before the fall, would have been, "Man is like God", but fallen man responds, "God is like me. I am God. No one is over me." All sin stems from this attitude of autonomy and rebellion. It results in every evil which we now experience on a daily basis throughout the world: mass murder on campuses, terrified refugees fleeing war by the thousands, hostile legal battles over personal rights, etc. Solutions elude us as a society because we fail to recognize the real problem. We have made ourselves gods, rather than to recognize Him, our eternal Creator as the One whom we must fear, love, and worship.

Paul, in writing to the Philippians, urges them to rejoice in the Lord. Perhaps their circumstances did not contribute to a joyful atmosphere. Never mind. Rejoice in the Lord. He tells them to be reasonable, and then follows that with "The Lord is at hand." The petty divisions and quarrels they were having revealed a lack of conscious awareness of God's presence (Phil. 2:1-5; 4:2-3). Ignorance of God, who He is, and how near He is, results in gloom at best and great acts of presumptuous evil at worst.

Think about It

Many of our troubles stem from sin, and all sin stems from failure to recognize that God is God. He is near, yet He is far above us, holy, infinite, eternal, and unchangeable. Peace, joy, and reasonableness will characterize those who heed Paul's admonition to be conscious that "the Lord is at hand." The gospel of Jesus Christ tells us that God came in human flesh to save us from our sin, to reverse what our first parents did. Make that gospel your focus today. Believe in Him. Live in Him.

Why Nothing is Going Wrong

Today's Reading: Isaiah 41-42; Colossians 1

Selected Verses

Behold my servant, whom I uphold,
my chosen, in whom my soul delights;
I have put my Spirit upon him;
he will bring forth justice to the nations.

Isa. 42:1

For in him all the fullness of God was pleased to dwell, and through him to reconcile to
himself all things, whether on earth or in heaven, making peace by the blood of his cross.

Col. 1:19-20

Reflections

Yesterday I suggested that everything is going wrong. I tried to summarize the cause. But there is more to the story. In truth, nothing is going wrong, because all things are under God's control and all things will culminate according to His plan and will.

Isaiah wrote to Judah and Israel, the divided kingdoms, where it seemed that their existence was hanging by a thread. He called Israel "His servant" (Isa. 41:9), but what a flaky servant she is! She cannot be trusted to be faithful to the Lord. Israel is quick to worship idols. She is blind to her own calling and history (Isa. 42:18-25). What does God do? He chooses a new servant. Well, He is not *really* new, because we learn He is the Son of God, the Messiah, the Lord Jesus Christ.

This Chosen Servant has the Spirit of God upon Him. He will bring justice to the nations. He will not wear out or give up before accomplishing His work in the earth. How gracious of God to find Someone to do what Israel could not or would not do!

Paul writes much about Jesus, showing who He is and what He has done (see also Eph. 2-3). Paul prays that the Colossians will grasp the truth about Jesus, because it is through His suffering on the cross that He has made peace and reconciled all things to Himself. Through Christ we "have redemption, the forgiveness of sins" (Col. 1:14).

Think about It

We need to recognize the trends and problems of our society today and do what we can to forestall corruption. Yet more than that, we need to recognize that nothing intimidates or frustrates God. Jesus will not grow faint or discouraged before accomplishing His work of redemption in the earth. Should we? Take heart. From God's viewpoint, nothing is going wrong.

Complete in Him

Today's Reading: Isaiah 43-44; Colossians 2

Selected Verses

But you have burdened me with your sins;
you have wearied me with your iniquities.
I, I am he
who blots out your transgressions for my own sake,
and I will not remember your sins.

Isa. 43:24b-25

For in him the whole fullness of deity dwells bodily, and you have been filled in him, who is the head of all rule and authority.

Col. 2:9-10

Reflections

Isaiah describes the sorry spiritual state of Israel. He expresses God's weariness with their empty religiosity but also the Lord's mercy towards them. Yes, He has had enough of their hypocrisy. They have demonstrated again and again that they only go through the motions of repentance as they offer sacrifices. Their best is worthless. But God will not let them go. He will do for them what they cannot do for themselves. He will not blot them out. No! Instead, He will blot out their sins, the sins which have burdened Him. This is the grace and mercy of God.

But how will He do that? Later, Isaiah will explain how God will do this, without compromising His holiness and justice (Isa. 53).

Fast forward to Paul's letter to the Colossians. We find the Apostle laying out for his readers the glories that are found in Jesus Christ. All the deity of God is in Christ. God is fully and completely with us in Christ. Christ is God incarnate, deity in human flesh. He is filled with wisdom, so we need never seek other philosophies. He died and was raised from the dead, so that in Him we are raised to life. In Him we are complete, filled, with nothing more to need or long for.

Think about It

This plan of God revealed partially and progressively in the Old Testament and fully and finally in the New brings God all glory and His believing people salvation, forgiveness, and eternal life. Let nothing and no one delude you, says Paul. Keep walking with Him deeply rooted and built up in Him (2:6-7). Resist the attraction of anything that promises to fill you apart from Christ. In Him alone we are complete.

God Wins; Don't Fight Him

Today's Reading: Isaiah 45-47; Colossians 3

Selected Verses

> *Turn to me and be saved,*
> *   all the ends of the earth!*
> *   For I am God, and there is no other.*
> *By myself I have sworn;*
> *   from my mouth has gone out in righteousness*
> *   a word that shall not return:*
> *"To me every knee shall bow,*
> *   every tongue shall swear allegiance."*

Isa. 45:22-23

Put to death therefore what is earthly in you: sexual immorality, impurity, passion, evil desire, and covetousness, which is idolatry. On account of these the wrath of God is coming.

Col. 3:5-6

Reflections

Isaiah predicts with detail the deliverance of Judah by Cyrus, king of Persia, an event that remained some 150 years in the future. God will do what He wills with mighty Babylonia. Judah will be conquered and taken into captivity by that empire, but then Babylonia would succumb to Persia and Cyrus would become the deliverer of Judah. God, through the prophet, keeps telling them "besides me there is no God" (45:5, 22; 46:9). When are they going to get this?

Paul calls the Colossians to holiness of life, beginning with their mindset. In order to focus on things above where Christ is, they are certainly going to have to turn away from the things below, earthly things like "sexual immorality, impurity, passion, evil desire, and covetousness." Sexual sin—for most of us men —is easy to spot. Guilt can be quickly detected and hard to ignore or suppress.

Covetousness, however, is more subtle. It is idolatry! We want things that others have because we love stuff. We rely on things to make us happy. Stuff seems to fill the emptiness in our hearts left by an earthly mindset. In reality, when we covet, we replace the worship of God with material things. God's wrath is going to be unleashed on those who practice that sin. It is not a harmless, little snake, all cute and cuddly. It is a deadly serpent whose venom kills. Put it to death, Paul tells them.

Think about It

The final victory of God over all evil and rebellion against Him is indisputable. He wins! What is not clear is whether we will bow before Him now, calling for His mercy and salvation, or later when we come kicking and screaming before His judgment. Don't fight God. Seek to set your mind on Him, now and always.

Life Under Surveillance

Today's Reading: Isaiah 48-49; Colossians 4

Selected Verses

Because I know that you are obstinate,
and your neck is an iron sinew
and your forehead brass,
I declared them to you from of old,
before they came to pass I announced them to you,
lest you should say, "My idol did them,
my carved image and my metal image commanded them."

Isa. 48:4-5

Walk in wisdom toward outsiders, making the best use of the time. Let your speech always
be gracious, seasoned with salt, so that you may know how you ought to answer each person.

Col. 4:5-6

Reflections

Paul concludes his letter to the church at Colossae with some final charges. They are to live wisely in their relationships with outsiders, that is, unbelievers. Two areas for concentration and care are the management of time and the quality of their speech. If a professing Christian is careless with his use of time, he enables unbelievers who observe him to discount either the genuineness of his profession or the veracity of his doctrine. More often than not, it is the latter option which prevails. By the same token, if the believer speaks in ways that are coarse, hurtful, lacking grace, or even corrupt (i.e. salt-less), he gives evidence that the gospel he professes is either not true or is powerless to change lives. Clearly, unbelievers are quick to grasp inconsistency in Christians to buttress their case against the call of the gospel.

God through Isaiah addressed another tendency of His disobedient, faithless people in Israel. The Lord tells them that His prophecies are designed to remove their claims that the deliverance which He planned for them was the work of their idols. It was a tendency in Isaiah's day, and it continues to the present, for unbelievers to take credit for anything good that occurs, but to use problems and tragedies as an excuse to blame God or reject His existence.

Think about It

If you are identified with Christ, your life is under constant surveillance, not just by the Lord but, by your agnostic and pagan friends, relatives, co-workers, and neighbors. Be sure your life shows consistency with your profession. They may not believe because of you, but avoid making it easier for them to disbelieve.

The Extent of Salvation

Today's Reading: Isaiah 50-52; 1 Thessalonians 1

Selected Verses

> *The Lord has bared his holy arm*
> *before the eyes of all the nations,*
> *and all the ends of the earth shall see*
> *the salvation of our God.*

Isa. 52:10

For not only has the word of the Lord sounded forth from you in Macedonia and Achaia, but your faith in God has gone forth everywhere, so that we need not say anything. For they themselves report concerning us the kind of reception we had among you, and how you turned to God from idols to serve the living and true God, and to wait for his Son from heaven, whom he raised from the dead, Jesus who delivers us from the wrath to come.

1 Thess. 1:8-10

Reflections

There are two dimensions to God's salvation: the geographical dimension and the spiritual dimension. God saves people everywhere and those He saves are so completely saved that they turn from idols to serve God.

Isaiah records the intention of God to show His power to all the nations of the earth. He would show this by revealing His salvation—His ability to redeem men and women, boys and girls from every tribe, tongue, and nation. This was always His plan. Isaiah passes on more information about the details of this plan, which we will see in tomorrow's reading.

With the coming of Jesus Christ, that salvation was more fully revealed. The kingdom of God was near. The apostles proclaimed the good news. The church was scattered throughout the Roman Empire taking the gospel to Jews and Gentiles on its way to the ends of the earth. Paul brought the message to Thessalonica. The people heard and believed. They received the salvation that is in Christ. Here we see how completely God saves people. They "turned to God from idols." Why? They turned "to serve the living and true God." Not only that, they set their attention on waiting "for his Son from heaven, whom he raised from the dead, Jesus who delivers us from the wrath to come."

Think about It

The gospel proclaims salvation everywhere. Those who believe experience the beginning of a complete transformation. They continue to be changed by it throughout their lives. This is the message which the world needs to hear in every generation until Jesus returns from heaven. Pray, send, give, and, if God wills, go that the blind may see and the deaf hear the truth.

The Victory of the Gospel

Today's Reading: Isaiah 53-55; 1 Thessalonians 2

Selected Verses

For as the rain and the snow come down from heaven
and do not return there but water the earth,
making it bring forth and sprout,
giving seed to the sower and bread to the eater,
so shall my word be that goes out from my mouth;
it shall not return to me empty,
but it shall accomplish that which I purpose,
and shall succeed in the thing for which I sent it.

Isa. 55:10-11

For you yourselves know, brothers, that our coming to you was not in vain.

1 Thess. 2:1

Reflections

Isaiah gave Israel and the world the greatest message in all of history in chapter 53. The Servant of the Lord would bear the sins of His people and "make many to be accounted righteous" (53:11). This truth, that One who is holy and righteous has taken the just wrath of God for sinners, is at the heart of the gospel message.

This is the best news ever told, but would this news get to the world? Would those who desperately need hope for forgiveness and reconciliation with God hear about this? The answer is "yes!" Nothing can stop God's word from going forth. Plenty of forces mounted up against it in Paul's day and in ours. The Apostle suffered in Philippi. They treated him shamefully (1 Thess. 2:2). Did he give up? No! He went right on to Thessalonica. There he continued to preach the word and this letter shows that the message bore amazing fruit in the lives of the people. Then, those new believers preached it to the surrounding region.

Think about It

We live in an unprecedented time of global communication. This is both a blessing and curse, since much of the communication is evil and deceptive. But technology also helps proclaim this gospel. And despite all kinds of opposition, God's word can never be defeated. Are you confident in the power of the gospel to change lives? Are you certain that God will open doors for His word—that He will use it to accomplish its every purpose? Fear not! God's word will triumph. Proclaim it with confidence wherever you can. God guarantees the victory.

Distress and Comfort

Today's Reading: Isaiah 56-58; 1 Thessalonians 3

Selected Verses

For thus says the One who is high and lifted up,
who inhabits eternity, whose name is Holy:
"I dwell in the high and holy place,
and also with him who is of a contrite and lowly spirit,
to revive the spirit of the lowly,
and to revive the heart of the contrite.

Isa. 57:15

But now that Timothy has come to us from you, and has brought us the
good news of your faith and love and reported that you always remember
us kindly and long to see us, as we long to see you— for this reason, brothers,
in all our distress and affliction we have been comforted about you through
your faith. For now we live, if you are standing fast in the Lord.

1 Thess. 3:6-8

Reflections

Paul was anxious about the Thessalonians. Twice he uses the phrase "[we or I] could bear it no longer" (3:1, 5). He wanted to know how those new believers were doing. He finally sent Timothy to them and learned that they were not only standing firm in the gospel but were impacting the whole region.

Isaiah describes how God who is high and lifted up also dwells with the one who is "of a contrite and lowly spirit." If God is with us, assuming we qualify as having "a contrite and lowly spirit," do we need anything more? No, not really. God is enough. The psalmist said, "Whom have I in heaven but you? And there is nothing on earth that I desire besides you" (Ps. 73:25).

Yet Paul could not bear the distress of not knowing if the young Thessalonian disciples were doing well, not reverting to idol worship. Did Paul lack faith? Did he focus too much on being successful? No. We can see that Paul had a tender heart toward those he taught. It was natural, not sinful. He made the sacrifice of sending Timothy to inquire about them. There was nothing wrong with doing that. We would not expect a sincere minister or missionary to be cold and uncaring about those he has served in the gospel.

Think about It

So we are right to be concerned, even worried, about those whose spiritual lives could be in jeopardy. We are right to do what we can to care for them and to keep up with their circumstances and progress. In the final analysis, however, our greatest comfort and joy will be that "the One who is high and lifted up, who inhabits eternity, whose name is Holy" dwells with us and revives our hearts. Don't be unfeeling toward others, but let God's presence be the bedrock of your spirit to comfort you in distress.

Sin—Why We Can't See God

Today's Reading: Isaiah 59-61; 1 Thessalonians 4

Selected Verses

Behold, the Lord's hand is not shortened, that it cannot save, or his ear dull, that it cannot hear; but your iniquities have made a separation between you and your God, and your sins have hidden his face from you so that he does not hear.

Isa. 59:1-2

For God has not called us for impurity, but in holiness. Therefore whoever disregards this, disregards not man but God, who gives his Holy Spirit to you.

1 Thess. 4:7-8

Reflections

Sin has been the problem since our first parents listened to the serpent and ate of the forbidden fruit. What did they get? They got the knowledge of good and evil and with it death! In our flesh we all find sin attractive. It may be as subtle as a snarky put-down or as grotesque as murderous rage, as imperceptible as a flirtatious glance or as devastating as serial adultery. Sin comes in many colors and shapes, all of them tempting and soul-killing but none of them truly satisfying. Worst of all, it results in our not seeing or hearing God. We tend to conclude He is not there.

Isaiah wrote to ancient Israel telling them that their sin was blocking their eyes and ears from seeing and hearing God. It was not God who was hiding from them. He is there in plain sight, seen and heard in His acts of Creation and Providence and in His revealed Word.

Paul admonished the church in Thessalonica with the words, "For this is the will of God, your sanctification" (1 Thess. 4:3). He then specifically mentions abstinence from sexual immorality for the next five verses, topped off with a paragraph about brotherly love.

In case they don't see the urgency of this, he turns to the subject of the return of Christ, His descent from heaven, the cry of command, the sound of the trumpet, and the resurrection of the dead. When Christ returns, all eyes will see Him. There will be no vacillating. We will be exposed at last. The shouts of rejoicing will mix with the cries of remorse.

Think about It

Is there hope for sinners? Yes, indeed! For God has done what no human being could do. "His own arm brought him salvation" writes the prophet (Isa. 59:16). In the end, "Nations shall come to your light, and kings to the brightness of your rising" (Isa. 60:3). The dead in Christ will rise first followed by those who are still alive and "so we will always be with the Lord." But the time is now. Do not assume there is no God. Assume that it is your sin that blinds your eyes. But He may be found because "all who call upon the Lord will be saved" (Rom. 10:8-13). Call on Him, today.

Don't Put Out the Fire of the Spirit

Today's Reading: Isaiah 62-64; 1 Thessalonians 5

Selected Verses

> *But they rebelled*
> *and grieved his Holy Spirit;*
> *therefore he turned to be their enemy,*
> *and himself fought against them.*

Isa. 63:10

> *Do not quench the Spirit.*

1 Thess. 5:19

Reflections

Need we be concerned about our responses to the Holy Spirit? Is there a danger we will in some way offend, resist, grieve, or quench the Spirit of God? Are we not secure in our relationship to God through faith in Christ? Could we, although believers, act in ways that seriously jeopardize our fellowship with Him? Both Isaiah and Paul tell us the answer is "yes"!

Isaiah described the attitudes of Israel as those of rebellious children, laden with iniquity, and despisers of the Holy One of Israel (Isa. 1:2-4). God's people will go into captivity because they have turned the Lord against them through their rebellion and grieving of His Holy Spirit.

Paul commended the Thessalonians as those who "turned to God from idols to serve the living and true God." Certainly, they had been born again and delivered "from the wrath to come" (1 Thess. 1:9-10). Nevertheless, Paul was concerned about their spiritual well-being and, now in his concluding words, he charges them not to quench the Spirit. He would not be warning them unless there were a danger that they could actually do it. He gives them several instructions as to their relationships with their leaders, their brothers who may be struggling, and their enemies. He tells them to rejoice, to pray, and to give thanks. Then he adds, "Do not quench the Spirit." He warns them about two wrong responses to prophecies: despising them and believing them without testing them. He urges them to hold fast what is good and reject all evil.

Think about It

Yes, we are secure in our relationship to God (Father, Son, and Holy Spirit) through faith in Jesus Christ. But our fellowship with Him varies in quality as we work out our salvation in obedience (Phil. 2:12,13). Where salvation through faith exists, there will be obedience and, as needed, prompt confession of sin and repentance for disobedience.

The Holy Spirit has been identified with fire (Luke 3:16; Acts 2:1-4). Paul is warning his readers about the danger of pouring water on that fire in their lives through ungodly attitudes toward others, selfish living, prayerlessness, and other evils. The Spirit of God is Holy and never leads us into such behaviors. Beware of quenching or grieving Him.

What God Wants

Today's Reading: Isaiah 65-66; Second Thessalonians 1

Selected Verses

Thus says the Lord:
"Heaven is my throne,
and the earth is my footstool;
what is the house that you would build for me,
and what is the place of my rest?
All these things my hand has made,
and so all these things came to be,
declares the Lord.
But this is the one to whom I will look:
he who is humble and contrite in spirit
and trembles at my word.

Isa. 66:1-2

They will suffer the punishment of eternal destruction, away from the presence of the Lord and from the glory of his might, when he comes on that day to be glorified in his saints, and to be marveled at among all who have believed, because our testimony to you was believed.

2 Thess. 1:9-10

Reflections

In the closing chapters of his prophecy, Isaiah describes the coming new heavens and new earth. Every pain, every disappointment, every sorrow of this world will be eliminated and forgotten (Isa. 65:17). Who will enjoy this new creation? Who will have God's favor? Surprisingly for those who don't know God well, it is not those who have pompously tried to impress God. God doesn't need our works. He doesn't need a "house." He inhabits the universe. There is nothing we can build for Him that would adequately reflect His glory.

But there is something in humans that gets God's attention: a humble and contrite spirit that shows itself in trembling at His word. God is glorified properly by all who bow before Him and who take His word seriously. They may also be used by Him to do great things, but the key element of their lives is a heart that bows in worship before Him.

Paul, in his second letter to the Thessalonians, puts his call to holiness in the context of the return of Jesus Christ in judgment. Believers suffer at the hands of those who neither know God nor obey the gospel of Christ. Paul wants his readers to focus on living in a way that is worthy of the kingdom of God, worthy of His calling. He prays to God to work in them to this end, and he charges them to make every effort in this direction, too.

Think about It

God looks for the contrite, humble heart, one that fears no one but God. Does He find that in you?

The Meaning and Purpose of Life

Today's Reading: Jeremiah 1-2; Second Thessalonians 2

Selected Verses

Now the word of the Lord came to me, saying,
"Before I formed you in the womb I knew you,
and before you were born I consecrated you;
I appointed you a prophet to the nations."
Then I said, "Ah, Lord God! Behold, I do not know how
to speak, for I am only a youth." But the Lord said to me,
"Do not say, 'I am only a youth';
for to all to whom I send you, you shall go,
and whatever I command you, you shall speak."

Jer. 1:4-7

But we ought always to give thanks to God for you, brothers beloved by
the Lord, because God chose you as the firstfruits to be saved, through
sanctification by the Spirit and belief in the truth. To this he called you
through our gospel, so that you may obtain the glory of our Lord Jesus Christ.

2 Thess. 2:13-14

Reflections

Jeremiah heard God speak to him, but the message took some time to sink in. God told Jeremiah that He formed him in the womb, but even before that, God knew him and consecrated him (ie. set him apart for a designated purpose). What purpose? To be a prophet to the nations. Jeremiah offered two excuses: his age and his lack of speaking ability. God answered his excuses promising to send him. Jeremiah had no authority from a human point of view. He lacked maturity and experience. But he needed neither because God was sending him. Secondly, God would tell him what to say. Jeremiah did not need to write powerful communiqués to the people. He only needed to report the messages God gave him.

Paul had a similar view of the work of God in the lives of the Thessalonians. Like Jeremiah, they were chosen by God and set apart by the Spirit. When they heard the gospel, they believed it and were saved. God had called them through the gospel and they responded. The ultimate result of this would be that they would obtain the glory of our Lord Jesus Christ.

Think about It

Many today hold a worldview that sees our lives as essentially a result of a random evolutionary process. There is no accountability and no boundaries, but also no purpose or meaning. Rejoice, if you know God has chosen you, called you, and set you apart as a recipient of His mercy, grace, and love. If He has forgiven and adopted you as His child to serve Him, praise God. Give yourself fully to Him. Glory awaits us.

God's Plan; Our Part

Today's Reading: Jeremiah 3-4; Second Thessalonians 3

Selected Verses

*And I will give you shepherds after my own heart, who will feed you
with knowledge and understanding. And when you have multiplied
and been fruitful in the land, in those days, declares the Lord, they shall
no more say, "The ark of the covenant of the Lord." It shall not come to
mind or be remembered or missed; it shall not be made again. At that
time Jerusalem shall be called the throne of the Lord, and all nations
shall gather to it, to the presence of the Lord in Jerusalem, and
they shall no more stubbornly follow their own evil heart.*

Jer. 3:15-17

*Finally, brothers, pray for us, that the word of the Lord may speed ahead
and be honored, as happened among you, and that we may be delivered
from wicked and evil men. For not all have faith. But the Lord is
faithful. He will establish you and guard you against the evil one.*

2 Thess. 3:1-3

Reflections

Jeremiah paints a sad picture of the spiritual adultery of Israel and Judah,
but, against that backdrop, he superimposes the triumph of God's plan to gather
to Himself all nations, redeemed and righteous, before Him. Again and again,
the prophets assure us that God will win and His plan will succeed.

When we turn to Paul's second letter to the Thessalonians, we find him
diligently laboring to instruct them in the gospel of Jesus Christ and to exhort
them to live holy lives. He requests prayer so "that the word of the Lord may
speed ahead and be honored." Paul worked with zeal, discipline, and knowledge.
But without God's working in the hearts of Paul's hearers nothing would occur.
God's workers must always pray because they need His power.

Think about It

God's purposes cannot fail for He is sovereign. At the same time, you and I
have a part to play. It may be to pray. It may be to go proclaim the good news of
life in Christ to your neighbor, coworker, or some unreached people around the
globe. God raises up shepherds to feed His people (Jer. 3:15) and He gifts each
one in His Church to serve (1 Cor. 14; Rom. 12:3-8). If you have not done so,
find your calling and do your part.

Conscience: Good or Bad?

Today's Reading: Jeremiah 5-6; First Timothy 1

Selected Verses

> O Lord, do not your eyes look for truth?
> You have struck them down,
>   but they felt no anguish;
> you have consumed them,
>   but they refused to take correction.
> They have made their faces harder than rock;
>   they have refused to repent.

Jer. 5:3

*The aim of our charge is love that issues from a pure heart and a good conscience and
a sincere faith. Certain persons, by swerving from these, have wandered away into
vain discussion, desiring to be teachers of the law, without understanding either
what they are saying or the things about which they make confident assertions.*

1 Tim. 1:5-7

Reflections

Jeremiah proclaims the Lord's judgment on Judah. He declares to them that
they have already received punishment and correction from God, but they have
ignored it. They have blown it off as nothing. They have dug in their heels and
determined not to repent. Punishment is not the final step in God's discipline
plan. He disciplines those He loves, but there comes a time when He no longer
disciplines but "gives them up" to their evil (Heb. 12:6; Rom. 1:24-28). They
assume that God is too weak or too merciful to bother chastising them, but they
are wrong. They then face only the wrath of God and eternal judgment.

Paul sent Timothy to Ephesus to correct some problems in the church
there. There were people affiliated with the congregation whose lives were off
track, not characterized by love, a pure heart, a good conscience, and sincere
faith. It was not enough that these people should go astray by themselves.
They had to bring the unsuspecting along with them. They did this by
attempting to teach things they did not really understand. Did their
uncertainty make them humble and tentative in their preaching? No, not at
all. They were making confident assertions about their lies and shipwreck of
their faith (1 Tim. 1:19).

Think about It

What are we to take away from this? Let God's word rebuke and correct you
as needed. Seek to be receptive to the Lord's discipline. Keep your conscience
tender. If it seems like God is tolerant of your unrepentant lifestyle, beware that

He may have given you up to your evil ways. Call on Him for grace to awaken your conscience and to make you repentant. Watch out for those who confidently proclaim that God won't judge sin. Flee to Christ from the wrath to come.

Healing for Sin-sick Souls

Today's Reading: Jeremiah 7-8; First Timothy 2

Selected Verses

For the wound of the daughter of my people is my heart wounded;
I mourn, and dismay has taken hold on me.
Is there no balm in Gilead?
Is there no physician there?
Why then has the health of the daughter of my people
not been restored?

Jer. 8:21-22

For there is one God, and there is one mediator between God and men, the man Christ Jesus, who gave himself as a ransom for all, which is the testimony given at the proper time.

1 Tim. 2:5-6

Reflections

Jeremiah was in grief over the sin of Judah. He had a message. It was from God. It was true, but it gave him no joy. He had to proclaim to the people their sin and failure. No wonder people called him "the weeping prophet." Sin has painful consequences for unrepentant sinners, but also for those who love them and can only watch them spiraling down into judgment. Jeremiah loved his fellow countrymen. He could call them to God, but he could not heal them when they refused to listen. In those days, Gilead was an area east of the Jordan known for its medicinal products. [13] The prophet longed for some balm or ointment to cure the sinful populace.

I remember an old spiritual we sang in my childhood. The refrain is:

There is a balm in Gilead
to make the wounded whole,
there is a balm in Gilead
to heal the sin-sick soul.

Amen! Paul had the happy work of proclaiming that there is healing in our Lord Jesus Christ. He is the One who gave Himself as a ransom. Our High Priest Jesus is the mediator between God and men. He took our sin upon Himself, dying on the cross, rising again, sending forth the Apostles to spread the news, and ascending to the right hand of God. Jesus cures not merely the physical body but the "sin-sick soul." Jeremiah longed to find such souls. But he found hard hearts, unreceptive to his diagnosis of their need.

Think about It

If you are sin-sick, find healing in Jesus who gave Himself for such as you (see Mark 10:45; Titus 2:14; 1 Peter 1:18, 19).

---

[13] *Reformation Study Bible*, note on Jeremiah 8:22, p. 1276

What a Church Leader Needs

Today's Reading: Jeremiah 9-10; First Timothy 3

Selected Verses

Correct me, O Lord, but in justice;
not in your anger, lest you bring me to nothing.
Pour out your wrath on the nations that know you not.

Jer. 10:24-25

I hope to come to you soon, but I am writing these things to you so that, if
I delay, you may know how one ought to behave in the household of God,
which is the church of the living God, a pillar and buttress of the truth.

1 Tim. 3:14-15

Reflections

Jeremiah was devastated by the sin of his people, God's people, but he did not become self-righteous. He knew that even as he preached against the sins of the nation, he himself needed God's guidance. He pleaded for God's just correction but with restrained anger. Jeremiah understood the power and holiness of God and his own failures that could bring him to nothing.

Paul, in writing to Timothy, instructs him in the standards for elders and deacons in the church. Their personal lives need to be exemplary in every way. These instructions cannot wait until Paul's next visit to Timothy. The matter of godly behavior is urgent. The Church, he writes, is "the household of God." God lives in His people. Furthermore, it is God's Church, not Timothy's, not Paul's. Finally, it is "the pillar and buttress of the truth." Although living in a different era, Jeremiah was the kind of man that Paul would have wanted Timothy to have as an elder or deacon in Ephesus.

Think about It

A local congregation must not have phony, hypocritical, self-righteous leaders. They will not be perfect, but they must be teachable, repentant, god-fearing men. God is a God of holiness and wrath. He will not let His name be associated with sin in His Church. It is a dangerous thing to be a leader of His church without a broken and contrite spirit.

If you are a church officer, do you seek to grow in conformity to these Scriptural standards? We who lead in the church must be teachable and repentant, recognizing our need for guidance and gentleness from our Lord. Do you pray humbly for yourself that God will correct you gently? As a church member, do you lovingly hold your officers to such standards knowing that we all stand in need of God's gentle correction? May we be diligent to honor God in our churches.

The Danger of Neglecting God's Word

Today's Reading: Jeremiah 11-13; First Timothy 4

Selected Verses

> *But if you will not listen,*
> *my soul will weep in secret for your pride;*
> *my eyes will weep bitterly and run down with tears,*
> *because the Lord's flock has been taken captive.*

Jer. 13:17

> *Practice these things, immerse yourself in them, so that all may see your*
> *progress. Keep a close watch on yourself and on the teaching. Persist*
> *in this, for by so doing you will save both yourself and your hearers.*

1 Tim. 4:15-16

Reflections

Jeremiah describes Judah as those who have become "accustomed to do evil" (Jer. 13:24). They have believed lies and lost the ability to do good. Doing evil feels normal. They worship idols without hesitation. The prophet says they have become useless like rotten underwear. They live under the imminent threat of God's judgment and their utter humiliation.

Is there any hope? They need a return to God's covenant, His law. They have neglected it both in the study of it and the doing of it. Centuries later it was still a problem in New Testament times. Paul addresses that subject with Timothy.

Paul charges Timothy with teaching the church in Ephesus. The goal is not merely that they get an education in the Bible but that they be trained in godliness. Timothy is to model this for them, despite his relative youthfulness. God calls pastors to grow and to make progress in the knowledge and practice of God's Word. Paul tells him to "immerse" himself in these things.

Think about It

If you are a pastor or church leader, do those you lead see your progress? Do you challenge them by a life wholly given to growth in godliness based on the Scriptures?

While this is especially important for pastors, this same exhortation applies to all believers. False teaching which is only slightly off-track from God's Word can easily deceive us. If we continue without course correction, over time we get farther and farther away from the truth. Like Judah, we can become accustomed to do evil until it feels normal. Beware of the life of your soul. Immerse yourself in learning godliness through the careful study and application of God's Word.

Competition for Glory

Today's Reading: Jeremiah 14-16; First Timothy 5

Selected Verses

Can man make for himself gods?
Such are not gods!
Therefore, behold, I will make them know, this once I will make them know
my power and my might, and they shall know that my name is the Lord.

Jer. 16:20-21

Command these things as well, so that they may be without reproach.

1 Tim. 5:7

Reflections

The messages in the prophecy of Jeremiah center around Judah's failure to honor and worship God and the judgment that was about to come upon them. This judgment would spill over into the whole earth as God always has all the tribes, families, language groups, and nations in view, not only the Jews. Again and again, the purpose of God to make Himself known to mankind comes piercing through.

In chapter 16, Jeremiah says, "to you shall the nations come" (vs. 19). The nations will come and confess that their fathers had believed lies and trusted in man-made gods. These were powerless and empty. God responds to this kind of confession and makes Himself known.

The Church of Jesus Christ has a special responsibility to be faithful to the Lord at every level, even in the matter of interpersonal relationships with older men and women, and younger men and women (1 Tim. 5:1-2). Paul goes into detail about the care of widows, balancing corporate responsibility with familial obligations. There is a place for the church to assume a major role in the care of the true widow. Her character must be godly. She must have no other sources of support and be beyond the age of remarriage and childbearing. There were dangers of condoning laziness and sloth but also of selfishly neglecting widows (or others) who were truly in need. Paul's thorough instructions aim to avoid excesses that would bring shame on the church.

Think about It

It's all about knowing and glorifying God. That is why Judah existed and it is why the Church exists. Indeed, that is why mankind exists. Is that your purpose? Beware of other gods that creep into our hearts: self-glorification, power, prestige, pride. "Such are not gods!" Let nothing compete for God's glory that you and—as far as it depends on you—His church be above reproach.

Flee Idols; Worship God

Today's Reading: Jeremiah 17-19; First Timothy 6

Selected Verses

*Then the word of the Lord came to me: "O house of Israel, can I not do
with you as this potter has done? declares the Lord. Behold, like the
clay in the potter's hand, so are you in my hand, O house of Israel."*

Jer. 18:5-6

*He who is the blessed and only Sovereign, the King of kings and Lord of lords,
who alone has immortality, who dwells in unapproachable light, whom no
one has ever seen or can see. To him be honor and eternal dominion. Amen.*

1 Tim. 6:15-16

Reflections

God reveals Himself in Scripture, but His revelation is not exhaustive due in
part to the limitations of human language. In today's readings, God compares
Himself to a potter and His people to a lump of clay (Jer. 18:5-6). Then in
Paul's letter to Timothy lofty language is used to describe Him. These
descriptions are true but of necessity are only able to capture partially all the
majesty and splendor of the Holy, Eternal God.

As the One who created us, God is our God. We owe Him our allegiance,
our obedience, our submission, our honor, and our worship. His Word should
be our command. The Lord showed Jeremiah that He had rights over Israel in
the same way a potter has rights over a lump of clay to make out of her whatever
seemed good to him. But Israel was rebellious and embraced false gods and
served them, totally disregarding their true and living God. They would pay the
price by defeat before their enemies.

Paul's words about God are set in the context of warnings about the dangers
of loving money and seeking to be rich. The Apostle urges his young disciple,
Timothy, to flee these dangers, to pursue godly qualities, to fight the good fight
of faith, and to live a blameless life. Why? Christ will return, He who is King of
kings and Lord of lords. He alone is immortal. He "dwells in unapproachable
light."

Think about It

We, too, owe our God everything we are and have. He is our potter and we
His clay. He is worthy of every exclamation of praise and every act of humble
service that we can offer to Him. Praise Him. Love Him with all your heart, soul,
mind, and strength. In so doing, you will be fleeing the idols of money and
pleasure.

The Calling to Carry a Cross

Today's Reading: Jeremiah 20-22; Second Timothy 1

Selected Verses

> *O Lord, you have deceived me,*
> *and I was deceived;*
> *you are stronger than I,*
> *and you have prevailed.*
> *I have become a laughingstock all the day;*
> *everyone mocks me.*
> *For whenever I speak, I cry out,*
> *I shout, "Violence and destruction!"*
> *For the word of the Lord has become for me*
> *a reproach and derision all day long.*
>
> Jer. 20:7-8

> *For this reason I remind you to fan into flame the gift of God,*
> *which is in you through the laying on of my hands, for God gave*
> *us a spirit not of fear but of power and love and self-control.*
>
> 2 Tim. 1:6-7

Reflections

As we saw yesterday, God is the potter, and we are the clay. That does not mean that we, who trust in and love Him, will automatically have smooth sailing through life. Both Jeremiah and Paul were imprisoned despite their faithfulness to God's calling. Their responses were different, but God's faithfulness to both was constant.

Jeremiah was beaten and imprisoned by a priest named Pashur. The next day, upon his release from the stocks, the prophet told Pashur that he would watch his friends die, then, he would go into captivity and die also. So Jeremiah seemed to be unaffected by Pashur's oppression. Nevertheless, following that episode, the prophet records his lament before God. He says the Lord "deceived" him. He was given a calling and a message from God which he could not silence in himself lest he explode. As a result of his obedience, he was the joke of society —the village idiot on a national level. He complains that he did not sign up for this.

Paul also was suffering imprisonment in Rome as he wrote his final epistle. There is some sadness and longing to see Timothy but no blaming of God. His focus is still on charging and encouraging Timothy to continued faithfulness in the ministry. "Don't be afraid. Don't be ashamed of my suffering," Paul writes with assurance of love and prayers. God has given Timothy His Spirit, His Word, a godly heritage, and a calling to His service.

Think about It

As a follower of Jesus Christ, are you prepared to suffer? How do you respond to undeserved suffering? Two faithful servants of the Lord demonstrate that whether you vent before God like Jeremiah or calmly keep serving Him like Paul, God is the potter and He will not let you go until He has made of you what He wills and used you as He pleases. Stay faithful, even when your cross gets heavy and you suffer injustice for His sake (Luke 9:23-25).

Christ, Our Righteousness

Today's Reading: Jeremiah 23-24; Second Timothy 2

Selected Verses

Behold, the days are coming, declares the Lord, when I will raise up for David a righteous Branch, and he shall reign as king and deal wisely, and shall execute justice and righteousness in the land. In his days Judah will be saved, and Israel will dwell securely. And this is the name by which he will be called: "The Lord is our righteousness."

Jer. 23:5-6

Remember Jesus Christ, risen from the dead, the offspring of David, as preached in my gospel, for which I am suffering, bound with chains as a criminal. But the word of God is not bound! Therefore I endure everything for the sake of the elect, that they also may obtain the salvation that is in Christ Jesus with eternal glory.

2 Tim. 2:8-10

Reflections

The prophet Jeremiah had the uncomfortable, but important, task of denouncing the failed, rebellious kings and prophets of Judah. God promised to punish them, but He also gave hope to the faithful among the people. Here we have a clear promise of a future king from David's line who would deal wisely, execute justice and righteousness, and bring salvation to Judah and Israel. This and other prophecies kept the believing remnant of Israel hopeful until Jesus Christ, the Messiah, came (see Luke 2:25-38). Jeremiah and his contemporaries probably could not have imagined in their wildest dreams the extent of this prophecy. God did everything He promised and far more by calling to Himself through Christ people from every tribe, nation, and tongue, all His elect down through history who in one voice confess, "The Lord is our righteousness" (1 Cor. 1:30).

Paul was concerned that the Church, which was beginning to reflect this global, cross-cultural composition, would be faithful to the gospel and to her head, Jesus Christ. He gives instructions to Timothy about preaching the word, appointing qualified godly leaders (1 Tim. 3:1-13), and insuring that the truths taught by the apostles to men like Timothy be passed on from generation to generation. Timothy needed to be careful about his own life, being watchful to avoid distracting worldly entanglements and foolish, ignorant controversies. He must do his best in handling the word of God. To do these things he will always need to keep Jesus Christ central in his mind.

Think about It

God's word proclaims that all have sinned and come short of the glory of God. But God declares all who call upon Him righteous in His eyes. They confess that "The Lord is our righteousness." Be sure that is your confession and hope, even while you seek to be faithful in your service for Him.

Preparing for the Bad, Last Days

Today's Reading: Jeremiah 25-26; Second Timothy 3

Selected Verses

[Jeremiah speaking] *"Only know for certain that if you put me to death, you will bring innocent blood upon yourselves and upon this city and its inhabitants, for in truth the Lord sent me to you to speak all these words in your ears."*

Then the officials and all the people said to the priests and the prophets, "This man does not deserve the sentence of death, for he has spoken to us in the name of the Lord our God."

Jer. 26:15-16

All Scripture is breathed out by God and profitable for teaching, for reproof, for correction, and for training in righteousness, that the man of God may be complete, equipped for every good work.

2 Tim. 3:16-17

Reflections

Paul writes to instruct Timothy in his pastoral duties and also to alert him (and all of us who have lived since him) as to the dangerous, difficult times that were and are to come. We read the list which begins with "lovers of self" and ends with "having the appearance of godliness but denying its power" (2 Tim. 3:2-5). Narcissism would be rampant with phony, hypocritical uprightness.

Paul didn't worry that Timothy would go astray. He knew the depth of character of his protégé. Not only that, Timothy had the Scriptures his whole life, the Word of God which brings wisdom for salvation and goes on to teach, reprove, correct, and train all who know it. Paul wanted Timothy to continue to rely on the Word for his own life and for his ministry in light of the expected difficulties ahead.

Jeremiah affirmed to the rebellious leaders of Judah that he spoke God's Word to them. They not only ignored it but pondered executing him for preaching it. He barely escaped death for standing on God's Word. He might have died for preaching the truth, but his enemies would and did die by it.

Think about It

How do we prepare for whatever may come? There's nothing wrong with stocking up on food, water, and firewood, but without a deep knowledge of the Bible it will be in vain. Be prepared God's way, by His Word, given to us that the man or woman of God "may be complete, equipped for every good work" including enduring the bad, last days. The Bible brings us spiritual growth as we allow it to teach, reprove, correct, and train us throughout the years of our lives. Make the daily study of Scripture your priority.

False Teachers: Why They Abound and What to Do

Today's Reading: Jeremiah 27-28; Second Timothy 4

Selected Verses

And Jeremiah the prophet said to the prophet Hananiah, "Listen, Hananiah, the Lord has not sent you, and you have made this people trust in a lie. Therefore thus says the Lord: 'Behold, I will remove you from the face of the earth. This year you shall die, because you have uttered rebellion against the Lord.'" In that same year, in the seventh month, the prophet Hananiah died.

Jer. 28:15-17

For the time is coming when people will not endure sound teaching, but having itching ears they will accumulate for themselves teachers to suit their own passions, and will turn away from listening to the truth and wander off into myths. As for you, always be sober-minded, endure suffering, do the work of an evangelist, fulfill your ministry.

2 Tim. 4:3-5

Reflections

Why would anyone listen to a false prophet? The answer is simple. People listen to false prophets and teachers because they prefer their message to the truth even when they suspect it is a lie.

In Jeremiah's day, he was opposed by those who claimed to be speaking for God. One such person was Hananiah. He directly contradicted what Jeremiah was saying. The false prophet told the people that Nebuchadnezzar would not suppress them or anyone else. He assured them that their king would be returned from captivity and the stolen items from the temple would all be brought back and replaced. Jeremiah said not only would Judah be subjugated but all their neighboring kingdoms would as well. Someone was lying. Jeremiah was proven right when he prophesied of Hananiah's death and it occurred on schedule. Would this convince everyone that Jeremiah was to be trusted? Read on and find out.

Paul was writing his final words to Timothy and to us. His warnings and charges are urgent. There would be difficult days ahead. People would not listen to sound teaching. Timothy would have to focus on fulfilling his ministry of preaching the word, including, reproving, rebuking, and exhorting. After all, that is what the Word of God does (2 Tim. 3:16).

Things have not improved in our time. Vast numbers of people still listen to those who tell them what they want to hear without checking to see what the Scriptures teach. "God is all love and everyone is going to heaven." No! That is not what Jesus or the rest of the Bible says. "God just wants you to be happy and healthy." No! God calls you and me to repentance and faith in Him. He looks for people with broken and contrite hearts, not presumptuous self-esteem (see Ps. 51:17; Mark 1:15).

Think about It

Study God's Word. Watch out for the false teachers and phony prophets. They will end up like Hananiah.

Our Role in Culture: Finding the Balance

Today's Reading: Jeremiah 29-30; Titus 1

Selected Verses

*But seek the welfare of the city where I have sent you into exile, and pray
to the Lord on its behalf, for in its welfare you will find your welfare.*

Jer. 29:7

*This is why I left you in Crete, so that you might put what remained
into order, and appoint elders in every town as I directed you.*

Titus 1:5

Reflections

While it is true that in Jeremiah's day the Jews went into exile under the
disciplinary action of God upon Judah, life for those exiles was not put on hold
as if it were meaningless or purposeless. They would not be coming back to
Jerusalem soon. The elderly among them would die before the seventy-year
captivity ended. False prophets told them to expect a quick return to their native
land. Jeremiah, by God's revelation, commanded them to settle down, plant
gardens, buy houses, have children, and seek the welfare of the land of their
captivity. In other words, God commanded them to do the regular activities of
normal life and to be good citizens as much as possible. Indeed, Daniel
exemplified this attitude and was a great asset to Babylon in both his personal life
and public service. We'll look at this when we get to the book of Daniel.

Paul wrote his letter to Titus whom he had left on Crete to organize the
church under godly leadership. The Cretan people had a bad reputation in
general, making it crucial that Titus adhere to the apostolic standards for elders
so that the church would not be tarnished by scandal. The church in Crete had
to have men above reproach to be their elders. They, like the obedient exiles in
Babylon, would stand against the culture of their day and make a difference.

Think about It

There is an ongoing debate among Bible-believing Christians about the role
of the Church in society. Should we seek to transform it or flee from it? Both
positions have a basis in the Scriptures. It is hard to be completely on either side
of this debate. God calls us to exercise wisdom that the Church not be consumed
with changing society and lose the gospel. Nor may we be so separate from the
world that our gospel witness is lost.

Pray for wisdom to fulfill the role of salt and light, (Matt. 5:13-16) of being
in the world but not of the world as Jesus prayed (John 17:14-19).

Good Attitudes about Good Works

Today's Reading: Jeremiah 31-32; Titus 2

Selected Verses

*I will make with them an everlasting covenant, that I will not turn away
from doing good to them. And I will put the fear of me in their hearts, that
they may not turn from me. I will rejoice in doing them good, and I will
plant them in this land in faithfulness, with all my heart and all my soul.*

Jer. 32:40-41

*Waiting for our blessed hope, the appearing of the glory of our great God and
Savior Jesus Christ, who gave himself for us to redeem us from all lawlessness and
to purify for himself a people for his own possession who are zealous for good works.*

Titus 2:13-14

Reflections

Jeremiah had a message from God that gave hope and perspective for the
people of Judah in the midst of imminent captivity. God promised to restore
them to their land, no matter how far He scattered them. Their disobedience had
brought His anger and wrath. They deserved His punishment. But His
commitment to them could not be terminated. He would do a new thing and
bring them back and establish them. They would have His word in their hearts
in that day. They would be stable in their faith and obedience. He would give
them a new covenant to replace the old one they had so miserably disregarded.
But God would not just do His people good. He would *rejoice* to do them good.
He promised to plant them in the land "with all [His] heart and all [His] soul."

That promised new covenant was brought about by the Messiah, the Lord
Jesus Christ. Paul had met Christ in a dramatic way and spent the rest of his life
proclaiming the good news of salvation through Him. He wrote to Titus to
remind him that God redeemed His people from lawlessness so that they would
belong to God and be "zealous for good works."

Think about It

Do you do good works with joy and delight? If we would be godly, we must
not merely do the right thing but be sure that action is accompanied by correct
attitudes. Seek to do good and to do it with a God-honoring spirit of grace and
love.

God's Love

Today's Reading: Jeremiah 33-35; Titus 3

Selected Verses

> *Give thanks to the Lord of hosts,*
> *for the Lord is good,*
> *for his steadfast love endures forever!*

Jer. 33:11b

For we ourselves were once foolish, disobedient, led astray, slaves to various passions and pleasures, passing our days in malice and envy, hated by others and hating one another. But when the goodness and loving kindness of God our Savior appeared, he saved us.

Titus 3:3-5

Reflections

Jeremiah's prophecy is peppered with indictments for Judah's persistent rebellion against God, His Law, and His prophets. But these lists of failures are also accompanied by reassurances that God will ultimately restore the people He has chosen for Himself. They will be blessed and they will be filled with praise and thanks to the Lord.

Paul wrote to Titus who had the unenviable task of organizing and teaching the congregation in Crete, a society known for being "liars, evil beasts, and lazy gluttons." Indeed, Paul identifies himself with a list of vices and character flaws that rivals that of the infamous Cretans. He says he and others who have now been saved could be described as "foolish, disobedient, led astray, slaves to various passions and pleasures, passing our days in malice and envy, hated by others and hating one another." It is not a flattering resume, to say the least.

Then God intervened. Everything changed. God the Savior came with His goodness and loving kindness and saved Paul and all upon whom He set His love.

Think about It

Many, like me, will agree that the more we know of God and of ourselves the more amazed we are of the goodness and loving kindness of the Lord. Words cannot describe the relief of sins forgiven, of salvation assured, of adoption as God's son, and of purpose and calling to serve God. Days spent in malice and envy are now filled with gratefulness and service. No, none who know Him would claim to be sinless or perfect, far from it. But it is all of God's grace and He will complete what He has begun.

Do you know the goodness and loving kindness of God who saves? If you do, lift up His praises today in all you do.

The Use and Abuse of Authority

Today's Reading: Jeremiah 36-37; Philemon

Selected Verses

As Jehudi read three or four columns, the king would cut them off with a knife and throw them into the fire in the fire pot, until the entire scroll was consumed in the fire that was in the fire pot. Yet neither the king nor any of his servants who heard all these words was afraid, nor did they tear their garments. Even when Elnathan and Delaiah and Gemariah urged the king not to burn the scroll, he would not listen to them.

Jer. 36:23-25

Accordingly, though I am bold enough in Christ to command you to do what is required, yet for love's sake I prefer to appeal to you—I, Paul, an old man and now a prisoner also for Christ Jesus—I appeal to you for my child, Onesimus, whose father I became in my imprisonment.

Philem. vv. 8-10

Reflections

Jeremiah received a message from God for the people of Judah. By God's instruction, he had his scribe Baruch write the message down on a scroll. Since Jeremiah had been banned from the temple area, the prophet sent Baruch to read the message to the crowd gathered to worship on a fast day. Word came back to the king's servants about this reading and they investigated further. As these officials of the king listened to Baruch read, they were gripped with fear (Jer. 36:16). They knew the king needed to hear the message, so they arranged to take the scroll, send Jeremiah and Baruch into hiding, and have the scroll read to King Jehoiakim.

The king listened to the reading, but had the scroll cut into sections and burned. Such was Jehoiakim's abuse of God-given authority. He would pay for it with the end of his reign and a shameful death without so much as a pauper's burial.

Paul, on the other hand, shows great restraint in the use of his authority over Philemon. He appeals to his friend to take kind and forgiving action toward his slave, Onesimus. In God's providence, Onesimus had met Paul and, through him, Christ. Paul wrote to the Colossian church, possibly about the same time, as to the proper attitudes of a master toward a slave (Col. 3:22-4:1).

Think about It

As king, Jehoiakim discouraged his officials from what appears to be an initial desire to obey God's word. Paul encourages obedience to his friend but without being heavy handed. Beware of ungodly authorities. Beware of the abuse of authority. Submit to God and to His authorities when appropriate. Use your authority with grace and restraint.

The Longed-For Kingdom

Today's Reading: Jeremiah 38-39; Hebrews 1

Selected Verses

The king of Babylon slaughtered the sons of Zedekiah at Riblah before his eyes, and the king of Babylon slaughtered all the nobles of Judah. He put out the eyes of Zedekiah and bound him in chains to take him to Babylon.

Jer. 39:6-7

But of the Son he says,
"Your throne, O God, is forever and ever,
the scepter of uprightness is the scepter of your kingdom.
You have loved righteousness and hated wickedness;
therefore God, your God, has anointed you
with the oil of gladness beyond your companions."

Heb. 1:8-9

Reflections

As I write this, it is Election Day in the USA, the first Tuesday following the first Monday in November. National Public Radio this morning reported on the rapid decline in religion in this nation. Belief in God is down. Identification with a particular church is down. It appears that hostility and disrespect frequently characterize public conversation about the political, social, and spiritual state of affairs in this country.

But we, reformed, evangelical Christians, do share some common dreams and longings even with those who do not agree with our theology. I think it is fair to say, we all long for a government led by honorable, just leaders, with laws that facilitate the flourishing of every person. Can anyone doubt that, if we somehow could achieve this utopia, we would want it to endure till the end of time?

Israel was not that utopia. The kingdom first established under King Saul benefited from the reigns of David and Solomon, but split in two, under foolish King Rehoboam. Neither the populace nor many of the rulers loved righteousness. Captivity devastated both kingdoms ending with the shameful capture and blinding of King Zedekiah.

But there was a promise. That promise was that a righteous king would rule on an eternal throne. That promise was fulfilled in Jesus Christ. His kingdom is forever!

Think about It

The readers of the Epistle to the Hebrews were painfully aware of the failure of their nation to establish a permanent, just kingdom. We, too, should know that our nation is not the fulfillment of the promised kingdom. The writer points us to the Only One who could fulfill it, the One who is the Son of God, the radiance of His glory and the exact imprint of his nature. I long for His return and the final fulfillment of the promise. Do you? If so, pray that we will be faithful until that day, and that it may be soon.

Drifter, Be Warned

Today's Reading: Jeremiah 40-42; Hebrews 2

Selected Verses

For you sent me to the Lord your God, saying, "Pray for us to the Lord our God, and whatever the Lord our God says declare to us and we will do it." And I have this day declared it to you, but you have not obeyed the voice of the Lord your God in anything that he sent me to tell you. Now therefore know for a certainty that you shall die by the sword, by famine, and by pestilence in the place where you desire to go to live.

Jer. 42:20b-22

Therefore we must pay much closer attention to what we have heard, lest we drift away from it. For since the message declared by angels proved to be reliable, and every transgression or disobedience received a just retribution, how shall we escape if we neglect such a great salvation?

Heb. 2:1-2

Reflections

The remnant of Judah—poor people and some armed bands left after the fall of Jerusalem—had seen the land devastated by war. Nebuchadnezzar allowed them to stay in the land under the appointed governor, Gedaliah. They were allowed to enjoy reaping whatever harvest there was. Jeremiah also chose the option offered to him and remained in the land. At Gedaliah's assassination the remnant got nervous. They went to Jeremiah for advice. "Should they go to Egypt?" They promised to do whatever Jeremiah said the Lord wanted them to do. They had good intentions. But when the answer came, it contradicted their preferences and they decided to go anyway. Jeremiah warned them of the grief they were bringing on themselves by their disobedience, but they would not listen.

The writer to the Hebrews warns his readers of the dangers of disregarding the gospel of salvation through the Son of God. There was a definite danger of drifting from it or neglecting it. We will learn that these readers were facing persecution and the author fears for their spiritual well-being.

It is easier to set out on a path of faith and obedience than it is to continue on that path when the trials and temptations arise. Jesus warned of this in His parable of the sower (Matt. 13:1-23). The remnant had Jeremiah telling them to stay in the land according to God's will. The Hebrews had the message of salvation "declared at first by the Lord, and it was attested to us by those who heard, while God also bore witness by signs and wonders and various miracles and by gifts of the Holy Spirit" (vs. 3-4).

Think about It

Beware of drifting away, of neglecting God's great salvation disclosed in His Word. Read it and heed it, every day. Fellow drifters, heed the warning.

The Confusing Faces of Sin

Today's Reading: Jeremiah 43-45; Hebrews 3

Selected Verses

[The remnant of Judah, speaking to Jeremiah]

"You are telling a lie. The Lord our God did not send you to say, 'Do not go to Egypt to live there,' but Baruch the son of Neriah has set you against us, to deliver us into the hand of the Chaldeans, that they may kill us or take us into exile in Babylon."

Jer. 43:2-3

Take care, brothers, lest there be in any of you an evil, unbelieving heart, leading you to fall away from the living God. But exhort one another every day, as long as it is called "today," that none of you may be hardened by the deceitfulness of sin. For we have come to share in Christ, if indeed we hold our original confidence firm to the end.

Heb. 3:12-14

Reflections

Defensive units in football excel by confusing their opponents with many different lineups, leaving the offense wondering what to expect. Satan is just as devious in hiding the true nature of sin, so that we confuse evil with good and good with evil. The deceitfulness of sin produces a hardened heart that is less, not more, sensitive to temptation.

When Jeremiah gave the remnant of Judah the message from God that they should not seek protection and security by going into Egypt, the leaders responded by accusing Jeremiah of lying. They even ascribed to him a motive for lying—that Baruch had pressured or bribed him into giving a false prophecy from God. Thus, those who were preparing to disobey God attacked the messenger, rejecting the message and impugning his motives. They deflected their own guilt by accusing the faithful prophet. Then they marched themselves down to Egypt filled with self-assurance and indignation towards Jeremiah.

The writer to the Hebrews warns his readers, whom he calls brothers, to "take care." He is concerned that they are about to fall away from the living God as a result of evil, unbelieving hearts, hardened by the deceitfulness of sin. In today's reading he describes various faces of sin: evil, unbelief, hardness of heart, rebellion, and disobedience. Our enemy does not want us to detect our own sin, but to see it is a good thing. God, however, calls sin by all those negative descriptors.

Think about It

Are you taking care to not be deceived by sin? Let us "exhort one another every day" but begin by exhorting ourselves through listening to God's Word. Take care. Do not be hardened by the deceitful and confusing faces of sin.

Confidence in the Worst of Times

Today's Reading: Jeremiah 46-48; Hebrews 4

Selected Verses

But fear not, O Jacob my servant,
nor be dismayed, O Israel,
for behold, I will save you from far away,
and your offspring from the land of their captivity.
Jacob shall return and have quiet and ease,
and none shall make him afraid.
Fear not, O Jacob my servant,
declares the Lord,
for I am with you.
I will make a full end of all the nations
to which I have driven you,
but of you I will not make a full end.
I will discipline you in just measure,
and I will by no means leave you unpunished.

Jer. 46:27-28

Let us then with confidence draw near to the throne of grace,
that we may receive mercy and find grace to help in time of need.

Heb. 4:16

Reflections

Jeremiah delivered God's messages of judgment on the nations. From chapters 46 to 51, the prophet declares both God's sovereignty over and His judgment upon the neighbors of Judah and Israel beginning with Egypt and ending with Babylon. But in the midst of these pronouncements, God reassures Israel of His salvation which He will accomplish. Jacob has nothing to fear. He "shall return and have quiet and ease." Jacob is still God's servant and will be kept while the other nations are laid low. Israel will be disciplined but not destroyed.

The original recipients of the Epistle to the Hebrews seemed to be struggling with fear. The writer tells them not to be like those of another generation who doubted God and rebelled against Him in the wilderness. There are similarities with the New Testament believers who face giants in a Promised Land of rest. We, too, need to learn from those who fell in the wilderness, not to doubt God. Jesus is our High Priest. We can come to Him and find mercy and grace to help in the worst of times.

Think about It

The trials you face today are not beyond God's knowledge and control. He will use them to discipline you for good. He will hear your pleas for mercy and grace and help you. Trust Him. Seek Him in prayer. He is able and willing to save you.

349

The Everlasting Covenant

Today's Reading: Jeremiah 49-50; Hebrews 5

Selected Verses

In those days and in that time, declares the Lord, the people of Israel and the people of Judah shall come together, weeping as they come, and they shall seek the Lord their God. They shall ask the way to Zion, with faces turned toward it, saying, "Come, let us join ourselves to the Lord in an everlasting covenant that will never be forgotten."

Jer. 50:4-5

In the days of his flesh, Jesus offered up prayers and supplications, with loud cries and tears, to him who was able to save him from death, and he was heard because of his reverence. Although he was a son, he learned obedience through what he suffered. And being made perfect, he became the source of eternal salvation to all who obey him, being designated by God a high priest after the order of Melchizedek.

Heb. 5:7-10

Reflections

Jeremiah watched while Judah followed Israel into ruins. God had decreed severe discipline upon His people who shamefully broke His covenant. Clearly, the old covenant and the old priesthood were not sufficient to save the nation. But God showed Jeremiah that there would be a new covenant—one that would never fail. What covenant? The one made with the sacrifice of the Son of God, Jesus Christ, who paid the ransom for all the sins of all who would obey Him.

The Aaronic priesthood could not save sinners, although (as we can now see) it was meant only to reveal the need for a better priesthood and a better covenant. The old covenant was not a failure. It actually fulfilled its limited and designated function. It pointed to the Messiah, the Holy One of Israel, who alone could make atonement for sins as He had none of His own for which to atone. The old covenant was not a failed experiment on God's part but a plan to reveal the greater glory that would come through the eternal never-to-be-forgotten covenant with Jesus Christ.

Think about It

The failures of Judah and Israel to obey the old covenant mirror our own failures to live in perfect holiness. Like Ancient Israel, we have all fallen short of the glory of God (Rom. 3:23). But by faith in Christ, we have a high priest, appointed by God, who will minister forever not under the weakness of Aaron's priesthood but after the order of Melchizedek. Be sure you are not dull of hearing but firmly and clearly grasp the basis of your salvation. Eternal life or death depends on it.

Vows of God

Today's Reading: Jeremiah 51-52; Hebrews 6

Selected Verses

The Lord of hosts has sworn by himself: "Surely I will fill you with men, as many as locusts, and they shall raise the shout of victory over you." It is he who made the earth by his power, who established the world by his wisdom, and by his understanding stretched out the heavens.

Jer. 51:14-15

For when God made a promise to Abraham, since he had no one greater by whom to swear, he swore by himself, saying, "Surely I will bless you and multiply you." And thus Abraham, having patiently waited, obtained the promise.

Heb. 6:13-15

Reflections

Just when all seemed lost forever, Jeremiah delivered a message from God to the exiles from Judah in Babylon. The Babylonians, by God's command, had desecrated and destroyed the temple in Jerusalem. All that was precious to Judah was in ruins. The kingdom was humiliated.

But God called them to turn their thoughts back to Him and back to Jerusalem. Babylon would pay for her devastation. Babylon was about to go into ruins. God had sworn by Himself to bring about this prophecy. This is the God who "made the earth by his power...and by his understanding stretched out the heavens." Nothing can stop Him. He does all that He decrees. He swears by Himself for there is nothing and no one greater.

The recipients of the letter to the Hebrews also needed reminding of God's faithfulness and trustworthiness. The writer recalled to them how God kept His covenant promises to Abraham. God made His covenant with Abraham unilaterally as a smoking pot and flaming torch passed between the severed carcasses of a heifer, a female goat, and a ram while Abraham slept (see Gen. 15). Like the displaced Jews of the Babylonian captivity and the aging childless Abraham, the readers of the epistle faced tremendous pressures to discouragement and even to renounce their faith. They needed to remember that God proved true then, and He would prove true again.

Think about It

If there is anything we can learn from the history of God's dealings with His people, it is that He always fulfills His vows. He swears by Himself and He cannot fail. Do you wonder if God will complete His promises in your life? Do not doubt. You do not know how or when, but all that He vows to do, He will do. Trust Him.

The Perfect and Eternal Priest

Today's Reading: Lamentations 1-2; Hebrews 7

Selected Verses

> He has laid waste his booth like a garden,
> laid in ruins his meeting place;
> the Lord has made Zion forget
> festival and Sabbath,
> and in his fierce indignation has spurned king and priest.
> The Lord has scorned his altar,
> disowned his sanctuary;
> he has delivered into the hand of the enemy
> the walls of her palaces;
> they raised a clamor in the house of the Lord
> as on the day of festival.
>
> Lam. 2:6-7

For the law appoints men in their weakness as high priests, but the word of the oath, which came later than the law, appoints a Son who has been made perfect forever.

Heb. 7:28

Reflections

The Book of Lamentations tells the sad, bitter story of the consequences of the sin of Israel and Judah. Despite the law of God which established the priesthood of Aaron, the sacrifices, the worship in the temple, none of this was done without sin. The glories of the past faded away as God sent Babylon to kill and destroy the city known as "the joy of all the earth" (Lam. 2:15). The writer of Lamentations was completely clear that this had occurred as a result of the sin of the people. God brought about the wreckage for the gross failures of king and priest and citizenry.

But He had another plan all along. He would send His own Son as a king and priest. The destruction only served to prepare the way for that Messiah who would come. The letter to the Hebrews explains eloquently how the ministry of Jesus Christ, the sinless and eternal High Priest, far exceeds the tarnished and mortal priesthood of the Mosaic Law.

Think about It

It was necessary for God to show the world that only Christ could be the High Priest that was needed—One who had no sin to atone for and who would live forever to make intercession for His people. All we need is Christ as our High Priest. His priesthood is after the order of the king of righteousness and the king of peace. In Him we find righteousness and peace forever. Look no further than our Lord Jesus Christ for the path to acceptance before the Holy and Eternal God.

Goodbye to the Good, Old Days

Today's Reading: Lamentations 3-5; Hebrews 8

Selected Verses

Restore us to yourself, O Lord, that we may be restored!
Renew our days as of old—
unless you have utterly rejected us,
and you remain exceedingly angry with us.

Lam. 5:21-22

But as it is, Christ has obtained a ministry that is as much more excellent than the old as the covenant he mediates is better, since it is enacted on better promises. For if that first covenant had been faultless, there would have been no occasion to look for a second.

Heb. 8:6-7

Reflections

The writer of Lamentations pours out his grief for Jerusalem which lies in ruins. The best he can imagine is some kind of return to the wonderful days of peace and prosperity, maybe the reign of Solomon when Israel was one kingdom, rich in wealth, politically dominant, free from oppressors. Ah, to return to those days again!

But Jeremiah had already prophesied that there would be a new covenant, not like the old one to which the people were unfaithful (see Jer. 31:31-34). The writer to the Hebrews reminds his readers that the new covenant made the old one obsolete. The good, old days were not so good, after all. The old covenant only served to show the sinful condition of the nation and the need for a better covenant, a better priest, and a better sacrifice. That is exactly what God did through Christ.

Think about It

Ecclesiastes 7:10 advises us:

Say not, "Why were the former days better than these?"
For it is not from wisdom that you ask this.

In the midst of difficult and trying times, it is easy to look back to some past era that seems to have been better. Resist that temptation and let go of the longing for some golden age of yesteryear. God, in Jesus Christ, has brought us a whole new covenant that far exceeds anything ever known. Pray that we may be faithful and live in anticipation of that day when His kingdom fully comes and all things are made new.

Two Traits of True Believers

Today's Reading: Ezekiel 1-3; Hebrews 9

Selected Verses

And he said to me, "Son of man, eat this scroll that I give you and fill your stomach with it." Then I ate it; and it was in my mouth as sweet as honey.

Ezek. 3:1

And just as it is appointed for men to die once, and after that comes judgment, so Christ, having been offered once to bear the sins of many, will appear a second time, not to deal with sin but to save those who are eagerly waiting for him.

Heb. 9:27-28

Reflections

God called Ezekiel to be a prophet to His people during the time of the Babylonian Captivity. Like Jeremiah, he would get a cold reception from his hearers, the exiled Jews. The Lord commissioned Ezekiel to deliver a message, but with the assurance that he would not be successful in changing their hearts and minds. All who are called to serve God, are called first of all, to be faithful. Success is up to God.

The prophet embraced his calling. The Lord instructed him to "eat this scroll that I give you and fill your stomach with it." He obeyed and found that—although the scroll contained a message of "lamentation and mourning and woe"—in his mouth it was "as sweet as honey." But would his hearers agree? No, not at all. God had already warned him that they were a rebellious people, impudent and stubborn (Ezek. 2:3-7).

The Hebrews, faced with pressures and trials, needed reassurance of the sweetness of the gospel of Christ, which is superior in every way to the Old Testament priesthood. Jesus Christ's High Priestly ministry resulted in a once-for-all dealing with sin and His exaltation into heaven where He intercedes before God on their behalf. They also needed reassurance that Christ would appear to them a second time to save those who are eagerly waiting for Him. The writer of the epistle gave them both of these reassurances.

Think about It

Two distinguishing traits of believers are: diligent intake of God's word which they find sweet, and eager anticipation of Christ's return which overrides the trials, distractions, and seductions of this world. We are not fully sanctified, but pray earnestly that these traits will describe you more and more.

Why the Good News is so Good

Today's Reading: Ezekiel 4-6; Hebrews 10:1-25

Selected Verses

Then lie upon your left side, and I will lay the punishment of the house of Israel upon you; for the number of the days that you lie upon it, you shall bear their punishment.

Ezek. 4:4

Therefore, brethren, since we have confidence to enter the sanctuary by the blood of Jesus, by the new and living way which he opened for us through the curtain, that is, through his flesh, and since we have a great priest over the house of God, let us draw near with a true heart in full assurance of faith, with our hearts sprinkled clean from an evil conscience and our bodies washed with pure water.

Heb. 10:19-22

Reflections

Ezekiel portrayed both the heinousness of the sin committed by Israel and Judah and also the means of atonement which God would make for them. Sin is as disgusting to God as eating contaminated food would be to us, bread cooked over a fire of human feces. Ugh! The punishment for sin is as painful and costly as laying for 390 days on one side. But notice that Ezekiel had done nothing to deserve this suffering. He was symbolically bearing the punishment for Israel and Judah—a picture of what Jesus Christ would do in reality several centuries later.

What Jesus did on the cross was to bring an end to the shadow of Old Testament sacrifices for sin. Jesus actually did bear the sins of His people in a way that Ezekiel could only act out. As Peter wrote, "For Christ also suffered once for sins, the righteous for the unrighteous, that he might bring us to God, being put to death in the flesh but made alive in the spirit" (1 Pet. 3:18). Those sacrifices pointed to Him and to the need for better sacrifices than those of bulls and goats. Indeed, His single sacrifice was better, so much better that it satisfied for all time the need for a sacrifice for sin.

Think about It

Why is the good news of the gospel is so good? We are forgiven in Him, but it does not end there. We are called to draw near to God, to enter the "holy places" of heaven "by the new and living way which He opened for us" not in fear and trembling but with confidence. That confidence is based on His faithfulness, not on our own.

Draw near, believing friend. Draw near to God with confidence for He is faithful. That gospel news is true—and it is good.

Holy Judge or Cosmic Cupcake?

Today's Reading: Ezekiel 7-9; Hebrews 10:26-39

Selected Verses

> Then he said to me, "The guilt of the house of Israel and Judah is exceedingly
> great. The land is full of blood, and the city full of injustice. For they say,
> 'The Lord has forsaken the land, and the Lord does not see.' As for me, my eye
> will not spare, nor will I have pity; I will bring their deeds upon their heads."
>
> Ezek. 9:9-10

> How much worse punishment, do you think, will be deserved by the one who
> has trampled underfoot the Son of God, and has profaned the blood of the
> covenant by which he was sanctified, and has outraged the Spirit of grace?
> For we know him who said, "Vengeance is mine; I will repay." And again, "The
> Lord will judge his people." It is a fearful thing to fall into the hands of the living God.
>
> Heb. 10:29-31

Reflections

Ezekiel was sent to proclaim the wrath and judgment of God upon Israel and
Judah. Why was He angry with them? They had committed abominable acts of
idolatry and murderous injustice growing bold in their sin. They were sure that
God had departed from them and did not see what they were doing. The Apostle
Paul would later ask: "Do you suppose, O man...that you will escape the
judgment of God? (See Rom. 2:3-5). The people of Israel and Judah certainly
assumed that they would escape the judgment of God. They could not see that
by their sin they were storing up wrath against themselves and going spiritually
blind because of their hard and impenitent hearts. The more they sinned the
more comfortable they felt sinning.

The writer to the Hebrews issues a stern warning to his readers. Some of them
are tottering on the edge of drifting away from the gospel, their only hope of
salvation. Could they not see what they were doing? Didn't they recognize that they
were not merely adjusting to the pressures of life in a hostile society but were about
to bring themselves under God's judgment with those who had trampled underfoot
the Son of God? Were they not terrified to profane the blood of the covenant by
which Jesus was sanctified? Did it seem nothing to outrage the Spirit of grace?

Think about It

God will judge. He will repay. Satan blinds the eyes of those who sin and
glibly say "the Lord does not see." Flee the company of those with hard and
impenitent hearts. Repent of all known sin. Believe in Jesus and find forgiveness.
You can only be saved by faith in Him, but you will be lost if, without Christ,
you "fall into the hands of the living God." He is no cosmic cupcake.

Arrogant Unbelief vs. Unwavering Faith

Today's Reading: Ezekiel 10-12; Hebrews 11:1-19

Selected Verses

*And the word of the Lord came to me: "Son of man, what is this proverb that
you have about the land of Israel, saying, 'The days grow long, and every vision
comes to nothing'? Tell them therefore, 'Thus says the Lord God: I will put
an end to this proverb, and they shall no more use it as a proverb in Israel.'
But say to them, 'The days are near, and the fulfillment of every vision.'"*

Ezek. 12:21-23

*These all died in faith, not having received the things promised,
but having seen them and greeted them from afar, and having
acknowledged that they were strangers and exiles on the earth.*

Heb. 11:13

Reflections

The people of Judah and Israel had heard the visions of the prophets but had
not seen their fulfillment. They grew impatient, then dulled, and, finally,
arrogant in unbelief. "Nothing is going to happen," they told themselves as they
went on with their idolatry, seeking power from pagan gods. All kinds of evil
arises when a society collectively begins to assume that there is no God or that, if
there is, He is powerless or complacent towards sin.

Ezekiel warned them of the soon coming fulfillment of the visions. All those
prophecies about the fall of Babylon, the rise of Persia, and the return of the Jews
to Jerusalem all came to pass on God's schedule. He showed them all up for fools
who demanded that God do their bidding on their schedule.

But our waiting patiently in faith for God to act pleases Him. Hebrews 11 is
a monument to those who trusted God to their dying day without seeing His
promises fulfilled. They were included with all who "draw near to God
[believing] that he exists and that he rewards those who seek him." (Heb. 11:6).

Think about It

Not everyone lives to see the fulfillment of God's promises. We are privileged
to live in the era of the last days, following the first advent of the Lord Jesus Christ,
including His life, death, resurrection, ascension, and the building of His Church
throughout the nations. Yet there is more—much more—to come.

Be sure you don't fall into the arrogant unbelief of the people of Ezekiel's
day who thought nothing would ever happen and who demanded that God
perform for them. Christ will return, but, even if not in our lifetimes, God will
be pleased as we draw near to Him in unwavering faith believing that He exists
and rewards those who seek Him.

Commended by God

Today's Reading: Ezekiel 13-15; Hebrews 11:20-40

Selected Verses

Because you have disheartened the righteous falsely, although I have not grieved him, and you have encouraged the wicked, that he should not turn from his evil way to save his life, therefore you shall no more see false visions nor practice divination. I will deliver my people out of your hand. And you shall know that I am the Lord.

Ezek. 13:22-23

And all these, though commended through their faith, did not receive what was promised, since God had provided something better for us, that apart from us they should not be made perfect.

Heb. 11:39-40

Reflections

We make much of awards and recognition in our society. But honors only hold meaning when either they come from an important source (like the Medal of Honor given by the President of the United States of America) or they reflect true achievement (e.g. the Eagle Scout award). My wife taught at an elementary school in Texas where at an end-of-the-year ceremony every student automatically got the "Shark Award" just for being enrolled in the school. It didn't reflect perfect attendance much less exemplary behavior or outstanding academic achievement. Even the youngest kids quickly understood that the award meant nothing.

God rewards and punishes mankind according to each one's performance. Through Ezekiel, the Lord told the false prophets of Judah that they had failed. Their so-called prophecies sent a deceptive message to God's people—discouraging the faithful and encouraging the wicked. God stopped them in their tracks and shut down this kind of evil influence.

In Hebrews 11, we read of those who were faithful to their deaths, faithful even though the final fulfillment of God's promises did not appear. God commended them for their unwavering faith. He calls them people "of whom the world was not worthy" (Heb. 11:38). Now that is a commendation worth getting!

Think about It

What recognition do you seek? Are you after a mere "Shark Award" or are you seeking to please God and receive His "well done"? No award in this world compares to hearing God's approval. Seek His commendation.

God Never Lets Us Go

Today's Reading: Ezekiel 16; Hebrews 12

Selected Verses

I will establish my covenant with you, and you shall know that I am the Lord, that you may remember and be confounded, and never open your mouth again because of your shame, when I atone for you for all that you have done, declares the Lord God."

Ezek. 16:62-63

And have you forgotten the exhortation that addresses you as sons?
"My son, do not regard lightly the discipline of the Lord,
nor be weary when reproved by him.
For the Lord disciplines the one he loves,
and chastises every son whom he receives."
It is for discipline that you have to endure. God is treating you as
sons. For what son is there whom his father does not discipline?

Heb. 12:5-7

Reflections

Ezekiel delivers a brutal message to the exiles of Judah, a message filled with emotion and grief for the sins of God's people in the face of His abundant mercy toward them. God poured out on them restoration and love when they were helpless and dying, but, as soon as they could, they responded with betrayal and spiritual adultery.

How did God respond to this? He cast them out of their land and sent them into captivity, but He did not forget His covenant with them. His punishment was discipline not rejection. There is a difference. God would restore them and keep His covenant with them. In fact, He would establish for them an everlasting covenant, a better covenant than the one they had broken. What's more He promised to atone for them for all that they had done (Ezek. 16:53-63). That is precisely what He did through the death of His Son, Jesus, on the cross.

The Hebrew believers, too, were experiencing God's discipline. The author of the epistle called them to count this discipline not as rejection but as evidence of God's love toward His sons. Instead of doubting the salvation that is in Jesus Christ, they were to "strive for peace with everyone and for holiness without which no one will see the Lord" (Heb. 12:14). When this is not the case and one or more of God's people fail to obtain the grace of God, a root of bitterness springs up and causes trouble. The whole church can be defiled as a consequence.

Think about It

Welcome discipline. Take difficulties from God's hand and let Him show you His grace to endure, to grow in holiness, and to be trained by it. Remember He atones for our sin, and He never lets us go. Never, despite our grievous sin. If we are His.

359

Ending Well

Today's Reading: Ezekiel 17-19; Hebrews 13

Selected Verses

*The righteousness of the righteous shall be upon himself, and the wickedness of the wicked shall
be upon himself. But if a wicked person turns away from all his sins that he has committed
and keeps all my statutes and does what is just and right, he shall surely live; he shall not die.*

Ezek. 18:20-21

*Remember your leaders, those who spoke to you the word of God.
Consider the outcome of their way of life, and imitate their faith.*

Heb. 13:7

Reflections

In Ezekiel's day, the people had a saying "The fathers have eaten sour grapes, and the children's teeth are set on edge" (Ezek. 18:2). The Lord rebuked them for using this proverb. He said that each person held responsibility for himself as to his obedience or disobedience. Whatever path a person chose, righteousness or sin, was his own and he would enjoy the blessings or suffer the consequences. A parent's sin could not make his child incur guilt, nor could a parent's obedience merit forgiveness to a sinful child. Each one stands alone before God with his own record.

But change is possible. No one is locked into a lifestyle of sin or righteousness based on choices in his youth. It's how you end up that matters. After a life of crime, the repentant thief on the cross pleaded for mercy and found forgiveness at death's door (Luke 23:39-43). It is also possible that one might prove to be unfaithful at the end of life. See? It's how you end up that counts. It is never too late to repent, but it's also never too late to rebel.

The writer to the Hebrews gives his readers an assortment of commands in light of all he has written. Several of them have to do with their relationship with their spiritual leaders, those who had taught them God's Word (Heb. 13:7, 17). They must observe the outcome of those godly lives and imitate their faith. How did those men's lives turn out? If they were faithful to the end, the outcome was good. If not, one ought to be forewarned that even those who at one time show some signs of true faith and obedience to God can veer off and prove to be unbelievers. This does not mean that anyone can lose his salvation. It does mean that anyone can act pious for a time and then fail to endure to the end (see Matt. 7:21-23; 13:1-23; 2 Tim. 4:10; 1 John 2:19).

Think about It

Be on guard against the schemes of Satan. Do not be presumptuous of your ability to resist every temptation and trap. We all know some who have not. May you and I endure faithfully and finish by ending well.

Why Does God Save?

Today's Reading: Ezekiel 20-21; James 1

Selected Verses

Then I said I would pour out my wrath upon them and spend my anger against them in the midst of the land of Egypt. But I acted for the sake of my name, that it should not be profaned in the sight of the nations among whom they lived, in whose sight I made myself known to them in bringing them out of the land of Egypt. So I led them out of the land of Egypt and brought them into the wilderness.

Ezek. 20:8-10

Of his own will he brought us forth by the word of truth, that we should be a kind of firstfruits of his creatures.

James 1:18

Reflections

Page after page, Ezekiel lays out the case against Israel and Judah. Their sin and unfaithfulness before a Holy God are an abomination. God would have been just and right to destroy them at the first failure, but He extended patience and relented again and again. Why? Three times (Ezek. 20:9, 14, 22), He says "I acted for the sake of my name, that it should not be profaned." Another time He says "And you shall know that I am the Lord, when I deal with you for my name's sake, not according to your evil ways, nor according to your corrupt deeds, O house of Israel, declares the Lord God." (Ezek. 20:44). The basis of God showing them mercy was the glory of His name—that His name not be profaned, and that Israel should know that He is the Lord.

God showing mercy to His elect people benefits us in two ways. One, all can see (if we are willing to) that He is able to save His wayward sheep. Two, His people come to know Him in truth. James sheds more light on the subject when he writes that "Of his own will he brought us forth by the word of truth, that we should be a kind of firstfruits of his creatures." Why did God save His people? Because He wanted to. It was of His own will. God has no constraints. He has no obligations. He is completely free. He can do what He wants consistent with His holiness. What did He want to do? He wanted to save a people for Himself, the beginning of a new creation.

Think about It

God wanted to save His elect people and that is what He did. Are you one of His? If so, marvel at the greatness of His grace and mercy to you. Remember, you are secure in Him because the reason God saves has nothing to do with you.

The Man Who Stood in the Breach

Today's Reading: Ezekiel 22-23; James 2

Selected Verses

And I sought for a man among them who should build up the wall and stand in the breach before me for the land, that I should not destroy it, but I found none. Therefore I have poured out my indignation upon them. I have consumed them with the fire of my wrath. I have returned their way upon their heads, declares the Lord God.

Ezek. 22:30-31

My brothers, show no partiality as you hold the faith in our Lord Jesus Christ, the Lord of glory.

James 2:1

Reflections

In Ezekiel's day, invaders broke through the walls of the city. The false prophets did not risk their lives to close these breaches or to stand in them (Ezek. 13:5). God looked, but there was no one who would do this. My study Bible notes refer to the contrast with Moses who, as a true and faithful leader, stood up in the spiritual breach for Israel when they crafted and worshiped a golden calf. Moses pleaded with God to spare Israel their just punishment and God heard him.[14] Now the so-called prophets ignored this need. God poured out His wrath on the nation.

Finally, God Himself took on flesh and lived among us to bring atonement for sin and mercy for His people. The Lord Jesus Christ is the Man who stood in the breach against our enemy. He is the Good Shepherd who did not flee when danger came. He bore the pain of death for us (John 10:7-18). James calls all who hold the faith in Him to reflect that faith in our actions and attitudes toward others. There should be no partiality based on socioeconomic classes. There should be no favoritism toward the rich nor discrimination against the poor. Those who have received mercy must be merciful or they show they deserve judgment.

Think about It

Be sure your relationships show mercy and not partiality. You have been saved by the Man who stood in the breach for us. Pride and haughtiness have no place in our lives.

---

14   *Reformation Study Bible*, p. 1415 (note on Ezek. 22:30-31).

Two Kinds of Wisdom

Today's Reading: Ezekiel 24-26; James 3

Selected Verses

For thus says the Lord God: Because you have clapped your hands and stamped your feet and rejoiced with all the malice within your soul against the land of Israel, therefore, behold, I have stretched out my hand against you, and will hand you over as plunder to the nations. And I will cut you off from the peoples and will make you perish out of the countries; I will destroy you. Then you will know that I am the Lord.

Ezek. 25:6-7

Who is wise and understanding among you? By his good conduct let him show his works in the meekness of wisdom. But if you have bitter jealousy and selfish ambition in your hearts, do not boast and be false to the truth. This is not the wisdom that comes down from above, but is earthly, unspiritual, demonic. For where jealousy and selfish ambition exist, there will be disorder and every vile practice.

James 3:13-16

Reflections

James warns his readers about the dangers that lie in the power of the tongue. While it may be attractive to be a teacher, one must beware of the danger of stricter judgment that will come to teachers. A teacher who lacks wisdom will lack meekness and will be subject to judgment. Godly wisdom is accompanied by a gentleness and humility not known in the world where those who are considered wise are frequently arrogant, boastful, bitterly jealous, and selfishly ambitious.

The Ammonites, in Ezekiel's day, demonstrated precisely that kind of earthly, demonic "wisdom" in their attitudes and statements at the time of the fall of Jerusalem. They rejoiced at the judgment upon the city and kingdom. God promised to bring worse judgment on them for this. They were not the only ones to receive God's punishment. In each case, the prophet concludes by telling them, "then you will know that I am the Lord."

Not knowing the Lord is at the heart of the problem because it is the foundation for not fearing the Lord. Since Scripture is clear that, "The fear of the Lord is the beginning of knowledge; [and] fools despise wisdom and instruction" (Prov. 1:7), it is obvious that those who lack fear of the Lord will be ignorant fools no matter how educated and esteemed they may be in this world.

Think about It

Beware of those modern-day Ammonites who boast about themselves and arrogantly look down on those wayward believers whom God is judging. The absence of the meekness of wisdom is the evidence of an earthly counterfeit wisdom we must avoid.

Humility before God

Today's Reading: Ezekiel 27-28; James 4

Selected Verses

Because you make your heart
like the heart of a god,
therefore, behold, I will bring foreigners upon you,
the most ruthless of the nations;
and they shall draw their swords against the beauty of your wisdom
and defile your splendor.

Ezek. 28:6-7

Come now, you who say, "Today or tomorrow we will go into such and such a town and spend a year there and trade and make a profit"— yet you do not know what tomorrow will bring. What is your life? For you are a mist that appears for a little time and then vanishes. Instead you ought to say, "If the Lord wills, we will live and do this or that."

James 4:13-15

Reflections

The prophet Ezekiel spoke for the Creator God, the God of all flesh. So he addressed the neighboring nations of Judah, like Tyre. God indicted Tyre for her arrogance and pride. She was prosperous and presumptuous. Tyre boasted of her greatness, her wealth, and her beauty. She elevated herself and brought on the judgment of God.

James warned his readers of the same danger on a personal level. Some were guilty of a total lack of humility before God. They set goals and made their plans and schedules as if they controlled their own destinies, as if they were immortal, unstoppable. Where is the recognition that we are all no more than "a mist that appears for a little time and then vanishes"?

Think about It

In centuries past, godly people routinely wrote D.V. in their correspondence when making plans—such as, "I will come to see you by New Years, D.V." I searched the internet for "D.V." in order to see what came up. On the third page of hits, I found a list of fifty possible options for D.V., things like Darth Vader, Death Valley, and Desktop Virtualization. Obviously, none of these were what the Puritans had in mind. About thirty-fifth in the list was "Deo Volente (Latin for 'Lord willing')." Yeah, that's it.

In our society, few know Latin and too few know the Lord who reigns and has the final say-so over our lives. I don't think the folks in ancient Tyre used D.V in their correspondence and neither do we, but, even if you don't write it or say it, my fellow mist, remember to keep it in your mind and heart as you make plans. Always seek to maintain humility before God.

God's Wrath

Today's Reading: Ezekiel 29-31; James 5

Selected Verses

Therefore thus says the Lord God: Behold, I will bring a sword upon you,
and will cut off from you man and beast, and the land of Egypt shall
be a desolation and a waste. Then they will know that I am the Lord.

Ezek. 29:8-9

Come now, you rich, weep and howl for the miseries that are coming upon
you. Your riches have rotted and your garments are moth-eaten. Your gold
and silver have corroded, and their corrosion will be evidence against you
and will eat your flesh like fire. You have laid up treasure in the last days.

James 5:1-3

Reflections

Who will be the target of God's judgment?

In Ezekiel's day, the Lord pronounced judgment on Egypt. What had they done? It was not so much what they had done or not done, but their arrogant attitude. They prided themselves in the things that God had done. They did not glorify Him but made idiotic statements like, "The Nile is mine, and I made it." Those who refuse to give God the glory He is due are in special trouble with Him. He would bring His judgment on them and they would know that He is the Lord.

Another target of judgment will be the fraudulent and heartless rich. James singled these people out for a stern warning. In the day of judgment, they would be in misery. The riches they trusted in would not serve them at all, but be rotted, moth-eaten, and corroded. There may have been a time when they could buy their way out of trouble but no longer. And take note, it is not the fact that they are rich but that they cheated their workers to expand their wealth. Furthermore, they trusted in their wealth and not in the Lord.

Think about It

Pride and autonomy rob God of His glory and bring His judgment. Beware of any tendency toward these quiet ways of rebelling. On that coming day of God's wrath, do not be found among those who have attempted to exalt themselves. As Isaiah wrote:

Seek the Lord while he may be found;
call upon him while he is near;
let the wicked forsake his way,
and the unrighteous man his thoughts;
let him return to the Lord, that he may have compassion on him,
and to our God, for he will abundantly pardon.

Isa. 55:6-7

Seeing Yourself Correctly

Today's Reading: Ezekiel 32-33; First Peter 1

Selected Verses

> You consider yourself a lion of the nations,
>> but you are like a dragon in the seas;
> you burst forth in your rivers,
>> trouble the waters with your feet,
>> and foul their rivers.
> Thus says the Lord God:
>> I will throw my net over you
>> with a host of many peoples,
>> and they will haul you up in my dragnet.

Ezek. 32:2-3

> *Blessed be the God and Father of our Lord Jesus Christ! According to his great mercy, he has caused us to be born again to a living hope through the resurrection of Jesus Christ from the dead, to an inheritance that is imperishable, undefiled, and unfading, kept in heaven for you, who by God's power are being guarded through faith for a salvation ready to be revealed in the last time.*

1 Pet. 1:3-5

Reflections

Pharaoh was one of those people who had a faulty and exalted opinion of himself. He saw himself as a "lion of the nations", but God had another view of him. Through Ezekiel, the Lord told the king of Egypt that he was no lion but a dragon who was fouling the rivers and who was about to be caught and destroyed.

Peter wrote that Christians are heirs of God. It is not their own doing. They didn't earn this status. God, by His mercy, has granted it to His people. There is a process.

First, He caused them to be born again. He did it. They did not will themselves to be reborn. Jesus told Nicodemus a new birth was an absolute prerequisite in order to see the Kingdom of God (John 3:3). Rebirth is a gracious gift from God's mercy. Second, because of that new birth, believers have a living hope through Jesus Christ's resurrection. Whatever they hoped in before is perishable, defiled, and fading. This new living hope is in an inheritance totally unlike any material and earthly inheritance. Third, they cannot lose this hope because the inheritance is kept in heaven (not Wall Street!) for them and they are guarded by God's power through faith for a salvation which they will see at the last time.

Think about It

Do you see yourself in the way Peter described, an heir of God with a living hope? You should, if you know the new birth has been granted to you and your faith is in Jesus Christ. Consider if your view of yourself is accurate and in accordance with the way God sees you. Remember seeing yourself correctly glorifies God.

The Soul Shepherd

Today's Reading: Ezekiel 34-35; First Peter 2

Selected Verses

I will rescue my flock; they shall no longer be a prey. And I will judge between sheep and sheep. And I will set up over them one shepherd, my servant David, and he shall feed them: he shall feed them and be their shepherd. And I, the Lord, will be their God, and my servant David shall be prince among them. I am the Lord; I have spoken.

Ezek. 34:22-24

He himself bore our sins in his body on the tree, that we might die to sin and live to righteousness. By his wounds you have been healed. For you were straying like sheep, but have now returned to the Shepherd and Overseer of your souls.

1 Pet. 2:24-25

Reflections

Not infrequently, the Bible uses the analogy of sheep to people. Sheep need constant care. They cannot survive without a shepherd. They are prone to make foolish decisions and get themselves in big trouble. Not being able to defend themselves, they are susceptible to predators.

Ezekiel condemns those who were supposed to be the shepherds of Israel and Judah. They looked out for themselves and neglected those in their care. God declared to them that He would rescue His flock and get them to safety. He would pronounce judgment. He would provide one shepherd who would feed them and faithfully fulfill the role of shepherd to them. This shepherd to come is identified as God's "servant David." Of course, David died four centuries before the time of Ezekiel, so the prophet would have been thinking of a descendant of David. We know Him as Jesus Christ, clearly of the lineage of David.

Peter refers to Christ as the Shepherd and Overseer of the souls of those to whom he wrote. It is Jesus who fulfilled the prophecy of Ezekiel and rescued His flock. He has fed His people with truth and He will come again to judge those who have rejected His Lordship and His Priesthood. Meanwhile, He calls those He has saved by His death and healed by His wounds to die to sin and live to righteousness. In the first century, the vast majority of the Jews rejected the Soul Shepherd that God had sent them. He didn't fit the stereotype they had imagined for their Messiah.

Think about It

Has the Shepherd rescued you from the agony of straying like sheep? Do you know the joy of returning to Him? If so, give Him all the praise and seek to live to righteousness until we enter His presence through death or His return for us.

Suffering before a Perplexed World
Today's Reading: Ezekiel 36-37; First Peter 3

Selected Verses

In accordance with their ways and their deeds I judged them. But when they came to the nations, wherever they came, they profaned my holy name, in that people said of them, "These are the people of the Lord, and yet they had to go out of his land." But I had concern for my holy name, which the house of Israel had profaned among the nations to which they came.

Ezek. 36:19-21

But even if you should suffer for righteousness' sake, you will be blessed. Have no fear of them, nor be troubled, but in your hearts honor Christ the Lord as holy, always being prepared to make a defense to anyone who asks you for a reason for the hope that is in you; yet do it with gentleness and respect, having a good conscience, so that, when you are slandered, those who revile your good behavior in Christ may be put to shame.

1 Pet. 3:14-16

Reflections

The persistent idolatry of Israel and Judah brought on their downfall, but did they learn from it? No! They continued to profane the name of the Lord by not admitting before their captors that God was punishing them for their sin. The God of the universe did not fail so that enemy armies overthrew and captured His people. So the captors scratched their heads and asked, "Why did this happen to them?"

Judah received a perfect opportunity to show repentance and to honor their God before pagan nations, but they failed. So Ezekiel declared their guilt to them. We will learn in the book of Daniel that there were at least a few Jews who were faithful to God while in captivity, but they seem to have been the exception and not the rule.

Peter wrote his readers—who were in a kind of captivity in the first century A.D.—that they should accept their suffering for righteousness sake. In other words, they should submit to undeserved persecution and maintain hope and trust in the Lord. He tells them to be ready "to make a defense to anyone who asks you for a reason for the hope that is in you." Hope in the midst of unjust suffering is as rare as it is hard to explain. The question they should anticipate is, "Why are these people still so hopeful under all this opposition?"

Think about It

How do we prepare for the possibility of suffering for righteousness sake? Should we prepare little sound bites or memorize trite phrases? Peter told his readers then and us now, to "honor Christ the Lord as holy." Do not be like the Old Testament Jews who profaned the Lord's name. Instead, by honoring Christ in your heart be ready to honor Him with your words. Create perplexity in the watching world.

Glory Revealed

Today's Reading: Ezekiel 38-39; First Peter 4

Selected Verses

*So I will show my greatness and my holiness and make myself known
in the eyes of many nations. Then they will know that I am the Lord.*

Ezek. 38:23

*Beloved, do not be surprised at the fiery trial when it comes upon you
to test you, as though something strange were happening to you. But
rejoice insofar as you share Christ's sufferings, that you may also rejoice
and be glad when his glory is revealed. If you are insulted for the name of
Christ, you are blessed, because the Spirit of glory and of God rests upon you.*

1 Pet. 4:12-14

Reflections

Israel and Judah were casualties in the cosmic battle of good and evil. As God's people they suffered for their sin and idolatry, but they would not ultimately be lost because God had chosen them for Himself. He promised to do a new thing with them, make a new covenant with them, and restore them. Here Ezekiel warns Gog, the enemy ruler, of the destruction which is coming upon him and his forces. God will show His greatness and His holiness and make Himself known to them.

In short, God would be glorified before the seemingly invincible forces of evil. What an encouragement to the exiles in the Babylonian captivity, far from Jerusalem.

Peter, too, assures the suffering believers of his day that God is not unaware of their plight. They suffer with Christ. They do not suffer as a means of discipline for their sin but rather as a means to show the power and grace of God. Blessing will be theirs, but, first, there is a time of trial to endure. While they are not suffering for sin but for Christ, they do have God's presence with them and assurance that their suffering will produce the purification of their faith (1 Peter 1:6-7).

Think about It

There will come a day when God's glory will be fully revealed, and His judgment will be finalized. Those who have suffered and been maligned for Him will be rewarded with vindication and their growth in purity of faith will bring glory to Christ.

Do you suffer for Christ today? Peter says be sure you suffer for Him and not for your sin. Meanwhile, entrust your soul to your faithful Creator because the day of glory revealed is coming.

The Sufferings of Christ

Today's Reading: Ezekiel 40; First Peter 5

Selected Verses

And in the vestibule of the gate were two tables on either side, on which the burnt offering and the sin offering and the guilt offering were to be slaughtered.

Ezek. 40:39

So I exhort the elders among you, as a fellow elder and a witness of the sufferings of Christ, as well as a partaker in the glory that is going to be revealed.

1 Pet. 5:1

Reflections

In Ezekiel's vision of the new temple, God took him into the inner chamber where there are tables for the washing and slaughter of the various kinds of sacrifices: burnt, guilt, and sin offerings. Such was the enormity of the sin of God's chosen people that He commanded the sacrifices to be repeated over and over with no seeming conclusion. Sin and sacrifices were the way of life on a daily basis. Talk about life on an endless treadmill!

Would there be no deliverance from the sin or the futility of the animal sacrifices? Yes, indeed, there would.

Peter witnessed that deliverance accomplished by the sufferings of Christ. The Apostle knew what those sufferings meant. "For Christ also suffered once for sins, the righteous for the unrighteous, that he might bring us to God, being put to death in the flesh but made alive in the spirit" he wrote (1 Pet. 3:18). Christ's sufferings meant that a sufficient offering had finally been made. Christ suffered *once* for sins. His one offering was sufficient because He was righteous. No other person and no sacrificial animal could accomplish what His sufferings accomplished which was to bring unrighteous people to God.

Peter counted himself as one of those unrighteous people graciously brought to God. He lived out the rest of his life and ministry in the light of the cross of Christ. When he appealed to the elders among his readers to be faithful and humble shepherds of God's flock, he did so as one who had never lost sight of the reason for Jesus' sufferings.

Think about It

Have you grasped the meaning of the sufferings of Christ? Leave aside any effort to earn forgiveness through any merit of your own, or any feeble offerings to God. They cannot suffice. Only the One who suffered for His people on the cross can bring us to God. Trust in the sufferings of Christ.

Keeping the Tension between Equality and Calling

Today's Reading: Ezekiel 41-42; Second Peter 1

Selected Verses

When the priests enter the Holy Place, they shall not go out of it into the outer court without laying there the garments in which they minister, for these are holy. They shall put on other garments before they go near to that which is for the people.

Ezek. 42:14

Simeon Peter, a servant and apostle of Jesus Christ,
To those who have obtained a faith of equal standing with
ours by the righteousness of our God and Savior Jesus Christ:
May grace and peace be multiplied to you in the knowledge of God and of Jesus our Lord.

2 Pet. 1:1-2

Reflections

In the new temple of Ezekiel's vision, God specified the priestly functions and designated the places for those functions. The priests took great care in the ordering of the ministry. They wore holy garments for their service and they were not to leave the Holy Place and mix with the people in those vestments. God was teaching them to respect His holiness and the service that they offered to Him.

What a contrast with the New Covenant! Peter identifies himself as a servant and apostle of Jesus Christ. Then he tells his readers that they "have obtained a faith of equal standing with ours." They, like him, have a standing based on "the righteousness of our God and Savior Jesus Christ." The members of the Church of Jesus Christ enjoyed an equality never known in ancient Israel. The old covenant people observed sacrifices that could, at best, point to the Lamb of God who would take away the sin of the world (Isaiah 53:7; John 1:29,35,36). All those who believed in Christ were and are on equal standing before God. As the saying goes, "the ground is level at the cross."

Of course, this equality is not absolute. There are differences in gifts and calling within the Church. Believers will distinguish themselves by their growth in God. Not everyone will "make every effort to supplement [their] faith with virtue (vs. 5)." Some will be more or less ineffective and unfruitful in the knowledge of Christ (vs. 8). Some, but not all, are called to shepherd the flock (1 Pet. 5:1-5). There are a variety of gifts given by the Spirit to the members of the Body (1 Cor. 12:4-31; Rom. 12:3-8; Eph. 4:11-16; 1 Pet. 4:10-11). The equality is not of gifts and calling but of standing before God based on the righteousness of Jesus Christ.

Think about It

Peter models both a respect for his office and a respect for all other believers who, like him, stand before God because of Christ alone. In your relationships with fellow believers, be sure to maintain the tension between the equality and calling each one has.

When Shame is Good

Today's Reading: Ezekiel 43-44; Second Peter 2

Selected Verses

As for you, son of man, describe to the house of Israel the temple, that they may be ashamed of their iniquities; and they shall measure the plan. And if they are ashamed of all that they have done, make known to them the design of the temple, its arrangement, its exits and its entrances, that is, its whole design; and make known to them as well all its statutes and its whole design and all its laws, and write it down in their sight, so that they may observe all its laws and all its statutes and carry them out.

Ezek. 43:10-11

Then the Lord knows how to rescue the godly from trials, and to keep the unrighteous under punishment until the day of judgment, and especially those who indulge in the lust of defiling passion and despise authority.

2 Pet. 2:9-10

Reflections

God gives Ezekiel a detailed description of the temple. Then He tells the prophet to pass these details on to the people of Israel so that they may be ashamed of their iniquities. The temple reflected God's glory so this description was intended to shame the Jews for their sin. Yet the temple also held a message of hope of salvation. Here, in this place of God's throne, provision was made for a sacrifice for sin. The gospel of Jesus Christ was portrayed in the temple, if we rightly understand it.

In Peter's time, there were false prophets and teachers who were completely insensitive to sin. He indicts them for their deceptions and schemes to lead believers astray. Peter shows how God in the past has brought judgment on those who rebelled against Him: evil angels, the wicked society of Noah's day, and Lot's neighbors in Sodom and Gomorrah. So God has shown that He is able to rescue the godly, like Noah and Lot, and keep the unrighteous under punishment until the day of judgment. Particularly those who indulge in the lust of defiling passion and who despise authority.

Think about It

If there is anything which describes our society, it is indulgence in the lust of defiling passion and the despising of authority. Our contemporaries see shame not as a good emotion leading to healthy repentance. Rather it is considered the result of poor self-esteem due often to a severe religious upbringing.

If this world is trying you, trust Him who knows how to rescue the godly from trials in amazing ways. Pray that God may grant our unbelieving loved ones shame for sin that leads to repentance and faith.

Stability in Spiritual Conflict

Today's Reading: Ezekiel 45-46; Second Peter 3

Thus says the Lord God: "Enough, O princes of Israel! Put away violence and oppression, and execute justice and righteousness. Cease your evictions of my people, declares the Lord God."

Ezek. 45:9

You therefore, beloved, knowing this beforehand, take care that you are not carried away with the error of lawless people and lose your own stability. But grow in the grace and knowledge of our Lord and Savior Jesus Christ. To him be the glory both now and to the day of eternity. Amen.

2 Pet. 3:17-18

Reflections

God had a special message for the princes of Israel through the prophet Ezekiel. They were not to abuse their power bringing violence and oppression on the common people. On the contrary, they were to execute justice and righteousness. They were to abide by the same laws as everyone else in such matters as worship and property rights. There was to be no privileged class in Israel, not even the royal family.

The political situation of God's people changed between Ezekiel's time and Peter's day. The Church did not live in their own designated land but was dispersed among the Gentile nations of the world (1 Pet. 1:1). Believers were subject to the ridicule of scoffers who openly doubted that the Lord would fulfill His promise to return. These unbelievers conveniently ignored the evidence of God's power and presence in the Creation and the Flood. This made it easy for them to dismiss the promised "day of judgment and the destruction of the ungodly" (2 Pet. 3:7).

Peter reassures his readers that the Lord is not time-bound as we are and that He will carry out all His judgment on His schedule. Meanwhile, he charges them not to be carried away with the error of the lawless who were given over to the lust of defiling passion and the despising of authority (2 Pet. 2:10). Instead, they were to focus on growth in the grace and knowledge of our Lord and Savior Jesus Christ.

Think about It

These two qualities, grace and knowledge of Jesus Christ, are bound together. By His grace He has made Himself known to us. By the knowledge of Him we grow in grace, being ever more assured that our faith is not in vain. Grow in the grace and knowledge of our Lord, and gain stability in the midst of our ongoing spiritual conflict created by abusive leaders and scoffing unbelievers.

Fellowship with God

Today's Reading: Ezekiel 47-48; First John 1

Selected Verses

And the name of the city from that time on shall be, The Lord Is There.

Ezek. 48:35

*That which we have seen and heard we proclaim also to you,
so that you too may have fellowship with us; and indeed our
fellowship is with the Father and with his Son Jesus Christ.*

1 John 1:3

Reflections

Ezekiel concludes the long description of the temple, the city, and the land with redistributed territories for the twelve tribes with the simple words, "And the name of the city from that time on shall be, The Lord Is There." What more can anyone desire than that the Lord should be there? Knowing that God is with us gives confidence in the face of huge danger and the threat of death itself (Deut. 31:6-8; Josh. 1:4-6; Ps. 23). Several Old Testament figures learned the devastating impact of being abandoned by God (Exod. 33:3, 15; 1 Sam. 4:21-22; Judg. 16:20). Not that they could actually ever be totally away from His presence, but they could be, and sometimes were, under His wrath and judgment and without His blessing and favor (Ps. 139:7-12).

The Apostle John also refers to the blessing of fellowship with God through Jesus Christ. God came to dwell among us, he says, and we saw Him. We touched Him. He came to give us eternal life and fellowship with the Father and the Son (see also John 1:14-17; 17:3).

Think about It

To know Him in truth and to be forgiven and accepted, that is what eternal life is about. The city which Ezekiel described points to that heavenly city, the New Jerusalem where God dwells and where His people live with Him. As John would write later: "And I heard a loud voice from the throne saying, 'Behold, the dwelling place of God is with man. He will dwell with them, and they will be his people, and God himself will be with them as their God'" (Rev. 21:3).

So whatever else we may say about the eternal state of believers, it will be unclouded, undiminished fellowship with God. Be faithful as you wait for His coming.

It's All Gonna Burn

Today's Reading: Daniel 1-2; First John 2

Selected Verses

And in the days of those kings the God of heaven will set up a kingdom that shall never be destroyed, nor shall the kingdom be left to another people. It shall break in pieces all these kingdoms and bring them to an end, and it shall stand forever, just as you saw that a stone was cut from a mountain by no human hand, and that it broke in pieces the iron, the bronze, the clay, the silver, and the gold. A great God has made known to the king what shall be after this. The dream is certain, and its interpretation sure.

Dan. 2:44

*And the world is passing away along with its desires,
but whoever does the will of God abides forever.*

1 John 2:17

Reflections

Daniel, a young Jew in the time of the Babylonian Captivity, was taken to Nebuchadnezzar's palace and given special training to assist the king. He was not among the "starting lineup" on the royal advisory team so he heard about his death sentence without knowing the reason. By God's grace and mercy, Daniel was able to save his life and that of other wise men by telling the king what his dream was and what it meant. No one else could do that. As a result, Nebuchadnezzar learned that his kingdom would one day be replaced by another, and that one by still another. Ultimately, none of those kingdoms would last because the God of heaven would set up an indestructible kingdom and crush all the opposing kingdoms of the earth.

To his credit, Nebuchadnezzar accepted the interpretation and honored Daniel with gifts and a promotion. Most importantly, he recognized the God of gods and Lord of kings of which Daniel had informed him. Even the most powerful king of Daniel's day bowed to the sovereign God of Israel.

John in writing his letter urges his readers to reject the love of this world and the things of this world. He tells them plainly that the world is passing away along with its desires. It's all gonna burn! What will last? "Whoever does the will of God abides forever."

Think about It

To abide forever we must do the will of God. But how do we know the will of God? We need to know God's word to know His will. Once a crowd asked the Lord, "What must we do, to be doing the works of God?" Jesus answered them, "This is the work of God, that you believe in him whom he has sent." (John 6:28-29). Our first duty is to believe in the One God sent to reveal the

Father to us and to be the propitiation (sacrificial offering to satisfy the wrath of God) for our sins. God looks for faith in His Son. That is what pleases Him (Heb. 11:6). Be sure you are trusting Him and nothing in this world. It's all gonna burn.

Everyday Persecution

Today's Reading: Daniel 3-4; First John 3

Selected Verses

*Nebuchadnezzar answered and said, "Blessed be the God of Shadrach,
Meshach, and Abednego, who has sent his angel and delivered his servants,
who trusted in him, and set aside the king's command, and yielded up
their bodies rather than serve and worship any god except their own God.*

Dan. 3:28

The reason why the world does not know us is that it did not know him.

1 John 3:1

Reflections

The Jews living in captivity in Babylon faced serious trials. Their faith and practice got them into trouble at times, but the message of Daniel is that God always saw them through vindicating their faith and His power.

Nebuchadnezzar needed repeated evidence that the God of Israel was truly God Most High. When he mandated worship of an idol, the three friends of Daniel refused to bow. He gave them one more chance to obey, but again they stood their ground. He threw them into the fiery furnace. Yet even that fire could not destroy them. They came forth without so much as the smell of smoke. Nebuchadnezzar was forced to honor God and reward Shadrach, Meshach, and Abednego.

The Apostle John instructs his readers about the life of one who has fellowship with God. There will necessarily be a qualitative difference in the person who loves God. It affects his relationships with others and his attitudes toward the trinkets of this world. He practices righteousness and loves his brother. "Do not be surprised, brothers, that the world hates you," he tells them (1 John 3:13). Why? Because the world did not know God.

Think about It

Daniel and his friends endured severe tests of their faith. They prepared themselves for death. But instead they experienced quick vindication (Dan. 3:18). Others will not be delivered from death but prepare to endure until they see Jesus Christ face to face "as he is." Be ready for everyday persecution, but, if it costs your life, anticipate transformation by Him when you see Him.

Safe in the Lions' Den

Today's Reading: Daniel 5-6; First John 4

Selected Verses

I make a decree, that in all my royal dominion people
are to tremble and fear before the God of Daniel,
for he is the living God,
enduring forever;
his kingdom shall never be destroyed,
and his dominion shall be to the end.
He delivers and rescues;
he works signs and wonders
in heaven and on earth,
he who has saved Daniel
from the power of the lions.
So this Daniel prospered during the reign of Darius and the reign of Cyrus the Persian.

Dan. 6:26-28

Little children, you are from God and have overcome them,
for he who is in you is greater than he who is in the world.

1 John 4:4

Reflections

God's people down through history have been tested and oppressed by evil forces in this world as was predicted in Genesis 3:15. They are not always delivered from those trials, but, by God's grace and power, they remain faithful to Him and even in death are not defeated

Daniel's political opponents set a trap for him. He resolved not to compromise his faith but to trust God to see him through the consequences of maintaining his practice of prayer. God protected him through a night in the lions' den. King Darius saw the power of God and decreed that all should tremble and fear before Him.

John reassured his readers of God's power in the face of opposing spiritual forces in the world. He called them "little children" perhaps because of his tender love for them but, probably, also because they were not spiritual giants. Nevertheless, he said they had overcome the false prophets, also called the spirit of antichrist and the spirit of error. Unlike those in the world, these little children did not listen to the false spirits.

Think about It

Daniel prospered under the pagan kings. Those John addressed were victorious against the forces of spiritual darkness. The faithful do not always prosper in this world. But all who abide in Christ know God's faithfulness and the ultimate deliverance of what Darius called the kingdom that shall never be destroyed. Stay faithful and confident. You are safe even in a lions' den.

Overcoming Faith

Today's Reading: Daniel 7-8; First John 5

Selected Verses

And to him was given dominion
and glory and a kingdom,
that all peoples, nations, and languages
should serve him;
his dominion is an everlasting dominion,
which shall not pass away,
and his kingdom one
that shall not be destroyed.

Dan. 7:14

For this is the love of God, that we keep his commandments. And his commandments are not burdensome. For everyone who has been born of God overcomes the world. And this is the victory that has overcome the world—our faith. Who is it that overcomes the world except the one who believes that Jesus is the Son of God?

1 John 5:3-5

Reflections

Daniel recorded here his visions of what was to come. He found them troubling because they were not easy to understand. We have the advantage of history and can draw some lines between the things he saw and what later occurred. The vision of the beasts seems to refer to the kingdoms of Nebuchadnezzar (Babylonia), Medo Persia, and Alexander the Great. The fourth is not so clear, but some believe it to be the Roman Empire.

What was clear was that none of these kingdoms would endure. The Ancient of Days gives the everlasting kingdom to the son of man, which points to Jesus Christ. His kingdom will not pass away.

John the Apostle knew the Son of Man, his and our Lord Jesus Christ. John wrote that He was the propitiation for our sins (1 John 2:2; 4:10). In Him we are given light and have fellowship with God and with all His people who also walk in the light with God (1 John 1:7). This fellowship with God results in a changed life. This changed life includes faith in Jesus Christ, love for God, and obedience to His commandments. Those changes demonstrate a new birth and results in victory over the world.

Think about It

Should we settle for a hum-drum spiritual life? No. Not according to John. We should expect substantial changes. No, not sinless perfection. We will always be going to Him to confess our sins and to be cleansed (1 John 1:9). If you do not see evidence in yourself of a new birth, call upon Him for mercy and grace to grant you overcoming faith.

There's a War On

Today's Reading: Daniel 9-10; Second John

Selected Verses

*The prince of the kingdom of Persia withstood me twenty-one days, but
Michael, one of the chief princes, came to help me, for I was left there with
the kings of Persia, and came to make you understand what is to happen
to your people in the latter days. For the vision is for days yet to come.*

Dan. 10:13-14

*For many deceivers have gone out into the world, those who do not confess the
coming of Jesus Christ in the flesh. Such a one is the deceiver and the antichrist.*

2 John v. 7

Reflections

Daniel was in a time of deep mourning for three weeks. He fasted and
prayed. God sent an angel to him, but, at first, he was more frightened than
strengthened. The angel addressed him kindly and called him a man greatly
loved. Daniel's prayers had been heard from the first day of that three-week
period, but the angel had been opposed by the prince of the kingdom of Persia.

John, in this second epistle, warns his readers about the deceivers in the
world. They are identified as those who do not confess the coming of Jesus
Christ in the flesh. *The Reformation Study Bible*[15] notes explain that a heresy
called the Docetism taught that Jesus did not have a real human body but was
some sort of phantom who only appeared to be human. John declared these false
teachers to be of the Antichrist.

Think about It

Once again in these passages, we see the very real nature of the spiritual war
going on around us. Satan and his forces wield a certain amount of power, but
God does hear His children when they pray. He does send aid. He will judge all
the hosts of wickedness and deliver His own safely to glory (Isa. 24:21; Eph.
6:11-12; 2 Pet. 2:4; Rev. 17:8; 20:10).

There's a war on, but God has all things under His control. Trust Him and
obey His truth. As we saw yesterday, His children will be victorious over the
world through Jesus Christ.

---

[15] *The Reformation Study Bible* (Sanford, FL: Reformation Trust, 2015), p. 2279.

Defying Authority

Today's Reading: Daniel 11-12; Third John

Selected Verses

And the king shall do as he wills. He shall exalt himself and magnify himself above every god, and shall speak astonishing things against the God of gods. He shall prosper till the indignation is accomplished; for what is decreed shall be done.

Dan. 11:36

I have written something to the church, but Diotrephes, who likes to put himself first, does not acknowledge our authority. So if I come, I will bring up what he is doing, talking wicked nonsense against us. And not content with that, he refuses to welcome the brothers, and also stops those who want to and puts them out of the church. Beloved, do not imitate evil but imitate good. Whoever does good is from God; whoever does evil has not seen God.

3 John vv. 9-11

Reflections

As we see in today's readings, the problem of defying authority is prevalent down through history and in all areas of life, political and ecclesiastical.

Daniel had a vision about a self-exalting king who lifted himself up above every other god and spoke against the true God of Israel. He would seem to be invincible for a time conquering kingdoms and amassing wealth, but in the end he would fall with no one to help (Dan. 11:45).

In John's time, there was a man named Diotrephes who had a similar defiant attitude. He disregarded the apostle and spoke against him. He treated strangers heartlessly and excommunicated those in the church who attempted to be hospitable. In short, the man was a picture of selfishness and pride. No wonder John tells his readers not to imitate evil but to imitate good. A person like Diotrephes can influence many to follow his wicked example.

Think about It

"Question authority" may be a popular bumper sticker but the solution to the abusive use of power is not to question the concept of authority. We need to submit to God's authority and to all duly instituted authority in the civil sector and in the church. Heed the warnings of Scripture (Rom. 13:1-7; Heb. 13:7, 17).

Contend for the Faith

Today's Reading: Hosea 1-4; Jude

Selected Verses

My people are destroyed for lack of knowledge;
because you have rejected knowledge,
I reject you from being a priest to me.
And since you have forgotten the law of your God,
I also will forget your children.

Hos. 4:6

Beloved, although I was very eager to write to you about our common salvation,
I found it necessary to write appealing to you to contend for the faith that was once
for all delivered to the saints. For certain people have crept in unnoticed who long
ago were designated for this condemnation, ungodly people, who pervert the grace
of our God into sensuality and deny our only Master and Lord, Jesus Christ.

Jude vv. 3-4

Reflections

In both readings today, we see God indicting those who have forsaken the truth and who misled those who looked to them for guidance.

Hosea, like other prophets, had a message of warning and hope for Israel and Judah. The Lord called him to depict God's mercy and grace toward His faithless people by taking a prostitute for his wife. God told them they were destroyed for lack of knowledge. Their teachers taught lies rather than God's law. The priests had facilitated national sin.

In a similar way, God called believers in Jude's day to contend for the faith, that is, the doctrine He gave the Church through the Apostles and Prophets. False and wicked teachers attacked this truth in their deceitful and treacherous ways. They misused God's grace as an excuse for sensuality. They denied the Lord Jesus Christ. Among other vices, they relied on their dreams. They claimed to get their truth by direct revelation, a practice Paul also condemned (Col. 2:18). [16]

Think about It

Truth matters. It matters what we believe, and, if we are in the position of teachers, it matters to all whom we influence for good or bad. Be sure you know the truth of God's word and that those you learn from contend for the faith and are not relying on the inventions of their minds.

---

[16] The Reformation Study Bible, Sanford, FL, Reformation Trust, 2015, p. 2292. See note on verse 8

From a Cloud to a Kingdom

Today's Reading: Hosea 5-8; Revelation 1

Selected Verses

What shall I do with you, O Ephraim? What shall I do with you, O Judah? Your love is like a morning cloud, like the dew that goes early away. Therefore I have hewn them by the prophets; I have slain them by the words of my mouth, and my judgment goes forth as the light. For I desire steadfast love and not sacrifice, the knowledge of God rather than burnt offerings.

Hos. 6:4-6

To him who loves us and has freed us from our sins by his blood and made us a kingdom, priests to his God and Father, to him be glory and dominion forever and ever. Amen.

Rev. 1: 5-6

Reflections

Hosea expresses God's view of His people. He laments their instability. Their unstable love is like a morning cloud or dew. It melts away rapidly. Their sacrifices and burnt offerings were unacceptable for they were not done out of steadfast love or from knowledge of God. They went through the motions. What? Did they think God could be fooled? So the Lord, through Hosea, says "What shall I do with you?"

God Himself answered the question. What He did was to send His Son to free us from our sins by His blood. Why? Because He loves us. His love is unchangeable and unstoppable. Not only that, He desired a kingdom for His glory. His purposes are wise and good. Although Israel failed to become what He called them to be, through Jesus Christ, all the nations have been called to be a kingdom and priests to Him. And He is glorified and has dominion forever and ever.

Think about It

Unregenerate man attempts to please God with fleeting love and phony sacrifices, but God graciously acts to redeem a people who know God, who are freed from their sins and made a kingdom. A cloud vs. a kingdom, what a contrast! Give praise to God for His love and wisdom

A Time to Love; a Time to Hate

Today's Reading: Hosea 9-11; Revelation 2

Selected Verses

> How can I give you up, O Ephraim?
> How can I hand you over, O Israel?
> How can I make you like Admah?
> How can I treat you like Zeboiim?
> My heart recoils within me;
> my compassion grows warm and tender.
> I will not execute my burning anger;
> I will not again destroy Ephraim;
> for I am God and not a man,
> the Holy One in your midst,
> and I will not come in wrath.

Hos. 11:8-9

But I have this against you, that you have abandoned the love you had at first. Remember therefore from where you have fallen; repent, and do the works you did at first. If not, I will come to you and remove your lampstand from its place, unless you repent. Yet this you have: you hate the works of the Nicolaitans, which I also hate.

Rev. 2:4-6

Reflections

God's love for His people is relentless, though He reveals in His Word how His heart recoils with the sinfulness of His people. Ultimately, God restrains His justice against His people and does not destroy them.

Hosea was sent to warn Judah and Israel of her impending judgment. This intervention by the Lord was another act of His patience and mercy. He gave them a chance to repent. He showed them through the sad, painful marital relationship of Hosea and Gomer, how God saw the unfaithfulness of His people toward Him. They repaid His goodness and blessing with idolatry and worship of false gods. Even after all that, God's compassion toward them was aroused. As He said through the prophet Ezekiel, "Have I any pleasure in the death of the wicked, declares the Lord God, and not rather that he should turn from his way and live?" (Ezek. 18:23).

The Lord gave the Apostle John messages for seven churches of Asia Minor. Most of them contain warnings of impending judgment for their sin. In the letter to the church in Ephesus, He commends them for several qualities including their hatred of a heretical group called the Nicolaitans. While it was good to hate evil, they were also found to have abandoned the love they had shown earlier. Jesus tells them to repent of this attitude lest they completely lose their standing as a church.

Think about It

Let this be a warning to us as well. Do not hate evil without maintaining deep love for God. There is "a time to love and a time to hate" (Eccl. 3:8). Pray for a heart that is tuned to God's, who both loves and hates perfectly.

The Danger of Prosperity

Today's Reading: Hosea 12-14; Revelation 3

Selected Verses

But I am the Lord your God from the land of Egypt; you know no God but me, and besides me there is no savior. It was I who knew you in the wilderness, in the land of drought; but when they had grazed, they became full, they were filled, and their heart was lifted up; therefore they forgot me.

Hos. 13:4-6

For you say, I am rich, I have prospered, and I need nothing, not realizing that you are wretched, pitiable, poor, blind, and naked. I counsel you to buy from me gold refined by fire, so that you may be rich, and white garments so that you may clothe yourself and the shame of your nakedness may not be seen, and salve to anoint your eyes, so that you may see.

Rev. 3:17-18

Reflections

It seems to be the experience of many that in difficult times faith flourishes and good character is strengthened, while in periods of ease and plenty laziness and arrogance grow. Can we handle prosperity?

Hosea delivered God's brutally honest message to Israel and Judah. The Lord told them that He was with them in the wilderness and in the land of drought, but, when they got to lush pastures and were filled, they grew proud and forgot God. This led them to a spiritual wilderness and desert and to the need to recognize their sin and unfaithfulness.

In the letter to the Laodicean Church, the Lord made similar comments to those who were rich and prosperous. They were actually spiritually blinded by their apparent success and security. He diagnosed their true condition as being "wretched, pitiable, poor, blind, and naked." They felt comfortable, but God found them lukewarm. Of course, being cold or hot does not feel comfortable. We prefer a moderate temperature, like lukewarmness. But God hates lukewarmness—spiritual lukewarmness, that is—in those who claim to be His.

God in His grace and mercy sends His truth to His people. There is always a remedy for prosperity-induced laziness, arrogance, and lukewarmness. That remedy is repentance and confession of sin.

Think about It

If these are not easy times, if you are in the wilderness or in dry lands, remember that the worst thing that can happen to you is not to suffer adversity but to forget the Lord. If these are good times in your life, be sure you are handling prosperity with humility and a God-glorifying focus. Beware the danger of prosperity.

The Day of the Lord

Today's Reading: Joel 1-3; Revelation 4

Selected Verses

The Lord roars from Zion, and utters his voice from Jerusalem, and the heavens and the earth quake. But the Lord is a refuge to his people, a stronghold to the people of Israel.

Joel 3:16

> *They cast their crowns before the throne, saying,*
> *"Worthy are you, our Lord and God,*
>   *to receive glory and honor and power,*
>   *for you created all things,*
>   *and by your will they existed and were created."*

Rev. 4:10, 11

Reflections

Joel mentions or alludes to the "day of the Lord" repeatedly (1:15; 2:1, 11, 31; 3:1, 14, 18). He says it is near. It is great and very awesome. "Who can endure it?" the prophet asks. It is a day in which the heavens and earth quake. Should we also quake at the thought of this day?

It depends. Joel says, "The Lord is a refuge to his people, a stronghold to the people of Israel." Those who are His people will find Him a refuge to run to, not a terrifying figure to run from. He is the only safe place for those who trust Him.

John receives a vision of what is to come. The door of heaven is opened and he looks inside. What does he see? He sees the One who is seated on the throne. He sees creatures and elders worshiping Him. These twenty-four elders cast their crowns before His throne in an act of adoration which signifies that they have nothing which He has not given them. Nothing they have can be withheld from Him. He is worthy of every possible honor. They cry out to Him of His worthiness, enthralled with His presence. They find Him majestic, glorious, honorable, and powerful.

Think about It

The day of the Lord is coming. Do you long for it or dread it? It depends on whether you will meet Him as your Refuge and Creator or your Judge. Be ready.

Who is Worthy?

Today's Reading: Amos 1-3; Revelation 5

Selected Verses

Hear this word that the Lord has spoken against you, O people of Israel, against the whole family that I brought up out of the land of Egypt:

"You only have I known
of all the families of the earth;
therefore I will punish you
for all your iniquities."

Amos 3:1-2

And no one in heaven or on earth or under the earth was able to open the scroll or to look into it, and I began to weep loudly because no one was found worthy to open the scroll or to look into it. And one of the elders said to me, "Weep no more; behold, the Lion of the tribe of Judah, the Root of David, has conquered, so that he can open the scroll and its seven seals."

Rev. 5:3-5

Reflections

In all kinds of human settings, we use rewards and punishments to attempt to encourage desired behavior or to inhibit undesired behavior. As any parent, teacher, or boss can attest, this approach yields limited success, but it seems to be the best option we have.

God did the same sort of thing, first, with our parents, Adam and Eve, in the Garden and then with Israel. He blessed them and He warned them. Their response was rebellion and sin. In fact, much of the content of the Old Testament points out this failure on the part of people. To turn against one's benefactor is a completely irrational act. To disobey God after being clearly warned about the consequences is the height of stupidity. Indeed, sin is stupid, always. Ungratefulness is more than stupid. Israel was guilty, but they were not the only ones. We all have sinned and have fallen short of the glory of God (Rom. 3:23).

When John got his vision of heaven, this truth, that all are unworthy before God, was confirmed. He saw a scroll with seven seals. An angel's cry went out, "Who is worthy to open the scroll and break its seals?" No one was found who qualified. John was appalled. He wept loudly. Such was the state of all mankind against the backdrop of God's mercy, grace, and holiness.

Then John saw the Lamb. He was declared worthy. He alone could open the seals of the scroll.

Think about It

How would you respond if you could see the true spiritual state of mankind before God in Heaven? Would you weep? Would you look to Jesus Christ, the Lamb who was slain and who alone is worthy? Look to Him and give Him the praise and glory He is due. He is the One who is worthy.

The Day of Wrath

Today's Reading: Amos 4-6; Revelation 6

Selected Verses

Therefore thus I will do to you, O Israel;
because I will do this to you,
prepare to meet your God, O Israel!
For behold, he who forms the mountains and creates the wind,
and declares to man what is his thought,
who makes the morning darkness,
and treads on the heights of the earth—
the LORD, the God of hosts, is his name!

Amos 4:12-13

Then the kings of the earth and the great ones and the generals and the rich
and the powerful, and everyone, slave and free, hid themselves in the caves
and among the rocks of the mountains, calling to the mountains and rocks, "Fall
on us and hide us from the face of him who is seated on the throne, and from the
wrath of the Lamb, for the great day of their wrath has come, and who can stand?"

Rev. 6:15-17

Reflections

If God poured out His terrible judgment on Israel, how much more will He pour out wrath on the whole earth which has rebelled against Him!

Amos continues to lay out for Israel how they have failed God. Repeatedly, he tells them that they ignored all of God's judgments. "Yet you did not return to me!" he says (Amos 4:6). Looking at Israel's history from a distance, it appears inexplicable. How could they not get the message? But they did not. But then, do we?

So Amos tells them to "prepare to meet [their] God."

John's vision reveals the contents of the scroll with the seven seals. One by one they are opened. All are frightening, but the sixth drives all the people great and small who are under the condemnation of the wrath of God and the Lamb to cry out for the mountains and rocks to fall upon them. Anything, they think, is better than to experience the full judgment of God.

Think about It

Here we have a picture of what is to come. The day of wrath of the One who is on the throne is before us. Will we prepare to meet our God as Amos urged? There is a way to prepare. Bow before the Lamb who was slain for sinners and repent of your sins. Ask for His mercy and forgiveness. By His grace, you will stand in the day of wrath.

Restoration after Tribulation

Today's Reading: Amos 7-9; Revelation 7

Selected Verses

> *I will plant them on their land,*
> > *and they shall never again be uprooted*
> > *out of the land that I have given them,"*
> *says the Lord your God.*

> Amos 9:15

> *Then one of the elders addressed me, saying, "Who are these, clothed in*
> *white robes, and from where have they come?" I said to him, "Sir, you know."*
> *And he said to me, "These are the ones coming out of the great tribulation.*
> *They have washed their robes and made them white in the blood of the Lamb.*

> Rev. 7:13-14

Reflections

The prophet Amos had a gloomy message for Israel. God's words through him moved the prophet himself. "O Lord God, please forgive! How can Jacob stand? He is so small!" he cries out again and again (Amos 7:2). But God relents and promises that all these dire warnings will not be final. There is a day of restoration and joy ahead. It will be permanent. There will be lasting prosperity and security.

Given the depth of sin and failure on the part of Israel, how is this blessing possible?

The gospel of Jesus Christ holds the answer. He is the Lamb of God whose blood atones for the sin of God's elect. They wash their robes in it. Those filthy robes are made white. They endure the pain and suffering of the great tribulation and though, as Amos admitted, they are small, yet they stand.

Think about It

Do not wonder if you suffer for a time. Some of it, we bring on ourselves by our sin and stupidity and some of it is the suffering of Christ that His people must bear because of their identity with Him. In the end, there is restoration. Be strong in the Lord, because tribulation is real, but it is not the end.

Silence in Heaven

Today's Reading: Obadiah; Revelation 8

Selected Verses

The pride of your heart has deceived you,
*   you who live in the clefts of the rock,*
*   in your lofty dwelling,*
who say in your heart,
*   "Who will bring me down to the ground?"*
Though you soar aloft like the eagle,
*   though your nest is set among the stars,*
*   from there I will bring you down,*
declares the Lord.

Obad. vv. 3-4

When the Lamb opened the seventh seal, there
was silence in heaven for about half an hour.

Rev. 8:1

Reflections

In John's Revelation, the Lamb opens six of the seven seals. When He comes to the seventh seal, something unprecedented occurs. There is silence in heaven. The saints were lifting up worship and loud praises to God, but now it stops. The guilty cry out in grief that the mountains should fall upon them to hide them. Then they all grow silent. It is as if they wait to see what the Lamb will do next. Then the judgment falls everywhere.

There was a time when the Edomites, the descendants of Esau, had grown so proud that they thought no one could bring them down. They vented their arrogance on suffering Israel. God sent Obadiah to warn them that He would judge them. That judgment would be more thorough and complete than anything they could imagine.

Think about It

The proud and foolish think that God, if He exists at all, has no interest or knowledge of people on earth. They see believers dying for their faith and do not know that the Lord receives them and keeps them safe. He reassures them that they will be avenged. The day of wrath comes.

What should be our attitude toward God? Should we not bow quietly before Him? Let all boastful pride be eliminated and replaced with prayerful humility and silence.

Sin: The Lethal Weapon

Today's Reading: Jonah 1-4; Revelation 9

Selected Verses

And he asked that he might die and said, "It is better for me to die than to live." But God said to Jonah, "Do you do well to be angry for the plant?" And he said, "Yes, I do well to be angry, angry enough to die."

Jon. 4:8b-9

The rest of mankind, who were not killed by these plagues, did not repent of the works of their hands nor give up worshiping demons and idols of gold and silver and bronze and stone and wood, which cannot see or hear or walk, nor did they repent of their murders or their sorceries or their sexual immorality or their thefts.

Rev. 9:20-21

Reflections

Jonah was sent to Nineveh, a city so evil that God decided to bring judgment on it. But first, He decreed that they should have one last chance to repent. So he chose Jonah to go. We all know the story. Jonah went in another direction, was intercepted by the big fish, and learned that God could stop him anywhere. Then Jonah, like Nineveh, got a second chance to obey God. This time he obeyed, sort of. Jonah proclaimed God's message to the city. Lo and behold, they repented, God relented and spared them.

Jonah was so angry he wanted to die. He appreciated what God had done for him, sparing him from a watery grave inside a fish. But now, he hated God's mercy toward Nineveh that wicked city. He wanted to die, but God mercifully discussed the matter with him. Jonah got yet a third chance to get it right. We are left to wonder if he did.

In Revelation 9, conditions following God's judgment were such that people were seeking death but for a different reason than Jonah. They sought death because they could not see any escape from the wrath of God. They had no hope. But they could not die, at least, not all of them. Did the survivors repent and call out for mercy, like the Ninevites before them? No! They persisted in their unbelief, their idolatry and demon worship.

Think about It

Why do some, under severe judgment, repent while others grow more hardened in rebellion against God? The answer is that God grants repentance to some and not to others. It is not a function of the severity of the trial or the eloquence of the preacher (Jonah was a reluctant preacher, at best). The difference is the sovereign work of God in the hearts of the hearers or sufferers. Here the Ninevites were wiser and more receptive than the fifth trumpet generation. Observe and learn from these examples: negative and positive. Without grace to repent, sin is lethal.

Foolish Presumption

Today's Reading: Micah 1-3; Revelation 10

Selected Verses

Its heads give judgment for a bribe;
its priests teach for a price;
its prophets practice divination for money;
yet they lean on the Lord and say,
"Is not the Lord in the midst of us?
No disaster shall come upon us."
Therefore because of you
Zion shall be plowed as a field;
Jerusalem shall become a heap of ruins,
and the mountain of the house a wooded height.

Mic. 3:11-12

And the angel whom I saw standing on the sea and on the land raised his right hand to heaven and swore by him who lives forever and ever, who created heaven and what is in it, the earth and what is in it, and the sea and what is in it, that there would be no more delay, but that in the days of the trumpet call to be sounded by the seventh angel, the mystery of God would be fulfilled, just as he announced to his servants the prophets.

Rev. 10:5-7

Reflections

Through Micah, the Lord indicts the leaders of Israel and Judah for their abuses. Officials take bribes and corruption rules. Priests and prophets disregard God's word but seek easy money. How do they commit these evils so glibly? Are they oblivious to the presence of the Lord? No! On the contrary, they actually presume on God's presence, that He is with them and will not touch them no matter what they do. "Is not the Lord in the midst of us? No disaster shall come upon us," they say in their foolish presumption.

In John's vision, he sees an angel straddling land and sea. This angel announces that "there would be no more delay" but what God had foretold by the prophets would come to pass. This is a message which is bittersweet. It proclaims the judgment upon all who have lived as if there were no God, or presuming that He is always on our side, but it also brings the end of the long delay that has extended down through human history since the serpent deceived Eve in the Garden.

Think about It

There is still time to flee to Jesus Christ and away from foolish presumption. Do not delay. The bittersweet message will be fulfilled. Seek the Light of the world who illumines our dark and foolish presumption (John 8:12).

Walking, Serving, Fearing

Today's Reading: Micah 4-5; Revelation 11

Selected Verses

> *And many nations shall come, and say:*
> *"Come, let us go up to the mountain of the Lord,*
> *to the house of the God of Jacob,*
> *that he may teach us his ways*
> *and that we may walk in his paths."*

Mic. 4:2

> *The nations raged,*
> *but your wrath came,*
> *and the time for the dead to be judged,*
> *and for rewarding your servants, the prophets and saints,*
> *and those who fear your name,*
> *both small and great,*
> *and for destroying the destroyers of the earth.*

Rev. 11:18

Reflections

The term "nation" in English shows up in both of the passages selected above, but they refer to quite different responses to God's revelation of Himself and His commands upon mankind.

Micah speaks of a day when the mountain of the Lord and God's house will be an attraction to all the nations of the world. People will stream there seeking to know God's ways so as to walk in His paths. If the "latter days" occur between the first and second advents of Jesus Christ (which I believe), then this is being fulfilled even today as the nations turn to Christ in faith. If we take the Church of Jesus Christ as the fulfillment of God's promise to Abraham to bless all the families of the earth in him (Gen. 12:3), it is easy to see how these promises in Micah are already being kept. There is a great host of people in every nation who trust in Jesus Christ as the Savior of the world and Lord of lords.

John heard the twenty-four elders worshiping and saying that the time had come for God's wrath in response to the raging of the nations. While Micah is talking about people from every nation coming to faith, the elders are speaking of the nations, perhaps on an official level, as they have rebelled against the Lord (Ps. 2). Even so, the elders have not forgotten that God's servants and those who fear His name have a sure reward. The judgment is a time in which God will winnow out the wheat from the chaff and apply rewards and punishment as required.

Think about It

What will God look for on that day? He will look for those who have walked in His ways, served Him, and feared His name. This is the way of life of the believer in Jesus Christ. Be faithful and be sure that those verbs describe you.

Choosing Sides in the War

Today's Reading: Micah 6-7; Revelation 12

Selected Verses

He has told you, O man, what is good;
and what does the Lord require of you
but to do justice, and to love kindness,
and to walk humbly with your God?

Mic. 6:8

Then the dragon became furious with the woman and went off to make war
on the rest of her offspring, on those who keep the commandments of God
and hold to the testimony of Jesus. And he stood on the sand of the sea.

Rev. 12:17

Reflections

Every human being is born into a war. In that war we are naturally born on the side of Satan. By grace through faith in Jesus Christ, we are transferred to His kingdom, and with that transfer we become enemy combatants to the dragon (John 8:39-47; Col. 1:12-14).

Revelation 12 gives us a graphic picture of the fury of the dragon that goes out to make war on the offspring of the woman. He rages and will not stop until he finishes, or a greater power overcomes him.

How does he recognize these children of the woman? Easy. They "keep the commandments of God and hold to the testimony of Jesus." In the midst of battle, it takes true faith to keep obeying and trusting the Lord. Some, in recent days as well as over the centuries, have been so severely tested that they had to choose between faith and death. I can only imagine the unleashed wrath of Satan as God's people defy him in favor of death with peace. I can only imagine the rejoicing in heaven as the saints and angels welcome the homeward procession of victorious martyrs.

Think about It

What does it mean to keep the commandments? Micah gave a simple three-point summary in Micah 6:8. Do justice. Love kindness. Walk humbly with your God. In other words, live out your faith in the midst of the war, but remember the dragon is after you and your faith will light you up on his screen. Be ready to incur his wrath as you bring glory to God.

Judgment: Does God Delay?

Today's Reading: Nahum 1-3; Revelation 13

Selected Verses

The Lord is a jealous and avenging God;
the Lord is avenging and wrathful;
the Lord takes vengeance on his adversaries
and keeps wrath for his enemies.
The Lord is slow to anger and great in power,
and the Lord will by no means clear the guilty.
His way is in whirlwind and storm,
and the clouds are the dust of his feet.

Nah. 1:2, 3

Also [the beast] was allowed to make war on the saints and to conquer them. And authority was given it over every tribe and people and language and nation, and all who dwell on earth will worship it, everyone whose name has not been written before the foundation of the world in the book of life of the Lamb who was slain.

Rev. 13:7-8

Reflections

The Bible from start to finish shows us that God is firmly in control of human history. Nothing escapes His knowledge, His presence, or His power. That does not mean that He watches human history as a disinterested bystander. He will act in His time to reward faithfulness and punish evil.

In Nahum's day, the nation of Assyria was imposing her power on the surrounding nations. Israel had already fallen to her and Judah, under King Manasseh, was a vassal state. Nahum proclaimed the power of God in the midst of this difficult situation. Assyria would fall, he assured them. God is slow to anger but not weak in power. He would pour out His wrath. Meanwhile, Nahum, whose name means comfort, reminded Judah that "The Lord is good, a stronghold in the day of trouble; he knows those who take refuge in him" (1:7).

John sees two beasts, one from the sea and one from the earth. These united with the dragon wreak havoc on God's people, who do not take the mark of the beast which gives access to commerce. It seems like a hopeless situation, yet God limits the time allotted to these beasts. God reassures all who refuse to worship the beast—their names were recorded before time in the Lamb's book of life.

Think about It

Let this bring comfort to us who believe but warning to all who confuse God's patience with any kind of weakness. His judgment will come in His time, not ours.

A Call for Endurance

Today's Reading: Habakkuk 1-3; Revelation 14

Selected Verses

Yet I will rejoice in the Lord;
I will take joy in the God of my salvation.
God, the Lord, is my strength;
he makes my feet like the deer's;
he makes me tread on my high places.

Hab. 3:18-19

Here is a call for the endurance of the saints, those who
keep the commandments of God and their faith in Jesus.
And I heard a voice from heaven saying, "Write this: Blessed are the dead
who die in the Lord from now on." "Blessed indeed," says the Spirit,
"that they may rest from their labors, for their deeds follow them!"

Rev. 14:12-13

Reflections

Down through the ages, the saints of God have been called to live by faith in His word. Often they have had to stand under intense opposition and persecution.

Habakkuk was perplexed about the spiritual state of Judah. Why did God seem to ignore the injustice and corruption in the nation? God responded that He would send the Chaldeans to discipline Judah. That answer drove Habakkuk to even greater confusion. How could God use such a wicked people to discipline His own people who while sinful were not nearly as evil as the Chaldeans? The Lord explained that when He was finished using the Chaldeans to discipline Judah, He would then turn His wrath on them, too.

Habakkuk gets it. He concludes with a psalm of praise and commitment to God. The prophet says he will trust God and rejoice in Him no matter what. Now that is an example of faith!

In Revelation, God gives John a picture of the things to come. There will be great trials. The saints must respond to the call to endure with obedience and steadfast faith in Jesus. Once that is over, they will be received into eternal rest where their deeds in this world will be remembered.

Think about It

Walk in faith and obedience, my brother, my sister. The time will come soon when the stress and pressure of this world will be over. Our reward is certain, so endure.

God: His Wrath and His Joy

Today's Reading: Zephaniah 1-3; Revelation 15

Selected Verses

On that day it shall be said to Jerusalem:
"Fear not, O Zion;
let not your hands grow weak.
The Lord your God is in your midst,
a mighty one who will save;
he will rejoice over you with gladness;
he will quiet you by his love;
he will exult over you with loud singing.

Zeph. 3:16-17

Then I saw another sign in heaven, great and amazing, seven angels with
seven plagues, which are the last, for with them the wrath of God is finished.

Rev. 15:1

Reflections

The prophet Zephaniah described the anger of the Lord against all the sin and corruption of, not only Judah but, all the nations of the world. He warns of the coming of the day of His wrath. That day would come and the judgment would be complete. Is there no escape? Yes, there is a hope for those who humble themselves before the Almighty.

Turning to Revelation, John's vision confirms that the wrath of God does have an end point. Seven plagues come upon the earth administered by seven angels. After this we learn that these seven plagues, "are the last, for with them the wrath of God is finished."

Finished.

What a good word to our ears! Zephaniah has given us a beautiful picture of the delight which the Lord has in His own. Several phrases show the completeness of His care and describe His presence (in your midst), His power (mighty one who will save), His joy (He will rejoice over you... exult over you with loud singing).

Think about It

If we are to be biblical in our understanding of God, we must grasp these realities of His being. He is absolutely holy and will not let the wicked go unpunished. He is also full of love and mercy and will save all who come to Him in faith through His Son, the Lamb of God, who took away the sin of the world.

Be sure your understanding of God is accurate. Seek to know Him in truth as He has revealed Himself in His Word because His attributes include His wrath and His joy.

Repent: Some Do; Others Don't

Today's Reading: Haggai 1-2; Revelation 16

Selected Verses

And the Lord stirred up the spirit of Zerubbabel the son of Shealtiel, governor of Judah, and the spirit of Joshua the son of Jehozadak, the high priest, and the spirit of all the remnant of the people. And they came and worked on the house of the Lord of hosts, their God.

Hag. 1:14

The fourth angel poured out his bowl on the sun, and it was allowed to scorch people with fire. They were scorched by the fierce heat, and they cursed the name of God who had power over these plagues. They did not repent and give him glory.

Rev. 16:8-9

Reflections

During Haggai's time, the people of Judah in captivity in Babylon had been allowed to return to Jerusalem. They settled down and began to build their comfortable and fashionable homes. Then God sent Haggai to tell them that He was not pleased with their wrong priorities. They had left the temple in ruins while they focused on their own houses. God sent them drought. The crops failed.

The message of Haggai and the failure of the crops got their attention. But in the case of the people living under the outpouring of God's wrath by the seven angels of Revelation 15-16, there is a completely different reaction. No matter what bowl of wrath is poured out the people do not repent and give God glory. They do not recognize His power and their sin. Their response is completely irrational. The only exception is the voice coming from the altar which gives God the praise for His display of justice and power (Rev. 6:9-11).

Adversity, in and of itself, does not produce repentance. As the bowls are poured out and one judgment is piled upon another, the cursing of God continues without diminishing. How do we explain this insane attitude toward the Sovereign and Holy God? Why did the people in Haggai's day repent after a crop failure while the people of John's vision dig in and curse God? The difference is that "the Lord stirred up the spirit of Zerubbabel the son of Shealtiel, governor of Judah, and the spirit of Joshua the son of Jehozadak, the high priest, and the spirit of all the remnant of the people." This turned them to obedience and service to rebuild the temple.

Think about It

Do not expect repentance and praise to God to come from rebellious sinners unless the Lord stirs up their hearts. Pray that God may show mercy to those who are under His wrath by not only sending adversity and a messenger with the gospel, but by also stirring up their hearts. That is why some repent and others do not.

God Rules

Today's Reading: Zechariah 1-3; Revelation 17

Selected Verses

Be silent, all flesh, before the Lord, for he has roused himself from his holy dwelling.

Zech. 2:13

And the ten horns that you saw, they and the beast will hate the prostitute. They will make her desolate and naked, and devour her flesh and burn her up with fire, for God has put it into their hearts to carry out his purpose by being of one mind and handing over their royal power to the beast, until the words of God are fulfilled.

Rev. 17:16-17

Reflections

My seminary professor, Steve Brown, used to quip, "Christians don't pray because they are afraid God doesn't exist. Atheists don't pray because they are afraid He does." Certainly, there are times when everyone doubts God's existence. Our experience can make us question whether our faith is based on reality. Is our experience a reliable basis for faith? The Scriptures tell us to trust what God has said, not what our hunches tell us.

Zechariah delivered messages to Judah assuring them that though their forefathers had brought God's judgment on themselves, they were not thereby automatically left without hope. Each person is responsible before God to repent of sin and turn to Him in faith. There are times when God may appear to be unengaged or sleeping, but that is an illusion. All the earth owes Him glory and honor. It is wise to keep silence before Him.

In John's visions, he sees that reality. There is chaos and wickedness in the world, but do not be confused. God is still ruling over all things. He puts His purposes into the hearts of those who hate Him, and they do His bidding without intending to.

Think about It

Our observations on the state of the world, if uninformed by Scripture, are not trustworthy. Let God's Word give you a solid basis for faith and life. You will know that, indeed, God rules.

Final Victory

Today's Reading: Zechariah 4-6; Revelation 18

Selected Verses

Then he said to me, "This is the word of the Lord to Zerubbabel: Not by might, nor by power, but by my Spirit, says the Lord of hosts. Who are you, O great mountain? Before Zerubbabel you shall become a plain. And he shall bring forward the top stone amid shouts of 'Grace, grace to it!'"

Zech. 4:6-7

Then I heard another voice from heaven saying,
"Come out of her, my people,
lest you take part in her sins,
lest you share in her plagues;
for her sins are heaped high as heaven,
and God has remembered her iniquities."

Rev. 18:4-5

Reflections

There have been many moments in history when it appeared that God's people had no hope of final victory. The Lord always sent messengers to reassure the Church that she would not be ultimately defeated.

In Zechariah's day, the temple was in ruins and God commanded its rebuilding. It seemed impossible and, in fact, it was. But it did not depend on the strength or might of human beings, even of those who loved the Lord and longed to see worship restored. Through the vision, the prophet understood that it would be successful through the Spirit of the Lord of hosts. God commands all the armies of angels and He does His will which no one can thwart.

John was permitted to see the fall of Babylon.[17] She had commanded the world, economically and culturally, and seemed invincible. All who dealt with her enjoyed wealth and pleasure. But her end is assured. She will be brought down to nothing. Her ruin will be mourned by those who depended on her. God called His people to come out and not to go down with her in judgment.

Think about It

What is your view of the dominant culture of our day? Are you optimistic that God's truth will ultimately triumph? If you are one who has been bought by the blood of the Lamb, flee both pessimism and compromise. Final victory is assured.

---

[17] *Reformation Study Bible*, note on Rev. 17:1–19:10, p. 2324.

The Bride's Dress

Today's Reading: Zechariah 7-9; Revelation 19

Selected Verses

Say to all the people of the land and the priests, "When you fasted and mourned in the fifth month and in the seventh, for these seventy years, was it for me that you fasted? And when you eat and when you drink, do you not eat for yourselves and drink for yourselves?"

Zech. 7:5-6

Then I heard what seemed to be the voice of a great multitude, like the roar of many waters and like the sound of mighty peals of thunder, crying out,
"Hallelujah!
For the Lord our God
the Almighty reigns.
Let us rejoice and exult
and give him the glory,
for the marriage of the Lamb has come,
and his Bride has made herself ready;
it was granted her to clothe herself
with fine linen, bright and pure"—
for the fine linen is the righteous deeds of the saints.

Rev. 19:6-8

Reflections

Zechariah was sent to confront Judah about her unacceptable service to God. Oh, she had fasted and mourned. She had put on an outward show of brokenness and repentance, but the Lord saw through the phoniness and hypocrisy. True service to God is performed with fear of Him, not some kind of self-serving motivation It is done by "small and great" since no one is exempt from responsibility before Him (Rev. 19:4). It is futile to attempt to perform outward acts of service to God that are not matched by inward piety.

John relates his vision of the marriage supper of the Lamb. What a joyous occasion it is! There is nothing quite like a wedding celebration where bride and groom are filled with love and hope for their future. They commit themselves fully to one another "till death do us part." But no matter how splendid the ceremony, the banquet, or the couple, nothing compares to the marriage of the Lamb to His bride, the Church.

Think about It

At weddings, the big question is always, "How will the bride look?" Through John's vision we are allowed the rare privilege of seeing the bride before the ceremony. Are you, like me, surprised by her attire? We expect it to be fine linen, bright and pure, but on closer examination we see that this linen is the righteous deeds of the saints. That is what she is wearing.

Fellow disciple of the Lord Jesus Christ, never underestimate the eternal significance of your righteous deeds done in fear of and love for Him. Your labor in the Lord is not in vain (1 Cor. 15:58).

The Key and the Book

Today's Reading: Zechariah 10-12; Revelation 20

Selected Verses

For behold, I am raising up in the land a shepherd who does not care for those being destroyed, or seek the young or heal the maimed or nourish the healthy, but devours the flesh of the fat ones, tearing off even their hoofs.

> *Woe to my worthless shepherd,*
> *who deserts the flock!*
> *May the sword strike his arm*
> *and his right eye!*
> *Let his arm be wholly withered,*
> *his right eye utterly blinded!*

Zech. 11:16-17

Then I saw an angel coming down from heaven, holding in his hand the key to the bottomless pit and a great chain.

Rev. 20:1

Reflections

In biblical prophecy, not every detail is clear. What is clear is that God reigns over all and that every person will stand in judgment before Him.

In Zechariah, God raises up leaders, both good and evil ones. He judges them and puts them down. God does not merely permit them to gain power but controls their ascendance, sometimes using it for His purposes to discipline His people. In the end, He judges these ungodly powers.

In Revelation 20, the key and the book depict God's control of the cosmos. The key, entrusted to an angel, opens the bottomless pit where the Lord holds Satan confined and impotent. He is completely wicked but not in control even of his own actions and destiny. We also see a book of life with the names of those chosen to live and not suffer the lake of fire.

Think about It

There are two possible responses to these passages: belief or unbelief. For believers in the Triune God there is great reassurance that all will be well for us.

Unbelievers may dismiss the assertions with ridicule or terror that they may be true. Without a Holy God who rules all things and who will judge all people, the universe is out of control and all life is meaningless—an unthinkable condition!

But praise God! He reigns in sovereignty and wisdom. He holds the key and the book. Let us believe Him.

All Things New

Today's Reading: Zechariah 13-14; Revelation 21

Selected Verses

*And the Lord will be king over all the earth. On
that day the Lord will be one and his name one.*

Zech. 14:9

And he who was seated on the throne said, "Behold, I am making all things new."

Rev. 21:5

Reflections

Zechariah's prophecy and the vision of John in Revelation intersect in today's readings. Here we can see:

1. God exercises authority over all things. He sits on the throne and there is no one who can compete with Him.
2. God deserves worship from all.

God makes all things new. The fallen world with sickness, sorrow, tears, and death gives way to a new heavens and earth where He restores all things.

Think about It

The Urban Dictionary defines the "now generation" as "people who want instant gratification." By definition Bible believers are not members of that group. We live for a day when His kingdom will come and the will of God will be done "on earth as it is in heaven" (Matt. 6:10).

Flee from the foolishness of the "now generation." They want what they want and they want it now. Don't fall for that illusion. Cling to the promises of God for a day when He will make all things new. The new year gives us an opportunity to consider how to make necessary changes to live more fully in the light of that day to come. How will you invest the year ahead to reflect an attitude of expectancy and faith in the day when the Lord makes all things new?

God's Perspective

Today's Reading: Malachi 1-4; Revelation 22

Selected Verses

*Then once more you shall see the distinction between the righteous and
the wicked, between one who serves God and one who does not serve him.*

Mal. 3:18

*Blessed are those who wash their robes, so that they may have the right
to the tree of life and that they may enter the city by the gates. Outside
are the dogs and sorcerers and the sexually immoral and murderers
and idolaters, and everyone who loves and practices falsehood.*

Rev. 22:14-15

Reflections

Malachi, like the other prophets, sees clearly the inward and outward sins of
the people he addressed. He goes into detail about their idolatry, their failures in
marriage, and their stealing God's money. The Jews presumed that either their
status as descendants of Abraham exempted them from obedience or that the
Holy One of Israel was unconcerned about righteousness in His people.

The prophet warns them that the day of the Lord is coming. They would see
that there is a distinction between the righteous and the wicked. It does matter
how one lives before God.

John points us to Jesus Christ, the Lamb of God. Those who are accepted
before God recognize their sinfulness and come to have their robes washed in His
blood (Rev. 7:14). These blessed ones do not presume upon God's mercy but
receive the salvation offered in the gospel. They have access to the tree of life and
enter the city by the gates. Meanwhile, those who remain in their sins—such as
immorality, murder, idolatry, and falsehood—are outside.

Think about It

Although Malachi wrote around 500 years before John penned his Revelation,
these writings converge in a harmonious and glorious view of the final end of all things.

All sin will be punished. Unbelievers remain outside the city where God
dwells with His people. Meanwhile, Jesus Christ has paid for the sin of His sheep
by His atonement. By His wounds they are healed (1 Peter 2:24). Be sure you
know that there is a distinction between the righteous and the wicked, between
the seed of the woman and the seed of the serpent (Gen. 3:15).

Epilogue

Thank you for walking with me through the Scriptures. These daily devotionals have only scratched the surface of the treasures of God's Word and His truth. My prayer is that you will continue to read, study, and meditate on His eternal revelation—the Bible. As Jerry White said in the preface, daily time with God in the Word and prayer is the primary spiritual discipline worth fighting to keep.

If we have not met here, may we meet in glory to worship forever the Triune God. Meanwhile, let us walk before Him in the light of His truth. *Soli Deo Gloria!*

Acknowledgments

It is risky to try to list all those to whom I owe a deeply felt "thank you" but I will take that risk while apologizing to those I have left out. I appreciate Jerry White's encouragement to me many years ago to write and his taking the time now to review this book and provide his gracious Preface.

I am grateful for the support and guidance of the Roanoke Valley Christian Writers group, especially our director, Mrs. Barbara Baranowski.

Thanks to our daughters (the selfless mothers of our grandchildren), Paula Acker (who is a great resource, especially when our conversations turn to what constitutes good writing), Alicia Henn (who is encouraging me to turn this into an audio book for a wider audience) and Ana Hasbrouck (who is challenging me to find my voice). Friends like Stella Davison (who suggested I write one devotional book—that turned out to be two), Duncan Rankin (who wrote the Foreword to my first book) and Joel and Rebecca Gurley (who read this book when it was still a blog and gave thoughtful feedback) were invaluable to me.

Mary's brother, Melvin Lackey, bought boxes of my first book and gave them out to everyone on Ruth's and his Christmas list! Thanks are due to dear friends in our former congregations at Christ Church (Katy, TX) and Central Presbyterian (Kingstree, SC) and our present congregation, Grace Church (Roanoke VA). Many thanks to those Navigators who are now with the Lord (like Dwight and Ruth Hill, Walt Henrichsen, Dean Troug, Gene Denler, Gene Tabor, and Fernando Gonzalez) who challenged me to put Christ in the center of my life and taught me how to spend daily time in the Bible and prayer.

Pastors and professors have marked my life: Bill Austin, Steve Bradley, Igou Hodges, Fred Greco, Tim Martin, and Charlie Evans. Several are with the Lord: Jack Arnold, Bill Larkin and John-Gregory Farrell.

Others who made a difference in my life include: Jim and Jeri White, Jim Petersen, Randy Weyeneth, Stephen Ansley, Terry Cook and my colleagues from the Argentina years (the Blakes, the Healeys, the Travises, the Klaases, the Ratchfords, the Clays, and the Egers). I am grateful to God for each of you.

Finally, I thank Mary, whose love, wisdom, and steadiness make me glad every day that God has allowed us to walk together with Him for nearly half a century. See you at Cooper's Monday, dear.

About the Author

The Rev. Dr. John Carroll is a member (honorably retired) of the Blue Ridge Presbytery of the Presbyterian Church in America. He was formerly associate pastor of Christ Church, Katy, TX, and pastor of Central Presbyterian Church, Kingstree, SC. He served for over two decades as a staff member with the Navigators on university campuses in the Philippines, Argentina, and various locations in the United States.

A graduate of Virginia Tech (BS), Columbia International University (M.Div), and Reformed Theological Seminary (DMin), John and, the world's greatest wife, Mary, have three married daughters and seven grandchildren. The Carrolls live on Thistle Dew Farm in the Blue Ridge Mountains of Virginia with a pretty good dog named Ocho. They enjoy hiking, gardening, time with family, touring historic sites and, of course, daily Bible reading.

John blogs at http://ThistleDewFarm.us.

CPSIA information can be obtained
at www.ICGtesting.com
Printed in the USA
FSHW010539271120
76243FS